Expert Praise for *Perfect Poison*

"A first-rate investigative examination into an unthinkable problem of growing concern: the healthcare professional who intentionally kills patients who have come to a hospital in search of medical care. M. William Phelps goes behind the headlines to show not only who the victims were—United States veterans—and how nurse [Kristen] Gilbert harmed them, but also, perhaps most frightening, the reasons why."

—Dr. Michael Baden, forensic pathologist, host of HBO's *Autopsy* series, and author of *Dead Reckoning: The New Science of Catching Killers* and *Unnatural Death: Confessions of a Medical Examiner*

"A horrific tale of nurse Kristen Gilbert's insatiable desire to kill the most helpless of victims—her own patients. Phelps renders the story expertly, with flawless research and an explosive narrative, and shockingly reveals that unimaginable evil sometimes comes in pretty packages."

—Gregg Olsen, bestselling author of *Bitter Almonds, Abandoned Prayers, Mockingbird* and *If Loving You Is Wrong*

"In the tradition of the very best true crime writers, M. William Phelps pulls back a curtain of illusions crafted by a clever psychopath and reveals a heartless narcissism more frightening than the murders themselves. A compelling account."

—Lowell Cauffiel, *New York Times* bestselling author of *House of Secrets* and *Forever and Five Days*

"M. William Phelps's *Perfect Poison* is true crime at its best—compelling, gripping, an edge-of-the-seat thriller. Phelps packs a wallop with his encyclopedic knowledge of police procedures."

—Harvey Rachlin, author of *The Making of a Detective* and *The Making of a Cop*

Other books by M. William Phelps:

Perfect Poison
Lethal Guardian
Every Move You Make
Sleep in Heavenly Peace
Murder in the Heartland

PERFECT POISON

A Female Serial Killer's Deadly Medicine

M. WILLIAM PHELPS

PINNACLE BOOKS
Kensington Publishing Corp.
http://www.kensingtonbooks.com

PINNACLE BOOKS are published by

Kensington Publishing Corp.
850 Third Avenue
New York, NY 10022

All Kensington Titles, Imprints, and Distributed Lines are available at special quantity discounts for bulk purchases for sales promotions, premiums, fund-raising, and educational or institutional use. Special book excerpts or customized printings can also be created to fit specific needs. For details, write or phone the office of the Kensington special sales manager: Kensington Publishing Corp., 850 Third Avenue, New York, NY 10022, attn: Special Sales Department, Phone: 1-800-221-2647.

Pinnacle and the P logo Reg. U.S. Pat. & TM Off.

First Printing: June 2003
10 9 8 7 6 5

Printed in the United States of America

For my children: April, Jordon and Mathew;
and my lovely wife, Regina, whose love, support and
patience have been a true blessing in my life.

Explanatory Note

Portions of dialogue and a number of events in this book were taken directly from trial transcripts. In other cases, court records, trial transcripts, medical records, search warrants, notes made by law enforcement, and exclusive interviews conducted with certain individuals relevant to this story were combined to reconstruct conversations and events that took place. As much as possible, the author has refrained from recreating scenes and putting thoughts into people's minds solely for dramatic effect; however, for the sake of keeping the narrative moving and to better communicate the story, in a few instances, dialogue was recreated based on the author's investigation. The end result had nothing to do with the integrity of the words spoken or the information presented. All thoughts attributed are, moreover, actual thoughts uncovered by the author.

Any name appearing in italics for the first time is a pseudonym. For good reason, that person has preferred to remain anonymous. Also, the author has chosen to keep the identities of Glenn and Kristen Gilbert's children, known as Brian and Raymond in the text, anonymous.

There are no composite characters in this book. Each person is real.

Through the reading of more than ten thousand pages of trial transcripts, court documents, pleadings and motions, audio and video tape transcripts, medical records, police reports, search warrants, affidavits, letters, e-mails, military reports, nearly one hundred interviews with dozens of people involved, and VA employee evaluations, along with scores of private documents the author uncovered over a two-year period, a comprehensive narrative has been put together that, in the author's opinion, best tells this story.

There were only a few times during the murder trial where conflicting versions of the same event occurred. The author has chosen to rely on the testimony that was believed by the jury of nine women and three men who sat through nearly five months of trial testimony and, ultimately, decided Kristen Gilbert's fate.

While conducting research for this book, the author uncovered several new pieces of information that had not previously been made public and were never reported. The author wishes to thank those individuals who came forward and told their stories for the purpose of giving a better understanding of why Kristen Gilbert did what she did.

They should be commended for their courage, intelligence and impeccable memory of the events. As it was explained to the author, "Psychotic behavior is hard to forget . . . when you fear for your life, you tend to remember how things happened."

Please visit *www.mwilliamphelps.com* if you wish to contact the author.

PART ONE

These seven victims, ladies and gentlemen, were veterans. They protected our country during war and peace. They were vulnerable, due to their physical and mental illnesses. Some were seriously ill. And some had no family. And because of that, ladies and gentlemen, they were the perfect victims. And when Kristen Gilbert decided to kill them or assault in attempt to kill them, she used the perfect poison.

—Assistant U.S. Attorney Ariane Vuono

PROLOGUE

There are sections of landscape bordering the quaint New England town of Northampton, Massachusetts, as flat as a table-top—acres of farmland that, from a bird's-eye view, might make one think this small section of the Northeast is no different from Indiana or Kansas.

And in many ways, there is no difference.

In May 1995, for example, the unimaginable happened. A tornado whipped through Great Barrington, Massachusetts, killing three people and injuring twenty-four. With a top wind speed of two hundred four miles per hour, farming tractors were tossed into the air and willow trees pulled from the ground and snapped in half as if they were plastic toys in a child's train-set collection.

Farmers and townspeople, in a matter of moments, were left devastated. Twisters, locals protested, were supposed to be con-fined to the Midwest and Deep South. Northampton, like Great Barrington, is located on the edge of the Berkshires, in mountain-ous terrain, fenced in by steep, rocky cliffs. It is a quiet place, full of agricultural history and laid-back living. Nothing ever happens there of any national interest—and residents like it that way.

From Interstate-91, the only hint that Northampton exists somewhere within the throng of massive pines, clapboarded homes and small businesses is the steeple of the old clock tower, which pokes through the tops of the trees like the point of a witch's hat.

On any given night, one can walk through downtown and see a wide variety of cultures mixing company. Passed on from generation to generation, Northampton, where Calvin Coolidge once sat in the mayor's chair, is rumored to be the lesbian capital of the nation. That distinction, however, is perhaps derived from the presence of Smith College, a prestigious liberal arts school for women.

Surrounding downtown, and split into three neighborhoods, or "villages," as the locals like to say—Leeds, Florence and Bay State—Northampton fits every bit of the Smalltown, U.S.A., image portrayed in many of nearby Stockbridge resident Norman Rockwell's paintings. There are old-fashioned ice cream parlors for the kids, cafes for the intellectuals and diners for the blue-collar workers. Coffee houses, art museums, book stores and pubs line Main Street. Street musicians are everywhere, shaking tambourines, strumming guitars, banging on bongos and tooting horns for tip money.

Made up of roughly thirty-thousand residents, Northampton encompasses some thirty-six square miles, with approximately one hundred and seventy miles of roadway intertwined through its thousands of raised ranches, colonials and rustic farms. One could easily agree it is every bit of what writer Tracy Kidder calls, in his book *Home Town,* a "quintessential landscape." Classic New England all the way: from its rolling hills to its maple syrup to its antique shops . . .

"Shake it," Kidder wrote, "and it snows."

Visible from just about anywhere in town, the Veterans Affairs Medical Center (VAMC) in Leeds has served the health needs of Massachusetts veterans since 1924. The main building of the hospital sits high atop Old Bear Hill, a rather steep stretch of land with a man-made duck pond at its base, perfect for sledding during winter months. Just off Route 9, the VAMC grounds rise out of the center of town like a monument and, to some extent, the main building looks a bit like a Victorian mansion. There are twenty-six smaller red-brick buildings, or "cottages," that doctors rent, spread over one hundred and five acres of some of the most sprawling landscape the Northeast has to offer. Perhaps deliberately, the entire compound resembles a military base rather than a full-facility hospital, where six miles of roadway snake around a piece of property that visitors who often come here say is but a small slice of "God's country."

On any given day, scores of vets stand and sit outside the main entrance, smoking cigarettes, drinking from brown paper bags, waiting for the VA bus to take them home. They wear tattered and torn camouflage Army jackets, berets and medals, and speak of their days in the war to anyone who will listen.

The VAMC provides "tertiary psychiatric and substance abuse services, as well as primary and secondary levels of medical care" to a veteran population of men and women in western Massachusetts of more than eighty-five thousand. With nearly six hundred thousand veterans statewide—twelve percent of Massachusetts's population—the one-hundred-and-ninety-seven-bed medical center at Leeds specializes in post-traumatic stress disorder and chronic mental illness, two ailments that often plague these men and women who sometimes return from overseas combat duty damaged for life by what they have seen.

"Our staff," an open letter to veterans reads, "is dedicated towards one purpose—fulfilling [a veteran's] needs as a patient. Veterans are the most important people in our Medical Center."

CHAPTER 1

By the time U.S. Army veteran Stanley Jagodowski turned sixty-six, on August 12, 1995, his reputation for being an uncompromising pain in the ass had already preceded his frequent stays at the VAMC.

During the past eight months, the Korean War vet had become a permanent fixture at the hospital, admitted three times since January because the sores on his feet and legs had become unbearable.

At five-foot-seven, two hundred and twenty-eight pounds, the gray-haired, brown-eyed former truck driver with the Jimmy Durante nose was severely overweight for a man his size and age. Because he smoked, drank, and maintained eating habits that were a nutritionist's worst nightmare, Jagodowski's doctors begged him to exercise, but he rarely did.

When he was transferred from the Providence, Rhode Island, VAMC and admitted to the Leeds facility on July 21, Jagodowski's doctors speculated that he wouldn't be returning home again. Not only had he suffered from non-insulin-dependent diabetes and high blood pressure, but he had enlarged heart ventricles and an irregular heart rhythm. Claire, his wife of nearly forty years, had recently told doctors she couldn't care for him anymore. They lived in a small, four-room ranch-style house in Holyoke, and Claire, who herself had just had a heart attack, took care of their two small grandchildren during the day. She just wasn't up to feeding, bathing, and helping a grown man go to the bathroom anymore. About a month before his VAMC admission, Jagodowski had fallen, and Claire had to call the police to help her pick him up off the floor.

A stubborn man, Jagodowski didn't believe his eating habits would ever catch up with him. Under a doctor's strict orders to sustain a healthier diet, he would hide snacks—candy bars, crackers, chips—under his bed so he could eat what he wanted, when he wanted. Nurses would ask him what he wanted for dinner off his restricted menu and, with his trademark sarcastic scowl, he'd snap, "Give me two eggs, bacon, sausage, hash browns and coffee."

Stanley Jagodowski just didn't get it.

Months before his latest admission, on April 27, 1995, the bad habits Jagodowski had developed throughout the years had finally gotten the best of him.

After an ongoing infection in his right foot failed to heal, doctors in Providence were forced to remove it. Three months later, on July 17, the infection spread throughout his entire right leg, and doctors had to amputate it just above the knee.

Jagodowski had been transferred to Leeds to recover from the amputation. Paranoid, confused and bitter, he often moaned because the sound of it, he claimed, made him feel better. To stir up trouble, he'd lay on the nurse's call bell until a nurse came into the room. As soon as she left, he'd do it again.

But Jagodowski's cynicism for life wasn't without merit or irony. He'd survived the Korean War, was discharged from the Army in 1954, and lived a quiet life as a truck driver for decades. Yet here he was now, confined to a hospital bed and wheelchair, dependent upon other people to help him move his bowels, watching diabetes eat away at his body as though it were rust on a car.

Despite his prior health problems, however, by August 21, 1995, things began to look up for the aging veteran. Only a month after his transfer from Providence, Jagodowski not only was feeling better, but he was looking healthier than he had in years.

The amputation had apparently done the trick. So much so, that for the past week, he had been free from any injectable medicines—which was a significant sign of improvement in it-

self. When pain did come on and his stump began to throb—as
Jagodowski would put it, "like five toothaches"—doctors prescribed oral treatments of Demerol, a painkiller.

A week earlier, on August 14, doctors had agreed Jagodowski was doing so well that he could leave Ward C—the
VAMC's chronic ward—and transfer to the long-term nursing
care unit of the hospital.

The only thing standing in his way was the availability of a
bed.

The Leeds VAMC has many different wards scattered
throughout its complex of buildings, with Ward C located in
the main building, Building One. The entire ward was shaped
like the letter T. Down at the end of the hall—the top of the T—
was a four-bed intensive care unit (ICU). There was a short
hallway between the ICU and the L-shaped nurse's station,
where the charge nurse sat. With about thirty beds, the ward
was split into teams and the workload divided up among the
nurses on duty.

At about 7:00 P.M., on August 21, 1995, respiratory therapist Michael Krason gave Stanley Jagodowski a treatment of
"three puffs of Albuterol," a drug that helped patients breathe
easier. Prior to August 21, Jagodowski had been receiving four
puffs of Albuterol, however. With over twenty-three years' experience, Krason agreed with everyone else that Jagodowski's
condition was improving. He wrote in his medical chart that he
was "alert, his breath sounds were clear, he [was] in no distress,
and his color [was] good." To top it off, Krason also noted that
Jagodowski showed no adverse reactions to the respiratory
treatment.

Near 8:00 P.M., Jagodowski's primary care nurse, Jeff
Begley, asked fellow nurse Beverly Scott to assist him in getting
Jagodowski ready for bed. Begley said he didn't want to deal
with the difficulties the heavyset Army vet was likely to create.

Scott agreed to help.

"Hi, Mr. Jagodowski," Scott said, entering his room. "How
are you tonight?"

"I'm fine, Beverly."

After straightening his bed linen and changing his gown, Scott and Begley switched Jagodowski's position in bed.

"I don't want to turn over. You're hurting me," Jagodowski kept repeating. "Stop it . . ."

"Oh, come now. Just help us out here, Mr. Jagodowski," Scott said. "We go through this *every* night."

Shortly after they were finished, Begley and Scott watched RN Carole Osman as she checked Jagodowski's IV to make sure it was in good working order. Osman said it looked fine. Like Scott and Begley, she also agreed that Jagodowski had no edema (body swelling) or mottling (graying of the skin because of lack of oxygen)—frequent ailments that plague diabetics.

After Osman finished, Scott and Begley, who had assessed Jagodowski as "stable," walked out of his room, stood outside the doorway and chit-chatted.

It was 8:20.

A short time later, as they continued to talk, twenty-seven-year-old Kristen Gilbert, a well-respected RN who had been working at the VAMC since 1989, came walking down the corridor toward them.

She was holding a syringe in one hand and an alcohol swab in the other.

Many of the nurses and doctors who had worked with RN Gilbert over the years agreed the good-looking bleached blonde was one of the most intelligent nurses on the ward. As far as codes or cardiac emergencies were concerned, Gilbert was probably the best the VAMC had to offer. Since she'd started working at the VAMC, Gilbert had built a stellar reputation for being the "go to" nurse during cardiac arrests, and many said she excelled during medical emergencies and had no trouble keeping her mind focused during all the chaos.

This was exceptional. In reality, codes weren't the picture-perfect, sterile scenes depicted on television shows like *ER* and *Chicago Hope,* where nurses and doctors acted in unison, always complementing each other's work. To the contrary, codes were disorganized and feverish. Nurses tripped over one another. Orders were barked out in desperation. Nurses and doctors made mistakes.

But Gilbert had become known as the "take charge" nurse. She'd give accurate orders at the appropriate times, and usually lead the emergency team the entire way.

Her expertise, however, went much farther. Her knowledge of medications was by far her strongest asset—which was one of the main reasons why she was assigned to the med cart and administered medications on most nights.

Nurses would often go to Gilbert with medical questions and she would always come through, giving a detailed description of each drug and its side effects as if she were, as one doctor later put it, a "virtual medical textbook."

Insofar as Begley and Scott were concerned, Stanley Jagodowski wasn't scheduled to receive any meds. But doctors would order medication all the time without letting the entire nursing staff know about it. So they assumed Gilbert was on her way to give him a shot that had been ordered by one of his doctors.

But less than a minute later, at 8:40, Begley and Scott's discussion was interrupted by a piercing scream.

"Ouch! Stop! Stop! You're killing me," Jagodowski yelled.

Just then, as if in slow motion, Gilbert walked out of the room and made her way up the hallway in an uneventful manner.

Startled by the outburst, Begley and Scott rushed into his room.

"Are you all right, Mr. Jagodowski?" Scott asked.

"Yes," Jagodowski said, holding onto his arm.

Yet Scott could tell by his facial expressions that he was in a great deal of pain.

"Everything okay?" she asked again.

"My arm hurts," Jagodowski complained.

There was no doubt that Stanley Jagodowski was a chronic complainer and generally had something nasty to say about everything the nurses did. But Scott had never heard his voice sound so troubled and panicky. What was more, why would Gilbert, an experienced nurse, after administering a shot, just walk out of the room while one of her patients was yelling out in pain?

It seemed odd.

Begley and Scott stayed with him for about five minutes to make sure he was okay and then continued on with their rounds. Jagodowski had no reason to be connected to a heart monitor, so the two nurses had no way to tell that his heart was, at that moment, beginning to flutter out of control.

Minutes later, at 8:43, Jagodowski went into sudden cardiac arrest.

Then his heart stopped.

With one RN in the bathroom, another in the lab, and Gilbert now in the ICU relieving RN John Wall, the emergency medical team responsible for responding to codes was, for two and half minutes, without the presence of a RN.

But even worse was that Gilbert, who had worn the "code" pager while making her rounds out on the floor, forgot to pass it off to Wall as he left the ICU.

Following a bit of confusion and delay, nurses soon piled into Jagodowski's room at a frantic pace. Security—which was required by hospital policy to send a representative to each code—arrived next. Within moments, a team of nurses, doctors and security personnel surrounded Stanley Jagodowski and began resuscitation efforts.

After several defibrillations, where the nurse in charge yelled "clear!" and then shocked Jagodowski with paddles, he was brought back to life, put on a ventilator, and transferred to the ICU—where his real troubles were about to begin.

CHAPTER 2

Stanley Jagodowski's daughter, Susan Lessard, received a phone call from the VAMC around 9:30 that same night.

"Your father's heart stopped," the nurse said. "Come to the hospital right away."

Lessard lived with her husband and two kids in nearby Chicopee, Massachusetts, about a twenty-minute drive from the VAMC.

Stunned by the news, Lessard and her husband stopped by her mother Claire's house to pick her up, and arrived at the VAMC at 10:30.

During the spring of 1995, Jagodowski had complained to Lessard about the pain in his legs just about every day. He had even lost his appetite, he'd complain, because the pain had become so severe.

But ever since the amputation in July, Lessard noticed, her father had been feeling much better.

"It was written on his face," she later recalled. "He looked one hundred percent better. He was more relaxed."

Lessard visited her father about five times a week while he was at the VAMC. In the middle of August, because he was doing so well, she decided to take a week's vacation with her family. She felt comfortable about leaving, she said later, because her father seemed to be in great spirits.

"I would not have gone on vacation unless he was improving."

On Friday, August 19, Lessard, her husband and two kids returned home to find that things hadn't really changed much. She checked with her mother and was told that her father's condition, if anything, had improved since she'd left.

Lessard was relieved.

But when she showed up at the VAMC three days later and first laid eyes on her unconscious father, she fell apart.

He looks so helpless, Lessard thought as she pulled up a chair next to his bed. With faint wheezing sounds coming from his mouth, she wanted to "pull him out of the state he was in" but realized it was impossible.

RN John Wall, a clean-cut, well-liked nurse who was often in charge of the ward, had admitted Jagodowski to the ICU at 9:00. Wall intubated him, placing a tube down his throat and into his lungs so he could breathe.

For the next few moments, Lessard sat with her father and held his hand while the machines around them buzzed and beeped. A ventilator to her right methodically kept her father alive as though it were a metronome counting down what little time he had left.

Every once in a while, Lessard would burrow up next to his ear and whisper, "Daddy, please squeeze my hand."

Jagodowski would, clamping down gently.

"See," Lessard would say to the doctor in the room, "he's not unconscious. He knows I'm here."

As the night progressed, RN Wall recommended that Lessard receive a sedative because she was so distraught over what had happened.

She refused.

For about forty-five minutes, she sat by her father's side hoping he would, through some miracle, come around.

But nothing happened.

Shortly before Lessard and her family had arrived to the ICU, RN Kristen Gilbert had come in and relieved Wall for a few moments. While Gilbert was there, she made a mandatory "progress report" of Jagodowski's code and his current condition.

Signed at 9:30, after briefly describing the code, Gilbert wrote:

> ... *[Jagodowski was] ... awaiting placement to a long-term care ward and developed some ... edema. ... Today, patient was noted to be confused and lethargic. Edema and mottling of upper extremities noted.*

Though no one caught it at the time, not one other nurse or doctor who had treated Stanley Jagodowski had made similar observations.

For some reason, RN Gilbert falsified the report.

Feeling a bit drained after the visit, Lessard prepared to leave the hospital. She stopped in Admissions downstairs and told the nurse she was feeling "light-headed" and "very warm"—and while explaining her condition, she fell back and passed out.

When she awoke several minutes later, Lessard found herself in an Admissions bed ... *being treated with a sedative.* Her father, she was told, had coded again while she had been out.

"It didn't look so good, Ms. Lessard," one of the nurses said.

Shortly after midnight, for the second time since Lessard had been admitted, Claire Jagodowski walked down to Admissions to give Lessard a status report.

After coding for a third time at 11:38, Stanley Jagodowski died. There was a priest up there now, Claire explained through tears.

It was all over.

CHAPTER 3

In 1978, Renee Walsh graduated from East Tennessee State, married a local serviceman, and moved to Germany, where she began working at the Frankfort Army Regional Medical Center as a staff nurse. When Walsh came back to the States two years later, she got a job at the Cape Fear Valley Medical Center's ER and trauma center, in Fayetteville, North Carolina. Eight years after that, she took a job at the local VA hospital.

In November 1990, Walsh's husband at the time was offered a job in Northampton, and she subsequently took a job at the Leeds VAMC.

By 1995, Walsh was a permanent daytime staff nurse on Ward C.

When the short nurse with black hair and an unmistakable Southern accent showed up for work on August 22, 1995 and heard that Stanley Jagodowski had died, she was curious about what had happened. Jagodowski had been sick—there was no denying that. But Walsh never expected him to just drop dead one night.

When Gilbert came into work later on that day, Walsh asked her about Jagodowski's code.

Gilbert and Walsh had become good friends through the years. Even though they no longer worked the same shift, they still socialized outside of work. Gilbert and her husband of six years, Glenn, owned a boat. They would often take Walsh and her young son out on the Connecticut River and go tubing.

"The Jagodowski code was really a sight, Renee," Gilbert said, rolling her eyes. "You should have been there."

"What do you mean?"

Gilbert smiled.

"Well, Claire Jagodowski began to have chest pains herself right in the ICU. So someone took her downstairs to get checked out. While she was down there, I got a call to go down because there really wasn't a real nurse around."

"She's okay, though, right?"

"We did an EKG . . . she's fine."

Gilbert began to laugh a bit louder.

"I wish you would tell me what's so darn funny, Kristen."

"Well, that's just it. While I was down there, Susan Lessard—you know, Jagodowski's daughter—she fainted! It was fucking hysterical. Here you have Claire Jagodowski nursing chest pains and the daughter is lying on the floor, completely out cold. . . ."

"What?"

"Claire was just standing over Susan saying, 'Get up! Get up! You have to go see your father upstairs! You'll never forgive yourself if you don't see him again.' "

Walsh was taken aback. She could clearly see that Gilbert was getting a charge out of telling the story.

Later, when Walsh got home and thought about it, she questioned how a nurse—of all people—could find humor in the death of one of her patients and the family's reaction to it.

On November 15, 1967, the Red Cross sent U.S. Coast Guard serviceman Richard Strickland, who was stationed on an island one thousand miles off the coast of Hawaii, a telegram. *It's a girl. Mother and baby are doing fine,* the terse note read. Strickland's first child, Kristen, the note went on to say, had been born two days before.

A few weeks later, a photograph arrived. There she was, little Kristen Heather Strickland, with her perfect oval face perched underneath a modest shock of dark brown hair, in the arms of her charming mother, the former Claudia Morgan.

Six months after Kristen was born, Richard got word that he was going home to Fall River, a tiny mill town on the southern coast of Massachusetts where he and Claudia had grown up. In May 1968, Claudia and baby Kristen, along with Richard's mother and father, welcomed him at Boston's Logan International Airport.

Just before Kristen turned three, the Stricklands enrolled her in the Christian Day School, a rather strict day-care center just outside of Fall River. Claudia was working as a substitute teacher then, and Richard was off pursuing a career as an electronics engineer.

After seven uneventful years, things abruptly changed for little Kristen. Seemingly overnight, she would now play second fiddle to her much younger sibling, Tara Morgan, who was born in 1974.

Kristen, perhaps now feeling the distance between her and her parents, began spending more time with her grandmother, Isabella Morgan, who lived down the street. Morgan and her husband, Claude, a thirty-year veteran of the Fall River Police Department, owned a small beach house in Little Compton, Rhode Island. Claude hated the water and disliked the beach. He bought the place for the kids. Because Tara was so little, Morgan would take Kristen to the beach every weekend—where she soon fell in love with the sand and surf.

Fall River is perhaps best known for being the birthplace of the world's most famous murderess, Lizzie Borden, who, despite continuing speculation of her guilt, was acquitted of butchering her parents with an axe in 1892.

For decades, children have played hopscotch and jumped rope to a schoolyard rhyme that has become synonymous with Borden's presumed guilt:

> *Lizzie Borden took an axe*
> *And gave her mother forty whacks.*
> *And when she saw what she had done,*
> *She gave her father forty-one*

As Kristen Strickland made her way through junior high, she began to embrace the notoriety of being born in the same town as Lizzie Borden. Whenever the opportunity presented itself, she'd brag to friends—and, later, her coworkers at the VAMC—joyfully claiming she was related to Borden.

"Imagine that—me being related to Lizzie Borden," she'd say with a sparkle in her eyes.

There is no evidence, however, of any blood relationship between the Stricklands, Morgans and Bordens. It was, like a lot of things in Kristen's youth, one more fabrication to add to a growing list. Kristen Strickland, the cute kid who used to bake fudge and sew quilts with her grandmother, was becoming a pathological liar.

In the early eighties, the Stricklands packed up their kids and moved to Groton, Massachusetts, a quaint little Hallmark-like New England town of about nine thousand, located just twenty miles south of the New Hampshire border.

They lived in an unassuming split-to-back ranch on the busy main thoroughfare of Boston Road. Although the Stricklands once took a trip to Disney World and frequently took the kids on weekend trips to New Hampshire and Vermont, it became, for Kristen and her younger sister, an "unaffectionate" household, as if Claudia and Richard were now robots, just going through the motions of parenting. They became strict and ran a regimented, disciplined household. Oddly, friends said, God and religion had no place in the Strickland home.

They were admitted atheists.

Kristen, as she grew into a young woman of fifteen, rebelled against her parents and spent a lot of time away from the home.

Richard, speaking of Kristen's formative years, later said she had, since childhood, lied just about everything. She "never had good relationships with women peers and tended to get into difficulties when she had friendships with men." One time, she even went so far as to convince some of her friends that her mother was nothing but a drunk who beat her up. But Richard said it was "absolutely not true."

The point, however, wasn't whether the stories were actually true; it was that Kristen had been saying they were and obviously had issues with both of her parents that went far beyond what most kids her own age go through.

Being popular, thin and attractive, sporting a lion's mane of curly, brunette locks that stretched a bit past her shoulders, Kristen had no trouble meeting friends at Groton-Dunstable Regional High School. Her yearbook picture shows a smug, smiling teenager, full of energy and life. In the notes next to the picture, she wrote of her love for red roses, ice cream and making new friends. "Vengeful people and fights," however, were on her shitlist, and she despised "cliques" and "fake people."

Although Kristen had a problem with lying, she wasn't stupid. For as she worked her way through her sophomore and junior years of high school, it became apparent that she was not an average student. Whatever she did, Kristen Strickland mastered with an almost effortless ease. She was in the top ten percent of her class and considered a gifted cornet player. She joined the marching band, orchestra and jazz ensemble. She became a member of the math team and whizzed through classes as if bored by the curriculum.

Still, as she grew older, a more vengeful, wicked side of Kristen Strickland emerged.

Pamela Erickson, a neighbor who lived across the street, became good friends with Kristen while the two rode the bus together and hung out after school.

Pamela's mother, however, wasn't too thrilled about her daughter's hanging around with the "Strickland girl."

"She was a habitual liar," a neighbor later recalled. "She would make things up on the spot. I could tell by just listening to her that she was lying."

A culmination of events got Pamela Erikson thinking that maybe Kristen wasn't the person she had originally thought she was. According to a story published in the *Boston Globe,* one day Kristen mentioned to Pamela that she was infatuated by the evil nurse, Amy Vining, on *General Hospital,* a popular long-running daytime soap the two girls used to watch together after school.

Amy was "conniving and backstabbing," Pamela recalled to the *Globe,* and would do anything to get her way.

"I like Amy," Kristen said one day.

"Oh, my God, why would you like Amy?" Pamela asked.

"I just like Amy," Kristen said with an obscure smile.

There was another time when Pamela couldn't find one of

her favorite shirts. When Kristen showed up at her house the same day, she was wearing it.

"That's mine!" Pamela snapped.

"No. You're mistaken. It's mine!"

These were little things, of course. But bigger things were on the horizon.

Exhausting all of her studies midway through her junior year, Kristen was graduated a year and a half before the rest of her class.

In 1984, with high honors, she left high school and was immediately accepted at Bridgewater State College, where she enrolled as a pre-med major at the age of sixteen.

As an added bonus, Bridgewater, located about twenty-five miles south of Boston, was closer to the one place Kristen had grown to love more than anything else: the beach.

Life seemed to be taking shape for young Kristen. Not only was she in college, but living so close to New Hampshire, she could spend a lot of her free time at Hampton Beach, a seaside resort tucked in the corner of the Massachusetts and New Hampshire state lines. It was only about an hour's ride from Bridgewater.

At the time, Kristen was juggling several men she had dated throughout college. She was never the one to end a relationship. It was always the men. Yet Strickland, besieged by ridicule and scorn, had to have the final say. She couldn't let go without getting even.

Even in high school, according to one ex-boyfriend, Strickland was "mentally unstable." She was an "intelligent manipulator," he later said, when it came to relationships. Whenever she felt she had lost control of a relationship, she first begged for forgiveness, claiming she would do anything to save it. But when that didn't work, she became malicious, at times becoming physically violent and verbally abusive.

While dating a boy in high school, Kristen left him a suicide note one day after he ended the relationship. Because of the breakup, she claimed she was going to eat glass.

Worried, the boy rushed over to her house.

But there she was, sprawled out on her bed, unharmed.

Then the harassing phone calls began at his house. The caller would breathe heavily and hang up. It had to be Kristen, he assumed. When he confronted her about making the threatening calls, however, she became enraged and gouged her fingernails through his right cheek, leaving him bloodied and confused.

Another boyfriend from around the same period said he had received the same sort of treatment. Yet calling and hanging up wasn't enough. Strickland tore the spark-plug wires out of his car, keyed both sides of it, and slit the tires.

In college, not much changed.

Several days after a boy she was dating broke it off, he got into his car and drove off only to find that someone had loosened the lug nuts on the tire rims.

Then there was the time when a boy at Bridgewater stood her up.

For days, seeing him in class, Strickland didn't say anything, pretending it didn't bother her.

But she had a plan, of course.

Finals were coming up. Being in the same class, they took finals in the same room. When the day came to take finals and the boy finished taking his test, she watched with an unforgiving eye as he walked up to the teacher's desk and put his test in the pile with the others.

After the boy left the room, Kristen finished her test and walked up to place it on the stack, but when she placed her test in the pile, she traded it with the boy's, took it home and burned it. When recalling the story years later to a friend, she said she got the biggest charge out of how calculating and cool she had been. She laughed about it. "He deserved it," she said. "I got him back! It took me a while, but I got him back."

How cruel, her friend thought. *How devious and vindictive.*

During the summer of 1986, after a year in college and several tumultuous relationships that usually ended under sour circumstances, Strickland met a rather plain-looking man from Northampton, Massachusetts, who was vacationing in Hampton Beach for the week. Glenn Gilbert was perfect. He was tall and lanky, yet attractive in a debonair, boyish way. Two years her senior, Glenn was taken right away by the outspoken seventeen-year-old blonde from Groton who was studying to be a nurse.

By the end of June 1987, after dating Glenn throughout the winter, Strickland transferred to Wachusett Community College in Gardner, Massachusetts, and then to Greenfield Community College—just a twenty-minute drive from Northampton—to continue studying for her nursing degree and, more important, to be closer to the man she had fallen in love with.

Northampton was a melting pot for some of the upper eche-lon of Massachusetts, full of lawyers, doctors, artists, writers, professionals and, like Glenn Gilbert, middle-class blue-collar workers.

One of the better places to live in the state, it only seemed fitting that the elegant and beautiful Kristen Strickland, now a well-educated woman of twenty, live among people she could relate to. After all, she was going to be a nurse soon. The prospect of living among the cultural elite in Northampton seemed appetizing to Strickland, who had, up until that point, spent most of her life in rural, backwater towns where not too much of anything ever happened.

But it was Glenn, after all, who fit a picture Strickland had of someone she could shape and mold into whatever she wanted. Glenn was blue-collar, and by no means a rocket scientist—yet, by the same token, was exactly what Strickland was looking for.

While attending classes at Greenfield Community College, Strickland took a job as a home health aide with the Visiting Nurses Association of Franklin County.

One of her first patients was a blind, deaf, mute, and severely handicapped young boy who lived with his foster family in Bernardston, Massachusetts. The family, who also had a younger foster child, had already had Strickland's coworker, a young woman in her late twenties, over to the house on several occasions to care for the two children and ready them for bed.

When Kristen and her coworker arrived one summer night in August 1987, the coworker introduced Kristen to the family, showed her where to bathe the retarded boy upstairs, and as-sured the foster parents they could take off.

"I am going to leave you with him and go get the other child ready for bed, Kristen. Okay?" the coworker said.

"Sure," Strickland said.

An hour or so later, the parents returned, and Strickland and her coworker left.

When the foster mother checked on the boy Strickland had cared for, she found his legs bright red and "demarcated by where the water level of the bathwater should have been."

The boy had been scalded over sixty percent of his body.

This was impossible to do by mistake. The family had specially ordered a faucet that was preset to a certain temperature. The only way to raise the temperature was to "unlock the faucet [and] adjust the faucet from its preset position."

The following morning, the foster mother called the VNA and said they "never had a problem with the faucet before" and, when the mother checked it out afterward, it had worked fine.

"Well, madam, we are—"

The foster mother interrupted. "We *never* want her to come into our home again."

By Christmastime 1987, Glenn and Kristen knew their relationship wasn't just some fly-by-night romance. It was time to take the plunge.

But a full-fledged wedding was out of the question. Richard Strickland had suggested they get married in Long Island, where he and Claudia had moved with Tara right after Kristen went off to Bridgewater. Strickland said he would spring for the entire bill.

But Glenn and Kristen were adamant: They wanted to elope.

"Our families wouldn't have gotten along," Strickland later told a friend. "Neither of us [was] particularly religious, anyway. It would have been nothing but a big hassle."

By the time January 1988 turned into February, Kristen Strickland had become Kristen Gilbert—and it wouldn't take long for Glenn to find out exactly whom he'd married.

A month after the wedding, Kristen nearly killed her new husband one night.

During an argument, she pulled an eight-inch butcher knife

out of a kitchen drawer and went after Glenn, chasing him from room to room in a tirade. Fearing for his life, Glenn locked himself inside a room and waited until she calmed down.

Perhaps it was an isolated incident? The stress of eloping? Or maybe her grueling schedule while studying to be a nurse had made her snap?

Regardless, Glenn would soon realize that it was the beginning of a marriage based on lies, deceit, adultery, threats and, in the end, another attempted murder that was almost successful.

CHAPTER 4

Kristen Gilbert's graduation picture from Greenfield Community College showed a cheerful woman of twenty-one, standing with a bouquet of flowers in one hand, her diploma in the other.

She looked content.

Shortly after graduating, she began her nursing career at the Leeds VAMC on March 6, 1989—but it didn't take long before a "black cloud" began to follow Gilbert around, hovering over many of the patients she came in contact with. As if she were cursed, it seemed Gilbert had the worst luck when it came to her patients. At unprecedented rates, one after the other, they began to drop dead.

Louis Trainor was one of the unfortunate.

Like many of the patients who came to the VAMC for long-term treatment, Trainor had his share of emotional problems. Yet despite the psychological effects of the self-inflicted wounds Trainor had put himself through, at fifty-one, he was in surprisingly good physical health.

Early in 1990, Trainor was admitted to the VAMC because he was having problems with his esophagus. Many years ago, he had swallowed Drano in an attempt to kill himself. He wasn't able to eat by himself because the chemicals had burned his throat so severely. Instead of reconstructive surgery, Trainor opted for a feeding tube in his stomach.

As grim as it may have seemed, Trainor's condition wasn't

life-threatening. He came to the VAMC only for preventative IV antibiotic treatments.

Including Gilbert, there were two RNs working the floor on the night Trainor had been admitted.

A schizophrenic, and a bit on the irrational side, shortly after being sent up to Ward C, Trainor began screaming at the top of his lungs: "Oh, God, just let me die. Let me die. God . . . please let me die."

But this was routine behavior for Trainor. He was delusional and suffered from manic depression. The nurses knew it was in his nature to scream, so they paid little attention to it.

Nevertheless, as he continued to carry on for about an hour, one of the nurses would periodically go in to check on him to make sure he was okay. Each time the nurse went in, Trainor would say, "I don't want to live anymore. Won't someone let me die?"

For some reason, on this particular night, he was acting a bit more irrational, and his behavior continually disrupted the nurses as they worked. Patients even began complaining. But no matter what the nurses said, Trainor wouldn't stop yelling. So they tried their best to carry on with their normal business and ignore the screaming that now played irritably in the background as if it were a car alarm no one could shut off.

Then, at one point, as one of the nurses was tending to another patient, she stopped what she was doing for a moment and realized that she hadn't heard Trainor yell for some time.

When she went in to check on him, Trainor was dead. There had been no code or medical emergency called. He was, as one nurse later put it, "Dead, dead, dead!" Just like that. "One minute he was alive and screaming at the top of his lungs, and the next he was dead. D-E-A-D. I remember it was the strangest thing."

One of the nurses later checked to see who his primary care nurse had been. It was Kristen Gilbert.

"It was weird because there wasn't any real reason for him to have died. He wasn't sick particularly," a nurse later recalled. "It didn't dawn on me that night, but years later, after I got to thinking about it, I know Kristen had something to do with it. She was the only nurse around."

* * *

Later that same year, a VAMC staff physician, while studying the charts of several of his patients who had died during the night-shift hours, realized that RN Gilbert's name kept showing up repeatedly for a majority of the deaths. By itself, it wouldn't have been alarming. But Gilbert was generally alone with the patients at the time of their deaths, and, more important, most of them were making good progress and weren't expected to die.

One morning, after finding out that another one of his patients had died while under Gilbert's watch the previous night, the doctor went in to see Melodic Turner, Gilbert's nursing manager.

He told her he didn't want Gilbert taking care of any more of his patients.

Although no disciplinary action was ever taken, word leaked that the doctor had said something about Gilbert. Shortly after the meeting with Turner, the nursing staff began to shun the doctor.

As the coincidences mounted and rumors swirled, Gilbert became known as the "angel of death." But it was a joke. No one took it seriously. The nurses teased her about the unfortunate luck and Gilbert lapped up the attention.

Yet, by the winter of 1991, a clerical worker at the VAMC, who was partly in charge of going through patient death records to insure their integrity, noticed a red flag while she was signing off on some of the previous years' deaths. There it was in black and white: Gilbert's name as the sole nurse who had found a majority of the patients on Ward C either in cardiac arrest or dead.

In fact, between 1990 and 1991, on Gilbert's shift alone, there were thirty-one deaths—more than triple the amount found on any other shift. Even more startling was that of those thirty-one deaths, Gilbert had found twenty-two herself. The next closest nurse had found only five. Which meant Gilbert was on duty and found approximately seventy-five percent of the deaths on her ward.

These were shocking numbers, by any account.

Upon a further look, the numbers of codes were even more staggering. Out of roughly forty codes called on Ward C between 1990 and 1991, Gilbert had found half of them: twenty, in fact. In 1990 alone, she had found thirteen, while her eight colleagues, *combined,* had found only five. Many of the nurses later admitted that throughout their entire tenures as nurses— some as long as twenty years—they had never even called a code, let alone seen them called on an average of one per week.

A statistician later concluded that the possibility of it being a coincidence that Gilbert had found and called that many codes was one in a million. There was just no way a nurse could have that much bad luck.

The perceptive VA worker, not sure of what to think, brought her findings to the attention of her supervisor.

"What are you accusing this nurse of?" her supervisor asked.

"Nothing," she said. "I'm just pointing out the fact that this nurse's name is on a majority of these deaths and codes. I'm not saying she did anything. . . ."

The supervisor told her to go back to doing her job and stop making false accusations against people.

Years later, when investigators caught up with the supervisor, she couldn't recall that the conversation had ever taken place.

CHAPTER 5

In December 1990, as gossip continued to center around her unfortunate luck with patients, a pregnant Kristen Gilbert took maternity leave to give birth to her first child.

After having a boy, *Brian*, she returned to work in February 1991. Gilbert began working second shift—4:00 P.M. to midnight. Despite her prior reputation as the "angel of death," Gilbert's colleagues considered her now a permanent member of what had become in her absence one of the tightest-knit groups in the hospital.

At twenty-four, Gilbert had been miraculously transformed from the angel of death into June Cleaver, it seemed, simply by giving birth. Married to a local man who was adored by her co-workers, she was seen now as nothing more than an impassive housewife, leading a mundane life in Northampton like the rest of them.

She was a bit on the chunky side now, her dirty blond hair cut conservatively about halfway down her back, usually propped up in a pink or purple bow. She relished the role of being perceived as the idyllic mother, and dressed like a Catholic schoolgirl: knee-high skirts, bulky sweaters, loose jeans.

"She was attractive in a motherly type of way," a former colleague recalled. "She was happy and loved her job."

As time went on, Gilbert and her coworkers began having

cookouts and went over to one another's homes for dinner parties. They took Gilbert's boat out on the Connecticut River. Gilbert threw baby showers for her pregnant colleagues. They met for lunch. They went out to the area clubs on their nights off. Gilbert's favorite band was the Cowboy Junkies, and she would drag many of her coworkers to their shows.

Everything was in place for an amiable life in suburbia.

But Gilbert never talked about her formative years: how her ex-boyfriends—and even her own father—had claimed she was nothing but "a manipulative, vindictive individual" who had spent her entire dating life harassing men, "making false rape allegations and damaging personal property when the relationships began to sour." Or that she was antisocial and narcissistic. Nor did anyone know she had threatened suicide on several occasions and even tried to stab Glenn. To her colleagues and friends, Gilbert was a caring nurse fulfilling the role of a soccer mom.

Then came the subtle signs when no one could deny that something was wrong.

One year, on Valentine's Day, while manning the phones at the nurse's station, Gilbert came running down the hallway screaming, "I just got a call from a guy who said he put on bomb on the ward."

Renee Walsh was working that night. *A bomb? . . . What?* she thought. It didn't make any sense to Walsh.

Who, she wondered, would go through the trouble of putting a bomb—of all places—on the second floor of a VA hospital?

"No kidding. I just took the call," Gilbert said when Walsh approached her.

"Okay, Kristen. Calm down," Walsh said. "I'll get David and have him call the police."

David Rejniak was the charge nurse that night. He was ultimately responsible for giving out orders if anything had gone wrong.

Soon the ward was inundated with police who, after looking in every corner of the ward, found nothing.

After the police left and things got back to normal, Renee Walsh was sitting at the nurse's station when she heard Gilbert, who had gone down the hall and around the corner near the janitor's closet for some reason, in a loud whisper, say, "David . . .

David . . . oh, David," as if she were playing peek-a-boo. "I think you ought to come down here. There's something in the closet I think you need to see."

Curious, Walsh then got up and walked toward Gilbert's voice. Rejniak was just coming back up the hallway after speaking with Gilbert.

"What is it, David?" Walsh asked.

"Kristen says she found a 'suspicious-looking' box in the closet."

"A box?"

"Yup. It's weird; it has a swastika on it."

A box with a Nazis symbol on it? Walsh thought. So she went down to see for herself.

Sure enough, it was a harmless-looking Kleenex box wrapped in white paper with a swastika drawn crudely in pen, Walsh noticed, on the side of it.

Rejniak, perhaps a bit embarrassed, called the police back and told them the good news: that they had to come back.

It had taken hours for the Massachusetts State Police bomb squad to arrive. While they were en route, the ward had to be evacuated and every single patient taken out of his room and brought to another ward.

Within moments, the bomb squad determined that it was nothing more than what everyone had presumed—a box of Kleenex wrapped in white paper.

The patients were then brought back into their rooms, and life went on.

The nurses later referred to the night as being their own little version of the St. Valentine's Day Massacre, for the simple reason that a tiny cardboard box painted to look menacing had caused so much confusion and panic.

Some of the nurses later speculated it was Gilbert who had planted the box.

Why?

So she could bask in the glory of finding it?

Still, in the eyes of many of her colleagues, Gilbert was the perfect mother. The perfect wife. The perfect nurse. She was a caring individual who spent time during the holidays setting up a Secret Santa program for area needy kids and volunteered at local homeless shelters. Having a separate room in her home dedicated to sewing, she loved to make Christmas stockings and quilts from scratch and give them away.

But it was all part of the façade.

At work, Gilbert told people her mother's real name was Tiesha, a name given to her by a royal family. She told people she had spent time as a child living and studying in England. She told people her parents were wealthy socialites. She said her family was connected to English royalty. All were lies.

"She was *so* Martha Stewart . . . *so* L.L. Bean-ish," former friends later said. "Kristen always had to have the best of everything. And she wasn't afraid to let you know about it when she got it."

As time went on, Gilbert, her coworkers began to notice, became obsessed with clothing and home items. Whether it was Gucci, Calvin Klein or Playschool, she not only had to have the latest in fashion and high chairs and toys for her kids, but it had to be the best. Even linens. Whenever someone came over, there she was, like a *Price Is Right* model, showing off whatever new bedspread, set of curtains or piece of furniture she had recently bought.

"You'll never believe what I just bought. Come on over and check it out," Gilbert would say.

Yet her buying habits became tangled in a web of something just short of fraud. She would order expensive clothing from magazines for an up-and-coming dinner party, work outing or night out on the town with friends, only to return them after the event was over.

She also felt the need to one-up just about everyone whom she felt threatened by in some way.

Rachel Webber was an attractive young nurse who had worked with Gilbert during the early nineties, and they became good friends almost immediately. Gilbert had thrown baby showers for Webber in 1992 and, later, in 1994. But something happened one day that gave Webber pause to think about how differently Gilbert had viewed the relationship.

At work one night in 1993, Webber told Gilbert that she was thinking of buying a new Jeep Grand Cherokee. Webber loved the new design, she said. But she wasn't sure her husband would agree. So she wrote it off as a pipe dream.

"Someday, Krissy," she said. "If it's the last thing I do, some-day . . . I'm going to get me that Jeep!"

Weeks later, Gilbert came into work and began talking about the vehicle as if she had engineered the thing herself.

"Wow," Webber said. "How do you know so much about it?"

"Consumer Reports!" Gilbert bragged. "I read up on it."

"Well, it *is* a nice vehicle."

"Sure is," Gilbert said. "Guess what, Rachel?" she added, and threw a set of keys on the table in front of Webber.

"What, Kristen? *What* did you do?"

"I went out and bought one today—come check it out."

"You're kidding me?"

As Webber walked around the vehicle, she could see Gilbert out of the corner of her eye, gloating. Webber took it as, *See what I have that you don't.*

"Nice vehicle, Krissy."

Walking back up to the ward as Gilbert drove off, Webber couldn't help thinking, *You bitch. Just because I wanted the thing, you had to go out and buy it.*

"She was always like that," Webber later recalled. "If you had it and she wanted it, well, she usually went out and bought it."

CHAPTER 6

November 13, 1993 was a special day in the Gilbert household. Not only was it Kristen's twenty-sixth birthday, but her and Glenn's second son, *Raymond,* was born.

For a good part of the early nineties, the Gilberts had led uneventful, middle-class lives. Sure, they argued and fought about the same domestic issues plaguing half of American marriages, but the arguments never materialized into much, and they usually just made up the old-fashioned way.

During the summer of 1995, however, the marriage began to pull apart at the seams, and was anything but the "Ozzie and Harriett" front Kristen would have liked people to think it was. She and Glenn were arguing now almost daily. Longer periods went by where they wouldn't talk. Although they had made a mutual decision years ago to forgo day care and work separate shifts so one of them could always be home with the kids, it just wasn't working anymore. They hadn't been intimate for some time, and the word divorce, usually coming from Kristen's mouth, was being thrown around the house at will.

Near the middle of the summer, her coworkers began to notice the change. Kristen went from being the model housewife and candid nurse who wasn't afraid to talk about anything to a secretive woman who rarely even opened her mouth to talk about her husband and kids. And if she did, it was to humiliate Glenn. "He's stupid, anyway," she'd say.

Then her entire appearance changed.

She began to lose weight, as much as thirty pounds. With her new buffed body, she dressed more provocatively. It was only tight jeans and tight blouses, as if she were a sixteen-year-old girl trying to impress the new boy at school. She wore more makeup and changed her hairstyle and color just about every other month. One day she even showed up to work wearing a fake nose ring.

For Glenn, he began to notice a change when, for the first time in their lives, his wife began bringing a change of clothes to work so she could go out afterward. And if she didn't work, she would still go out.

Glenn would question her about it, but the conversations would quickly turn into shouting matches.

Even more bizarre was that even though she was never much of a cook, Kristen had begun to prepare home-cooked meals for Glenn on a more regular basis—this at a point in her life when she was thinking of divorcing him. It was unusual because they both worked different shifts and rarely ever ate meals together. Further, they just weren't getting along anymore.

Why the Betty Crocker impression now?

The meals, Glenn began to notice, had a powdery taste to them, he later remembered, "similar to the taste of dissolving aspirin in your mouth." Of course, he couldn't say anything to his wife about it. They were constantly fighting. Telling her that her cooking tasted terrible would only make things worse.

To her friends at work, Kristen began to be more firm about her plans for the future.

"I don't love Glenn anymore," she told one coworker. "I want to be out of that house by Thanksgiving!"

Around the same time, the name of James Perrault, a young security guard at the VAMC, kept popping up in conversation at the Gilberts' home. She would tell Glenn that she wanted to fix Perrault up with her sister, Tara.

Glenn, at thirty, his brown hair beginning to recede, had a slight belly most married men develop after years of being attached to the old ball and chain. But he was good-looking in a plain sort of way, the kind of guy most women would love to bring home to Mom: tall, quiet and passive. He was an extraordinary father to his two children, spending every free moment he had with them. He was a hard worker who had twenty-five people working under him as the shop supervisor of a local optical lens firm.

But lately, Glenn had a big problem: James Perrault's name being mentioned on a regular basis in his house. Here they were, having marital problems, and Kristen was throwing around another man's name at will. It was beginning to upset Glenn.

Perrault was twenty-six when Kristen met him, and had been working at the VAMC since July 1994. A Gulf War veteran, at a slender, well-built six feet, one hundred and sixty-five pounds, Perrault was a hard body of a man, with dark eyes and kinky, military-cropped brown hair.

In other words, the total opposite of Glenn.

On the outside, Perrault was a young, innocent man fumbling through life just waiting for bigger things to happen. Before the VAMC job, he'd worked as a security guard for Milton Bradley. Becoming a VAMC police officer was a step in the right direction for Perrault, who wanted nothing more than to be a bonafide cop one day. The VAMC had even sent him to Little Rock, Arkansas, for a month-long training course. And because he worked on government property, Perrault was authorized to carry a gun.

All VAMC security personnel, whether they worked the day or night shifts, were kept to the same regimen. In Perrault's case, his schedule during the late summer months of 1995 had him showing up at 3:00 P.M. and going home around eleven. He would patrol the hospital grounds for two hours, and then take over at the security desk around 5:00 P.M. for two hours, while continuing to rotate with the other security guard on duty until their replacements relieved them at eleven.

It wasn't quite the same as cruising through Springfield, tracking down drug dealers and pimps. But the time went by fast, and it sure beat chasing shoplifters through the aisles of some department store.

When he wasn't driving the grounds, Perrault's job would take him into any number of unplanned situations. Aside from being responsible for the safety of staff and patients, VAMC security personnel were mandated by VA guidelines to assist during any medical emergencies—or codes—and/or psyche interventions. If a patient was unruly or disruptive, for example, it was up to security to contain him.

During the latter part of August 1995, Perrault began spending more time up on Ward C associating with Gilbert. The two seemed to flirt with each other on occasion—especially, nurses were beginning to notice, during codes.

Perrault seemed to enjoy the attention Gilbert gave him. He was single. He was having trouble meeting women, and Gilbert, perhaps, filled that void.

If there wasn't a code, he would go up on his breaks and visit while she worked in the ICU.

Perrault seemed to many of the Ward C nurses as being the cocky jock in high school who was full of himself, and most of them despised him for it.

"He wasn't the smartest individual in the world," one nurse later recalled.

But Kristen hadn't chosen Nobel prize-winners as lovers— and, as James Perrault would soon learn, for good reason: They were harder to manipulate.

CHAPTER 7

During the latter part of September 1995, one of the more pressing issues facing many of the nurses who had worked with Kristen Gilbert for the past six years wasn't the obvious trouble in her marriage, or even the new boyfriend she thought she was keeping secret; it was that her new lifestyle was beginning to affect her work. Gilbert wasn't as conscientious a nurse as she used to be. Her once-admired nursing skills had diminished over the course of the summer, and she didn't seem to care about patients anymore.

This was somewhat shocking because Gilbert had always been able to separate life and work. She always kept it together, and even fed off the attention a career in nursing offered. During codes, for example, Gilbert thrived, often demanding to be the "defibrillation" person on the team who got to yell "clear" before applying the paddles to a patient in cardiac arrest. She, along with others, had brought scores of patients back to life over the years.

But something had changed.

Back on March 23, 1995, without calling in, Gilbert showed up for work late. So her boss, Melodie Turner, asked why.

"I was at the Holyoke Mall. I saw an elderly man fall on the ground . . . his wife on top of him. The man, Melodie, then went into cardiac arrest. I gave him CPR with the assistance of a bystander for about twenty minutes. The ambulance showed up and brought him to a local hospital."

"What happened to him?" Turner asked.

"I stopped at the hospital on my way in to check on him . . . but he died, Melodie. I tried."

Turner was overwhelmed.

The next day, Turner sent out e-mail to VAMC staff explaining how Gilbert had acted as an "angel of mercy to the poor wife who fell over." The subject of the e-mail read "very nice job."

Turner ended the short note with, "Kristen is an excellent emergency nurse," before letting the staff know where Gilbert could be reached.

E-mails of gratitude poured in.

Priscilla McDonald, a colleague, called Gilbert a "hero."

"Even though the man you assisted died," wrote Denise Carey, "the wife would have been more distraught if no one had come to their aid."

Investigators later located the elderly man and his wife. Surprisingly, they both were alive and well and living in Springfield. The wife said she had, indeed, fallen on top of her husband at the mall, but no one stopped to help them.

It was even possible, investigators speculated, that Gilbert had seen the entire incident take place—but, in fact, did nothing.

By the first week of October, James Perrault had set himself a few goals—one of which, undoubtedly, involved getting into Kristen Gilbert's pants. Not a day went by without Perrault's showing up on Ward C at some point during Gilbert's shift.

"I'm not meeting anybody I feel I can spend a lot of time with," Perrault told Gilbert one night. He wasn't dating anyone at the time, he added, because there just wasn't anyone he "found interesting. I'm looking for something . . . solid."

"My marriage," Gilbert said, "is commonplace. I'm unhappy, too."

As the days passed, Gilbert started e-mailing Perrault on the VAMC computer system.

Soon after, they started planning all their breaks together, meeting in the library, in the basement near the boiler, or anywhere they could find a spot to be alone. They began meeting up the street after work at the local VFW. They went out for breakfast at area diners.

One night, Perrault was sitting at the VFW bar having a few beers with a bunch of friends and coworkers. The place was packed. By the time Gilbert strolled in, around midnight, there wasn't a seat available.

"Can I share a stool with you, Jimmy?"

"Sure."

After about an hour, Perrault said he had to go. So Gilbert asked him to walk her to her car.

When they got to Gilbert's car, without a word, they started kissing. Kathy Rix and Karen Abderhalden, coworkers and friends of Gilbert, were standing at the other end of the parking lot.

Worried that her coworkers had seen the kiss, Gilbert became upset, hopped into her car, and sped off.

Unsure of what had just taken place or where it was headed, a confused Perrault jumped into his truck and began driving toward his mother's house in Chester.

As he passed Ryan Road School in Florence, he noticed Gilbert's car pulled off to the side of the road on the grass. Gilbert's house, where Glenn and the kids were sleeping, was less than a mile away.

So Perrault pulled up behind her and flashed his lights.

As he shut off his truck, Gilbert got out of her car walked up to his driver's side window. Before Perrault could even get the window rolled down, Gilbert reached in, opened the door, hopped up, and straddled Perrault.

At first, Perrault didn't move. Then Gilbert began kissing him all over.

For about twenty minutes, they kissed and fondled each other. Then, just like that, Gilbert jumped out and sped off again without saying a word.

The following day, as Perrault was driving the grounds of the VAMC, he saw Gilbert coming out of the main door. She'd had the day off but had to stop by for something. When she saw him, she stopped and walked over to where he had parked in front of the main entrance.

"Last night was a big mistake," she said. "That shouldn't have happened. I'm sorry for misleading you."

"It's all right," Perrault said. "I understand. You're married."

"Can we go back to how things were and forget that it ever happened?"

Before driving away, Perrault said, "That's fine. If that's how you really feel, Kris, I have no hard feelings."

At eleven that night, shortly before Perrault was getting ready to leave, he got a phone call in the security office.

"Can you meet me after you get off work?" Gilbert asked.

"What's going on?"

"I need to talk to you."

"Sure," Perrault said. "Up the street at the commuter parking lot?"

"I'll see you then, Jimmy."

When Perrault pulled up, Gilbert came running over to his truck and said, "I want to be someplace alone with you . . . I know a place. . . ."

"Where?" Perrault asked, sticking his head out the window.

Gilbert didn't answer. Instead, she got into her car and took off.

Perrault followed.

She drove for about fifteen minutes toward Hatfield, a small farming town west of Northampton.

Far away from any residential neighborhoods, Gilbert turned off the main thoroughfare and drove down a dirt road by the edge of a cornfield, then continued on until they were far enough from the road where anyone driving by could not see them.

After turning off his lights, Perrault got out of his truck and walked toward Gilbert's car, while she walked over to the passenger-side back door and opened it.

"Get in!"

Neither said a word; they just started kissing. But after a moment, Perrault stopped her.

"No, Kris. Stop this."

"Come on, Jimmy."

"I don't know how far you want this to go, based on your conversation earlier today, Kris," Perrault said.

"All the way," Gilbert said. "I want it to go all the way."

CHAPTER 8

Kathy Rix began her VA nursing career in 1975 in Syracuse, New York, where she worked for ten years in the medical ward and two years as an emergency room supervisor. In 1988, Rix moved to Westfield, Massachusetts, married a local cop, and got a job working at the Leeds VAMC.

Rix was perceptive, a professional. Dedicated and cerebral, she took her responsibilities as a nurse with the utmost seriousness.

Not too much got by Kathy Rix.

At a lean five-four, with a slight red tint to her shoulder-length blond hair, Rix had an eye-catching attractiveness to her. She had been a nurse for two decades and knew her job better than most. When she met Gilbert, they immediately hit it off and not only developed a working relationship but also became friends.

Rix later said she had never met a nurse as attentive and qualified as Gilbert. She viewed Gilbert's clinical and patient assessment skills as being far beyond those of many of the nurses she had worked with throughout the years. Her knowledge of medications, Rix recalled, was "excellent. She was very efficient in documenting [events], and her notes seemed to be clear and easy to read."

In early October, several Ward C nurses went to Rix and began complaining about Gilbert's recent behavior. They felt they could depend on Rix. If they told her their concerns, they knew something would be done about it. In particular, Beverly Scott, April Gougeon, Lisa Baronas and Lori Naumowitz said they had a big problem with the way Gilbert was leaving the ward for extended periods during her shift.

When Rix confronted her, Gilbert said she would go off to the library to look up work-related things. Once, she said, she went to the security office to get a new parking sticker for her Jeep because the old one had been torn off in the car wash. She didn't understand what the big problem was.

The nurses knew they were lies; Gilbert was slipping away to meet her new boyfriend, James Perrault—and they were sick and tired of it.

Like everyone else Gilbert had worked with, Rix noticed the physical changes in Gilbert during the fall of 1995 as well.

As time passed, Rix began to become concerned about all the time Gilbert was spending at the VFW. She had never known Gilbert to frequent bars regularly, and watching her apply lipstick and put on a fresh layer of clothing at the end of her shift gave Rix reason to believe Gilbert was up to no good.

Shortly before Halloween, Gilbert called Rix at her home, and with one simple question let Rix know exactly what she was up to without even admitting to it.

"I have a friend who is having an affair," Gilbert said. "I want to know your thoughts about it, Kathy."

"Are you sure you're not talking about yourself, Kristen?"

"Oh, no. Why would you say that?"

"Well, you haven't had anything good to say about Glenn in a *long* time."

"I'm not talking about my situation, Kathy. Trust me," Gilbert said before ending the conversation.

James Perrault was wearing out his welcome on Ward C by the end of October. To the chagrin of most of the nurses, as codes became more regular, so did Perrault's presence. Many nurses noticed that the codes and medical emergencies happened only when Perrault was on duty, and, disturbingly, Gilbert and Perrault would flirt with each other while trying to save a patient's life.

They were seen rubbing their bodies together and touching

each other in a provocative manner. Gilbert would even smile at him and make eye contact while they worked.

Perrault loved the attention and noticed the bumping and grinding got more erotic as each code was called.

"You're good at what you do," Perrault said one night.

"Thanks," Gilbert said. "I enjoy watching your muscles while you do compressions. You do it better than most other officers."

Since that first night back in September, when Perrault and Gilbert physically consummated their relationship in the backseat of Gilbert's car as though it were prom night, they began meeting four to fives times a week at various places. Like two virgins discovering sex for the first time, they screwed their way through October.

They just couldn't get enough of each other.

On some days, they'd meet before work *and* after work. It wasn't in cheap motels or at Gilbert's home while Glenn was at work. Always under Gilbert's direction, they would run off to the old cornfield in Hatfield, down by the Connecticut River boat launch, or they would pull off on dirt roads Gilbert had discovered while four-wheeling with fellow nurse David Rejniak.

Close to the end of October, the nurses on Ward C decided they needed something to take them out of the funk that was overwhelming everything they did. The talk and focus had been centered on how much Gilbert had changed, the affair she thought she was hiding, and poor Glenn Gilbert, the "good guy" who was getting the short end of a very long stick.

With Halloween right around the corner, the Ward C staff decided to have a masquerade ball.

Days before the party, Gilbert dreamed up an idea and presented it to Perrault while they sat in the basement of the VAMC one night and talked.

"I want to fix you up with my sister, Jimmy. With the Halloween party coming, it'll be the perfect place for you two to get together."

"What about *us?*"

"Well, there can't be an 'us,' Jimmy. You know that. . . . Anyway, you've met my sister—"

"Yeah, she's attractive."

"You two will get along well."

Perrault didn't care one way or the other. He'd already had Gilbert; why not try out the sister, too? As a bonus, Tara was single. She could offer Perrault what he wanted: a steady, full-time girlfriend he could go out on the town with without worrying about being seen.

For the next few days, Gilbert went around the ward and told everyone the latest news. She was beside herself and seemed elated by the prospect. Miss Matchmaker. It was all her idea.

Just about everyone from Ward C showed up at the party: John Wall, Kathy Rix, Renee Walsh, Lori Naumowitz, April Gougeon, David Rejniak, the whole crew, including friends of the nurses, dates, husbands and wives.

Glenn Gilbert was, of course, a bit apprehensive about going, but thought maybe a night out with his wife would somehow help the marriage. He wanted nothing more than to have a life with Kristen.

Kristen dressed as a gypsy. She wore a loose-fitting, bright, blood-orange-colored costume with all the trimmings. The blouse part of the costume was cut right below her modest breasts, making her belly button visible. An expert sewer, she put the costume together herself. Her sister, Tara, went as a medieval maiden, dressed in a blue gown that accentuated her dirty blond hair and pale-white skin. Perrault, of course, being ever so preoccupied with how he looked, wore a simple two-piece suit, with a red tie and white shirt. He drank Budweiser from the bottle and worked the party as if he were a nightclub singer after a gig, schmoozing with whomever he could.

Kristen's night was dominated by trying to act as if the entire event had been her idea. She strutted around as the hostess with the mostest, catering to everybody's whim—with the exception of her husband's.

Tara and Perrault never hooked up, and many wondered if the idea had been a front.

Either way, Glenn had seen enough of his wife's following her sister and Perrault around.

"Kristen," Glenn said, pulling her aside, "why the hell are you so preoccupied with your sister and Jim?"

Kristen didn't respond.

"Can't you pay me any attention?"

Kristen walked away without speaking. Glenn, having seen enough, left the party and walked home.

Later on, Perrault approached Kristen, reminding her of her earlier suggestion that he meet her sister.

"So, when am I going to formally meet your sister?"

"No!"

"No? But you said . . ."

"I know what I said, but I'm jealous."

A few days later, Renee Walsh went up to Gilbert and asked her how the date between her sister and Perrault had gone. With the fuss that Gilbert had made over the date, and Walsh not even seeing them together once during the party, she was curious about what had happened between Perrault and Tara after the party.

"So, did your sister have a good time with Jim?"

"No, I wouldn't let her."

"What do you mean, 'you wouldn't let her'?"

"Jim was drinking . . ." Gilbert started to say. "He was a real asshole, anyway. I didn't want him near my little sister. I told her she couldn't go out with him."

CHAPTER 9

To be closer to his married girlfriend, James Perrault rented a one-bedroom apartment on Parsons Street in Easthampton on November 1, 1995. Renting the apartment, however, was only the first step. If Gilbert wanted to continue the relationship, Perrault soon made it clear, she would have to make a decision.

"You're the kind of guy I wish I could be with," Gilbert said one night. "I wish I never married Glenn in the first place."

"I like you, too, Kris. But—"

"He abuses me," Gilbert added. "He verbally abuses me and pushes me around."

It was a lie. Those who knew Glenn Gilbert knew he wouldn't lift a finger to anyone, let alone the mother of his children.

"You could get a restraining order against him, Kris. You know that, don't you?"

"No! I have to think about the kids."

"Well, in that case, you should go to counseling then. You know, try and save the marriage."

Gilbert was adamant. "No. Never. It won't work. It'd never work."

With that, Perrault was at a loss for ideas. He wasn't a marriage counselor. Far from it, actually. He was just trying to figure out where Gilbert's life was heading and where—and if—he fit into it somewhere. If she wanted to try to work things out with Glenn, it was okay with him. He hadn't really invested too much time in the relationship by this point, anyway.

"You have only one option then, Kris."

"What's that, Jimmy?"

"Move out."

But Gilbert didn't want to move out of her Drewson Drive home. She demanded that Glenn leave—and vowed to friends she would do whatever it took to get Glenn out of house so she could stay there with the kids.

When Glenn got home from work on November 5, he felt sicker than he had in years. For the entire day, he'd suffered from flu-like symptoms. Sweaty, pale and nauseous, by the time his wife had gone off to work at four, Glenn sat down to see if he could shake off whatever it was he had.

Throughout the night, he battled fatigue and muscle cramps until, finally, he began vomiting, feeling as though he were going to pass out. At around 10:45, he broke down and called his wife.

"I need you to come home and take me to the ER."

"I'll be right there."

While in the ER, as they drew blood, Glenn was wide awake, alert. There wasn't a doubt in anybody's mind that he was ill, but he was certainly aware of what was going on around him.

A short time later, the ER doctor came in and said that Glenn's potassium level had dropped to a "critically low level." In addition, "his heart was beating irregularly and exhibiting cardiac arrhythmias."

Potassium is found naturally in the body. It was unheard of for a man of Glenn's age and physical shape to have a low potassium level. A person would have to stop drinking water for days—and even then, the level of potassium would be higher than what Glenn was exhibiting.

Not having much of anything to say, Kristen stood by and watched as the nurses and doctors worked on Glenn. After a while, Glenn was released and given a prescription of potassium to get his level back up to where it should be.

Still feeling ill, Glenn took the following day off from work.

But after getting most of his strength back the next day, November 7, he was able to return.

"I'm not happy with how you were treated at the ER," Kristen told him later that night before she left for work. "I'll have the VA check your blood to make sure your potassium level is back up."

"How you going to do that?"

"I'll bring home the equipment, take a blood sample myself, and bring it back to the VA with me."

"Okay," Glenn said, and Kristen went off to work.

This was extraordinary. Hospitals, under strict guidelines, never test employees' blood samples, and VAMC policies strictly forbid it. Further, Gilbert had never even spoken to the lab technician, who later said she would have told her no, anyway.

Over the next several days, Kristen never denied the fact to her coworkers that Glenn had been ill.

"He should have coded," she told one friend, "due to his low potassium level. But he didn't." She also displayed her dissatisfaction about how the ER had treated him. "The hospital should have taken a blood sample to check his potassium level before they discharged him."

But the ER *had* taken a blood sample. Kristen had stood there and watched them do it.

Then she called her old friend, Rachel Webber.

"What happened?" Webber asked, after Kristen explained how sick Glenn had been.

"Oh, he played some volleyball, and his electrolytes were off. They had to replenish his fluids . . . they put him on an IV."

"Is he okay now?"

"He's fine."

Feeling a bit better, on November 10, Glenn went for an appointment at Kaiser Permanente, where his doctor checked his potassium level once again. It was, finally, back to normal.

Kristen had November 11 and 12 off. On the eleventh, while LPN April Gougeon was filling out some paperwork at the nurse's station, she looked up and spotted Kristen walking toward the medicine supply closet—or satellite pharmacy—which was directly across the hallway from the nurse's station on Ward C. Gougeon was surprised to see Gilbert. But there she was, dressed in a sweatshirt and jeans, rummaging through the medicine supply closet.

"Hi, Kristen, what's going on? What are you doing here?" Gougeon asked.

As Gilbert rushed by, she said, "Oh, I need to . . . get some more medication for Glenn. He didn't fill his prescription, and I need to get some more potassium."

Gougeon watched as Gilbert tore through the medicine cabinet and, after apparently finding what she was looking for, took off.

The following night, November 12, she showed up again.

This time, LPN Lori Naumowitz watched as Gilbert walked hurriedly by the nurse's station without saying a word, again en route toward the medicine supply closet.

As she entered the satellite pharmacy, Naumowitz followed her. Looking on from the doorway, she watched as Gilbert rummaged through the closet.

"Um . . . what are you doing?" Naumowitz asked.

"Oh, Lori . . . hi," Gilbert said. "Glenn got a prescription for potassium from the hospital, but he ran out. I'm just taking some potassium home for him. No big deal."

The VAMC stocked potassium on Ward C in many different forms, the most popular and easily accessible being tiny, clear ampoules similar to many of the other medications in the closet. Given in large doses, potassium is fatal. It is the final drug administered during an execution by lethal injection and stops the heart almost immediately upon impact.

After Gilbert left, Naumowitz pulled nursing assistant Lisa Baronas into an empty room and, privately, told her what Gilbert had done.

Baronas had her own story to tell.

A couple of days prior to November 11, she said she saw the strangest thing. As she walked into the nurse's locker room to use the restroom at the beginning of her shift, she noticed a funny-looking reflection on the wall. At first she thought it was from her watch because there was no curtain on the window and the sun, which was just beginning to set, had been reflecting off the floor. But after looking more closely, she saw that the reflection was being made by a couple of silver drug packet strips hanging out of Gilbert's coat.

So she walked over.

Immediately, she saw the VA symbol on the packets and knew that they were from the medicine cabinet. Without removing them from Gilbert's jacket, Baronas looked at the names printed on the back of each packet: nifedipine and captopril.

In all her years of nursing, Baronas had never seen nor heard of the drugs.

A few days later, while telling Beverly Scott over the phone what she had seen, the two nurses made a date to look up the meds in a reference book. What they eventually found out not only piqued their interest and confused them, but gave them cause for concern.

Nifedipine is a calcium blocker. Calcium blockers are used in the treatment of certain heart conditions and victims of stroke. It causes the blood vessels and heart muscles to relax and dilate. The type of nifedipine Gilbert had in her pocket, however, had never been authorized or prescribed for any patients on Ward C.

Captopril is used in the treatment of cardiovascular diseases, hypertension and congestive heart failure, generally for lowering blood pressure.

Combined, both drugs can lower the heart rate of a healthy person to an extremely dangerous level—and, if given in a large enough dose, can cause death.

CHAPTER 10

A week or so after the initial incident that had landed Glenn in the ER, Kristen, without notice, came home from work during her dinner break one night toting a large canvas bag. She had a simple request for Glenn: As she had promised, she wanted to take a sample of his blood back to work and have it tested. She said she didn't trust the doctors. She wanted to be sure his potassium level was where it should be.

Here they were discussing divorce and having arguments every other day about who would stay in the house and who would leave, and now Kristen was coming home to make sure Glenn was okay?

Something didn't fit.

Kristen brought the canvas bag into the bathroom.

"Come on in, Glenn," she said, and took a large syringe out of the bag. It was filled with a clear liquid.

Glenn looked at the needle.

"It's saline," Kristen said. "I need to flush your vein first, before I take blood from you." She had another syringe that was empty. Glenn guessed it was for the blood she was going to draw.

After wrapping a tourniquet around his arm, she inserted the larger needle "into the crook of his left arm and began injecting the clear liquid."

Glenn hadn't thought of it at the time, but anyone who had

ever gotten blood drawn knew that the vein was never flushed because it would dilute the blood.

As the fluid entered Glenn's body, his fingertips went numb and, growing cold, his "hands, arms and chest drain[ed] of color and [became] translucent."

What the hell is going on . . . ?

As Glenn tried to pull away, Kristen pinned him with her hip against the wall and hurriedly pushed the injection into his vein until the syringe was at least half empty. At the same time, she ripped the tourniquet off his arm so the fluid would quickly enter his bloodstream before he could do anything.

In seconds, Glenn's legs locked. As he began to lose consciousness, he slowly slid down the side of the bathroom wall he had been leaning on like some drunken bandit in a spaghetti Western who had been hit over the head with a bottle.

Within a few moments, he came out of it and saw Kristen scrambling around the bathroom in a frenzy. She was gathering up the syringes and putting them back into the bag.

"This isn't going to work," Kristen said as Glenn came to. "You must have fainted at the sight of the needles."

Even so, while her husband lay helpless on the floor, Kristen walked out of the house and returned to work as if nothing had happened.

When she returned, she ran into Lori Naumowitz and gave her version of what had happened back at home.

"You just left him there . . . and came back to work?" Naumowitz asked.

"He's fine. He just fainted."

"We have to call him, Kristen. We have to make sure he's okay."

"He just fainted, Lori. He'll be fine."

The next day, Glenn confronted her.

"What the hell happened here last night?"

"You fainted. Everything's fine. It happens all the time. It's no big deal, Glenn."

"Jesus. What the . . . ?"

"You're fine. But listen, don't tell anybody about it, okay?"

In his naivety—or perhaps denial—Glenn let it go.

* * *

Oddly enough, just a week before, Gilbert had called the family veterinarian. She said that their Labrador, Mindy, suffered from car sickness. "Could I come in and get some Acepromazine? We're taking a car trip pretty soon."

"Sure," the doctor said.

Gilbert showed up some time later and picked up five twenty-five-milligram tablets of the drug.

Acepromazine is similar to Valium. It's a stimulant for dogs that are stressed out. It can also be used to prepare an animal for an operation; it stabilizes the rhythms of the heart. An overdose, given in one large dose or over an extended period of time in smaller doses, will drastically reduce the heart rate of an animal or human being.

In time, it will cause death.

Glenn Gilbert later recalled that they weren't planning any road trips at the time. They may have been planning on getting divorced, but a trip was the last thing on their minds. Also, he said, Mindy had been in the car plenty of times, and not once had she ever gotten carsick.

James Perrault sat down one evening and decided to write Gilbert a letter. He knew the only way he could get her full attention was to put his thoughts down on paper and read the letter to her aloud the next time he saw her. If Gilbert didn't like where a conversation was headed, she had a way of manipulating it so it swung back in her direction. Perrault wanted to make sure that didn't happen.

The next morning, he met Gilbert for breakfast at a local mall.

After they got a cup of coffee and had something to eat, Perrault told her to sit down.

"What is it, Jimmy?"

He pulled out the letter and read it aloud from beginning to end. It said that he wasn't happy with the way things were, or where they appeared to be heading. He urged her to move out of her house so they could see if there was anything between them. The way things were now, he couldn't do it much longer.

"Yes, Jimmy. We could have a future together," Gilbert said, taking the letter.

As she read it, Gilbert began to cry. Perrault had mentioned in the letter that he would end the relationship if something wasn't done soon.

"Don't . . . Jimmy . . . don't . . . please," Gilbert begged.

From Perrault's point of view, it was do-or-die time for Gilbert. She couldn't have it both ways any longer.

"If you don't leave Glenn, Kristen, I'm leaving you," Perrault said.

Gilbert jumped up from her seat and took off toward a pay phone.

"I'm calling Glenn right now," she screamed.

Perrault went after her.

"Is Glenn there?" Perrault heard Gilbert say to whoever was on the other end of the line.

After a pause, Gilbert said, "It's me. I just want you to know that I am not happy anymore. It's over. I want a divorce."

Perrault was impressed. She was finally taking charge.

"What?" Glenn asked on the other end.

Gilbert hung up, turned toward Perrault and smiled. She began crying, hugging him as if they'd just hit the lottery.

Several days later, Glenn proposed counseling. He said he still loved her and wanted to save the marriage for the sake of the children. Seven years was worth a counseling session or two, if only to get directions on how to end the marriage.

They went to counseling one time. When they got home, Kristen lashed out at him.

"You move out!" she said. "I'm not leaving this place."

"Fine, then. I will."

For the next few days, Kristen lived the life of a single woman, seeing Perrault whenever and wherever she wanted to.

Weeks later, without a fight, she changed her mind and moved out of the house.

CHAPTER 11

Shaped like a horseshoe, with the open end facing Northampton Street (Route 10), the apartment complex James
Perrault helped Kristen Gilbert move into on December 1, 1995,
provided the perfect spot in town for divorcées, single mothers
and newlyweds. Rent was cheap. Retail and grocery stores were
nearby. And for some of those who worked in Springfield or
Holyoke, it was the best of both worlds: community-oriented,
small-town living with the benefits of big-city life just up the
road.

For Kristen Gilbert, Northampton Street was the perfect location. Not only was Glenn's work just a two-minute ride down
the road, but Perrault lived only two miles away.

The kids stayed with Glenn. Kristen didn't even make it an
issue. She would see them every day, of course, because Glenn
worked so close by. He would drop them off in the morning and
pick them up after he got out of work.

It appeared to be the perfect setup for everyone involved.

Perrault and Gilbert's relationship took on a new dimension
now that they were free to come and go as they pleased. They
went to the movies. Attended plays. Went bar-hopping and had
romantic dinners.

Perhaps it was love after all for James Perrault.

* * *

By the end of 1995, codes on Ward C had become an outright problem. Nurses were beginning to mention to each other that there was a "marked increase" in the past few months, but now it seemed as though they were happening weekly. And for some reason, most of the codes were being called during the busiest times—say, for example, when they were understaffed—and, lo and behold, on Gilbert's tour of duty.

Here it was December, and already there had been about thirty-five codes for the year on Ward C alone during Gilbert's 4:00 P.M. to midnight shift. Even more shocking was that Gilbert had found twenty of the codes herself. The closest nurse behind her had found only five. By comparison, during the previous year, 1994, there had been a total of fifteen codes, yet Gilbert had found half of those, too.

But even more alarming was the number of deaths.

By December 7, Ward C had lost thirty-seven patients on Gilbert's shift alone. There was no comparison with the two other shifts: The day shift had lost only six patients and the overnight shift ten. But the most significant factor in the second-shift deaths was that Kristen Gilbert had found twenty, more than half of them, herself.

In 1995, Henry Hudon, from Westfield, Massachusetts, was a thirty-five-year-old schizophrenic who liked to smoke cigarettes, drink beer and, shortly after being admitted to the VAMC, run away from the hospital whenever the opportunity presented itself.

"I'm going out for a smoke," Hudon would say, never to return.

A frequent visitor to the VAMC's psychiatric ward, Hudon was an Air Force veteran who had "demonstrated excellent performance in all phases of his duties," his sergeant, Thomas Harrington, wrote about him in 1980.

Growing up in East Longmeadow, Massachusetts, Hudon lived the average life kids in Springfield's most reclusive suburbs did during the seventies. He graduated from East Longmeadow High School in 1977, an above-average student. He took the postmaster's daughter to his high school prom and the police chief's daughter to the senior banquet, and was a member of the high school's swim and golf teams.

Born prematurely on February 5, 1960, in Holyoke, Hudon embodied the persona of an all-American military boy, created in the image of his father, a twenty-four-year Air Force vet who had fought in World War II.

When it came time, deciding on a career in the military was an easy decision for Hudon, who looked up to his father. So, years later, the scrawny, blond-haired boy with thin lips and an imposing smile enlisted.

Hudon's outgoing personality, strong moral fiber and easy-going attitude, however, landed him in a vegetative state not too long after he arrived at the Royal Air Force Station, in Lakenheath, England.

As Hudon, an assistant physical therapist, and two friends walked into a local London pizza joint one night, the base commander, with his wife, children and another couple, stopped Henry at the door. There were two men fighting in the back of the restaurant, the commander said. He asked Henry if he could break it up.

"I'll do my best, sir."

Henry was known throughout his company as a peacemaker, a guy who didn't like to see people argue and fight. So he walked over to where the men were yelling and pushing each other and tried getting in the middle, demanding that they stop fighting.

But someone watching the fight didn't appreciate Hudon's can't-we-all-just-get-along attitude. While he was trying his best to separate the two men, Hudon was struck in the back of the head with a beer bottle, and his paralyzed body fell to the ground. The impact his head had made with the cement floor was so powerful it detached a retina from his right eyeball and shattered his front teeth.

Henry Hudon would never be the same.

For the next three weeks, he lay in a coma, incoherent and nonresponsive. But Hudon was a fighter. After several surgeries, and plenty of prayers on the part of his family, surprising even his doctors, Hudon fought his way out of the coma.

Unfortunately, he was a different person.

Before the accident, Henry Hudon was a guy who never argued with anyone and took orders from his commanders as the letter of the law. Now, Hudon would become enraged at the drop of a dime and had a hard time listening to anyone.

"He looked the same," Julia Hudon, his mother, recalled, "but he was *not* the same."

He became emotional. He "heard voices" and saw things that weren't there. He accused people of stalking him. While on certain medications, Henry's hands shook as if he suffered from Parkinson's disease. Within a year, he was honorably discharged and sent back to the United States under the official diagnosis of suffering from paranoid schizophrenia.

Not knowing what to do, Julia Hudon had her son committed to North State Hospital a year after he returned, but realized soon after that the VAMC in Leeds had similar services available.

Once a healthy, twenty-year-old member of the United States Air Force with a promising career ahead of him, Henry Hudon would now live out the rest of his life dependent upon a cocktail of psychiatric medications and frequent visits to the VA hospital whenever he felt his mental health spiraling out of control.

Between 1986 and 1995, his mental status fluctuated from being "out of control" to "in control," which landed him in and out of the VAMC at Leeds more than three dozen times. He'd take his medication as prescribed, and it would work wonders. But the effects wouldn't last. Three or four times a year, he'd show up for a new prescription or an adjustment of the meds he was already on, and end up spending anywhere from ten days to three weeks, and, one time, nearly a year.

Throughout the fall of 1995, Henry's condition worsened. None of the medications he was prescribed worked. Doctors couldn't find the right mix. Not only that, but he developed "tardive dysdiadochokinesis," a syndrome, caused by the medication, that made his body shake uncontrollably. He developed TMJ, which made his face sag and his speech slur. Spending so much time at the VAMC, Hudon began hanging around with other VA patients and started smoking pot once in a while with them outside. When he didn't take his medication regularly, he would get nasty.

"You're the one who's sick, not me!" he'd snap.

Julia Hudon would clean her son's apartment daily and sometimes find his medication thrown all over the place. It was a double-edge sword: When he was sick, he felt he didn't need the medication, which was, in fact, the time he needed it the most.

On December 7, 1995, Julia Hudon was sitting at home when she picked up the phone and was startled to hear Henry's voice.

"You're home?" Julia asked. For all she knew, Henry had been on the locked ward of the VAMC for the past few days.

"Yes, Momma . . . I don't feel good, Momma," he said.

Although he was thirty-five years old, Henry always referred to his mother as "Momma," and the sound of it never got old to Julia Hudon.

"What's wrong, Henry?" she asked.

"I've been throwing up . . . I have diarrhea, like when I had the flu. I feel so sick. I've been throwing up, Momma."

"Well, you're going to have to go back to the VA. You're not stabilized!"

"Oh, Momma . . ."

"Do you want me to come over and get you now?"

"I just want to sleep, Momma. Please, can I just go back to bed and sleep?"

Julia Hudon didn't answer.

"Come and get me tomorrow morning," Henry suggested.

"All right. But if you need me tonight, call."

CHAPTER 12

Henry Hudon spent the night of December 7 vomiting and having diarrhea.

"Momma, I still feel sick," Henry said over the phone the next morning. "Take me back, Momma. I'm still throwing up."

Julia Hudon noticed the weakness in his voice. But she was relieved that he was alert and aware enough to call her.

Henry lived in a small, one-room efficiency apartment on Mill Street in Springfield. It wasn't much, but it sure beat living on the street in his car, where he had recently lived.

When Julia arrived, she could tell by looking at her son's apartment that he'd had a rough night. From one end of the room to the other, the floor was slick with bodily fluids. Yet Henry was up and around, walking back and forth.

"You need to eat something, Henry," Julia said as they made their way to her car. "I'm stopping at McDonald's."

But Henry didn't have an appetite, and wasn't likely to keep anything down. So he sat in his mother's car and tossed French fries to the sea gulls that were flocking around the parking lot.

"They're beautiful, aren't they, Momma?"

"They sure are, Henry."

As Henry continued to feed the gulls, Julia Hudon thought about how she was going to get her son readmitted to the VAMC. She knew the hospital was going to hassle Henry about taking off the previous day, and thought it was even likely that they would deny him a bed.

So she hatched a plan.

"Listen, Henry," she said. "If you have to tell them you took pills—red, yellow, green, whatever—you tell them anything. *Just get that bed.*"

Henry understood he needed to be back on his medication and that whatever he said would have to be convincing. So after parking the car and speaking to an orderly, Henry and Julia walked into Admissions, and Henry showed the clerk at the desk the bracelet he still had on from the previous day.

"I took thirty red pills last night and twenty this morning," Henry said. "I drank a twelve-pack of beer."

"Okay . . ." the clerk said, and handed Henry some paperwork to fill out.

As Henry and his mother sat and waited for a nurse, Henry said, "I have to go to the bathroom."

"You better hurry . . ."

By then, RN Cynthia Galante had been briefed about what Henry had said.

As Julia waited outside the bathroom, she could hear Henry dry-heaving and gagging to the point of choking. When she saw Jack Harris, a security guard Henry had known, Julia yelled, "Hey, Jack, can you go in there and check on my son?"

Harris then went over and knocked on the bathroom door.

"Are you okay, Henry?"

Getting no answer, he used his master key to unlock the door, and walked in.

"Are you okay, man?"

Henry got up off the ground, wiped off his mouth on his shirt sleeve, and said, "I took an overdose of drugs because I want to kill myself."

"Come on, Henry. Let's go get you some help."

While helping him into a wheelchair, Harris, a trained medical emergency technician, noticed that Henry had a "steady gait, his speech was not slurred and his pupils were not dilated or constricted." When Harris looked into the toilet bowl to see if there was any blood, all he saw was "white sputum," but it had no odor and didn't smell of alcohol. Added to the fact that, besides vomiting, Henry wasn't impaired in any way, Harris became curious.

As Cynthia Galante watched Harris wheel Henry into Admissions, she stopped what she was doing, took the wheelchair from Harris, and led Henry into the triage room, where he was placed on a stretcher.

Harris filled her in.

A few minutes later, at 12:05, Galante took Henry's vital signs for the first time. His temperature was 97.9; pulse 80; respiratory rate 28; and his blood pressure 138 over 84.

Henry Hudon had the vital signs of a healthy twenty-year-old.

Galante also noticed that he appeared to be alert, coherent and cooperative. She noted that his intake vital signs were normal and, oddly enough, "did not exhibit the symptoms of a drug overdose."

"I am used to seeing a patient who is unable to respond," Galante later recalled, referring to veterans who come in drunk, or on drugs. By contrast, Henry was talking and having no problem answering questions.

"Mr. Hudon," Galante asked, "what's going on with you?"

"I took an overdose of pills . . ."

"Why?"

"Because of increased pain."

For the next thirty minutes, Henry was assessed and his vitals were monitored. His condition never changed. At one point, he told Galante that his arm and chest hurt because he had been in a fight just days ago and had gotten punched in the chest.

Then Dr. William Smith came in and made the determination that Henry was admitted for a "drug overdose for pain," but he was "not suicidal," and that he took the "pills for a sore arm." Dr. Smith asked Henry several questions, but Henry refused to answer, only saying that his right elbow was sore.

Waiting patiently in the triage room, Julia Hudon finally got the answer she had been hoping to hear since she picked Henry up hours ago—that he would be admitted to Ward C.

Moments later, Jack Harris pushed Henry over to the elevator so he could be taken up to the ward and formally admitted.

"Momma, I don't want to die," Henry said as the elevator doors began to close.

"It's a hospital, Henry. They are going to make you better. You go back up and get stabilized. I'll bring you one of your Christmas gifts tomorrow when I come back."

The frosty air outside the hospital enveloped Julia Hudon as she opened the door and headed for her car. The sun was propped up just behind the pointed peaks of the Berkshire Mountains, and the blood-red sky was getting ready to give way to the night over the horizon. It was a quiet and beautiful winter day in the mountains of New England, and Julia Hudon could now rest assured that her son was in good hands.

CHAPTER 13

On December 8, RN Elizabeth Corey worked the dreaded 6:00 A.M. to 6:00 P.M. shift. That it was a Sunday only added to the day's longevity. When she admitted Henry Hudon to the four-bed ICU of Ward C at around two o'clock, she too noticed right away that something wasn't quite adding up.

It was obvious that Henry Hudon had lied about his condition. He was not showing any signs of a drug overdose or drunkenness. And sure enough, a breathalyzer test administered when he had first come in had now come back negative and his preliminary blood test results came back negative for both alcohol *and* drugs.

At 2:15, Corey gave him a shot of benadryl, "to help him rest." Profuse vomiting during the last twenty-four hours was taxing on the human body. A few hours of uninterrupted sleep would do Henry some good.

Shortly after giving him the shot, Corey checked his vital signs. Again, they were normal and stable. His heart rate, with a normal sinus rhythm, was about seventy to eighty. Perfect. Henry Hudon was a typical healthy, physically fit, thirty-five-year-old schizophrenic suffering from a severe case of the flu.

Nothing more. Nothing less.

As hospital protocol dictated, RN Corey had checked Henry's vital signs once again before she handed him over to Gilbert at about five o'clock. His heart rate and rhythm, Corey noted, were, again, normal and stable. For the three hours Corey had spent with Henry Hudon, his condition hadn't changed one bit.

Dr. Gregory Blackman was a young and energetic radiologist when he began working at the VAMC in April 1993. Working full-time at Baystate Medical Center in Springfield, Blackman, the father of two kids, moonlighted at the VAMC to help make ends meet.

Ever since he'd started his second job, Blackman had worked the weekend evening shift. While on duty, his responsibilities included making the rounds through the ER and Admissions. He wore a pager so he could respond to any codes called in the hospital during his shift.

His first night at the VAMC back in 1993 was a night Blackman will likely never forget.

After an unsuccessful code, Blackman got upset that one of the nurses didn't "bay the patient properly," meaning that the nurse, by his estimation, had failed to ventilate the patient accurately. Although it wasn't the nurse's fault that the patient died, afterward Blackman snapped at her.

"Next time, you need to bay him correctly!"

As Blackman was leaving the room, Gilbert grabbed him by the arm and pulled him aside.

"You need to adjust your attitude," she said. "We are not at the university anymore. This is a VA hospital . . . *doctor.*"

It was the first time Dr. Blackman had met Kristen Gilbert.

On Sunday, December 8, 1995, Blackman got to work around 5:15. Within an hour, it would be another night he would never forget—and, notably, it would involve Kristen Gilbert once more.

Making his rounds, Blackman went into Henry Hudon's room around 5:30 and, like everyone else, assessed him as being "alert and comfortable." By this time, Henry had seen eight people. Each person had agreed that, aside from being in the throes of schizophrenia and suffering from a bout with the flu, there was nothing else wrong.

"Henry wasn't drowsy or sleepy at all," Blackman later recalled.

For about two minutes, Blackman watched Henry's heart rate on the telemetry monitor RN Corey had hooked him up to before she left, and decided that there was nothing out of the ordinary. The only danger Henry Hudon faced was himself: He needed to stop running away from the hospital and get his meds stabilized. After that, everything would fall into place.

The previous night, Gilbert and Perrault were down at the VFW throwing darts with some friends. One time, Perrault purposely botched a shot and nicked Gilbert's toe. She had been teasing him about it the entire day, on December 8, before they got to work.

At 5:18, Perrault sent Gilbert an e-mail on the VAMC's computer network. He said he felt bad about what had happened at the VFW, but he knew that she wasn't *really* mad at him, and that it was all just a cute little act.

"[B]ut please don't remind me of what I did. I didn't want to hurt you. . . ."

The remainder of the e-mail consisted of Perrault's telling Gilbert about some chicken he had put in the oven before he left for work. Then he went on to explain about an upcoming Christmas party he was going to in Worcester, Massachusetts, on the following Sunday. It was a yearly military outing. He wanted Gilbert to meet him after his maneuvers so she could attend the party with him.

Thirty minutes after Perrault sent that first e-mail, for no apparent reason, Henry Hudon's condition dramatically changed. His heart rate, doubling, went from 80 to 160, and his blood pressure went from 138 over 84 to a whopping 200 over 120, all in a matter of moments.

After Hudon went into sudden cardiac arrest, Gilbert called a code and began resuscitation efforts as staff poured into the room. Henry Hudon, a young man who had come into the VAMC merely five hours ago suffering from the flu, was now fighting for his life.

"He had a seizure. . . ." Gilbert said when Dr. Blackman came into the room. "He's asystole. . . ."

Asystole is not something a doctor wants to hear when arriving on the scene of a code. It is a "cardiac standstill with no car-

diac output and . . . eventually occurs in all dying patients."
There is no heart activity. The heart is flatlined . . . and it is almost impossible to get a patient back once his heart is in asystole.

Blackman was beside himself. It was shocking to hear that Hudon, a man he had just seen, was now, suddenly, this close to death. But not only that, Gilbert had said he'd gone into a seizure. Seizures don't cause asystole; one can get respiratory arrest from a seizure, but even then, it's rare.

Nothing was making any sense.

To get air into his lungs, respiratory therapist Michael Krason intubated Henry right away. They couldn't shock Henry's motionless heart because once the heart is in asystole, a defibrillation shock can cause death. The only other thing the doctor could have done at that point was give the patient a drug called epinephrine, a synthetic form of the naturally occurring drug adrenaline. Epinephrine will shock the still heart of a dying man back into some sort of rhythm. Doctors order it all the time during codes.

Given to a healthy man, however, it would kill him.

Dr. Blackman ordered five "bristo-jet" packages of epinephrine to be pumped directly into Henry's IV.

After twenty-five minutes, Blackman and his crew brought Henry back to life. The young doctor was shaken, but he was overwhelmed by Hudon's desire to fight, and couldn't believe they had brought him back. Within moments, Hudon was opening his eyes and responding. Not only had they gotten him back, but it was evident that being dead for fifteen to twenty minutes hadn't affected Hudon's brain function.

When Blackman saw Henry open his eyes, he wanted to walk around and high-five each member of the crew. They had done the unthinkable. *What a job!* Henry Hudon was going to live.

Gilbert, watching Blackman celebrate, walked over and said, "Dr. Blackman, slow down a little . . ."

"Excuse me?" Blackman said.

"Don't be so happy. It wasn't *that* great of a save."

"What?"

"He's a schizophrenic, you know."

Blackman was shocked. *How dare she ruin such a moment!*

But instead of confronting Gilbert under these tremendously exhilarating circumstances, he simply said, "I still think it was a good thing."

Before he left the room, at about 6:15, Blackman gave strict orders to keep Henry medicated and on a ventilator. "And one last thing: make sure to notify me immediately if his condition changes."

CHAPTER 14

About forty-five minutes after Henry Hudon had first coded, Gilbert got online and e-mailed Perrault an answer to his previous question. In her terse note, Gilbert mentioned nothing about the dramatic cardiac arrest that had just taken place in her presence less than an hour ago. Instead, she wanted to make sure she had the correct directions to the Christmas party, which she suspected Perrault had mixed up.

Gilbert had a patient in ICU who had literally been dead for about twenty minutes before being brought back to life, and she still hadn't taken any of his vital signs since she'd started her shift nearly three hours ago. It was odd that she would remember to e-mail her lover but forget her duties as a nurse, especially since Hudon had been through so much.

Nurses in ICU were required to record vital signs every hour on the hour and include strips of the patient's telemetry heart monitor that best described the condition of the patient's heart during the course of the night. If a patient went into cardiac arrest, most nurses included three, four or even a half-dozen strips. But here was Gilbert, three hours into her shift, and she hadn't recorded *any* vital signs whatsoever, and had cut and pasted only one small section of Henry's heart strip to his chart.

A few moments after she finished sending Perrault an e-mail, Gilbert called a second code on Henry.

As the same team worked to resuscitate him, Dr. Blackman,

with Gilbert right beside him, reached into his medical tool box and took out a drug he rarely—if ever—used: bretylium.

Bretylium is not a first-line drug used to shock a patient's heart into beating again. It is a last-resort drug used only after everything else—including epinephrine—has failed.

When Gilbert saw him pull it out, she said, admiringly, "I've never seen 'bret' used before, doctor."

"How 'bout that?" Blackman shot back.

The bretylium worked. Hudon was brought back to life for a second time.

Blackman ordered him to be put on Valium for comfort. If anything—*anything*—went wrong, Blackman said, he wanted to be notified right away.

At 7:21, Perrault responded to Gilbert's e-mail: "Oops. You're right as always," he wrote, regarding his mix-up with the directions.

By this time, Dr. Blackman had gotten Henry's definitive test results back from the lab. It was confirmed that there were no barbiturates in his system when he had been admitted seven hours ago. The entire scope of his blood work was negative.

At 7:30, Gilbert called a third code on Henry.

Shocking everyone in the room, Dr. Blackman once again brought him back to life—but this time Henry remained unconscious. His body, because of all the fighting it had done, was beginning to shut down.

Dr. Blackman again ordered Henry to be kept on a heart monitor, but he also wanted him placed on a blood pressure machine.

Twenty minutes later, Gilbert wrote back to Perrault. She wanted to know what time she should meet him and what she should wear.

By 7:58, Perrault responded. Between 12:00 and 12:30, he wrote. "I'll be in jeans and a T-shirt."

A minute later, at 7:59, Gilbert wanted to know how late they were staying.

Perrault must have been away from his desk, because he didn't respond until 8:10. "Who knows?" he wrote. "Why, do you have to be home at a certain time?"

Gilbert didn't respond immediately. She must have been away from her computer doing something else. So Perrault wrote back at 8:18 trying to get a response. He said he really "needed that kiss." Then, "I love you." He added that the kiss "felt so right." He wanted to know if they could go out later that night.

By 8:43, Gilbert was back online. She said she would love to go out. "You're welcome for the kiss."

By 9:00, when she hadn't heard from Perrault, Gilbert wrote back asking if they were going out. "Should I meet you?" She seemed to be worried that he wasn't answering right away.

Between each e-mail, Perrault and Gilbert had seen each other during Henry Hudon's three codes. Perrault had been the one cop to respond. But Gilbert hadn't seen nor heard from Perrault for quite some time now, and she was likely wondering what was going on, where he was, and why he wasn't responding.

At 9:35, she called one more code on Henry Hudon. But within moments, Dr. Blackman made the sullen determination to call off resuscitation efforts. Henry wasn't responding . . . he was totally unconscious . . . the telemetry showed a flatline.

Still, for the next twenty-five minutes, Dr. Blackman and his team tried everything they could to revive him.

Blackman decided at 10:05 to stop efforts. Henry Hudon, at thirty-five, was dead.

Julia Hudon had not been notified once that her son, for approximately five hours, was fighting for his life. As far as she knew, Henry was sleeping off the terrible effects of the flu.

CHAPTER 15

Julia Hudon was used to getting phone calls from the VAMC at all hours of the night. Henry would go out for a smoke, hop on a bus near the hospital's entrance—as he had done on December 5—and never return. The VAMC would call Julia and explain what had happened.

"I'll go get him," she'd say.

A little after 10:00, on December 8, Julia Hudon's phone rang, startling her awake.

"Mrs. Hudon. It's Dr. Gregory Blackman."

"Yes?" Julia Hudon said. She was still half asleep.

"Your son is gone," Blackman said matter-of-factly.

"Fine. I'll go and get him more food," Julia said, and hung up.

She wasn't the least bit alarmed by Blackman's words. She figured Henry had just walked out of the hospital again. She had gotten calls like this for the past ten years and was at a point in her life where she almost expected them whenever Henry was in the hospital.

After hanging up with Dr. Blackman, Julia prepared to take her second trip of the day to Henry's apartment. But no sooner had she hung up the phone than it rang again.

"Mrs. Hudon . . . don't hang up," Dr. Blackman said in a panic. "What about food?" he asked. "I told you he's gone!"

"I heard that. I'll get him food or whatever he needs," she said. "And I'll try to get him back to you as soon as I can."

"No, Mrs. Hudon. I mean Henry's gone." He spelled it out: "Like D-E-A-D . . . dead!"

The following day, after allowing the blow of Henry's death to sink in, Julia phoned the VAMC and asked for Ritchie, the orderly she and Henry had come to know throughout the years. She said she wanted all the records from the time her son had been admitted to the time of death.

"Who was with him, Ritchie?" Julia wanted to know. "I can't believe he's gone." She was hysterical. "Who can I talk to? I need to speak to someone . . . *anyone.*"

"If you call back later," Ritchie said, "ask for his nurse, Kristen Gilbert."

Ritchie gave her the direct phone number to Ward C.

Though the horror of her son's death still hadn't sunk in, Julia Hudon suspected foul play from the start. If nothing else, she at least wanted some answers.

So she called the number Ritchie had given.

"Hello?" Gilbert said.

"This is Mrs. Hudon, Henry's mother. Can you tell me anything about my son . . . please, please, what were his last words?"

"It was fast. I have just come on duty and have to go," Gilbert snapped before hanging up.

Part of Gilbert's job, as the ICU nurse that night, was to file the heart monitor recordings of Henry Hudon's four cardiac arrests. These papers, no doubt, would have shed light on what had happened to his otherwise healthy heart as it beat wildly out of control.

To no one's surprise, those records were never found.

Years later, after she learned the details of Henry's fateful night, regarding Gilbert and Perrault's e-mail correspondence throughout the night, Julia Hudon told the *Hampshire Gazette* newspaper that Gilbert "was e-mailing her lover while my son was dying."

CHAPTER 16

Like many of his comrades, seventy-two-year-old Army veteran Francis Marier never claimed to be a war hero—just one of the lucky ones. On D-Day, June 6, 1944, when soldiers were being killed on the beaches of Normandy as if they were skeet targets, Marier escaped without a blemish.

As the decades after the war passed, Marier developed problems one might assume were a manifestation of his days in combat. He became obsessed with food. For the past several years, the six-foot-one, two-hundred-and-ninety-pound Marier would sit down with his brother and knock off ten pounds of corned beef in a weekend. His doctors warned him about overeating and placed him on an 1800-calorie-a-day diet, punctuated by extensive exercise, but Marier rarely adhered to it. Adding to his problems, "Buck," as he liked to be called, lived on the second floor of a small efficiency apartment that didn't have a kitchen. This forced him to eat at local restaurants for the better part of his life.

When he was admitted to the VAMC during the fall of 1995, Buck Marier was suffering from "a history of adult onset diabetes mellitus maintained on insulin," along with Chronic Obstructive Pulmonary Disease (COPD), a respiratory illness brought on by smoking that generally evolves into emphysema. Patients with COPD have trouble breathing. They wheeze. And a deep recurring cough hampers their daily life.

By December 5, 1995, the VAMC had Marier's diabetes under control and discharged him a few days later. Knowing he was unable to care for himself, Marier planned on going to live with his nephew, Raymond Marier, in Chicopee. His right foot had been amputated at the ankle some time ago, and he had trouble maneuvering the stairs where he lived.

One of the primary problems that landed Marier back at the VAMC had nothing directly to do with his blood sugar, COPD or heart. It was his repeated bouts with cellutitus. Diabetics fight a constant battle with circulation. Cellutitus is a byproduct of the disease. Ulcers develop on the surface of the skin and can get out of control if not contained.

After just a few weeks of being home, on December 19, Marier once again admitted himself to the VAMC, after developing an acute ulcer on the lower extremity of his left leg—a hole about the size of a pea. If it wasn't treated immediately, Marier was smart enough to know he could lose the entire leg.

As with all diabetics, Marier's blood sugar level (BSL) was checked and monitored upon his admission. Even though it came in at 155, which was somewhat higher than normal, his doctors agreed it wasn't that big of an issue because Marier had a strong heart and no history of heart problems.

It became apparent from that same initial examination that Marier had, at least for the past two weeks, taken heed to his doctor's orders and had been watching his diet. For he now weighed two hundred and seventy-seven pounds, almost fifteen pounds less than his previous admission.

Nevertheless, Marier's condition was unusual. Many of the vets admitted to the VAMC with similar problems weren't so lucky. What separated Buck from most others was that he was not totally dependent upon the care of the Ward C nurses. He could shave himself, eat on his own, move around fluidly in a wheelchair, and get dressed by himself.

RN John Wall was Marier's nurse on the night of December 19, and even Wall noticed how well he was doing.

"He was on bed rest . . ." Wall later remembered, "[he] had a snack after dinner—as most diabetics do—and had even wheeled himself into the restroom to shave."

The following day, Marier woke up, ate breakfast and, not

being one to associate with the other patients, isolated himself in his room.

Getting the cellutitus under control was the only reason Marier admitted himself to the VAMC, and his dosage of insulin upon admission reflected that. Because he wasn't being treated for diabetes during this particular visit, Marier's meds had been adjusted to counteract the fact that he was on a restricted diet and antibiotics for the ulcers. What was more, low *or* high blood sugar was not one of his problems. Nor was anything having to do with his heart.

In fact, a doctor later calculated the risk factor percentage for Marier's having sudden cardiac arrest—as so many of the Ward C patients around him were seemingly having—as being "less than one percent." Diabetics don't generally go into cardiac arrest, no matter how low their blood sugar is. Even if a hypoglycemic event occurs, where the BSL dips to dangerous levels, cardiac arrest is unlikely. There has never been a correlation between cardiac arrest and low blood sugar. "One does not cause the other, period," a doctor who later assessed Marier's condition said.

As the charge nurse, John Wall worked the 2:00 to 10:00 P.M. "T shift" on December 20, 1995, while Gilbert, who handled the med cart, and Kathy Rix, who spent the night working in ICU, were scheduled for four to midnight. As usual, Bonnie Bledsoe, a respiratory therapist who had been dating and living with John Wall at the time, April Gougeon and Lisa Baronas were also on board. Renee Walsh, who had been scheduled to leave at four, was still there. Since Ward C was understaffed, Wall had asked Walsh to hang around and help out where she could.

The nurses were split into teams. Since Marier was in the room directly next to the nurse's station, he was on Gilbert's team. She would be responsible for giving him his meds for the night. Wall, seeing they were shorthanded, also volunteered to give out meds and look after a few patients. Since Marier was in the room across from the nurse's station, Wall decided to take him on as a patient.

During the day, Marier had been seen by several nurses. One

of them, Frank Bertrand, a burly man about the same size as Marier, had befriended Buck. Bertrand called him "a woodsman—a guy who played hard and perhaps lived hard, too."

Before he left for the day, Bertrand had taken Marier's vital signs. With a temperature of 97.9, a heart rate of 85, and his blood pressure at a near perfect 126 over 80, Bertrand noted he was fine.

Between four and six o'clock, Marier's vital signs were checked again. He was "stable," "normal," one nurse recorded. His mental status was "alert and orientated." Francis Marier was, by all accounts, recuperating from the ulcers on his left leg. On top of that, Marier wasn't shy when it came to ringing the call bell. With a deep, thunderous voice, if something was bothering him, he would gladly let the nurses know about it.

At 8:00, Wall looked in on Marier for about the eighth time that night, and noted that although he "denied any change in the sensation of his leg where the infection was, his appetite was one hundred percent."

Furthermore, Wall reported, Marier showed no signs of hypoglycemia, a common illness among diabetics. When hypoglycemia sets in, diabetic patients almost instantly become weak, drowsy, confused and hungry. Turning pale, they get dizzy and develop headaches. They become irritable. They sweat, tremble, and their heart beats rapidly.

To the contrary, Francis Marier was calm and relaxed, getting ready to go to bed. He'd even shaved himself.

Around 8:15, Wall checked his BSL and found it to be within normal limits. Again, Wall noted that he was "alert and orientated."

After Wall finished up in Marier's room, he returned to the nurse's station and continued to catch up on his clerical work for the night.

Gilbert, walking toward Marier's room, stopped by the nurse's station for a moment.

"John, you got a second?"

"Shoot, Kristen."

"Can I leave early?"

"No," Wall said. "Absolutely not."

They were short on staff as it was. If Gilbert left, Wall would have to go back out on the floor and help the other nurses. It was the same old story with Gilbert lately. All she wanted to do was leave early so she could go see James Perrault.

At a few minutes before 10:00, Gilbert once again approached Wall, who was himself preparing to go home.

"John, I really need to leave early . . . can I go?"

"No, Kristen. We're shorthanded. I'm on my way out the door myself, anyway."

Gilbert became enraged and stormed off down the hall.

He can leave early, but I can't?

What Gilbert didn't realize was that Wall wasn't going home early. He had come in at 2:00; by 10:00 he'd already logged his eight hours.

After checking in on Marier once more, Wall left. If for some reason Marier had shown any disturbing signs, Wall would have never gone home, he later said.

Only minutes later, Gilbert walked into Marier's room and found him to be "lethargic and mumbling incoherently," she later wrote. She then checked his BSL and said it was at an unprecedented 44. Even for diabetics, this was unheard of. A 44-count is well below the scale many nurses usually see. Plus, Marier had been fine only moments ago when Wall checked him. How could his BSL drop nearly one hundred points in the span of just a few minutes? A person with a 44-count would literally be in a comatose state.

It was almost impossible.

Gilbert later said that after she pricked his finger and found his BSL that low, she decided to administer an ampoule of D-50, which is a concentrated, syrupy form of sugar that can be pushed directly into the vein. Nurses give D-50 to diabetics who are in a diabetic coma. It generally perks them right up.

When Gilbert pumped the D-50 into Marier's arm, she said he went into "full cardiopulmonary arrest."

Another improbability.

Because of its thick consistency, and the fact that it comes in such a large syringe—one slightly smaller than a tube of caulking—it takes two hands to administer D-50. Even under the most perfect conditions, nurses say, it takes about two minutes, sometimes even longer, to push the entire ampoule into the vein. One needs strong arms. For a nurse to ascertain that a pa-

tient had suffered a cardiopulmonary arrest during the push of a
syringe of D-50, she would have to be taking his pulse at the
same time. The only other way to know would be if the patient
had been hooked up to a heart monitor. And because Francis
Marier hadn't had any problems with his heart, he wasn't on a
monitor.

At 10:17, Gilbert called a code on Marier, and resuscitation
efforts began.

Many later agreed that the only way a person could end up
with a BSL of 44, in the short time frame that had occurred in
Marier's case, was if someone had given him an overdose of insulin.

CHAPTER 17

It wasn't the throbbing pulse of a fifteen-year-old boy, but after about four minutes of giving Francis Marier CPR, nurses and doctors were able to get his heart beating again on its own. A moment later, one of the nurses heard faint breathing sounds coming from his mouth.

"He's alive!"

After being stabilized, he was transferred to the ICU, where Kathy Rix, Renee Walsh and April Gougeon were waiting for him.

All three nurses agreed they had never in their lives seen a patient who had a BSL as low as Francis Marier's.

"I was stunned. Shocked. I had never seen a patient not respond to [one] push of D-50—and certainly if not one, the second one would do it," Renee Walsh later said.

Gilbert said that after checking his BSL, and finding it at 44, as she gave Marier an ampoule of D-50, he coded. But Rix did another finger prick test in the ICU shortly after Marier's code, but his blood level was at a staggering 37. It had actually gone down.

Restless and agitated, Marier was thrashing around the bed, in danger of disconnecting several tubes and IVs that had been hooked up. They tried restraining him, but he just wouldn't calm down.

At 11:15, Kathy Rix gave Marier a shot of Valium . . . but it did nothing. Then she gave him another ampoule of D-50, and his BSL immediately shot back up. Contrary to what had happened an hour before with Gilbert, Marier didn't go into cardiac arrest when Rix pushed the D-50 into his system. Instead, as if it had been the first ampoule of D-50 he'd been given, his BSL rose to 76.

One brick of D-50 generally did the trick for comatose diabetics. But here was Francis Marier, who had maintained a BSL of 155 for the past twenty-four hours, just now responding to what was seemingly a second ampoule of D-50.

What the hell was the problem?

Checking his chart, Rix noticed that at five, Gilbert had administered a scheduled dose of long-acting NPH insulin. This type of insulin is designed to begin working about four or five hours after it is injected, then peak about eight hours later, and begin to decline after that.

Rix realized that between 10:00 and 11:00—the time Marier had gone into cardiac arrest and ultimately ended up in her ICU—the NPH would have reached its peak effect.

Many now questioned how much insulin Gilbert had given him.

Near midnight, Kathy Rix stepped out of the ICU and yelled down the hall, "I need some help down here." She was still having problems restraining Marier.

With no response, Rix ran down to the nurse's station while April Gougeon stayed with Marier and the other two patients in ICU. Carl Broughear, a third-shift RN, and Gilbert were standing around chit-chatting. Rix noticed that Gilbert was all dolled up, wearing bright red lipstick, a skin-tight blouse and pants to match.

"I need some help," Rix yelled, and ran back to the ICU.

By this point, Gilbert and Broughear must have realized it was serious, because they rushed right down after hearing Rix scream.

Marier was still restless, thrashing around, waving his arms and legs, while the nurses fought with him to keep his tubes in place.

While trying to calm him with the help of April Gougeon and Carl Broughear, Rix turned to Gilbert and said, "Why don't you write up the ICU note so we can all leave closer to on time?"

Nodding, Gilbert agreed.

Not only had Marier's BSL remained low, but his heart rate continued to climb throughout the night, reaching anywhere from the mid-150s to as high as 175.

There was no reason for Francis Marier to have an actively increasing heart rate and low blood sugar. It made little sense to his nurses and doctors.

Kathy Rix's last note of the night established that Marier's heart rate had decreased considerably to about 145 by 11:55, with his blood pressure at about 170.

Like Henry Hudon, Marier was tough. He was a fighter. Oddly enough, though, his BSL remained at 76.

Carl Broughear took over for Rix in the ICU after she left. At one A.M., he checked Marier's BSL, and it had gone back down.

Forty-one?

While sweating profusely and sustaining a rapid heart rate, Marier continued to thrash around, kicking and waving his arms. This, Broughear thought, was strange, because patients— at least by his experience—with low blood sugar levels were far less active.

A few minutes after one, Broughear gave Marier another push of D-50. His BSL immediately rose to 78 . . . but only for a few minutes . . . then dropped back down to 48.

Marier's doctor came in and ordered two more ampoules of D-50. Broughear administered them and then checked Marier's BSL right away.

It shot right up—

—but only to 99.

Damn, it should be much higher, Broughear thought as he looked at the results.

As if something inside Marier's body were consuming the D-50 as fast as Broughear could pump it in, a few moments later, his BSL dropped back down to 47.

Near 2:30, Marier's doctor ordered even more glucose. "And check his BSL with the machine from Ward D," the doctor told Broughear. Perhaps there was a problem with Ward C's machine?

But Broughear got the same results.

Confused, not believing the BSL results in front of him,

Marier's doctor ordered a sample of Marier's blood be sent to another hospital to be double-checked.

It was almost 5:30 in the morning,

Something is wrong here, the doctor thought as he wrote up the order. *Maybe our machines aren't working?*

CHAPTER 18

RN John Wall, who had celebrated his forty-third birthday in September, had a movie star air about him. A trim, one hundred and fifty-five pounds, Wall was well respected among his VAMC superiors and colleagues. At six foot one, with a full head of kinky brown hair that he kept pushed back, and bushy eyebrows to match his thick, Tom Selleck-like mustache, Wall didn't quite match the stereotypical image of most nurses.

There wasn't a nurse who worked with Wall who could dredge up a bad word about him.

"He was an excellent nurse," Renee Walsh later said. "Very dedicated."

"He was very caring and diligent with patients," April Gougeon later noted.

Working with Gilbert, Wall had gotten to know Glenn Gilbert throughout the years and they had become pretty good friends.

There was one time in the middle of October when Glenn had stopped by Wall's house to help him out with his boat, and the two got to talking.

"You guys have been really, really busy up at the hospital lately, huh, John?" Glenn asked.

Wall didn't know what to say. They hadn't been any busier than usual. So he just went along with Glenn. "Yeah, I guess there's some overtime available."

"Kristen has been working till two and three in the morning."

Wall knew then that Kristen had been lying so she could get out of the house and run off somewhere with Perrault.

Wall's proficiency reports mimicked the saintly consensus he had among staff. Each year, he was heralded as a nurse who was rising up through the ranks on his way toward a managerial position. While in his sixteenth year of nursing—thirteen of which spent at the VAMC—Wall's nursing manager, Melodie Turner, wrote of his performance throughout 1995 that he "routinely exceed[ed] expectations to an exceptional degree . . . is professional and accountable. He serves as a leader. . . . He is [thorough], accurate [and] timely in documenting and reporting administrative and clinical information. . . . Mr. Wall has made significant contributions," Turner went on to write, "to the nursing profession. . . ."

There was no doubt about it: John Wall loved his job, valued the responsibility of being a nurse, and took every part of the job seriously. Codes, Wall later recalled, were especially trying on him because the patient who was being resuscitated was usually a patient he had gotten close to. But with the astonishing rate codes were occurring lately, Wall, like Kathy Rix and Renee Walsh, was beginning to worry that there was more to it than just coincidence.

Respiratory therapist Bonnie Bledsoe, a cute blonde from a well-to-do family in Western Massachusetts, took a job at the VAMC in early 1991, and began dating John Wall almost as soon as they met.

Bledsoe was tall, about five-nine, big-boned, like a volleyball player or swimmer, and seemed to carry a cheerful disposition wherever she went.

By October 1991, Wall had asked Bledsoe to move into his Northampton home, and she gladly accepted.

As their relationship blossomed, Bledsoe and Wall found out that they had a lot more in common than long walks on the beach and working in the same hospital.

They both had huge appetites for illegal drugs.

For Bledsoe, it was heroin. It started in the fall of 1994, when she fell into a trap Wall had been caught in already for some years.

Together they had been using between five and ten bags of heroin a day each. They would use in the morning, before work, and at night, after work. Although Wall never admitted to using at work, Bledsoe did.

How could, one might wonder, two VAMC employees use between $250 and $500 of heroin every day and not one of their colleagues—especially their nursing manager, Melodie Turner—pick up on it?

Bledsoe later explained.

"When you first start using heroin, you have to—when you take it, you get kind of a euphoric high. The more you use heroin, the less of an effect it has and the more you need, the more the body becomes physically dependant upon the drug, and eventually you're taking the drug just not to get the withdrawal symptoms, but you don't get high anymore."

Bledsoe claimed her drug use never affected her job performance, and many who worked with her over the years, along with her performance evaluations, agreed with her contention.

In April 1995, quitting heroin came easy to Bledsoe . . . but not for long. Because by late August, she had fallen in love with crack cocaine—and never looked back. While Wall stuck to using heroin, Bledsoe began using crack three or four times per week, spending anywhere between $100 and $200 dollars per use. Although she said never used crack at work, whenever she did use, she usually took the following day off to recuperate.

Still, Melodie Turner's work evaluations of Bledsoe and Wall thrived with praise.

"Exceptional and fully successful," one report noted of Bledsoe's performance between April 1995 and March 1996. "I have received compliments," Melodie Turner wrote of Wall in 1996, "from peers and clinicians on his professionalism and nursing knowledge. . . . I expect Mr. Wall to become the Acute Medical Laboratory problem resolution expert."

For her entire life, Bledsoe had been asthmatic—and one of the only things that really worked for the severe asthmatic fits she sometimes had was a shot in the arm of epinephrine. What's more, no one knew it just yet, but there were enough ampoules of epinephrine missing from Ward C lately to start a small pharmacy.

Was it Bonnie Bledsoe who was stealing them?

CHAPTER 19

Early in the morning on December 21, a nurse at the VAMC called John Wall and explained to him what had happened to Francis Marier the previous night. As far as Wall was concerned, Marier had shaved, showered, eaten his dinner and fallen asleep. The only worry Francis Marier had was falling out of bed in his sleep.

Concerned, Wall went to work early and reviewed Marier's chart. He was "stunned and shocked" to find out how much D-50 had been pumped into Marier's system throughout the night without any response—a total of eight ampoules—and that he'd had a cardiac arrest just moments after Wall left his side.

Wall soon learned that Marier had also been put on a D-5 and later a D-20 drip, which were the same as the D-50, except they came in a drip form and were hooked to a patient's IV. For the entire night, Marier's BSL wouldn't climb. And by six the next morning, it still wasn't anywhere near where it should have been, taking into account he'd had enough glucose pumped into his system during the night to crystallize his blood.

Something wasn't adding up.

But the most striking aspect of the night's events occurred around nine A.M. After several hours of the D-20 and D-5 drips, Marier's BSL suddenly shot back up to a normal level, as if whatever had been in his system eating up the glucose somehow dissolved.

Wall then went to Kathy Rix with a scenario.

"I think she might have sabotaged my patient because she was angry at me for not letting her go home early last night," Wall said, referring to Gilbert.

Rix confided in Wall that she, too, was developing suspicions. In fact, she had been watching Gilbert for some time. Since November, Rix explained, she had been keeping track of the medical emergencies on Ward C, and the one nurse who kept popping up on her list was . . . well, she didn't even have to finish her sentence . . . *Gilbert.*

When Renee Walsh arrived, she was overwhelmed by the news that Carl Broughear had spent eight to ten hours trying to get Marier's BSL to rise. When she thought about it, the only thing that made sense was that somebody had given Marier a mass dose of insulin.

By December 22, Francis Marier had made an impressive recovery and was transferred out of the ICU and back into the regular population on Ward C. Later that afternoon, he was given a clean bill of health, scheduled for an outpatient follow-up on February 29, and discharged.

For the past twenty years, sixty-one-year-old Korean War vet Thomas Callahan had consumed upward of a quart of whiskey per day. There were times when he couldn't even remember his own name. A two-pack-a-day smoker, Callahan had developed a severe case of COPD and was a frequent patient at the VAMC because of it.

Yet it was a battle with schizophrenia that consumed most of Callahan's medical care.

When he was admitted to the VAMC on January 18, 1996, Callahan had a simple request for the admitting nurse.

"Where's my whiskey?"

After he failed to get the answer he'd perhaps hoped for, he cursed the nurse and said, "I was trying to call home . . . they kept saying, 'Go back to Oz. Go back to Oz.' "

Before this, "Tomcat" Callahan had spent two days in the ICU at Baystate Medical Center. He'd been admitted with "right lower lobe pneumonia," along with a "severe exacerbation of his COPD," which he had been battling for the past eight years.

For the nurses who treated him, Callahan was extremely high maintenance. "Eccentric" and "gregarious," one nurse remembered. "Difficult" and "loud," another recalled. Since 1986, he'd been hospitalized at the VAMC at least twenty times. Calling him "Father Callahan" behind his back was a running joke because he liked to take confession from anyone who entered his room.

While fighting pneumonia in the ICU on January 22, 1996, Callahan's body began to detox violently from its addiction to alcohol. During the daytime hours, nurses in the ICU fought continuously with him to keep a biPAP mask attached to his face. His emphysema was chronic. He had pneumonia. The biPAP mask helped him breathe. While he continually grabbed at his IV, at one point, it took three nursing assistants to restrain him. Yet not once while this was happening did Callahan's heart rate rise. He did have a history of heart disease, but he had never been admitted to a hospital for it. Further, the only medication he was taking was for his pneumonia, mental illness and COPD.

His heart condition was not even an issue.

As usual, Gilbert came into work on January 22 at 4:00. John Wall was again the charge nurse, and he ordered Gilbert to work in the ICU. Kathy Rix was in charge of distributing meds to Teams One and Two.

On January 18, RN Liz Corey, who had been Callahan's nurse during the day shift, made a note that Callahan had been in ICU coughing for a good portion of the day, but his heart rate, throughout the entire day, had not changed.

The next day, respiratory therapist Michael Krawiec gave Callahan a treatment and noted that he had "a productive cough and that he tolerated his treatment with no adverse reaction." Later that same day, RN Frank Bertrand noticed that he was "highly agitated," but his heart rate was "sinus rhythm to sinus tach . . . [he had] no irregular heartbeats" and was running at a rate of "90 to 110."

A stickler for detail, RN Rix saw Callahan later that night and assessed his condition a little more differently. Like many of her colleagues, Rix was dedicated to providing the next shift with as much information about a patient as possible. All the nurses were required to give extensive written and/or tape-recorded reports of each patient they cared for so the patient's doctor and the nurse on the following shift would know exactly what was going on.

The only nurse who hadn't been routinely doing this was Gilbert.

Nursing manager Melodie Turner had even sent the nursing staff e-mail messages reminding them of the "importance of charting" patients and including rhythm strips in medical files.

But again, neither Turner, nor anybody else in the VAMC administration, went any further than that. Awareness, apparently, was enough; following up and checking the actual medical files to see who was adhering to protocol and who wasn't would have been the obvious next step, but no one did it.

Back on December 8, it would have taken only one look to notice how poor Gilbert's record-keeping was. She had found Henry Hudon in cardiac arrest four times. Even an inexperienced nurse would have known to include no fewer than eight heart strips from Hudon's telemetry monitor on his chart, so his doctor—if no one else—could see what had transpired during Hudon's codes. But Gilbert placed only two strips in his file: one at the beginning of her shift—before the first code—and another when Hudon was dead, a flatline.

Then there were the vital sign records. Turner had clearly spelled out in countless memos how the system was supposed to work: Patients' vital signs in the regular population, during an eight-hour shift, were to be taken and recorded no less than two times; in the ICU, it was mandatory that they were checked and recorded every hour.

A quick glance at many of Gilbert's patients throughout the past few months would have shown that she rarely recorded *any* vital signs.

But again, those who should have did nothing about it.

Thomas Callahan remained stable throughout the day on January 22. During that afternoon, RN Ann French sat with Callahan in the ICU and watched him eat. She noticed that he was shoveling the food in his mouth as fast as he could, and she feared he might choke.

Sure enough, Callahan began gagging, but quickly spit out his food before any more problems arose.

Gilbert had come on duty at four and, by seven, had spent the better part of three hours with Callahan. Other than the earlier choking incident, French explained, his condition went unchanged.

By 7:15, Gilbert had made her first assessment: he was "alert and orientated to person [and] place, but not time. Less agitated this evening, but [he] remains very manic."

At 7:17, Callahan began singing "Ave Maria" at the top of his lungs and had eaten "one hundred percent of his meal," Gilbert noted.

A readout coming off his telemetry monitor reflected that, at 7:25, Callahan's heart rate was sinus tach, 100 to 115, which was normal under the circumstances. Dr. Michael DiBella, Callahan's attending physician, had even come in and ordered a transfer for him out of the ICU back into the general population as soon as the next day.

But at 7:45, while Gilbert stood by his side, Callahan began "coughing forcefully," she later wrote, and then yelled, "I think I'm going to die."

His scream was so loud that it rang throughout the entire corridor. Many were startled but quickly wrote it off as another one of his manic episodes.

Gilbert claimed that as Callahan began coughing, his heart rate more than doubled: from 100 beats per minute to a deadly 240. When this happened, Gilbert yelled for help, as Callahan continued to scream.

For about fifteen minutes, Gilbert and several nurses monitored him closely. His blood pressure hovered at around 191 over 116, and his heart rate at about 215 to 200, but he never coded.

By 8:10, Callahan's heart finally calmed down to 115, and it appeared that everything was going to be fine.

As Kathy Rix stood by the nurse's station, Mike Krawiec came walking by, shaking his head.

"What is it?" Rix asked.

"She's at it again. . . ." Krawiec muttered under his breath.

Rix bolted for the ICU. When she got there, Callahan's episode, just winding down, seemed to be under control. Although Rix was a bit disheveled and confused, she logged the situation in her growing mental bank of emergencies and went back to her assignment.

In her progress note, Gilbert implied that Callahan's cardiac event had been brought on by the coughing fit he'd had. But cardiologist Dr. Thomas Rocco later summarized that it was impossible for a cough to cause a heart attack. And since Callahan had been singing "Ave Maria" right before his heart rate doubled, Rocco further acknowledged, "[he] was improved to the point where he could sing."

Gilbert also wrote that she obtained a full twelve-lead EKG, which meant she would have stuck twelve round leads all about Callahan's chest and feet and thus taken a full readout of his heart rate. She also said she called the on-duty physician to examine him.

But there was no evidence that she had done any of it.

When a nurse in the ICU takes an EKG, she makes three copies of the results: One goes into the record at the patient's bedside, and two get placed in the hospital mail to be sent to the EKG department, where a doctor officially reviews the results, initials them, and then places them in the patient's permanent record.

Soon after Callahan's cardiac event ended, Gilbert went on a scheduled break and RN Wall relieved her. When Rix found out that Gilbert had gone on break and Wall had taken over, she ran down to the ICU to see what she could find out.

"Let's take a look at the heart strips," Rix suggested.

Wall agreed.

After reviewing the strips, Wall and Rix decided to search the room. Other than the obvious, they were looking for any possible reason why Callahan's heart rate could have doubled.

"John," Rix asked, "what kind of medication could have possibly been given to him that might have caused his heart to go into such a fast rhythm?"

Half-joking, Wall said, "Wouldn't it be funny if we looked in the needle-collection container and saw EPI . . ." referring to the drug epinephrine.

Besides potassium, Rix and Wall made the determination that epinephrine was the only other drug that could have made Callahan's heart rate, along with that of a growing list of other patients, ascend out of control. They had checked what medication he had been on since being admitted and knew from experience that none of it could have caused his heart rate to climb like it had.

"What about potassium?" Rix asked.

Potassium was another drug, like epinephrine, that was extremely taxing on a healthy heart.

Inside the ICU, there was a red and tan needle-disposal bucket attached to the wall similar to those on the counter in any doctor's office. There was also one inside Callahan's room, one on the IV cart, one on the crash or "code" cart, and one in the medicine cabinet where medications were stocked under the cupboard.

Rix looked inside the one in the ICU first, but because of its small oval cover, she had a hard time seeing past the top. After carefully pushing the lid down, she didn't see anything.

Then she walked over to the bucket underneath the medicine cabinet.

As soon as she looked inside, there they were: three broken glass ampoules, each one about the size of a Magic Marker cap, lying on the bottom. The glass was the same texture and color of a beer bottle—only thinner and more brittle. Easy to see, stretched across the front of the white label, were three hot-pink-colored stripes, as if to warn the person thinking of using it that it was a powerful, life-threatening drug. Staring at Rix across the top of the vials was the word EPINEPHRINE in capital letters. On the bottom were the numbers 1:1000, which meant it was one of the highest concentrated forms of epinephrine available. Shaped like an hourglass, or a miniature Coke bottle, with a thin and breakable neck, an ampoule of 1:1000 epinephrine could be snapped in an instant if a patient had had an allergic reaction to food, a bee sting, or was suffering from a severe asthmatic fit.

Epinephrine—or "EPI," as those in the medical field call it—is produced naturally in the body's system, more commonly called adrenaline. It causes the blood pressure to rise, the heart to race. It is stocked in two forms at the VAMC: a large bristo-jet pre-filled syringe, 1:10,000 strength, used mainly during cardiac emergencies for patients found in cardiac arrest; and, a 1:1000 form packaged in a smaller glass ampoule, used for treating people with food and bee sting allergies or asthma.

An overdose of the drug causes the heart to beat faster and faster until it cannot sustain the rate, thus collapsing it into *v-fib,* where it quivers without beating.

Epinephrine is extremely hard to detect in the human body. Not because the body produces it naturally, but that it is the first drug given when a person goes into cardiac arrest.

If one were in the business of killing people, it could be said that EPI is the *perfect poison.*

A thought occurred to Rix as she looked at the broken vials in disbelief. In over twelve years on the job, she had never known anyone to use the drug in that form.

Quickly, Rix opened up the medicine cabinet to see if there were any other drugs stocked that, in appearance, even remotely resembled the three broken vials of epinephrine she had just seen. Maybe there was another answer?

There were none.

After the initial shock set in, Rix grabbed a piece of paper and jotted down how many unused ampoules of EPI were in the medicine cabinet.

Eighteen, she wrote as her hand trembled.

From that point on, Rix decided she was going to keep track of the EPI inventory herself. With a drug like EPI, which was rarely ever used, it wouldn't be hard to figure out if Gilbert was, as Rix and Wall now highly suspected, using it to poison patients.

"I can't believe it," Rix said to Wall in a whisper after she realized what could be happening. "I just can't believe it . . ."

CHAPTER 20

John Wall and Kathy Rix didn't need much more convincing. Patients at the VAMC were dying at alarming rates, and medical emergencies were being called just about every other day on what seemed to be only during the second shift—and Kristen Gilbert's signature was all over them. The questions plaguing Rix and Wall, however, were a bit more difficult: What should they do about the spent epinephrine ampoules they had found in Callahan's room? Whom should they go to? Was it even proof of anything?

Rix was scheduled to leave for vacation on January 26. So whatever she and John Wall were going to do would have to wait until she got back a week or so later. Wall, of course, wasn't going to act on anything alone. If this thing went as far as he and Rix thought it would, once it became known, Wall himself would have some explaining to do. He was addicted to heroin, he had been using the drug for years, and he had been lying about it to everyone around him. The last thing he wanted was to draw attention to himself.

The day before Rix left, she removed all the disposal needle buckets and replaced them with new ones.

"If I find any spent ampoules of EPI when I return," she told herself, "I'll know they aren't from the Callahan incident."

It seemed like a good plan.

Then she took out her pad and counted the ampoules in the medicine cabinet.

Bonnie Bledsoe, on January 28, 1996, was working in Ward D, which, being in another building altogether, was a considerable distance to walk from Ward C. Gilbert was alone in the ICU with one patient, Michael Cascone, a seventy-five-year-old World War II vet who, like Callahan, had been admitted to the VAMC with a severe case of pneumonia. Cascone, a big man, had spent twenty-eight years in the Army, reaching the rank of master sergeant, and was well respected by anyone who wore camouflage green.

Because she was the only respiratory therapist on duty that night, Bledsoe would be responsible to show up for any codes called on Ward C.

At 7:00, Gilbert called a code on Cascone, and Bledsoe rushed over from Building Two. No sooner had she made it back to her post in Building Two after she helped Gilbert get Cascone out of trouble, than Gilbert called a second code.

When Bledsoe made it back to her post in Building Two after the second resuscitation effort on Cascone had been successful, her pager went off again—sure enough, for a third time, Michael Cascone was fighting for his life.

After things calmed down and Cascone was out of trouble for the third time, Bledsoe walked toward the door in the ICU to leave, but stopped for a moment.

She had something to say.

"If I have to run over here one more time, Krissy, I'm going to start wheezing."

Bledsoe was an asthmatic. She and Gilbert had been out with their significant others on a number of occasions, and because she knew Gilbert was so knowledgeable in medicines, Bledsoe brought up her asthma all the time.

Standing about ten feet away from Gilbert in the ICU, Bledsoe explained how all the running back and forth was making her asthma act up. When she finished talking, Gilbert reached into the front pocket of her smock and pulled out a small vial of some type of medication.

Gilbert flashed the vial. "Do you need some EPI, Bonnie?" she asked. Then, quickly, put it back into her pocket.

"*No,* thank you," Bledsoe snapped and walked away.

As for Michael Cascone, his heart wasn't as strong as Francis Marier's. After a fourth code was called later that same night, he died.

CHAPTER 21

A proud father, former Navy crewman Walter Cutting watched his son, Kenny, play football for the Lunenburg High School Blue Knights during the early seventies, perhaps dreaming of him one day becoming the next all-star running back for the New England Patriots.

A clean-cut kid with bushy, Groucho Marx-type eyebrows set above his sad brown eyes, Kenny was motivated to succeed at anything he did. Marrying his high school sweetheart on January 26, 1976, Kenny joined the U.S. Army a year later. In a matter of weeks, he was off to Fort Leonard Wood, Missouri, for recruit training. It was a far cry from the Yankee confines of Lunenburg, Massachusetts, but it was what Kenny wanted. On April 11, only months after he left, Jeffrey Cutting, Kenny's son, was born.

After boot camp graduation, Kenny was transferred to the 39th Engineers Station at Fort Devens, which worked out perfectly, because Fort Devens was located in Ayers, a mere stone's throw from the new ranch-style house he and Nancy bought in Leominster.

He was living the life he had only dreamed about. But shortly after Cutting arrived at Fort Devens, tragedy struck.

For the past few years, he had been experiencing stiffness in his legs and his eyesight had been poor. But it never amounted to anything. While in training, only about fifteen months into his military career, Kenny called his father at home with some rather grim news.

"My doctor just informed me that I'll be dead in a few years . . ." Kenny said, not a speck of worry, discontent or concern in his voice.

"What?"

Kenny wasn't overly emotional or tattered in the slightest by what appeared to be the worst news a married man of twenty could ever imagine hearing from his doctor.

"They say I have multiple sclerosis," Kenny continued.

At the time Kenny was diagnosed, little was known about the affliction his father would later tag a "horrendous disease." Many doctors, in the late seventies, had equated MS with a death sentence.

Nonetheless, each day after the initial diagnosis offered a new set of problems for Kenny. His body deteriorated quickly as the disease grew at an extraordinary rate—and within only a couple years after being discharged, Kenny was having trouble walking and seeing.

Like almost everyone who had ever entered Kenny's life, his in-laws adored him. Kenny always had something nice to say and never once complained about having been dealt a deck of cards that might end his life years before he'd planned. He vowed to fight the disease with everything he had.

By 1980, it was obvious to Nancy that caring for Kenny at home was going to be almost impossible. One day, shortly after he first started using a wheelchair, Nancy wheeled him out on the front porch so he could enjoy a promising summer afternoon. Kenny loved just sitting, soaking up the sunshine. After a while, Nancy went out to check on him and found the skin on his feet stuck to the cement, as if they had melted to it like a piece of gum. The roughest part for Nancy was that Kenny was oblivious to what had happened; he couldn't feel his feet.

After that, the Cuttings placed Kenny in a long-term care program at a Jamaica Plain VA hospital. Within days, he began saying how uncomfortable it was. The Cutting family thought that for a man like Kenny Cutting, who was as gentle as a falling leaf, a man who never once complained about *anything,* to begin fretting, the conditions in Jamaica Plain must have been deplorable.

The VAMC in Leeds was a long drive from Leominster, but it had a reputation for being one of the best VA hospitals in the state. Perfect for Kenny's situation, the VAMC had both short- and long-term care units, an acute medical ward, and a staff of doctors that could help make Kenny's life as comfortable as possible.

Before moving him into the VAMC, Nancy had once again tried taking care of him at home, but by this time he was bedridden, his eyesight nearly gone. And one of his main problems brought on by the MS was bowel obstruction, which was usually accompanied by fever and infections.

His muscles just didn't want to work anymore.

Throughout all of it, though, Kenny's spirit never wavered. He stayed focused on the good in his life.

"He never fussed," Walter later said. "He was always cheerful. He was [a] very happy . . . happy man."

As he began to get comfortable at the Leeds VAMC, Nancy and Walter soon realized that they had finally found a place where they could feel comfortable about leaving Kenny.

"He could not have had any better care," Walter later said.

Nurses at the VAMC fell in love with Kenny and his angelic attitude, and he soon became a favorite patient of many nurses.

"Everyone loved Kenny," Rachel Webber recalled. "He had these big, brown eyes, and he would look at you and [say], 'You look beautiful tonight . . . you look so beautiful.'"

A favorite saying of Kenny's to all the female nurses was, "Can I tell you something? You're looking very beautiful today."

By the fall of 1995, he was being spoon-fed and had lost total use of his hands and legs. But, as if he had accepted his fate and made peace with the outcome, he never looked back.

In late October, Cutting had been sent back to the Jamaica Plain VA hospital for small bowel obstruction surgery, where he underwent an "exploratory laparotomy." But after opening him up, doctors found "no mechanical obstruction . . ."

Being cleared for surgery and subsequently undergoing it

without any cardiovascular problems was significant for someone in Kenny Cutting's condition because coronary artery disease and myocardial infarction—heart disease—are equally the
number-one cause of death during general surgery. This was
why doctors did extensive research beforehand, profiling patient risks for cardiovascular disease. A quick check of Kenny's
medical history showed that he didn't have the disease, and
there was no history of it in his family. Many people confuse
MS with some of the more common diseases. MS patients, at
the end stages of the disease, deteriorate in increments, each
organ—liver, pancreas, kidneys, etc.—failing, in succession,
like dominoes. After that, respiratory failure slowly develops,
and, finally, death.

Although Kenny's organs weren't the same as, say, a healthy
forty-one-year-old male's, by all accounts he had a healthy
heart—which is one of the only organs unaffected by the on-
slaught of MS.

On November 1, 1995, Kenny had a complete colonoscopy.
It showed no lesions, but did indicate he had multiple infections. So he was then put on antibiotics, eventually recovered,
and was transferred back to the VAMC in Leeds—a place that
he had literally called home for the past fifteen years.

By November 20, settled back into his room in the long-term
care unit of the VAMC, Kenny was assessed as "alert" and in
"fair physical condition." He had no problems with his heart,
lungs, or anything else related to his organs. He was having the
same mild seizures he'd had for years, but that was it.

Things got a bit more complicated by late January, though.
His persistent bowel obstruction was back, and along with it an
infection and fever of 104 degrees.

Since 1985, Kenny had been on what is called a "DNR [do
not resuscitate] status." Nancy figured that if it was his time to
go, she should let him go, and never winced at making the decision. She knew there was no cure for his MS; why fight the in-
evitable when it came time?

Back on December 3, 1995, Gilbert, who, like most of the
VAMC nurses, knew Kenny pretty well, noted in his chart that
his "abdomen remain[ed] distended and firm . . . [But will] continue to monitor bowel sounds . . . [patient was] resting quietly."

The following day, Kenny's daytime nurse recorded his blood pressure at 160 over 85; his pulse regular at 100; and there was "no report [from the patient] of pain." With the exception of his bowel obstruction and a slight fever, Kenny was stable.

Running a high fever because of an infection, on January 26, 1996, he was transferred to the Ward C ICU. A few days later, nurses took him off the oxygen he had been on, and he began breathing on his own.

For the next week, his fever seesawed, and with it, his heart rate.

By Thursday, February 1, Gilbert wrote that he "remain[ed] unresponsive to all stimuli"—verbal interaction, prodding, poking—"[and] opened his eyes spontaneously . . . [but] not as a result of stimuli."

This change was drastic compared to what Nancy, Kenny's now-grown son and Kenny's mother had witnessed the previous day, January 31. When Nancy first entered the room that day, Kenny said the same thing he had a thousand times before, "You look exquisite, Nancy."

He was groggy and tired, sure. But he answered all of her questions and talked to everyone in the room.

For the next twenty-four hours, nurses in the ICU monitored Kenny's fever and bowel movements. After hearing faint bowel sounds over the course of the day, it appeared Kenny's system was responding to the antibiotics.

During the early morning hours of February 2, Kenny's fever had gone down, and there was even more movement in his bowels. He had good color. He was alert.

It was an old story where Kenny Cutting was concerned: He would get transferred to the Ward C ICU and do battle with whatever part of his MS decided to act up, and, after fighting it with every ounce of strength he had left, his condition would return to as stable as it would get.

Kenny Cutting was a fighter. No one denied him that.

But no matter how hard he was willing to fight this time around, Kenny's fate was sealed later that same afternoon when Gilbert approached James Perrault with plans for later on that night.

Before leaving for work at half past three, on February 2, 1996, Gilbert told Perrault she would meet him at his house at around 10:00 so they could go out on the town.

This was an odd time—because Gilbert's scheduled shift didn't end until midnight.

CHAPTER 22

By February 2, 1996, the Northeast had all but finished digging out of what was being billed as "the Blizzard of '96," a mid-January winter storm that had dumped nearly two feet of snow in the Northampton region, and about three feet just to the south, in New York and New Jersey. It had been one of the worst winter storms the East Coast had seen in some seventy years, claiming twenty-three lives by the time it had done its damage and whipped out to sea.

But weather records, storm-related deaths and snowfall amounts were far from the minds of nurses John Wall, Kathy Rix and Renee Walsh. For months now, they had been watching and questioning Gilbert's every move. But with Rix still away on vacation, nothing had been said or done. And Renee Walsh, although highly suspicious, was still keeping her thoughts to herself.

The death rate on Ward C had risen so sharply within the past few months that for anyone who had even glanced at the data in passing, it would have been impossible to deny that something highly irregular was going on. In the past twenty-four months, there had been more than one hundred deaths on Ward C alone, which, by itself, should have been enough to spark someone's interest.

But no one in management noticed.

Broken down even further, the available data were even

more shocking. During the past two years, there had been twenty-three deaths during the midnight to 8:00 A.M. shifts, and twenty-two deaths during the 8:00 A.M. to 4:00 P.M. shifts, which was not out of the ordinary for a hospital the size of the VAMC. But during the hours of 4:00 P.M. and midnight—Gilbert's shift—there had been *fifty* deaths, more than double. In fact, since 1991, when the "angel of death" moniker became attached to Gilbert, there had been approximately one hundred and sixty-one deaths on Gilbert's shift alone, not even close to the one hundred and twenty-one deaths recorded on *both* the first and third shifts throughout that same period.

As for codes, the numbers were even more stunning. During that same two-year period—1995-96—there bad been forty-five codes on Ward C. Gilbert, however, had found thirty of them herself. In what should have further inspired suspicion, since she'd starting working at the VAMC back in 1989, Gilbert had found seventy-two codes herself, whereas during all other shifts—all the nurses combined—her colleagues had found only seventy.

Finally, between August 1995 and February 1996, employees in the VAMC pharmacy had delivered approximately one hundred and fifteen ampoules of 1:1000 strength epinephrine to Ward C, yet not one doctor or nurse had administered the drug. Further, the pharmacy did not maintain any type of record to keep track of its deliveries; it simply restocked the drug whenever the satellite pharmacy, medicine cabinet or anywhere else the drug was stored ran low.

Apparently, the dead were speaking from their graves; the only problem, however, was that no one in VAMC management or quality control was listening.

Throughout the day on February 2, Kenny Cutting's condition had somewhat improved, with the exception of a high fever. There was no mistaking that Kenny was ill. But he had been down this road before and pulled out of it without any major problems. His daytime RN, Corrine Rourke, later said that Kenny "was quite sick [on February 2] . . . but . . . he was going to pull through." Assessing him later on that same day, Rourke added that he was "just beginning to turn the corner and he had a good chance of getting back to, partially, his normal life." Rourke had cared for Kenny many times in the past while he had suffered from the same set of problems, and he always, she later said, "pulled through."

During the early morning hours of February 2, Kenny's blood pressure remained at 120 over 80.

Nearly perfect.

Around 5:00 A.M., Kenny's 103-degree temperature went down to 101, and his blood pressure dropped to 103 over 76, then to 100 over 64. But his heart rate remained a bit high.

The antibiotics were beginning to work.

At 6:50, RN Rourke noticed that Kenny's heart rate had increased into the 130s, but there was no "ectopy," extra beats. This was a bit high, of course. But Kenny's fever had gone back up, too—and when a fever rises, the heart rate is generally not too far behind.

By ten o'clock, Kenny's temperature had dropped a few degrees, and his heart rate soon followed, dropping back down into the 110s. Sometime later, his temperature rose again, and his heart rate was right behind.

In terms of mechanics, the body is like a machine. Doctors call it "radiational cooling." The blood and arteries work like the coolant and hoses in a car engine: the hotter the engine gets, the harder the system works to cool it off. The fact that Kenny Cutting's heart rate increased during the duration of his fever indicated that his cardiovascular system was doing the job it was designed to do.

At about 3:30 P.M., the night shift began filing in. When John Wall arrived, he learned he had been designated Team Leader, instead of charge nurse. His colleague and friend, David Rejniak, who lived down the street from Gilbert when she lived in Florence with Glenn, had been elected charge nurse for the night. Rejniak knew Gilbert pretty well, and some said he'd even had a crush on her.

It was a slow night on Ward C. Usually, the census was about twenty to twenty-five patients, but tonight there were only eleven beds filled. Carole Osman and Lori Naumowitz were assigned to work the floor, while Gilbert was told to report to the ICU, where her only patient of the night was Kenny Cutting.

Around six, Rejniak reported to the ICU to relieve Gilbert, who was getting ready to go on her dinner break. With Rix on vacation and Wall now working the desk for Rejniak, Gilbert and Rejniak were the only nurses qualified to stay with Kenny Cutting.

When Rejniak showed up, Gilbert filled him in. "He's doing the same now as . . . before," she said before walking out of the room.

As she sat and ate her lunch, John Wall came into the break room.

"Kenny isn't looking so good tonight, John," Gilbert said nonchalantly. "If he dies, can I use some of my comp time and leave early?"

Protocol among the nurses dictated which nurse could leave early on any given night. If a nurse wanted to leave early, he or she would first have to clear it with the others. Gilbert, who had been working part-time for the past few months, had lost her seniority to ask if she could leave early. Full-timers had the opportunity to use any accrued comp time before part-timers did.

After thinking about it for a moment, Wall said, "I don't care, Kristen."

At first, he had been taken aback by her request. He knew Kenny was sick, but for crying out loud, was the man suddenly on his deathbed? But seeing that Gilbert had spent the past two hours with him, maybe she knew something Wall didn't.

According to Gilbert's own assessment, however, which she had just written in Kenny's chart before she sat down to eat, he was "stable" when she had left him. His doctor, Theodore King, even checked in on him earlier that night and made the same assessment.

After finishing her dinner at about 6:25, Gilbert returned to the ICU and relieved Rejniak.

"How's he doing?"

"The same," Rejniak said.

While Rejniak had been with him, Kenny's heart rate had remained between 110 and 130.

Fifteen minutes later, Gilbert called Rejniak at the nurse's station.

"Kenny's taken a turn for the worse," she said.

"I'll be right there."

When Rejniak arrived, Kenny's heart rate, at 75, was considerably lower that it had previously been.

"He just didn't look good," Rejniak later recalled.

About twenty minutes after returning to the nurse's station, Rejniak decided to go back and check on Kenny again. When he arrived, he was amazed to find that his heart rate had dropped even lower.

It was now down into the 50s and 60s.

But at 7:00, Gilbert documented that Cutting's heart rate had jumped back up to the "120s–130s." His telemetry monitor, however, just moments before, had recorded it at 107—and in Gilbert's check of his vital signs back at 6:00, right before she left for her break, it was in the low 100s.

Only minutes after Rejniak left the room, Gilbert claimed Kenny's heart rate tripled, and then went into v-fib, a state in which the heart loses its capability to function as a pump . . . and, then, asystole . . . and, finally, flatline.

Because Kenny Cutting had been on a DNR status, there was nothing anyone could do except watch him die.

Within seconds, he couldn't breathe. Then he had no pulse. A minute later, at 7:15, Kenny Cutting was dead.

When a patient at the VAMC dies, post mortem care must be administered immediately by his nurse: clean up the body, place it in a black body bag, and transport it to the morgue in the basement.

At 8:10, Gilbert and Rejniak wheeled Kenny's body down to the morgue; then Gilbert went back upstairs, put on her coat, and sat down to write her final note of the night.

"Transferred to ICU for treatment of seizure . . . and fever. . . . Since admission, patient never regained consciousness, and continued to spike fevers . . . 103 temperatures, despite antibiotic therapy. . . . Tonight," she wrote, "Kenny's heart rate [went up to the] 140s."

All of it was lies.

Nowhere in her note had Gilbert written that Kenny's heart rate had, as Rejniak had witnessed, dropped down into the 70s and 80s and then the 50s and 60s. Further, Cutting had been transferred to the ICU because he had developed a fever due to his bowel obstruction. Seizures were never part of the equation. On top of that, he wasn't unconscious for his entire stay in the ICU. One of the third-shift nurses noted at one point that he was trying to say something but just couldn't get the words out. Nancy, Kenny's son, Jeffrey, and his mother-in-law had spoken to him only a few days before his death. And Kenny's fever had decreased several times during the past several days, at one point dropping down as low as 99 degrees.

Gilbert never mentioned any of it.

Finally, there was no evidence of his heart rate ever being in the 140s. On the previous night's note, Gilbert had written that the "monitor shows [heart rate]" of "120s to 130s," but the telemetry monitor again disagreed—because the one strip Gilbert chose to include in Kenny's chart indicated his heart rate was 107.

After she finished writing up Kenny's final report, Gilbert went down to the nurse's station and dialed up Nancy Cutting at her home.

"I'm a nurse from the Veterans Affairs Medical Center," she said.

"Yes . . . okay."

"Your husband has passed away!"

Nancy dropped the phone.

After Gilbert hung up, she went looking for David Rejniak. It was approaching nine.

"David," she said, "can I take sick leave from now until midnight?"

"I guess so . . ."

Early for her date with James Perrault, Gilbert showed up at his Parsons Street apartment a few minutes before ten o'clock.

CHAPTER 23

Since the Francis Marier episode back on December 20, Renee Walsh had been looking for some solid evidence that Gilbert was up to no good. She had a feeling that something was amiss where Gilbert and medical emergencies were concerned. The coincidences were just too many.

By the end of the day on February 3, Walsh had all the proof she needed. First, when she came in that morning, Walsh couldn't believe Kenny Cutting had died.

"Who was Kenny's nurse last night?" she asked a colleague. But before the nurse could even answer, Walsh chimed in, "No, don't tell me . . . Kristen, right?"

Then, later that morning, Walsh ran into one of her favorite patients, a middle-aged Hispanic man, *José Velasquez,* she had come to know throughout the years. Velasquez would come into the VAMC once a month for an IV antibiotic treatment the hospital was giving at the time to its AIDS patients.

The previous night, Walsh had bumped into Velasquez downstairs in the triage room. He would show up during the day and get the treatment down in the outpatient clinic, but for whatever reason, he had come in late, just as Walsh was leaving.

The treatment itself was a snap. A nurse would insert an IV into his forearm, hang a bag of the antibiotic, and Velasquez would sit and read a magazine while the medication worked its way into his system. The entire procedure took about an hour. After that, Velasquez would sign out and leave. It was a painless procedure that, besides having an IV hanging, a patient wouldn't even know was taking place.

For some reason, Velasquez couldn't make it in for his normal time on February 3. The outpatient clinic closed at four, and by the time he had shown up it was about 5:30. The Admissions nurse, after checking, told Velasquez that someone in Ward C would take him, and sent him on his way.

At six, preparing to leave, Walsh stopped in the ICU to pick up a book she had forgotten. Once there, she bumped into Gilbert as she was making her way to dinner.

"Hi, Kristen, anything going on?"

"Not much, Renee."

Out of the corner of her eye, Walsh spotted Velasquez; he was sitting, an IV in his arm, reading a magazine.

"What's *he* doing up here?"

"Oh," Gilbert said, "José . . . Well, Admissions sent him up. The clinic was closed when he came in. I only have one patient, Kenny Cutting. I told them it wouldn't be any trouble."

It seemed like a logical explanation.

After Walsh and Gilbert discussed work-related issues, Walsh went home.

The next morning, shortly after hearing about Kenny Cutting's untimely death, Walsh bumped into Velasquez, who was wandering aimlessly in a daze out in the hallway near Ward C.

She couldn't understand if he had spent the night at the hospital, or if he had come back for something he might have forgotten.

So she asked him.

"Hello, Miss Walsh," Velasquez said. He was a bit nervous and fidgety. He looked pale and weak. "Boy," he added, "did I ever have a strange experience last night."

"Excuse me?"

"Yeah, I'm still not feeling too good from what happened."

"Really," Walsh said.

"I was just sitting there, you know, getting my treatment and reading my magazine. Well, I finished the treatment and that nurse, Kristen—"

"—Gilbert," Walsh said.

"Yeah. Well, she came over, flushed my IV and, all of a sudden, well ... I ... I ... I can't really tell you what happened next, Miss Walsh ... I felt hot ... sick, like I was going to pass out—"

"Relax, José. Take your time."

"Well, I *did* pass out!"

Whenever an IV treatment like the one Velasquez had received ends, the attending nurse has to flush the line. With a catheter sticking out of a patient's forearm, a syringe filled with saline solution is inserted and, with one plunge, the port of the IV is cleared to insure that every last bit of the medicine makes it into the patient's body. It's a routine procedure, one nurses do thousands of times throughout their careers.

"Continue, José," Walsh urged. She was horrified.

"I don't know, Miss Walsh. I felt sick. I must have passed out. But a few minutes later, I must have come back around and, after picking myself up off the ground ... the weirdest thing happened."

"Go ahead."

"She's just standing there staring at me. You know, looking down at me."

"What?"

"She looked at me and said that I must have had some type of allergic reaction to the treatment."

Walsh knew it was impossible. The drug Velasquez had been receiving had been dripping into his body for about an hour at the time he had passed out. An allergic reaction would have taken place within minutes of its first being administered. But more important to Walsh was that Velasquez had gotten the treatment more times than she could count and had never had an adverse reaction to it. She'd given him the treatment herself just last month, and the month before that, and the ...

As Walsh listened, her mind began to race. *That's it,* she thought, *I have to do something.*

"What else happened, José? What did you do then?"

"Well, I felt better, you know, after a while. So she took the IV out, and I went home."

Walsh put her arm around Velasquez, gave him a hug, and told him to take it easy.

You can't let this go on any longer. Something has got *to be done,* Walsh said to herself as she left the building

CHAPTER 24

World War Two veteran Angelo Vella had lived in Westfield, Massachusetts, his entire adult life. At sixty-eight, he had been retired from the Marine Corps for decades, yet still kept in touch with the boys down at the local VFW. Vella was a respected volunteer firefighter, but earned his living operating a concession stand in town, serving fried dough, baked potatoes, pasta and antipasto. Whatever Angelo Vella's customers wanted, he was happy to deliver.

Like a lot of veterans his age, Vella suffered from COPD, and had spent many years in and out of area hospitals.

Treating his COPD, Vella had gone to the VAMC numerous times. Gilbert, like a lot of the nurses on Ward C, had gotten close to Vella's family throughout the years because he had spent so much time up on the ward. According to Vella's daughter, Mary Vella, Gilbert was the "friendly nurse with the short blond hair and colorful smocks with different-color cartoon characters . . . on them."

Mary Vella and her family liked Kristen Gilbert.

On February 4, 1996, at 7:00 A.M., Vella was admitted to Ward C. Because he had been complaining of "shortness of breath," Vella was given a room on Ward C right next to the nurse's station. Based on his condition upon admission, Vella's doctors thought it was the best room for him. He could be monitored more closely.

* * *

Originally from Northern Ireland, Mary O'Hanlon was the traditional motherly type of nurse. A short, petite woman, she had a very noticeable Irish accent.

O'Hanlon conducted an "admission assessment"—a routine form filled out when patients are admitted to the ward—of Vella after he was admitted. She recorded all of his vital signs, applied oxygen, and checked his skin for abrasions. Vella had been involved in an auto accident back in 1959 and had multiple scars on his lower legs. "His skin was dry . . . tattoo on right arm. His admission weight: one hundred and ninety-three pounds," O'Hanlon wrote.

Most of the information had come from Vella himself, who was, O'Hanlon noted, "alert and stable."

Vella was well educated about his disease. He had been involved in the Chronic Lung Disease Support Group and Pulmonary Rehab program the VAMC offered. The program taught patients to gain control, through education, of their disease. Vella worked hard. He wanted to learn about his condition and help the nurses wherever he could.

But one of his chief medical problems was out of his control. Edema, or the "swelling of soft tissue as a result of excess water retention," had plagued Vella for years. O'Hanlon, along with his doctors, were keeping a close eye on it, and he was responding well to a treatment of Lasix, a diuretic designed to fight the onset of edema.

By the end of O'Hanlon's shift, it was obvious that the Lasix had worked—because Vella's edema had begun to subside.

For quick IV access, his arm was fitted with a hep-lock. When O'Hanlon checked it before she left, it was "patent"—free from any obstruction—and "showed no redness, no swelling or tenderness," she wrote.

Gilbert, who had just come on duty as the medicine nurse, took over for O'Hanlon at around four o'clock. Being a Team Leader that day, before O'Hanlon left, she was obliged to tape-record a report of Vella:

"He is in no distress. He seems comfortable and alert . . . good color, and his vital signs are stable."

At five, Lisa Baronas, who was just down the hall from

Vella's room, waiting for the dinner trays to be delivered, looked up and saw Gilbert standing by the entrance to his room.

Adjusting her eyes, Baronas noticed that Gilbert was drawing a syringe, but she couldn't really make out what she was filling the syringe with because it appeared as though Gilbert was trying to hide what she was doing.

After the syringe was full, Gilbert entered Vella's room.

Respiratory therapist Bonnie Bledsoe had just finished giving Vella a treatment, in which, afterward, she checked his heart rate.

It was normal.

With her back to the door, while she was washing the nebulizer she had just used on Vella in the sink, Bledsoe heard Gilbert walk in. She then looked over her shoulder, noticed the syringe in Gilbert's hand, spied the med cart outside the door and, without worry, continued with what she was doing.

John Wall was the charge nurse, with Baronas, Jeff Begley, Liz Corey and Frank Bertrand working the floor. Although she was assigned to the ICU, Gilbert was responsible for administering meds to several patients. Angelo Vella, however, wasn't one of them—and hadn't been scheduled to receive any type of injectable medication, anyway.

Seconds later, as Frank Bertrand stood by the nurse's station, he heard Vella's heart monitor alarm go off. Bledsoe, still standing by the sink in Vella's room, turned when she heard a scream.

"Ow, it hurts . . . it burns!" Vella yelled.

The ward was busy at this time of the night. Shifts were overlapping.

When Bertrand heard Vella scream, he raced into his room, while the other nurses in the vicinity looked on. Bledsoe rushed to Vella's bedside, while Gilbert, frozen in her tracks for the moment, just stood there in some sort of daze.

Bertrand, a twelve-year employee of the VAMC, was related to Gilbert by marriage. Bertrand had married Glenn Gilbert's cousin.

Entering Vella's room, Bertrand saw Gilbert at his bedside, standing by his left arm. She had a syringe in her hand.

Just then, Vella's heart rate began to race uncontrollably—as much as 300 beats per minute.

Vella, however, remained conscious.

"Mr. Vella?" Bertrand asked. *"Mr. Vella?"*

"She did it!" Vella lashed out, pointing at Gilbert. "It started when she flushed my line . . ."

A moment later there was a flatline . . . and soon . . . Vella's pulse stopped.

Bertrand then called a code because Vella was now in full cardiac arrest.

The small crowd that had congregated over by the nurse's station swarmed into his room.

Bertrand immediately began resuscitation efforts as one of the nurses, in what had become a routine lately, called in the chaplain to administer last rites.

Meanwhile, Melodie Turner and Lisa Baronas, who were back at the nurse's station, began watching Vella's cardiac episode as it was being recorded on the telemetry monitor at the nurse's station. Although it was a Sunday, and Turner wasn't supposed to be there, she had attended an annual ceremony in the VAMC's chapel earlier and decided to make a pit stop by the ward before she went home.

"Grab all of that tape," Turner ordered Baronas. "Grab every single bit of the rhythm strips off that monitor. I want them saved."

John Wall had run down to Vella's room from the ICU when he heard the alarm. When he entered, he saw Bertrand at Vella's bedside, trying to get him to respond. Gilbert was leaving as Wall walked in.

When Vella regained consciousness, he was frantic. Although he had just had a massive cardiac event, the first thing he did when he came out of his comatose state was look at the doctor in the room and shout, "When she put that in my arm, it burned and my chest was heavy."

The doctor was speechless. No one could believe that here he was, only moments after being resuscitated, talking about what had just happened.

"The burning sensation happened," Vella kept insisting, nearly out of breath, "after she injected it into my arm."

* * *

Although he was still in the ICU and being monitored continuously, by 5:30, Angelo Vella was out of immediate danger. Frank Bertrand's quick thinking and years of experience had saved Vella's life.

When Vella began to talk about what had taken place shortly before his code, it would shed an entire new light on what Kristen Gilbert had been doing up on Ward C.

CHAPTER 25

Mary Vella was at a friend's house when her mother phoned with the horrible news.

"Your father has just been given his last rites," the former Mrs. Vella said. "Go down to the [VAMC] right away."

When Mary walked into the ICU, the first thing she saw was her weak-looking father, lying serenely in his bed. He looked colorless and gaunt, machines buzzing around him, tubes coming out of his body. On the face of it, though, Mary knew her father well enough to know that he wouldn't give into death without a fight.

It wasn't just the heart attack, Mary thought as she stared at him. *Something else was wrong.*

Vella's wife, stepdaughter and stepson were there, too.

"It happened when she put something in my arm," Vella whispered to everyone as they gathered around him.

"What, Daddy?" Mary asked, leaning over.

"Angelo, get some rest," his wife said, gently wiping sweat off his brow.

"Are you all right?" Mary asked. "What happened?"

"It began as numbness," Vella continued in a raspy tone, "in my legs and arms. Then my heart felt like it was about to explode."

Mary thought how vulnerable he looked just lying there trying to explain what had happened. Her dad, she thought, had always carried a lot of inner strength. "He was very tough," she later recalled. "He just seemed so scared . . . frightened."

Mary's stepsister, Joann Sell, then leaned in to tell him to be quiet and get some rest. Being a nurse, Sell was surprised he was so alert.

"How are you?" she asked.

"I'm okay. . . ."

"What happened?"

"I'm not quite sure," Vella began to say. He took breaks while speaking. It seemed as if it took everything he had just to get the words out. "The nurse came in, and she was putting something . . . she was flushing my IV and"—he stopped for a moment to swallow—"I felt flushed and had some chest pain. Then there was a lot of activity going on around. Frank was saying something about pulling the IV out. I can't remember anything else until I woke up." He stopped for a moment to catch his breath. Then, "But Frank . . . Frank saved my life."

Vella was clear about those crucial moments before his cardiac episode. He had spent enough time in hospitals throughout his life to know procedure. He had no doubt that when Gilbert flushed his IV, with what he presumed was nothing more than a harmless saline solution, something went wrong.

Just then, Frank Bertrand and Gilbert entered the room. Bertrand walked over to the family to offer his support.

"Glad to see you're doing better, Mr. Vella."

Gilbert walked toward a table near the back of the room and shuffled some papers around, trying to look busy.

"Thank you for saving my father's life," Mary Vella said, in tears.

"It's okay," Bertrand said.

Gilbert was paying no attention to what was going on. But Mary wanted to thank her for what she presumed at the time was a noble effort on her part. So she walked over and extended her hand.

"Thank you," she said in her sweet and calm voice.

Gilbert wouldn't look into her eyes, much less shake her hand. She seemed cold and distant. This struck Mary as odd, because Gilbert had always been so friendly and cordial in the past.

* * *

When Kathy Rix returned to work on February 6, one of the first things she did was check the ICU medicine cabinet to see if any of the eighteen ampoules of epinephrine she had counted before her vacation were missing.

On December 6, 1995, a box of twenty-five ampoules had been delivered to Ward C. About six weeks later, another box of twenty-five had been delivered because the first box was gone. Since August 1995, one hundred and thirty-five ampoules had been dispensed to Ward C.

But again, no one questioned where they had been going.

Epinephrine was one of one hundred and ten medications delivered under Automatic Ward Stock procedures to Ward C. Having such a large amount of the drug available on the ward was merely a precautionary measure—so that when the hospital pharmacy was closed, the ward could have access to whatever it needed, whenever it needed it. After the ampoules arrived on the ward, nurses and doctors were allowed to use them at their own discretion. According to a later audit by the office of Inspector General, Criminal Investigations Division of Veteran's Affairs, there was "no accountability."

There was no accountability.

Kathy Rix knew what she was going to find before she opened the doors to the medicine cabinet. Her gut had told her for the past two weeks that something was amiss with Kristen Gilbert, as far as the increasing amount of codes and the drug epinephrine were concerned. Although several patients had survived sudden cardiac events during her absence, several more had died. To Rix, there were just too many coincidences adding up for her not to continue looking for an answer.

She still wanted some sort of proof, nonetheless. Rix's husband was a cop. She understood procedure and policy, and lived by it.

Epinephrine was rarely—if ever—used on Ward C. The majority of the patients who required a dose of epinephrine came in through the triage room, or ER. The epinephrine used during medical emergencies came in a different form, a bristo-jet. The smaller ampoules that Rix had been keeping track of were for injection by syringe only.

When Kathy Rix opened the medicine cabinet, she saw just

three ampoules of 1:1000 strength epinephrine, which meant that in just two weeks' time, fifteen ampoules of the drug had been used.

"Fifteen," Rix gasped. *Oh. My. God.*

CHAPTER 26

Renee Walsh had given up on the notion of ever getting a good night's sleep. As a nurse with over fifteen years experience, concentrating on her normal everyday activities lately was becoming almost impossible. Like a shadow, wherever she went, whatever she did, the troubling notion that a colleague could be killing patients right under her nose haunted her, so much so that it pained Walsh to see Gilbert in a patient's room anymore.

Still, there was an outside chance Gilbert hadn't done anything at all. Walsh considered that perhaps she was just being paranoid, looking too deeply into what amounted to a set of circumstances that had placed Gilbert, simply by association, in the shadow of guilt. What if she were wrong? Gilbert had been employed at the VAMC for seven years. Not only would Walsh be an outcast for falsely accusing a colleague of being a murderer, but it would be impossible for her to work with her ever again.

Still, for the past few weeks, Walsh had looked under bed sheets, in garbage cans, in needle-disposal buckets, and anywhere else she thought might have been a good hiding place for evidence of a crime. She wasn't sure what she was looking for, but she knew there had to be an answer. The José Velasquez incident had been at the forefront of her mind, gnawing at her, for about two weeks now. Another near miss with Angelo Vella.

Who was next?

At first, Walsh was on the lookout for potassium. Potassium was another drug, she knew, that could wreak havoc on the human body if given in the form of an overdose. Walsh had no idea the VAMC had even stocked the 1:1000 ampoules of epinephrine.

Though she didn't find anything that night, Walsh became even more convinced of Gilbert's guilt after receiving a phone call from her one night shortly after that.

For most of the day, Walsh had cared for a patient who, being "very, very ill," was probably going to die, she thought, within a few weeks, and she had expressed to many of her colleagues, including Gilbert, how much she would miss him.

A few hours after Walsh got home, Gilbert called.

"I just wanted to let you know that [your patient] died right after you left," she said without emotion.

"What?"

"I know he was one of your favorite patients, Renee. I just wanted to call you and let you know."

Hours after she had hung up, having trouble falling asleep, Walsh couldn't stop thinking about the worst.

For John Wall, Angelo Vella was "the final straw," he later said. He and Kathy Rix were now talking almost daily about what they should do.

With Rix running around counting ampoules of epinephrine and Walsh looking under every nook and cranny of the ward for anything she could find, they feared Gilbert was going to catch on to what was they were up to soon enough, anyway.

And then what?

Walsh had an inkling that Rix was up to something. She had known Rix for quite a while, and was convinced by the second week of February that she wasn't herself since she had returned from vacation. For the past few days, Walsh had wanted to approach her with her own concerns, but she was having trouble finding the right words and place to do it.

But on February 13, the opportunity presented itself.

Staying late because they were shorthanded, Walsh entered the break room and saw Kathy Rix just sitting there alone, staring blankly into the muddy whirl of cream and sugar swirling around in her coffee cup. When Walsh thought about the events of the past few weeks hard enough, it seemed almost ridiculous that no one else had come forward, or at least said *some*thing. Since February 2, just eleven days ago, four patients had died on Ward C: Kenny Cutting, Leslie Smith, Jack Knightlinger and Henry Cormier.

How many more would it take?

Kathy Rix didn't say anything as Walsh entered the room and walked toward the counter to make a cup of coffee.

After ripping open a small pouch of sugar, Walsh turned and looked at Rix, who just stared back at her with an exhausted look on her face.

"You know how it's always kinda been a joke about Kristen being the angel of death . . . how we're always joking about it?"

"Yes," Rix said, nodding her head slowly.

"Do you ever think that maybe it's not a joke? That maybe things are really going on?"

The silence in the room was deafening.

"I think about it all the time, Renee . . . all the time," Rix said, dropping her head down on top of the table.

"Maybe we should talk."

For the next few minutes, the two nurses swapped stories about what they had seen, heard, thought and felt. They left nothing out. It was like uncorking a bottle of demons that had built up for months. Yet, when everything set in and they realized what was going to have to happen next, that enormous weight had been replaced with a terrible sense of responsibility and confusion.

Where do we go from here?

No sooner had Rix and Walsh begun to vent their concerns, than John Wall walked in as though the meeting had been preplanned.

But Walsh abruptly stopped talking. Even though Rix and Wall had been discussing what to do for some time, Walsh, who didn't know about it, was scared.

Rix then turned to Walsh and whispered, "I think we can trust John, Renee. He has his suspicions too. We've been talking about this for quite a while now."

"Oh?" Walsh said, surprised.

"He has some of his own stories to tell."

Worried that someone might walk in at any moment, the three nurses swapped a few stories and began discussing a plan.

"Should we go to Melodie?" Walsh asked. "The FBI? The Northampton Police Department? Who? Where?"

"No," Wall said. "Who knows what she'll do with the information."

The nurses had every reason to believe that Melodie Turner, being management, and, remarkably, oblivious to what had been going on, would somehow try to cover it up. They were scared. Confused. This was serious now. The entire thing was about to explode, and they were going to be at the center of it. It had to be done right. If security found out, James Perrault would know. And they couldn't chance that.

So they agreed to sleep on it for a few days and think about what needed to be done next.

CHAPTER 27

Northampton High School graduate Melodie Turner began working at the VAMC in 1979, after spending eight years at Northampton State Hospital, a psychiatric facility. Beginning her VA career as a staff nurse in psychiatry, in 1981, she was transferred to the acute medical ward. In 1983, armed with a bachelor's degree in public health, Turner landed a position as nursing manager of psychiatry. Five years after that, the VA made her nursing manager of Ward C.

"But I don't have any medical nursing experience," a co-worker later recalled Turner telling her bosses when they approached her with the idea. "I have never worked in an ICU in my life!"

"We don't need a medical nurse; we need a manager. And you are a good manager . . . that's what we want."

This was, perhaps, one of upper management's biggest mistakes: hiring a person who knew very little about what everyday life was supposed to be like on an acute medical ward to run the show.

So Melodie Turner, equipped with some rather impressive academic credentials, entered Ward C as nursing manager, according to some, knowing little about the medical side of nursing. She wasn't qualified in ACLS. She didn't know how to read a monitor or EKG. And she had no idea how to start an IV.

Now, however, she would be the person to decide if her staff was doing these basic nursing procedures accurately.

What was more, Turner had very little experience in codes and medical emergencies. Medical emergencies and codes rarely ever occurred on a hospital's psychiatric ward. And if they did, nurses would call in the medical personnel.

Ignorance, however, ran all the way up the VAMC management chain. Turner's bosses, others claimed, were no more knowledgeable in these areas of medicine than she was. The VAMC, for the most part, was a psychiatric hospital. In terms of beds, the psychiatric side of the hospital dwarfed the medical side by about three to one. Most of the people in management had been working at the VAMC—in the same office, in the same position—for their entire careers. As one nurse later put it, "They wouldn't know what death statistics were if you hit them over the head with [them]."

Turner usually worked the 7:00 A.M. to 5:00 P.M. shift, so her hours dovetailed with each of the three shifts she was now responsible for. She was married with two kids, and her husband also worked at the VAMC. In her late forties, tall and skinny, with bleached-blond hair that was turning gray as the years piled up, Turner was extremely high-strung and, from day one, relished the role of being head nurse.

"Drama queen," is how one of her former underlings described her.

As the staff got to know her, they learned quickly that her preoccupation with her looks fell in line with her controlling managerial style. She was never, for instance, shy about letting her minions know who the boss was. She put high standards on most of the nurses she had seen promise in— particularly Kathy Rix, John Wall and Renee Walsh—and always kept an eye on how they conducted their business. For this, some of the staff applauded her. Yet others considered her one of the toughest bosses they had ever worked for and complained that she had often abused her power and took her responsibilities to an impossible level—especially where discipline was concerned.

"She loved chaos and things being stirred up," recalled an old colleague of Turner's. "This way she could fix them—which she was really good at."

"She could be intimidating," another nurse later said. "Very, very controlling."

At times, her managerial practices even bordered on harassment, and Turner often went out of her way to be overly insensitive while lecturing certain members of the staff.

"She would bring you to the point of tears, belittling you and your work, and then, when you started to cry, she'd tell you it was okay," Rachel Webber later recalled.

Funny and witty, Turner enjoyed the larger-than-life persona she so desperately tried to project. Being estranged from her "mentally ill" mother for more than thirty years, some claimed, probably gave rise to her demanding absolute perfection from her staff.

One time, during the winter of 1993, personal phone calls became an issue on Ward C.

Earlier that day, Turner had been given a copy of all the long-distance phone calls that had been made on the evening shift for the past several weeks. After learning that some of the calls were as long as thirty minutes, she became "infuriated" and demanded to know who had been making the calls.

Rumor had it that one of the nurses, who had friends and family across country, had been calling home.

To find out who was responsible, Turner called each nurse into her office one by one. The nurses speculated that Turner knew who was making the calls, but couldn't, in all fairness, make accusations without any solid proof.

Living up the same code of silence many cops adhere to, the nurses got together beforehand and agreed they would play the "I have no idea" game and leave Turner guessing. It would likely enrage her to the point where she would leave them alone and forget about the incident. In turn, the guilty nurse would stop making the calls, and life would go on.

After getting nowhere with her interrogation, Turner came out of her office and called everyone to the nurse's station. She had something she wanted the staff to hear.

Pausing for a moment before speaking, Turner said, *"What am I going to do with you guys?"* Then, with a flip of her head, stormed off.

After that, whenever there was a problem and one nurse covered for the other, Turner would gather the staff together and, jokingly, say, "This evening shift is so close . . . [you guys] would probably cover up a murder."

Not everyone agreed that Turner was so bad, however. One of her former colleagues recalled that although she didn't see Turner as the best boss she'd ever had in her decade and a half as a nurse, she certainly didn't agree with the sentiments of some of the others. The nurses who had problems with Turner were the same people who managed to piss her off in some way. Turner was, the nurse insisted, one hundred percent behind the nurses on Ward C—providing, that is, they stayed on her good side.

"She hated slackers and liars. If Melodie was behind you and respected your work, she would . . . stick up for you right down the line."

By the beginning of 1996, Turner had had it with Gilbert. Although she saw her as an excellent code nurse, more knowledgeable in medicines than most, she had caught Gilbert in so many lies throughout the years that she'd lost any bit of professional respect she had left for her. She felt Gilbert could have been more "self-directed" and wanted her to seek out more work, responsibility, and uphold the "policies and frameworks" they had worked under to a greater degree.

Gilbert, of course, always let her down.

But besides noting it on Gilbert's performance evaluations, Turner never took it any further.

As far as Gilbert's name being on approximately seventy-five percent of the codes and fifty percent of the deaths since 1989, one might ask why Turner hadn't been compelled by the numbers at least to speak to Gilbert.

It seemed odd that she hadn't.

But what was even more peculiar was that for the past year Turner had sat on what was called the Medical Emergency Committee, along with representatives from the pharmacy, security, and supply and distribution departments. Headed by a physician, the group met once a month to review the previous month's medical emergencies "for needs that might have come up in carrying out the medical emergencies [and] the whole deportment of the medical emergency." They would discuss how the codes and emergencies were played out. They would make sure there was enough medication on hand during the episode, make a judgment as to how the code team responded, and rate how the overall code had been carried out.

One would have to assume the increasing amount of codes would have raised a red flag during one of these meetings.

But it never did.

"The Medical Emergency Committee," a member of law enforcement later said, *"including* Melodie Turner, didn't think that a serial killer was wandering through the halls of Ward C—so they certainly weren't looking at these codes with a suspicious eye."

Nevertheless, the roof was about to cave in on Melodie Turner.

CHAPTER 28

Late in the day on February 13, Renee Walsh and Kathy Rix got together to talk about their next move.

As they spoke, it became obvious that talking at work about such sensitive issues was probably not a good idea. The last thing Walsh and Rix wanted was for a rumor to start floating around that they were getting ready to turn Gilbert in.

So after a few moments, they decided to table the discussion for a later time. Walsh, however, had been treading water now for weeks, losing sleep, not eating. She suggested that whatever they decided to do had to be done quickly.

"Okay," Rix said. "Don't worry. I'll call you at home later."

The following day, Rix once again counted the epinephrine ampoules in the ICU and satellite pharmacy. In the ICU there were three; the satellite pharmacy still had twenty-two. Since she'd returned from vacation a week ago, there had not been a drop in the count. But that made little difference to her and John Wall. Because during the past week, while the epinephrine count in the ICU and satellite pharmacy stayed the same, there had been only one medical emergency, on February 11, and Gilbert was nowhere in sight when it occurred.

That, however, was all about to change.

* * *

Ed Skwira was born in Holyoke, Massachusetts, on May 25, 1927. Eighteen years later, he entered the U.S. Army, became a truck driver, and, after being discharged from the Army in early 1947, joined the local chapter of the Teamsters Union.

Not long after that, Skwira married a local gal, Stacia, and started a family, having three kids right off the bat.

Pushing six feet, two hundred and fifty pounds, with his greased back, jet-black hair, "Big Ed," as the family called him, became known around the house years later as "The King."

For whatever reason, ever since he had been discharged from the Army, Skwira had developed a hearty taste for hard liquor. And by February 1996, at sixty-eight years old, when he was admitted to AdCare Hospital in Worcester, Massachusetts, for alcohol abuse, Skwira admitted that he had been drinking scotch on a daily basis for fifty years.

His chief complaint when he arrived at AdCare on February 6, 1996, was alcohol dependence. But he was also suffering from diabetes, along with several other problems either directly or indirectly related to his years of abusing alcohol. Overindulging in hard liquor for five decades doesn't come without a price, both physically and socially. Yet despite the health problems he had, Skwira's alcohol abuse, remarkably, had little effect on his home life. At the time he was admitted to AdCare, he and Stacia had been married for forty-eight years, having celebrated their twenty-fifth and fortieth wedding anniversaries with extravagant parties.

Skwira had detoxed himself once before, two years earlier, and managed to stay sober for about six months, but then began drinking again.

After a quick assessment at AdCare, save for his drunkenness, Skwira checked out pretty well. He showed no signs of jaundice. His vision was good. He had no hearing problems. No chest pain. No shortness of breath. No palpations. No wheezing. And no diarrhea or constipation. He had no memory loss and, answering questions at will, could concentrate suitably. His vitals checked out incredibly well: his blood pressure was 150 over 90; temperature 96.8; pulse 100; and his heart had a regular rhythm and rate, with no rubs or murmurs. He wasn't experiencing hallucinations, nor had he any thoughts of killing himself.

If he could beat his addiction to alcohol, everything else might just fall into place.

Within a few hours, however, Skwira would learn just how severe an alcoholic he was, and, because of that, his doctors planned on detoxing him "in a safe environment to prevent [any] medical or psychiatric complications."

There was no getting around it: The next few days in Ed Skwira's life would be hell.

For the next week, doctors kept him heavily medicated, trying to ward off the multitude of complications associated with withdrawal. But it being a seven-day program, by the end of the week, Skwira's time had run out at AdCare, and the hospital couldn't keep him any longer.

As a veteran of the U.S. military, however, Skwira was entitled to long-term care for his alcohol abuse, and on February 15, 1996, was transferred to the Leeds VAMC to begin what everyone had told him would be the fight of his life.

CHAPTER 29

A quaint little Southern belle, Renee Walsh believed things in life happened for a reason. Being a devout Episcopalian, she had always turned to God for comfort and guidance during times of uncertainty. The Lord gave a person only what they could handle—no more, no less. Lent was right around the corner. Perhaps more than any other year, it was time for Walsh to cleanse herself of the demons that had been haunting her now for weeks.

*Some*thing had to be done. It couldn't wait any longer.

She was scheduled to leave work early on Thursday, February 15. Before gathering her things and signing out, Walsh pulled Kathy Rix into the locker room, took a quick look to see if anyone else was around and laid it on the line.

"It can't go on any longer," Walsh urged. "The longer we sit on this, the more it's going to happen. I've made up my mind, Kathy. I think the best thing we can do, in order to be safe, since we're government employees, is to go to see Melodie."

For the past few days, the entire ordeal had caused Walsh a considerable amount of anxiety. She was still second-guessing what they were about to do. "What if I'm wrong?" she would ask herself while staring at the ceiling trying to fall asleep. "What if I'm so far off base . . . what if there's some other explanation?"

Part of it was not wanting to believe it was possible.

Northampton was akin to Mayberry, the fictional town where television's *The Andy Griffith Show* was set in. Almost everyone knew one another. People stopped you at the gas station and asked how your kids were. Locals hung around the coffee shops and talked about taxes, Little League and upcoming elections. Who wanted to believe they had been living in the same community—or, worse, working side by side—with a serial killer?

What was more, what if they *were* wrong? Walsh worried the entire incident would end up in the newspapers if they went to the police. Anyway, the VA had always insisted that if a nurse had suspected some type of negligence, or had a complaint about another employee, the right thing to do was to go to one's immediate supervisor and report it. If one didn't get any satisfaction there, keep going up the chain of command.

"Yes," Rix agreed, "we need to do something—*soon.*"

"I'm going to Melodie," Walsh said. "That's it! If you and John don't want to take it any further, I'll understand."

"Don't go alone, Renee," Rix advised. "I'll go with you. And call John. I'm sure he'll go, too. You shouldn't have to do this by yourself."

"I'll call Melodie tonight."

When Ed Skwira arrived at the VAMC on February 15, he wasn't feeling all that well. Inside the VA van during the ride over, he had been experiencing some mild chest pain. But chest pain—or "angina"—was something he had suffered from for decades. He'd even been taking nitroglycerin pills for quite a few years now to ease the pain.

Admitted shortly after 2:00 P.M., Skwira was mentally confused and "appeared . . . hypotensive," meaning his blood pressure was low. This was Skwira's first time at the VAMC. Maybe the thought of what was ahead scared him?

Upon a further check of his medical history, doctors learned that Skwira had developed some serious cardiovascular problems throughout the years. Maybe it wasn't anxiety and stress causing his chest pain after all; perhaps it *was* a heart attack.

Ed Skwira had suffered from hypertension for many years; coronary artery disease; peripheral vascular disease; and carotid artery disease with hypercholesterolemia. In the late

1980s, he'd undergone abdominal aortic aneurysm repair surgery. Common in patients with hypertension, the large blood vessel going through the diaphragm to the abdomen becomes engorged, like a backed-up garden hose, and has to be relieved. Although he went through the surgery without any complications, the continuing angina pain Skwira suffered from was an indication he still had some blockages, which limited blood flow.

The admitting doctor, after examining him, noted there was a "slight change on his EKG." With Skwira now acting confused and restless, this worried the doctor.

Maybe he is *having a heart attack?*

But heart attacks don't, normally, come on as suddenly as they did to people on television or in the movies. Often, a heart attack was days in the making, and sometimes people didn't even know they had one.

Not taking any chances, the doctor ordered some fluids, got Skwira stabilized, and sent him up to the ICU in Ward C to be monitored more closely.

It was about 2:30.

When Gilbert came in at four, she was assigned to the ICU, where now, mildly sedated, Skwira rested comfortably.

Placing him in the ICU was a precautionary measure. His EKG readings were normal, but the admitting doctor wanted to be sure there was nothing else wrong. By this point, Skwira had even stopped complaining about the chest pain he'd had, yet the doctor still wanted to rule out the possibility, he later said, of a heart attack.

Shortly after four, Dr. Nabil Raheb, the attending physician, came in and ordered Gilbert to give Skwira a chest X-ray and full body CAT-scan. There was a slight chance, Raheb contended, that Skwira's aorta had a tear in it.

Radiology was on the same floor as Ward C, but with Skwira being as heavy as he was, there was no way Gilbert was going to lift him up on the gurney herself. So she called nursing assistant Lisa Baronas in for some help.

When they got down to Radiology, Lisa helped Gilbert lift the overweight vet off the stretcher and onto the table.

"Call me when you're done, Kristen. I'll come back and help you."

"Thanks."

It was now 4:15.

Within the hour, Lisa Baronas was summoned back to the CAT-scan room, where she helped Gilbert return Skwira to his room in the ICU and, when they finished, left the room and continued preparing the supper trays she was getting ready to distribute.

Dr. Raheb learned quickly what all the fuss had been about. Ed Skwira, Raheb diagnosed, had a "bulge in [his] aorta." Medically speaking, it was called a "thoracic aortic aneurysm."

After studying Skwira's X-rays and CAT-scans, Dr. Raheb thought there was a possibility he also had a tear in his aorta, which meant disaster. Blood can leak into the chest cavity and cause all kinds of problems, resulting in a drastic drop in blood pressure and, ultimately, death.

Dr. Raheb saw the bubble in Skwira's chest, put that together with his low blood pressure and confusion, and thought, *Dissection! This patient has a dissecting aortic aneurysm.*

The VAMC wasn't equipped for emergency open-heart surgery. So a decision had to be made right away.

At the same time, however, a tear in the aorta was extremely painful. And Skwira hadn't complained of any chest pain in a number of hours. In fact, since his admission, he'd been seen by several doctors and nurses and his condition hadn't changed one bit.

A decision was soon made to have Skwira transferred to Baystate Medical Center, a full-facility hospital more equipped to deal with a patient in his condition. If nothing else, doctors at Baystate could make a more calculated diagnosis and take things from there.

Alone now, while Lisa Baronas handed out dinner trays, Gilbert monitored Skwira's status in the ICU.

It was pushing five o'clock.

The charge nurse, David Rejniak, was down at the nurse's station doing some paperwork when Gilbert called him from the ICU.

"Call Dr. Raheb," Gilbert said. "Ed is having chest pain."

She sounded excited and anxious. So Rejniak called Dr. Raheb right away.

Moments later, at 5:07, Gilbert called a code, and efforts began to resuscitate Skwira immediately afterward.

Soon, the room filled with all sorts of medical personnel and, of course, the one guy who seemed to be on duty whenever a code was called: Gilbert's lover, security guard James Perrault.

In her notes, Gilbert wrote that Skwira had gone into "sudden cardiac arrest" for no apparent reason. Nowhere in the note had she written that he had been experiencing chest pain right before he coded, as she had told David Rejniak. Nor had Dr. Raheb reported it. This was odd, because with all the confusion surrounding his condition for the past several hours, knowing that he was going to be transferred to Baystate, Skwira's nurses would want to document anything—and everything—that happened so his doctors at Baystate could have a clear picture of what had been going on.

But Gilbert didn't see fit to add any information above and beyond the fact that he had coded.

Down at the other end of the ward, Kathy Rix had been going about her normal nightly duties when the team pager she was wearing went off.

Looking down at the blinking light, Rix shook her head. *Here we go again.*

Shortly after she arrived for work at four, Rix had, without telling anyone, gone directly into the ICU medicine cabinet and, once again, counted the ampoules of epinephrine.

There were three—same as there had been for the past week.

As Rix entered Skwira's room shortly after his code, she was told the situation was under control. But before leaving the room, Rix took a look in the medicine cabinet to see if the three ampoules of epinephrine she had counted an hour or so ago were still there.

As she approached, she hoped her suspicions were off base. But here she was now, faced with the prospect of Gilbert calling yet another code.

She had to find out.

Please be in there, please, please, Rix kept thinking as she went for the drawer.

But it was empty.

Her knees buckled, and she felt sick to her stomach.

"I was useless," Rix later recalled. "I was sure I couldn't function anymore. To me, that made it positive that there was something going on."

CHAPTER 30

When Renee Walsh got home on February 15, she picked up the phone, dialed John Wall and explained the conversation she'd had with Kathy Rix earlier that day.

"Okay," Wall said. "I'm with you guys."

After that, Walsh phoned Melodie Turner.

"Melodie . . ." Walsh said apprehensively, pausing for a moment. "Okay, here it is. John and Kathy and I . . . we need to talk to you professionally about something very serious, and it's very important that we do it as soon as possible."

"What's wrong, Renee? What is it?" Turner, wild with curiosity, asked.

"I'd rather wait until we're all together, Melodie. We need to have absolute confidentiality with this. No one can know that we're meeting with you, or even talking right now. We have to meet in a secure place—*not on the ward, though.* We can't been seen coming and going."

"Just tell me, Renee. What's so important that the three of you need to speak to me? I need to know *now.*"

Walsh knew Turner hated being left in the dark about things. But as much as she would have liked to, she couldn't tell her.

"You'll have to wait!"

A few minutes after they hung up, Turner called back. She was even more anxious and impatient. Walsh had never heard her act like this before.

"What is it that could be *so* serious? Just tell me, Renee."

"No!" Renee said. "Wait until we can all get together."

The following day, February 16, wasn't going to work. It would have to be the day after. It was the only day Wall, Rix and Walsh could meet together.

On the morning of the sixteenth, Turner called Walsh again.

"Can't we push this meeting up . . . maybe have it today?"

"No," Walsh said. "We're busy, Melodie. It'll have to wait."

"What about tonight?"

"No."

For the next twenty-four hours, Turner called half a dozen more times, demanding to know what the problem was. But Walsh repeatedly told her no.

"Well, I guess if you're going to talk to me about something so serious," Turner finally said in defeat, "I can't think of three finer people to come and talk to me besides you and Kathy and John. I'm sure you have something very important and worthwhile to say, but can't we do it any sooner?"

"Absolutely not."

Any anxiety and fear Walsh had been dealing with now seemed to be doubled. She kept thinking about Gilbert, Glenn, and their kids. She had known Gilbert as a friend, colleague. It wasn't every day someone accused a coworker of murder.

But ultimately, it came down to the patients: as a nurse, Walsh had a responsibility, both professionally and ethically, to do something. As a person, she had a moral obligation. How, she wondered, could she look at herself in the mirror every day if she didn't do something?

On the other hand, if Gilbert was indeed a cold-blooded murderer, what would she do to Walsh and her family if she ever found out what Walsh was planning? Walsh knew it was possible that Gilbert had tried to "do something" to Glenn. If she was capable of trying to kill her husband, Walsh thought, what wasn't she capable of?

The entire situation scared the hell out of all three nurses. But underneath the apprehension and fear was a layer of suppressed anger that had compressed over time. They were upset that they were the ones who had to come forward. Where was

upper management in all of this? Why didn't Melodie Turner
see it? Why didn't Turner's boss, Priscilla McDonald, notice the
increasing number of codes, deaths and medical emergencies?
What about Quincy Garfield, the Chief of Nurses? The Medical
Emergency Committee? The Chief of Medicine? The Chief of
Staff?

Where in God's name was Quality Management?

CHAPTER 31

After unsuccessfully intubating Ed Skwira for a fifth time, Dr. Raheb decided they couldn't wait any longer for his transfer to Baystate Medical Center. He had to go now. Something was dreadfully wrong. He wasn't responding to treatment.

By this point, Skwira's family had been notified about his code and were en route to Baystate. While awaiting his transfer, Skwira coded again and underwent CPR. Within moments, the team at the VAMC got his heart to beat at a normal rhythm. He was then sedated, where his blood pressure remained at 141 over 91, his heart rate at 100.

Shortly after six o'clock, Phillip Skwira, Skwira's youngest son, showed up at the VAMC and followed his father's ambulance to Baystate.

Meanwhile, Dr. Raheb had made the diagnoses that Skwira had suffered a "dissecting descending aortic aneurysm"—a fatal condition.

But the doctor was wrong.

As it would later be proved, Ed Skwira had been showing all the classic signs of epinephrine poisoning—and now his killer, undoubtedly worried sick that he was still alive, was riding with him in the ambulance to Baystate.

* * *

After Skwira was gone, Kathy Rix went back into his room.

While putting the medical equipment away, Rix grabbed the needle-disposal bucket near his bed and looked inside to see what she could find out about his code. Being a nurse for almost two decades, Rix knew that during codes doctors ordered 1:10,000 bristo-jet plunges of epinephrine, not the 1:1,000 ampoules she had been counting.

Rix couldn't believe it, but when she opened the bucket, there were three broken ampoules of 1:1000 epinephrine in the bottom of it.

Her legs went numb.

Before she finished cleaning up, Rix went around and picked up the various portions of heart rhythm strips that, like a fax machine, had spit out of Skwira's telemetry monitor during and after his code. It was a detailed account of what had happened to his heart as it spiraled out of control.

Rix collected them, rolled them into a scroll, and left them near his chart. This way, she thought, when Gilbert returned from Baystate, she could go through and cut out certain sections that best depicted the codes.

It never occurred to Rix that Gilbert might want to dispose of what would ultimately be incriminating evidence against her: the rhythm strips. Rix was confused, scared. After seeing a second round of spent epinephrine ampoules, she had a hard time concentrating on anything else. Plus, she had no idea if Gilbert was falsifying medical records and failing to follow policy on top of everything else.

Between the time Gilbert returned to the VAMC after escorting Skwira to Baystate and the next morning, those heart telemetry strips Rix had collected had disappeared—and Gilbert had not even cut and pasted one section to Skwira's chart.

At 6:30, on February 15, 1996, Ed Skwira was admitted to Baystate Medical Center and, oddly enough, doctors quickly ruled out the possibility that he'd had a heart attack. Moreover, after only a few tests they concluded that he, in fact, had a normal functioning heart.

Yet on learning of his sudden cardiac event back at the

VAMC, doctors believed that he had developed a "possible tear in his aorta," a condition that, added to his thoracic aortic aneurysm, was a recipe for death. Then, upon further evaluation, they suspected that he also had a "perforated viscus."

Bad news all around.

A perforated viscus is a tear in the wall of the stomach, which results in germ- and bacteria-laden air bleeding into the abdominal cavity. It was likely due to Skwira's first code and the arduous time the VAMC staff had intubating him.

For a person who had just suffered sudden cardiac arrest and now had a possible tear in his stomach, an operation to repair it carried a one hundred percent mortality rate—and Ed Skwira's doctors were totally against doing it.

But now they had to break the bad news to Skwira and his family, who were waiting patiently in his room for a status report.

As Stacia and Phillip stood by, Skwira's doctor came into the room and gave it to them straight.

"Mr. Skwira, I'm sorry, but you're going to die. There's not much we can do for you."

Skwira began to cry. Stacia took his hand and kissed him on top of his head. Phillip, having trouble digesting it all, just stood there, stone-faced, waiting for someone to tell him it was all a joke.

Under the misbelief that he had a swollen thoracic aortic aneurysm, doctors convinced Skwira and his family that the cardiac medication he was on should be stopped right away. It wasn't doing him any good.

This was a crucial decision, because the meds Skwira had been on were basically keeping his heart stable.

Next, doctors suggested that he begin morphine treatment right away to make him more comfortable as he passed on.

Skwira and his family agreed it was probably a good idea.

Unfortunately, this type of painkiller actually suppresses respiration and "makes the heart muscle more irritable." The morphine would, undoubtedly, put Skwira in another world and allow him to be comfortable as he died, but coupled with everything else that had happened, it would also help in killing him.

*   *   *

The next day, Phillip went to see his father early in the morning. Skwira appeared to be well-rested when Phillip arrived, but was still showing signs of discomfort and, strangely, had developed a new set of symptoms.

Every once in a while, Skwira would begin to have hallucinations and become fidgety, sitting up and lying down in his bed.

His doctors had already decided to have him transferred back to the VAMC, where he would be more comfortable during his final days.

Later that night, Skwira's entire family visited. Time was short. It seemed like just weeks ago he was out in his garden tending to his vegetables and flowers, walking around the house watering his plants and cracking jokes.

Now he was waiting to die.

Some years ago, Skwira had asked someone in the family to take a picture of him standing at the base of a favorite maple tree he'd planted in the front yard. An avid bird-watcher, he had placed a bird feeder next to the tree that he wanted in the picture too.

"Why?" his family asked when he said he wanted the picture taken.

"Because . . . I just want a nice picture for all of you to remember me by."

As the others went out to get some coffee, or just take a break from the emotion of being in Skwira's room, Phillip watched as his father forced himself up in bed, looked straight up at the ceiling, and said, "I don't want to die," before falling back into bed, as if he had just taken his last breath.

Skwira had suffered a tremendous amount of pain the entire day. He would sit up, lie down, and move around. No matter what he did, he just couldn't seem to get comfortable. And the hallucinations continued.

"He was agitated," Phillip recalled later. "He was in a lot of agony . . . a lot of pain."

Two days later, on February 18, 1996, Edward Skwira died

early in the morning, shortly before his family, who were planning on visiting him, had a chance to make it to the hospital.

A year later, toxicology tests determined that Ed Skwira's
system was loaded with the drug ketamine. Ketamine is an
anesthetic used therapeutically for children and adult asthma
patients. On the street, it's commonly referred to as "Special
K," and kids take it mainly for its hallucinatory side effects.
Given to someone improperly, ketamine can cause hallucinations, which Skwira clearly suffered from during his final days.

More of a concern to investigators, however, was that the
VAMC had never purchased or stocked ketamine, and not a single doctor or nurse—from AdCare, in Worcester, where Skwira
had been detoxed, to Baystate—had prescribed or authorized
the drug.

CHAPTER 32

With all that had happened at the VAMC the past seven months, Kristen Gilbert would have to step up to the plate sooner or later and explain herself—because Renee Walsh, Kathy Rix and John Wall were en route to a meeting with Melodie Turner and there wasn't anything Gilbert could do to stop it.

Melodie Turner insisted the meeting take place in the office of her boss, Priscilla McDonald. Tucked away in the back of Building Two, McDonald's office was off the beaten path. It being a Saturday, the hospital was deserted anyway. There was a good chance no one would see them entering or leaving the building.

With Renee Walsh off, Wall and Rix were scheduled to work later that day, as was Gilbert.

It was about one P.M. when the meeting began.

"Would one of you like to start?" Turner asked as she closed the door.

With that, the accusations began.

All three nurses laid out their concerns where the frequency of medical emergencies and percentage of cardiac arrests occurring on Ward C and its ICU were concerned—and that most of the cardiac arrests happened more often when Gilbert was the patient's primary nurse, when she was alone with a patient in ICU, or when she relieved another nurse for dinner or break.

Turner looked as if someone had drained the blood from her body and replaced it with milk.

"We want to emphasize, Melodie, that none of us has any proof," Walsh wanted to make clear.

Rix and Wall nodded.

"None of us have witnessed her doing anything," Walsh added, ". . . but, nevertheless, we're worried."

"Read [Angelo] Vella's code note," Wall spit out.

Turner made a note.

"There have been more codes on the ward than I have *ever* seen in my career," Rix said.

"We request that a study be done as soon as possible," Walsh urged. "We want someone to look at the percentage of cardiac arrests occurring on the ward when Kristen was on, as opposed to any other nurse."

They waited for Turner to respond, but she didn't have much to say. There was no doubt she was concerned, as they had figured she would be. And Walsh could tell by looking at her face that she knew they were serious.

"I will take this information directly to my superiors," Turner said. "But we want to keep Kristen away from the patients as much as possible."

They agreed. But the question was, how?

For the next few minutes, they devised a plan whereby John Wall would try to convince Gilbert to be the charge nurse when she showed up for work. Being charge nurse would strap Gilbert down to the nurse's station. If she wasn't sitting, doing paperwork and going through patient files, she would be answering phones and ordering supplies. If by some chance she decided to go roaming around the ward, John said he would tail her.

It was the perfect plan. All they had to do was get Gilbert to agree to it.

"I'll take care of staffing on the ward," Turner said. "John, you go to the ward, and I want Kristen to be off . . . we're going to get her off duty." In Turner's mind, she wasn't going to allow Gilbert, who was scheduled to come in at four, to work at all.

Before the meeting was over, Turner had one more suggestion.

"Go out and get attorneys for yourselves."

After Wall, Rix and Walsh left the meeting, Turner picked up
the phone and called Ward C. It was shortly after four
o'clock.

As fate would have it, Gilbert answered.

"Kristen, when John comes in, the two of you can work it
out, but one of you can take the night off."

This must have tipped Gilbert off that something was going
on because Turner had just scolded Gilbert a few days before
for taking Saturdays off, and here she was now offering her the
night off on a silver platter. It was totally out of character for
Turner.

"Okay," Gilbert said, and hung up.

For the next hour or so, Turner wondered how she was going
to get Gilbert off the ward.

When Wall finally ran into Gilbert at about 4:30, he just flat
out asked her if she wanted to be the charge nurse for the night.

"No!"

Wall asked again.

"No!" Gilbert said. "I want to be Team Leader."

This meant she would be in charge of handing out meds—
the last thing Wall wanted to hear.

As Gilbert worked her way around the ward, handing out
meds, Wall made sure to be right around the corner from wherever she was. He felt responsible for the well-being of her patients. He had been having nightmares for weeks now. There
had been enough death in the past several months on Ward C to
last a lifetime.

No more.

But as he stealthily made his way in Gilbert's shadow, Wall
felt she knew what he was up to.

Meanwhile, Turner was in her office stewing over the fact
that a serial killer could be wandering through her ward at that
very moment and there wasn't a damn thing she could do about
it.

No sooner had Turner thought about calling another RN in to cover for Gilbert, than the evening coordinator called her office to say that Gilbert had just gotten injured.

Injured?

Shortly before 6:30, Gilbert had walked into Joseph Gallante's room to give him his nightly injection of medicine. Within a few moments of being in the room, crying hysterically, Gilbert came running out.

"John," she said holding her arm, "look what happened."

Wall came around the corner, and Gilbert came up to him. She claimed that Gallante, all of about five-foot-six, one hundred and forty pounds, had, like a bully on a schoolyard playground, "grabbed her right arm, rotated it inward, and twisted it up behind her back." When that happened, Gilbert claimed, not only did she hear something in her shoulder pop and a separation occur, but she said the needle she was holding had pricked "the lower thumb area of her right palm."

Although it seemed all too perfect, Wall wasn't going to argue with her.

Next, Wall had her fill out an accident report. While she was doing that, Karen Abderhalden called Perrault at home and told him what had just happened.

"I'll be right there," Perrault said.

During the ride home, Gilbert explained to Perrault how she had awakened Gallante to give him his medication, but must have startled him somehow. Already in a sling, Gilbert went on and on about how violent he had become.

After he was sure Gilbert had left the building, Wall went into Gallante's room to see if he could find out what happened.

Wall was overwhelmed, he later said, to see the seventy-two-year-old Gallante "lying on his back, supinely, in soft restraints." Gallante was an Alzheimer's patient who had suffered from dementia for years. Many of the nurses who had cared for him described him later as a "very docile individual who did not have a history of violence." No one could believe he could overpower Gilbert.

As time went on, the nurses put it all together.

Gilbert was famous for putting on grotesque contortionist displays in front of the nurses as they stood around during coffee break. Even James Perrault would later explain how he had seen her do it a number of times just for the fun of it, or, as he recalled, "like Mel Gibson in the movie *Lethal Weapon.*"

Obviously double-jointed, Gilbert would pop her arm out of its socket at the shoulder and let it hang until someone told her to put it back in. She would laugh about it. It was a joke.

As her story unfurled during the coming days, Gilbert claimed to have sustained the needle prick in her *right* palm during the altercation she'd had with Gallante. But because Gilbert was right-handed, many would later find this difficult to believe, since she claimed Gallante grabbed her right arm and twisted it behind her back.

The more pressing question of the moment, however, was: Who had tipped Gilbert off someone was on to her? And now that she'd been fingered, what would she do next?

Within the next few days, special agents from the Washington and Boston Veterans Affairs' Inspector General Offices converged like paratroopers down on Northampton and began to unravel what had been going on inside Ward C for the past seven years.

PART TWO

Fire-brand *(fir'brand')* \ n. 1 : a piece of burning wood; 2 : a person who creates unrest or strife: AGITATOR

—The New Merriam-Webster Dictionary

In every life, joy flashes gay and radiant across the sorrows of all sorts of which the web of our life is woven. . . .

—Nikolai Gogol, *Dead Souls*

CHAPTER 33

When John Wall, Kathy Rix and Renee Walsh, nurses with more than fifty years of cumulative experience, met with their nursing manager on February 17, 1996, and voiced their concerns regarding the possibility of a colleague's harming patients, they had no idea they had cast a stone into a pond that, they would soon learn, seemed to have no bottom.

The ripple effect created by that stone, however, was just now being felt by anyone who had ever come in contact with twenty-nine-year-old Kristen Gilbert. Word had hit Ward C like a pinball, ricocheting off anyone who had ever worked with Gilbert throughout the years. Gilbert was being investigated for murder, people were whispering.

Yes . . . murder!

Not a series of accidents or mercy killings, but cold-blooded murder. Kathy Rix had found broken ampoules of epinephrine. The rash of codes and medical emergencies. Gilbert's affair with James Perrault. Glenn Gilbert's being sick back in November.

It was all adding up.

But Gilbert took to the offensive right away, beginning a phone campaign to proclaim her innocence: There were people—nurses!—she pleaded during one phone call after the other, out to frame her. They were upset, she repeated to anyone who would listen, because she had cheated on Glenn with

James Perrault. Gilbert's only problem, however, was that her plea of innocence was drowned out by one lie after the next.

It started with the injury she said had been sustained on February 17. She changed her story three times. Mr. Gallante, Gilbert had first claimed, had "grabbed her arm, tugged it, and then twisted it." Then, a few days later, she told someone else he "grabbed her wrist, forced it behind her back until it touched the back of her neck." Her most bizarre claim came later, when she said that Gallante had "... flung her across the room."

The initial report detailed the needle stick in her right palm; and then later, in an official report to the Labor Board, Gilbert wrote that it happened in her left palm.

James Perrault's boss, Timothy O'Donnell, the VAMC Chief of Security, wasn't going to waste any time. There needed to be some type of criminal investigator on the scene—and fast. Things were spiraling out of control. Accusations and rumors were flying around like buzzards, tainting the integrity of potential witnesses.

O'Donnell wanted order.

Several agents from the quality-control side of the VA's Inspector General's Office (IGO), in Washington, DC, were already en route to the VAMC, based on information O'Donnell had received concerning the meeting Melodie Turner had had with Wall, Rix and Walsh. O'Donnell placed a call to the VA's Bedford, Massachusetts, IGO early in the morning on February 29, 1996.

Special Agent Steve Plante, after being briefed about the call, phoned O'Donnell right away.

"Listen," O'Donnell said, "there are several agents coming in from Washington to investigate a recent rash of medical emergencies and deaths up here at the Leeds Medical Center. They're having a meeting later on today. You might want to be here."

"I'm on my way," SA Plante said.

The VA-IGO was broken down into several groups, each with its own set of responsibilities. The Criminal Investigations Division (CID), for example, investigated fraud, waste, criminal conduct and abuse within its own agency, similar to that of the internal affairs division in any police department.

Thirty-nine years old, in perfect physical shape at five-five, one hundred and forty pounds, with a full shock of thick black hair and a flawlessly trimmed mustache to match, SA Plante had worked for the CID as a criminal investigator out of the IGO's Bedford office for the past six years.

Living in Bedford with his wife and kids, Plante had normally been assigned cases in and around the eastern New England area: Providence, Rhode Island; West Haven, Connecticut; Worcester, Massachusetts. Northampton was a world away from Bedford. On top of that, he had broken his leg while on a skiing trip just weeks before and was sporting a full leg cast. The thought of dropping everything and going to Northampton might have never occurred to a less experienced agent. But O'Donnell's phone call interested Plante. He had never investigated the type of case O'Donnell had described, and he wasn't about to let his leg, or a massive Nor'easter snowstorm that had pummeled the region for the past few days, stop him.

After graduating from Dartmouth High School in the late seventies and spending four years in the Coast Guard, where he was bitten by the law enforcement bug while patrolling a two-hundred-mile stretch of water out in the wide-open Atlantic, boarding and searching boats from all over the world, Special Agent Steve Plante enrolled at Stonehill College, just outside Boston, in 1979. He was the first and only one of his siblings to attend college and, under the GI Bill, received a bachelor's degree in criminal justice. Following a two-year stint in the INS from 1983 to 1985, Plante transferred to the Department of Agriculture's IGO and spent the next four years learning how the feds investigated all sorts of crimes against the public.

In 1988, Plante entered the VA-CID and fell in love with the work. Soon his superiors noticed he had a meticulous knack for studying documents and records, and they started assigning him fiduciary cases, white-collar crimes: fraud and embezzlement.

* * *

It was obvious to SA Plante when he arrived at the VAMC that the nurses were reluctant to talk. Many were scared, he later said. "But the three main players"—Kathy Rix, John Wall and Renee Walsh—"all good people, definitely wanted to tell their story."

Later that same day, Dell Levy, a ten-year healthcare inspector from the Washington, DC, Office of Healthcare Inspection (HCI), showed up. Separately, she interviewed Wall, Rix and Walsh. Seeing that SA Plante was already on the scene when she arrived, Levy knew her role: to make sure policy and procedure had been followed correctly by staff members, nothing else. It wasn't the HCI's job to conduct investigations. It was more interested, Levy later said, in the "overall running of the medical center" in the same way FDA inspectors kept tabs on the public food supply.

The first thing SA Plante did when he got there was gather together as many medical records of dead patients as he could, secure a room to store them in, and get started going through them to see if something stood out right away. He was looking for clusters of deaths: several deaths on the same ward, signed off by the same nurse.

Plante's next job was to develop a rapport with his three main sources, Wall, Rix and Walsh. He wanted them to know right away he was on their side and that they shouldn't feel threatened in any way. Plante's style wasn't to bully witnesses. He wasn't brassy and demanding. He just wanted to know the facts.

Meanwhile, Levy began to bring in VAMC personnel so she could ask the appropriate medical procedure questions. Kathy Rix, during her first interview, wouldn't stop crying, Levy later recalled.

"Relax, Ms. Rix. It's okay," Levy reassured her. "You know, it's okay to talk to me."

But Rix continued to cry.

"I'm scared," she whispered. "I'm scared."

As the investigation progressed over the course of the first few days of March, Walsh, Rix and Wall began to grow increasingly impatient. SA Plante aside, the HCI inspectors, Walsh insisted, were more concerned with procedure and the overall behavior of the staff rather than looking into what the three of them were accusing Gilbert of.

They were confused and didn't know the difference between the HCI and the VA-IGO's Criminal Investigations Division, assuming HCI inspectors carried the same authority as SA Plante and his office.

But as Walsh and the others would soon find out, there was a big difference.

SA Plante was on to something from the get-go. From speaking with Rix and Wall, SA Plante and Dell Levy kept hearing the same name pop up: Thomas Callahan. John Wall, often uneasy and restless during his interviews, would say, "Check Callahan's chart for January twenty-second. Please. Check it out!"

So SA Plante burrowed his way to records department in the basement of the VAMC and began digging through the thousands of medical files, looking for Thomas Callahan's case history. He knew that each VA hospital had a separate EKG department where a patient's entire EKG history was stored. All he had to do was look up January 22 to see what Wall was referring to.

When Plante located Callahan's file, his EKG for January 22—the day he had coded—was missing.

CHAPTER 34

The biggest worry John Wall, Kathy Rix and Renee Walsh faced right away was the VAMC's own security office. Timothy O'Donnell and his crew were involved from day one, and Rix, Walsh and Wall worried themselves sick that Gilbert would somehow find out what they had been saying. With Gilbert practically living with Perrault, there was a strong possibility he was acting as her mole. Whatever he learned at work, they assumed, he was likely taking home and sharing with Gilbert.

Little did they know at the time how right they were.

"Keep your eyes and ears open," Gilbert told Perrault one night in early March. "Report back to me anything important you hear. Make sure you find out who the investigators are talking to and how long those interviews are."

Perrault, of course, obliged.

David Levin, the head of the VAMC's Quality Management Department, had requested a meeting with Wall, Rix and Walsh a day or so after they had met with Melodie Turner. Chief O'Donnell said he wanted to meet with them, too, separately, and tape-record each interview.

They refused. Either they met as a group, or forget it. And no one was going to tape-record anything.

On March 1, Dell Levy sat down with Walsh and wanted to know what her main concerns were.

For about an hour, Walsh told Levy exactly what she had

told Melodie Turner a few weeks back, but went into more detail where specific patients were concerned.

The HCI was designed to keep track of patient care and make sure VA patients were receiving proper care from medical personnel employed by the VA. But Walsh didn't know this. She thought she was talking to a criminal investigator.

As Levy continued asking questions, Walsh became irritated, feeling that Levy wasn't the person Walsh thought she was. Levy's questions were geared more toward whether the nurses had been following proper procedures and giving out medications correctly.

"When," Walsh asked, interrupting Levy, "are we going to get around to talking about what I'm really concerned about?"

"Well, Ms. Walsh, what is it that you're so worried about?"

"The reason why I wanted to talk to somebody in the first place was because I'm worried that this nurse I work with . . . Kristen Gilbert . . . I think she may be killing people. I'm worried, Miss Levy, that something is happening . . . our cardiac arrest rate is out of sight."

"Maybe, Ms. Walsh, we should have you talk to somebody else. That's not really my field."

After three days on the scene, Levy was summoned back to Washington to report to her superiors what she had learned. After telling her boss upon returning that she needed more time and the assistance of another healthcare inspector, Levy's boss sent her back to Northampton with colleagues Rayda Nadal and Irene Trowell-Harris. A day or so after they arrived, on March 5, Sandra Willis, yet another HCI inspector, joined them.

At first, Levy thought they would be there only another two or three days. But as they began to conduct interviews, it became clear they needed more time.

Meanwhile, SA Plante began to throw around his authority.

"Any interview you conduct," he told Levy upon her return, "from now on, I want to be there."

Because he was a criminal investigator, SA Plante had jurisdiction over everyone. Anyone in the VAMC, even the director of the hospital, had to answer to him. All it took was one phone call.

* * *

During the next week, a horrifying picture began to emerge from the wreckage of medical records and interviews SA Plante and inspectors Dell Levy, Rayda Nadal and Sandra Willis conducted. Levy didn't see it at first, but Plante picked up on it immediately: Kristen Gilbert was running in circles trying to cover up one lie after the next.

During one interview with Nadal and Levy, Gilbert denied even being involved in the care of many of the patients in question. She said her name was on the code notes only because she had been summoned to the codes by other nurses and nursing assistants—and because she was more experienced in code situations and had a reputation for being a "conscientious" code nurse, the nurses had asked her to document the codes, which she said she gladly did.

But as the nurses filed in and told their stories, not one said he or she had sought Gilbert out during codes because of her "supposed" talents. Furthermore, many of the nurses said that even if they had wanted to, there were many times where Gilbert couldn't be found, because she was always off somewhere smooching it up with Perrault. Besides, it was Gilbert who had been calling most of the codes in the first place.

Already armed with testimony from several of Gilbert's colleagues who had admitted to knowing exactly where ampoules of 1:1000 strength epinephrine had been kept on the ward, SA Plante, after being briefed by the HCI inspectors, asked Gilbert during one interview if she had ever used the drug in her career at the VAMC.

"I didn't even know they had it in the hospital," Gilbert said.

CHAPTER 35

Like many of the nurses on Ward C, Lisa Baronas had developed her own suspicions about Gilbert. In her late twenties, Baronas had been a nursing assistant at the VAMC for years. She liked her job. It was satisfying, and she felt as if she was making a difference in the lives of those patients she had touched. Her coworkers considered her a "hard worker" and "very dependable."

While Baronas was working one day in March, to her surprise, she looked up from what she was doing and spied Gilbert standing by the elevators. Gilbert didn't know it then, but Baronas had just come from an interview with HCI inspector Dell Levy.

"What are you doing here?" Baronas asked.

"I'm going for an interview with the investigators. Listen, Lisa. They're probably going to ask you about Ed Skwira," Gilbert said. "Now, you remember being in the room with me when he coded, don't you, Lisa?"

"No. I wasn't, Kristen."

"Don't you remember? You were in the room with me at the time," Gilbert insisted.

"No, *Kristen*. I wasn't!"

Gilbert then walked into the elevator without saying anything more as Baronas, amazed by what she had just heard, went back to work.

The day after Gilbert had approached Baronas, SA Plante called Baronas in for a second interview. He now wanted her version of Ed Skwira's code.

Baronas didn't think she had much to offer.

"I wasn't even there," she said. Yes, she had helped Gilbert transport Skwira to Radiology. Yes, she then helped Gilbert transport him back to his room. "But I plugged in his blood pressure machine, locked the wheels on his stretcher, and left."

"I would have remembered if I was there when somebody coded," Baronas later recalled.

When SA Plante realized Gilbert had lied to him, he first wondered what she was trying to hide. People, Plante knew, wouldn't generally lie unless there was a payoff. But at the same time, he worked hard to maintain an impartial perspective. Baronas, he thought, could be stretching the truth as well. He had to make sure there wasn't an obvious solution for all the codes, medical emergencies and deaths, maybe something in the ventilation system, a healthcare issue, or malpractice. For all Plante knew, some of the nurses could have been handing out the wrong medications and trying to cover their tracks.

So he began looking into things even deeper.

Still wearing a sling and bandage from the injuries she had supposedly sustained on February 17, Gilbert began calling and e-mailing anyone and everyone she used to work with to see what she could find out about the investigation.

"What are they asking you?" was one of her favorite questions. Along with, "Who else is being interviewed? Tell me what you know."

Around the same time, she also began keeping a detailed notebook on the progress of the investigation. Her first entry, dated the "end of February," indicated that the two inspectors from HCI who had interviewed her had asked questions "mostly about policy and procedure."

Her notes regarding her second interview a few days later were more detailed, however. The same two investigators were asking questions, she noted, along with SA Plante, about the bomb scare back in 1993 and several fires that had occurred throughout the years on Ward C. Between March 10, 1990, and May 6, 1993, there had been eleven fires on Ward C, and Gilbert was on duty for eight of them—even though her shift had changed several times during that same period.

After looking further, Plante found out that Gilbert had found eight of the fires herself and even extinguished a few of them. In one instance, she had even received an award for putting out a fire that had gutted an entire bathroom. Plante, along with many nurses, speculated it was Gilbert who had started the fires in the first place.

Why?

So she could extinguish them and be the hero.

Next to her notes about the fires and bomb scare, Gilbert wrote that Plante had asked her if she had a "theory" about the recent rash of codes and deaths; then he told her that "125 epinephrines [ampoules] were missing"; asked her to "review [the code] note in Skwira's chart," explaining in detail the "sequence of events"; and, finally, she wrote that Plante had asked her to take a polygraph test, which she refused.

During that same interview, Plante revealed to Gilbert perhaps his most compelling piece of evidence to date. Regarding the sequence of events surrounding Ed Skwira's death, Gilbert's notes indicated that Plante posed a hypothetical question at one point during the interview: "What if I were to say that I have somebody who counted the [EPI ampoules] before you came on duty . . . ?" Plante then acknowledged there had been "three ampoules." And when "this person" checked the medicine cabinet, "this person" saw that they went missing, but then later spotted the broken ampoules in the needle-disposal bucket.

Gilbert didn't write any conclusion to SA Plante's query. Instead, her notes about that part of the interview ended abruptly.

On another page, under the heading, "What other people have told me was asked," Gilbert kept a list of the nurses she had spoken to and the information they had given her. Under the title "Lori" [Naumowitz], for example, Gilbert noted that Lori "said somebody saw pills in my coat pocket . . ." Then she wrote "who was angry at me," regarding her divorce. Ending

Lori's heading, Gilbert wrote that Melodie Turner had asked Lori if she and Gilbert were still friends. When Lori said she was, Turner, according to Gilbert's recollection, then told Lori to "rethink that—you wouldn't want to go down with a sinking ship."

Under the heading "David [Rejniak]," Gilbert listed the same items as she had for Lori, except it was obvious that Rejniak had been a little bit more open with Gilbert about what he had discussed with SAs Plante and Levy. Rejniak, according to Gilbert, said "the investigators tried *very* hard to convince him that [she] was capable of wrongdoing in order [to] illicit [sic] info from him." Rejniak also told Gilbert that he felt the investigators "had convinced other people" of the same thing.

If Gilbert had been keeping a tally of the people she could and could not trust, the last page of her notes sprang to life with two nurses Gilbert hadn't really paid any attention to throughout the seven years she had worked at the VAMC: Carole Osman and Ann French.

At the time, French, who was nicknamed "Yosemite Ann," in her late fifties, was a member of the NRA whose one highlight in life was hunting. It was odd that Gilbert and French had anything in common. Plus, many of the nurses said she had no love for Gilbert whatsoever.

Under the heading "Carole," Gilbert noted that Osman had "refused to answer personal questions," and that the investigators had asked her to "speculate" and "theorize."

Ann French, who had already warned SA Plante that if he wanted to speak with her about anything, it had better not affect the upcoming hunting season, Gilbert wrote, "refused to take a polygraph."

It was clear Kristen Gilbert was keeping a scorecard. The mistake she was making, possibly without even realizing it, was that she was helping Plante document a potential murder case against her, effectively giving away her entire game plan.

When Renee Walsh finally heard about the broken and missing ampoules of epinephrine Kathy Rix had discovered, she felt a bit disappointed that Rix hadn't shared the information with her sooner. Walsh didn't even think that Gilbert might have been using epinephrine. She had always assumed it was potassium, as she had told SA Plante. Yet now that she knew, it made more sense why so many of the patients in question had screamed out in pain right before their codes. Epinephrine, when injected in the arm, is extremely painful. It burns. The area around the shot goes numb. The heart races. Blood pressure skyrockets.

By March 5, it was clear that the focus of the investigation was now centered on Gilbert and dozens of missing ampoules of epinephrine. In fact, as the second week of March approached, most of the questions now being asked were straight to that point: "What type of drug do you think [Gilbert] used? How does epinephrine come [packaged] on to the ward? Where is it stocked? The IV push [bristo-jet], is that the only way [the drug] comes?"

When Walsh heard this question, she immediately said no.

"It also comes in a much smaller concentrated version [1:1000]. But I've never given it here."

"You've never given it?" SA Plante asked.

"No."

"Let me ask you this: What would happen if you gave it to someone in an IV?"

"Nothing good, I would imagine."

"You've never known anyone to give it in an IV?"

"No."

"Is it available on Ward C?"

"I've never had to go and look for it, so I really don't know," Walsh said.

SA Plante kept asking if Walsh had ever—*think hard, think really, really hard*—given it to *anyone* at *anytime*. But Walsh kept insisting that she hadn't.

"I have never even seen an order for it."

SA Plante got up from his seat and extended his hand.

"Ms. Walsh, you've been a big help to us. I'll be in touch."

When Plante closed the door and thought about the interview, a sigh of relief washed over him. Walsh had stood up to his grilling and kept her ground. She was certain about what she had seen. She hadn't been intimidated. That meant only one thing to Plante: She was telling the truth.

Things were beginning to point in one direction—a direction, SA Plante would soon learn, the boys in Washington wouldn't be too happy about once they found out.

CHAPTER 36

At about 8:00 P.M. on March 6, after attending a Lenten service at her local church, Renee Walsh opened the door to her apartment to the sound of a ringing telephone. Without even turning on the lights or taking off her coat, she picked up the receiver.

"Hi, Renee. It's Kristen."

Walsh was breathless. She hadn't seen nor heard from Gilbert since before she had turned her in.

Act normal . . . act normal, she told herself. *Just take it easy and see what she wants.*

"Kristen? Oh, you caught me off guard . . . I just got home."

Gilbert didn't waste any time.

"What did they talk to you about? What do they want to know?"

What can I say that will sound right?

With her mind racing, Walsh said, as calmly as she could, "Well . . . they are asking a lot of questions regarding policy and procedure. They wanted to know about certain drugs we use during codes."

As Walsh said this, she turned on the light and took a piece of paper out of the drawer and began jotting down what Gilbert was saying.

"There's been an increase of codes, Kristen," Walsh said when Gilbert fell silent. "And they felt the need to look into it."

"They talked to you for three hours about *that?*"

"How do you know they had me in there for three hours?"

"Carole [Osman] told me."

Walsh remembered seeing Osman on the ward as she got called down to talk to SA Plante. She made a mental note: *Tell Kathy and John to stay the hell away from Carole Osman.*

"Well, Kristen, I don't know what else to say," Walsh said.

Gilbert's tone became more aggressive. She spoke fast.

"I have to tell you this makes me paranoid as hell, Renee. If they start looking at the records, my name is all over seventy-five percent of the deaths."

"There are a lot of other names are on those charts, Kristen. It's not just yours."

"I wonder why they feel they have to investigate this now."

"I have no idea."

"You don't think that the family of one of the patients [who] died filed a wrongful death suit, do you?"

"I haven't heard anything like that, Kristen."

"You know how everyone always jokes and teases me about being the angel of death and always being there when someone has a cardiac arrest? You don't think anyone would be stupid enough to say something like that to the inspectors, do you?"

"No, no, no," Walsh said. "None of the questions have [lent] themselves to that. That's not what they talked to me about, anyway."

Gilbert wouldn't let up.

"What *did* they ask you about then . . . for three hours?"

"Just a broad range of things. You know, Kristen, they wanted to know how well we're staffed. How things work on the ward. Stuff like that."

"But why? Why do they want to know this?"

"There's been an increase in the number of deaths lately, Kristen. That's no secret."

"Why, though?"

"I don't *know,* Kristen. Listen, I have to get going. I am not even out of my coat yet. I need to eat dinner. I'll talk to you later."

"Yeah," Gilbert said. "If I'm not in jail!"

* * *

By March 13, all of the HCI inspectors summoned to the scene since February had been sent back to their offices in Washington, and SA Plante, now alone, was left to sift through a mountain of documents and interviews. After quickly ruling out the possibility of malpractice, improper patient care or poor ventilation, Plante carefully began to put flesh on the bones of what he now considered a criminal investigation.

For SA Plante, as he went through the scores of interviews and studied each of them meticulously, his focus was drawn toward the many lies Gilbert had told.

She had met with Dell Levy and Rayda Nadal between March 8 and 13, and they had asked her to explain Francis Marier's and Thomas Callahan's codes. On both occasions, Plante learned, Gilbert went out of her way to mislead them.

Lie number one.

Regarding Marier, Gilbert said that because Marier had been on a restricted diet, and on his usual dose of insulin, he was getting too much insulin for the amount of food he had been taking in, and thus he had gone into shock and coded because of that. This was in total contrast to her earlier story about Marier's blood sugar level being at 44 when she said she checked it shortly before he coded.

Lie number two.

As for Callahan, Gilbert claimed she had contacted the on-call doctor, and he had come in to check on Callahan right before he coughed and coded. A quick look at Callahan's chart told Plante that no doctor had come into the room because there was no note written by any doctor.

On March 12, during an interview with SA Plante, after he had informed her about the "statistical analysis and the correlation between the increased number of patients' deaths and the times she was on duty," Gilbert said, "The deaths and codes came in spurts. It was probably just a coincidence [that I was on duty]. It was just my time to be involved."

Plante then grilled her about why she thought she had been around so many codes.

"The LPNs and nursing assistants frequently called on me and reported to me crisis situations, thus increasing my numbers."

Plante knew already from talking to several of the LPNs and

nursing assistants that this was a lie. It didn't matter who found a patient in an emergency situation; that person would call the code. One didn't have to be a nurse to call a code.

This, of course, wasn't evidence that Gilbert had killed anyone. Plante was smarter than that. But it did make it clear she was trying to hide something.

When Dell Levy returned to Washington, she was surprised when she was given only twenty days to complete a report based on what she found at the Leeds VAMC.

In her ten-year career working for the government, Levy had been given upward of a year or more to conclude her findings regarding cases of this magnitude. Why the change all of a sudden?

The VA was in a panic. It realized that the biggest problem it faced right away was that there had been zero accountability for the ampoules of epinephrine that went missing. Armed with that information, the VA sent out a memo to all of its facilities stating its concerns, making sure to let each center know to begin some sort of inventory regarding its supply of epinephrine.

Levy said later that the simple fact the VAMC in Leeds "lacked any ability to review trends in deaths and codes on a particular ward that could be associated with a particular healthcare employee" was also of great concern to her bosses upon her return. They were afraid what happened at the VAMC in Leeds could be happening elsewhere, and no one would know about it unless a whistle-blower had come forward.

None of this, however, was of any concern to SA Plante. His job was to catch a killer—and now, with the mounting evidence he was accumulating against Gilbert, it seemed as if it was only a matter of time.

CHAPTER 37

Going through boxes and boxes of medical records, SA Steve Plante's gut instincts told him that he could be investigating the most successful serial killer the Commonwealth of Massachusetts had ever seen. During Gilbert's seven-year tenure at the VAMC, three hundred and fifty patients had died. She hadn't killed them all, of course. But even one, Plante thought, was enough to keep him looking for more.

By the end of March, Plante moved his case off "the hill" and took it into town. It was time to start banging on doors.

Back in February, Kristen had phoned her estranged husband, Glenn, and told him that an investigation by the IGO "regarding a high number of deaths on a certain ward" was under way at the VAMC. She said SA Plante would likely be calling.

"You don't have to say anything if you don't want to, Glenn."

Knowing that Plante was sooner or later going be knocking on Glenn's door, in a bit of a panic one afternoon in late March, Kristen called again. She wanted Glenn to be prepared.

"You have spousal privileges, you know, Glenn," she said. *"What?"*

"Marriage protects one spouse from incriminating another. The privileges are there, Glenn, if you want to use them."

Glenn was still in the dark about a lot of things; he didn't really understand what his soon-to-be former wife was talking about, because he didn't really think that she was involved.

This was the first time Kristen had flat-out asked Glenn to keep quiet. For the past six weeks or so, she would call and just express her anger toward whoever had been cooperating with the investigation—mainly John Wall, Kathy Rix, Lori Naumowitz and David Rejniak.

Kristen felt they had betrayed her.

Regarding Lori, she said, "How could that bitch speak to those people, Glenn?"

But now she was telling Glenn there was going to come a time when he would have to make a decision about whose side he was on.

"Yeah, whatever," Glenn said and hung up. He wanted to be left alone.

SA Plante, as Kristen had promised, paid a visit to Glenn around the first week of April, but Glenn didn't say much. He wasn't hostile or rude. But he made it perfectly clear that he wasn't going to be talking about his soon-to-be ex. They had kids. The kids needed their mother, even if they were no longer living together.

Plante didn't push Glenn. He knew that if it came down to it, he could have him subpoenaed. Then he'd have to talk.

SA Plante faced a number of obstacles as spring approached. Most of the people he'd reached out to were not all that thrilled about answering questions about Gilbert, yet they continued to help. But Glenn Gilbert and James Perrault—the two people he needed most, if he was going to begin to understand the kind of person Gilbert truly was—weren't talking about their personal relationships with her. Perrault would answer any questions related to the VAMC—"He had no problem with that," Plante later recalled—but when it came to his personal or sexual relationship with Gilbert, which was still burning strong as ever, he continually said it was off limits.

"He knew his rights. He was being well informed."

What was it going to take, Plante often wondered, to get these guys to talk? He knew that ninety percent of the evidence he needed for a conviction was in the medical records at the

VAMC. But he also knew that if he was going to understand that evidence, he would have to get into the minds of those who knew Gilbert best: Perrault and Glenn.

As Plante contemplated what to do next, Gilbert went on the move.

During one of her frequent calls to Glenn to find out what he'd heard, Kristen mentioned that the investigation had been centered on a "certain type of drug."

This piqued Glenn's interest.

"What kind of drug?"

"Epi," Gilbert said.

"Epi . . . what is that?"

Gilbert explained. Then she said, "If they're looking for it in these bodies, well, they're *going* to find it!"

Glenn was confused.

"Because," Gilbert said. "Because . . . they're focusing on it as the reason these people died. . . . [But]," she insisted, "it would be hard to prove."

She was correct, of course.

All human beings have epinephrine—more commonly known as adrenaline—in their tissue. Whenever a person becomes startled or scared, his blood pressure rises and he feels anxious.

That is adrenaline at work.

Detecting excessive amounts of it in one's system, however, was not clear science at the time. There was no definitive way to test for it—and any results would be vehemently challenged in court.

Plante decided that he had to present Glenn Gilbert and James Perrault with some hard facts if he was going to convince them that Gilbert was the malicious serial killer he now thought her to be. He would have to show them in black and white the evidence he had without giving away his case. Yet, before he could do that, it was time to start thinking about getting the US Attorney's Office involved.

Gilbert, on the other hand, was acting stranger than ever.

Near the end of May, as she was wandering around the grounds of the VAMC looking for Perrault one afternoon, she ran into RN Karen Abderhalden, whom she had known quite well and still considered a close friend.

"Karen," she said, "have you seen Jim? I have his dinner."

"No."

"Listen, Karen, do you think you can get me a needle and syringe?"

"What? Why, Kristen?"

"I need to draw some blood from Mindy [her and Glenn's dog]. Glenn and I are short on cash. We need to have Mindy checked for heartworms. We can save some cash if we bring the blood to the vet ourselves."

"Absolutely not, Kristen. You're crazy for even asking such a thing during the middle of an investigation like this."

CHAPTER 38

Shaped like an inverted L, the US Attorney's Office, located on the third floor of the Federal Building in downtown Springfield, is a stuffy office space tucked into the northeastern corner of the building. About the size of a gas station kiosk, the reception area of the office sports an American flag, a rather large picture of the attorney general and, next to that, a picture of the president of the United States.

On June 21, 1996, Assistant United States Attorney William Welch, after coming in from one of his semi-daily jogs around downtown, sat down to man the "duty" phone, or whistle-blower hotline that handles calls from citizens or law enforcement who want to report a crime, open an investigation, or need assistance in an investigation. When Bill, as everyone in the office called him, picked up the phone at around two P.M., SA Jeff Leonard, who wasn't working with SA Plante on the Gilbert case, but had been briefed about it by Plante, was on the other end of the line.

"I'm with the VA-IGO in Bedford. How are you, Mr. Welch?"

"Fine. What's up?"

"We have an agent in Northampton right now investigating some suspicious deaths up at one of our medical centers, and we believe we have a serial killer on our hands. We'd like to maybe open up a grand jury investigation."

Bill Welch, himself a Northampton resident, was stunned. It

was, up until that point, a casual Friday afternoon. Watching the
clock tick down all day, Welch sometimes cut out early and had
a few beers with his friends at a local bar. US attorneys worked
exhausting hours. There were many times when fifteen-hour
days turned into ten-hour nights and sleep came in the form of a
nap in the conference room.

"Can you come in—or have your agent on scene come in—
today?" Welch asked.

"Sure."

A graduate of Princeton University and Northwestern
University Law School—where Welch, at six-two, two hundred
and twenty pounds, felt more comfortable on the football field
than he did stuffed inside a classroom—he joined the
Springfield US Attorney's Office early in 1995. He was sworn
in as US attorney in 1991 and worked in Reno, Nevada. For the
most part, he was assigned criminal tax section cases, but soon
got involved with major drug cases. In one case, Welch tried
several defendants who had a major methamphetamine and cocaine distribution center in northern Nevada. The case, which
garnered national attention, took thirteen months to try.

Two of the defendants got mandatory life sentences.

Law was injected into attorney Welch's blood, from as far
back as he can remember, by his father, the honorable
Massachusetts Superior Court Judge William H. Welch.

When SAs Leonard and Plante showed up at the US Attor-
ney's Office that Friday, they brought with them memos from
Plante's interviews with Kathy Rix, John Wall and Renee
Walsh.

Welch was overwhelmed by the allegations. Trying drug,
murder-for-hire, fraud, extortion and mob cases was one thing,
but going after a nurse for the deaths of her patients was something Welch had never imagined. It didn't seem possible. Welch
lived in Northampton. He had driven by the VAMC and gone
mountain biking in the hills just beyond it ever since moving
into town. To think that a nurse had killed multiple patients was
incredible. Yet, he told himself after reading the notes from the
interviews, there had to be something to it, seeing that the three

nurses had more than five decades of experience among them, which alone gave the substance of their allegations credibility.

"What is your biggest concern right now?" Welch wanted to know.

"Well," Plante said, "it's the boyfriend, James Perrault. He's a cop up there. He hasn't been all that cooperative. . . ."

The first thing Bill Welch did, after deciding they might have a case, was open up a grand jury investigation.

The next thing he did was issue a subpoena for James Perrault.

Days later, Plante and Welch met again.

"We have to review each death and come up with, as morbid as it sounds, a Top Ten list of suspicious deaths," Welch advised.

"Dr. Mike Baden," Plante said, "has been doing that for the past few days. He's on the scene now, going through the medical records."

Along with renowned forensic pathologist Dr. Baden, Welch made a few calls and enlisted the help of Dr. Mark Nelson, a VA doctor who had reviewed records in a couple dozen deaths that occurred between March and August 1992 at the Harry S. Truman Memorial Veterans Hospital in Missouri.

Dr. Michael Baden, a product of the 1930s Bronx, had a career as a forensic pathologist spanning some four decades. By the time he was called in to study the medical records in the Gilbert case, working on VA poisoning cases had become a forte of his. Resident Agent Bruce Sackman, the top dog himself, in charge of IG offices in Boston, New York and New Jersey, had taken an aggressive position in the Dr. Michael Swango murder case and the Missouri VA hospital murders.

In March, when the Gilbert case was put in front of Sackman, he took the same stance, knowing exactly whom to call.

"We have this funny case up in the Northampton, Massachusetts, VA hospital," Sackman told Baden during that first phone call. "We think one of the nurses may have been doing harm to the patients. We need you to take a look."

Baden's expertise had been instrumental in helping to get the US Attorney's Office in New York to open a case against Dr. Michael Swango, the debonair, blond-haired, blue-eyed doctor who was ultimately convicted of murdering three patients in a New York VA hospital and one woman while he was an intern at Ohio State University Hospital.

It was because of Bruce Sackman, Baden recalled, that Swango was brought to justice. The former US attorney in New York, who had refused the case several times before she took another job in the private sector, had for years failed to see what Sackman had. But as soon as she left her post, the US attorney who took her place jumped right on the case and pursued it.

"As much as everybody wanted that case to go away," Baden recalled, "the IGO—Bruce Sackman in particular—didn't. If it weren't for Bruce's persistence . . . nothing would have happened to Swango."

In his book *Dead Reckoning: The New Science of Catching Killers*, cowritten with Marion Roach, Baden labeled himself an atheist.

"It's hard for me to believe in a God who would not only tolerate Hitler but also allow people to do the horrible things they do to one another," he wrote.

When he enters the "autopsy suite" to look into a person's life and death, Baden wrote, he has to leave God at the door and rely on science. It's the only way to get through it all.

Conducting more than thirty thousand autopsies throughout his career, working part of his career in the Office of the Chief Medical Examiner in New York City, Baden has no doubt seen everything imaginable.

Sporting a partially receding swath of wiry gray hair, at seventy, Baden was reminded daily of how cruel the human race can be to one another—an issue that started for him shortly after he was born, when fourteen of his mother's siblings were murdered in Auschwitz.

Baden's credentials spoke for themselves. He had been involved in O.J. Simpson's defense; the autopsy of actor John Belushi; the re-autopsy of Medgar Evers; the autopsy of New York Yankee Billy Martin; the autopsies of Mary Beth Tinning's nine kids; the re-examination of the Lindbergh kidnapping and murder; and the investigation by the Congressional Select

Committee on Assassinations into the deaths of JFK and Martin Luther King, Jr.

Married, with three grown children, he lived in New York City, where he hosted a show on cable's Home Box Office called *Autopsy*.

Bruce Sackman knew he was calling in the best when he got Baden involved in the Gilbert case. If the truth was there, Baden would find it.

Within a few days after arriving at the VAMC and reviewing one tedious medical file after the next, Baden realized that several of the patients under suspicion had suffered unexpected *sudden* deaths. SA Plante had already narrowed the initial list of the three hundred and fifty deaths down to three dozen. A lot of the records in question, Baden noticed, were from patients who were either expected to be released from the VAMC in a matter of days, or who had been receiving treatment for conditions unrelated to their hearts.

His approach was three-pronged: First, he looked at the medical care of the patient. Second, what disease, if any, did that particular patient have? And, finally, most important, should that person have died *when* he died?

He quickly saw that many of the patients were scheduled to leave the VAMC within days of their death, and, to make matters worse, they were getting better.

The one way to rule out foul play, Baden suggested, was to exhume the bodies and have a look.

CHAPTER 39

Bearing a strong resemblance to actor Robert Loggia, with his sun-drenched skin and receding hairline, Massachusetts State Police Detective Kevin Murphy, at six-two, two hundred and ten pounds, fit perfectly into the tough-guy cop mold created by many television shows. In his late forties, Murphy was tall and unassuming, street-smart, unruly and gruff. Throughout his career with the state police, he had seen just about everything: dead babies left in Dumpsters; bloated and unidentifiable bodies strewn about the banks of the Connecticut River; junkies dead from overdoses left to rot in rundown warehouses and crack dens; kids with their heads blown off during drive-bys; hangings; burned bodies; and bodies stabbed, shot and mutilated.

The only crime Detective Murphy hadn't come across in his twenty-four years on the job was serial murder.

On paper, SA Plante and Detective Murphy were a peculiar match. One was a street cop who had been somewhat soured by the years on the job. The other was full of fire, even though he had chased paper cases for his entire career. Murphy, rough around the edges, drank beer and smoked. Plante, clean-cut, went to the gym every morning before work. Murphy was the first to say he didn't take any "bullshit" from sources who held back on him. Plante took it all, he admitted, providing it moved his case along.

At an early age, Murphy learned how disappointing life

could be when one of his four brothers developed Hodgkin's disease and struggled with the illness for four years before losing the battle in July 1961. Murphy's uncle, NYPD cop James Murphy, was once featured in a magazine article as "The Toughest Cop in New York."

Nailing speeders on the Interstate and chasing down drunk drivers wasn't Murphy's bag. But beginning on January 10, 1972, he did it, without regret, for the first nine years of his career. After that, he moved on to Homicide and Death Investigation. In the late eighties, he worked with the FBI on a joint terrorist task force that eventually captured several fugitives responsible for the murder of Phil Lamonica, a New Jersey State Trooper.

"Being involved in that task force," Murphy recalled, "solidified my resolve in the benefits of being a team player. No matter how hard you work or how smart you think you are, that job taught me that you always need other people. . . ."

During another murder case he pursued for nearly three years, the perp ended up committing suicide, addressing his suicide note to Murphy—who was about to arrest him any day.

In late June, Murphy sat with his notebook in the Northampton DA's office listening intently to SA Plante as he presented the case he had been developing against Gilbert. Sitting beside Murphy were US attorneys Bill Welch and Kevin O'Regan, DA Elizabeth Schiebel and her two top assistants, Michael Goggins and David Angier.

The purpose of the meeting was to discuss a possible collaboration between local and federal law enforcement. SA Plante needed help. The case against Gilbert was overwhelming him. Juggling all the interviews he still had to conduct, the medical files that still needed reviewing, and the footwork that was undoubtedly ahead was more than one man could handle.

As it was, Plante was away from his family five days a week, commuting home only on the weekends. This was the first time in his career he had ever done that for such an extended period of time. In addition, he was working around the clock, also something he had never done before. Every day seemed to turn up new leads, new accusations, and new possibilities.

When Plante finished his spiel in the main conference room, Murphy walked over, introduced himself, and invited the well-dressed special agent upstairs for a cup of coffee.

"Let's forget about all this administrative rhetoric," Murphy said as they made their way. "This can-you-help-our-guy-and-we'll-help-your-guy *bull*shit! Do you *have* a case or not? I want to know how you feel about it."

Murphy was referring to the promises the feds and locals had made to each other. They had discussed deputizing a DA from the state as a special US attorney. Both agencies would share credit equally. They would agree to keep it all hush-hush for the time being . . . and all that other political mumbo-jumbo Murphy had no interest in. When it came down to brass tacks, Murphy was a cop. He knew the area. He had developed sources through the years. He could help.

Cruising through downtown Northampton now, Murphy looked over at Plante and told him he would help.

"But the administrative nuances of all this we don't care about, right?"

Plante nodded.

"We gotta get the bad guy, Stevie," Murphy said. "If she's innocent, we'll prove it! If she's not, we'll find out."

CHAPTER 40

The first thing SA Plante did was introduce Murphy to everyone up on the hill. By all rights, no one who worked at the VAMC had to answer to local law enforcement because it was a federal institution. This also proved to be a very serious situation for Gilbert. If the case made it to court, since the crimes had been committed on federal property, Gilbert could face the death penalty.

Ironically, if convicted, she would die by lethal injection.

Plante made it clear to everyone, including Perrault and his boss, that when Murphy came up on the hill to get something or ask questions, he had better be taken seriously, or Plante would step in and, wielding his authority as a government agent, make damn sure he was.

Plante and Murphy needed some type of case management plan. Documents were piling up by the boxful. Without any type of order, mistakes could be made, critical information possibly overlooked, and they ran the risk of doing things twice.

"What sort of paperwork do you want us to generate?" Murphy asked Bill Welch one afternoon.

A cop who knew the legal ropes fairly well, Murphy also knew that within the state system, everything he wrote down was discoverable. Defense attorneys would sooner or later get hold of it, and a harmless note to himself could be turned into some sort of startling piece of defense evidence. Also, if Plante wrote up a report about a certain incident and, for some reason, Murphy had written one without telling him, they had to be sure the reports jibed.

"Make your own personal notes," Welch advised. "But I don't want you writing anything down as far as a 'report' is concerned. Steve has written plenty of them. He knows the federal system. Let him handle it."

Glenn Gilbert was living under a pretty well-laid out routine by the time July 4, 1996, came around. He went to work, dropped off the kids at his estranged wife's apartment along the way, got out of work, picked up the children, settled in at home, and just tried to forget about what had happened between him and his wife. Couples split up, marriages dissolved.

Kristen, on the other hand, was beginning to crack under the pressure of the investigation. Now, with Perrault scheduled to testify in front of the grand jury in about a week, and the evidence against her mounting daily, she could feel a certain shift in Perrault's demeanor.

He was thinking things over. Starting to talk less. Gilbert didn't like that.

Perrault wanted to be a bonafide cop one day. What he did the next couple of months would, undoubtedly, have an effect on his future in law enforcement. He had to be careful.

Plante had done a mind-numbing study of the medical records to put some sort of statistical spin on everything. If nothing else, at least he could present in lay terms what he had to Perrault and Glenn, and maybe get them to finally open their eyes.

What Plante found turned out to be devastating.

Between February 17, 1996—the day Gilbert went out on medical leave—and the first week of July, there had been only *four* deaths and *two* medical emergencies on Ward C. Comparatively speaking, from October 1995 to February 17, 1996, there had been *twenty-three* deaths and nearly *thirty* medical emergencies. Plante's study went as far back as 1989, when Gilbert was working several different shifts. That year, the deaths for each of the three shifts were "randomly distributed among each shift and averaged between ten to fifteen deaths per

shift per year." Later in 1989, and the early part of 1990, however, when Gilbert began working solely the midnight-to-eight
A.M. shift, the numbers during the day and evening shifts "remained essentially constant" while the midnight-shift numbers
doubled. Throughout the next five years whatever shift Gilbert
worked, the numbers followed her, while they stayed virtually
the same on the shifts she hadn't worked. Dr. Stephen
Gehlbach, Dean of the University of Massachusetts School of
Public Health, ran the numbers for Plante and calculated that
the probability of Gilbert's "being on duty for such a large number of patient deaths per shift," given the fact that she had sometimes worked part-time, was ". . . a chance occurrence [of]
1:100,000,000." Regarding all the codes she had been on duty
for, Dr. Gehlbach came up with the exact same numbers: one in
a hundred million.

This wasn't smoking-gun evidence. But the probability that
she didn't have something to do with the deaths and codes was,
at least according to Dr. Gehlbach, astronomically small.

Now all Plante and Murphy had to do was get Glenn to believe it.

Cops know, however, that denial can put blinders on a
spouse. They sometimes see only what they want to. What husband wanted to believe his wife was a serial killer? With Glenn
being the Gomer Pyle type, innocent and naïve, still rapt under
Kristen's spell, they knew the chances of his coming around
were slim, but they had to keep trying.

"Let *me* go talk to him," Plante said to Murphy.

"That might be better," Murphy said, and smiled.

Murphy could be somewhat pushy and impatient. Yet Plante
had developed patience and poise as a sixth and seventh sense, and
the nurses he was interviewing were becoming quite comfortable
with him. With his heavy Boston accent—*pock the cah near the
bah*—his personable, New England charm oozed from his pores.

Maybe Glenn would finally see it, too.

Back in early May, before Murphy was involved, Plante had
made a house call to Glenn, coming up on him as he worked in
the yard one day. Plante filled him in on what he could without
giving away too much.

Glenn listened, but didn't offer anything.

"If you want to talk, Glenn," Plante said, handing him his card, "give me call."

Immediately after he left, Kristen called, as if she had been casing the place.

"Why didn't you just slam the door in his face?" she asked.

"I didn't say anything, Kris! He did all the talking."

After discussing it a bit more, Plante and Murphy both agreed that they needed to get anything they could from Glenn: a lead, a name, something she had done.

Anything.

But when Plante showed up again shortly after the July Fourth holiday, Glenn still didn't want to talk about anything.

"Can't help you. Sorry."

Since he was feeling the heat from both sides, it was time for James Perrault to make a decision. Gilbert was pestering him almost daily, asking him to find out what he could and report it back to her. On occasion, she would even ask if anyone had been talking about "epinephrine." Perrault was becoming more reluctant to do anything anymore, especially since he had been subpoenaed to testify in front of the grand jury on July 16, just a few weeks away. In fact, he was even thinking of breaking off the relationship. Things weren't making sense. He needed some space to think things through.

One day, while they were just hanging around Gilbert's apartment, Perrault saw a "yellow kit" lying on the coffee table and asked Gilbert what it was. It had been the second time he had seen the thing.

"I'm allergic to bee stings," she said. "It's a bee-sting kit."

"Is that epinephrine?" Perrault asked, pointing to a brown ampoule in the pouch.

"Oh, yes. That. I need it for my allergy to the bees."

A few days later, Perrault contacted SA Plante and told him what he had seen.

Armed with that information, Plante and Murphy began to examine Gilbert's medical history. Back on June 16, they found out, she had been admitted to Cooley Dickinson Hospital to get some work done on her shoulder. When Murphy and Plante obtained those medical records and matched them up against her medical records throughout the years and her pre-employment medical examination, nowhere did Gilbert indicate she was allergic to bee stings. To the contrary, she made it a point to note that she was allergic only to penicillin. When they interviewed Melodie Turner, who had been taken out of her supervisory post and reassigned, as one person later recalled, "to a job that was akin to watching paint dry," Turner said she was "completely unaware of Gilbert's allergic reaction to bee stings."

Another day, another path to explore.

CHAPTER 41

By July 8, James Perrault had seen enough. His head was spinning from all the allegations and statistics Plante had laid on him. All the coincidences. He wanted no part of Gilbert any more.

Later that night, after they had gone out for dinner, Perrault mentioned to Gilbert that he thought their relationship hadn't been going so good over the past few weeks. Maybe it was time to separate.

As Perrault expected, she didn't take the news so well. She became upset, rushed into the bathroom, locked the door, and began bawling hysterically.

Listening to her sob, Perrault went into the bedroom to sit down and collect his thoughts. Breaking up with her wasn't as easy as he thought it would be. He still loved the woman.

A few moments later, Perrault heard the toilet flush, and Gilbert stormed into the bedroom and threw an empty bottle of Fiorinal, a migraine medication she had been taking, on the bed.

Perrault stood up.

"Now look what you made me do," Gilbert stammered. She seemed drunk, slurring her speech, stumbling around.

Then she took off running.

Concerned for her safety, Perrault chased her. But approaching the end of the hallway just outside his door, where a set of stairs led to the outside parking lot, he stopped, went back inside his apartment, and phoned the Easthampton Police Department.

While he was on the line explaining what had just happened, Gilbert rushed back into the apartment and, when she figured out to whom he was talking, began grabbing at him, screaming and yelling.

When she realized it was impossible to overpower him, she ran out the door.

After Perrault hung up, he looked out the door and saw Gilbert sitting outside on the front steps.

She hadn't run anywhere.

"Listen, I called the cops because I'm worried about you, Kris."

"That's fine. When they get here, I'll just tell them you beat me up." She turned toward him, "I'll have *you* arrested!"

The cops showed up and—as they do in all domestic disturbance cases—separated the two lovebirds. One cop took Perrault off to the side and began asking him questions, while the other stayed with Gilbert.

Perrault came clean right away. He told the officer what Gilbert had in mind. Sizing up Gilbert's present condition, the officer agreed with Perrault; he hadn't laid a finger on her.

After both cops had a brief meeting with Gilbert while Perrault waited in the wings, one of the officers approached him.

"Can she spend the night at your apartment?"

"Absolutely not!"

Perrault said he was worried she might, sometime during the course of the night, again make false allegations against him for abuse.

First thing the next morning, July 9, Perrault woke to the sound of Gilbert banging at his door. She was "in a daze," Perrault noticed, acting as if she were under the influence of drugs or alcohol. He thought she might have taken a second bottle of pills and was coming back to reach out for help.

So he invited her in.

He realized immediately he wasn't going to get through to her. She needed to be under a doctor's care. She was a danger to herself, if not others. But instead of calling the cops, Perrault decided to do something he thought for the life of him he would never be faced with: calling Glenn at work to ask him to come over and see if he could have her committed.

The two men had never spoken at any length before. What does one man who took another man's wife away from him say? It was awkward, to say the least. But for Perrault, it was the only option he had left. Gilbert had been acting as he had never before seen her. Her neighbor, *Samantha Harris,* whom Perrault had come to know pretty well throughout the summer, referred to Gilbert, when she was in this state, as "manic." But Perrault had never really understood the comment until now. Gilbert, Harris said, would become delirious and frenzied as if she had no idea what she was doing.

As Perrault went into his bedroom to call Glenn, Kristen retreated to the kitchen, where she curled herself up in a fetal position on the floor and began to prove just how manic she could be.

As he dialed Glenn's number, Perrault could hear her moaning.

"I didn't do anything . . . you have to believe me," she kept saying over and over.

"What the hell are you talking about?" Perrault, walking back into the kitchen, asked after hanging up with Glenn.

Kristen didn't answer. She just kept repeating the same thing: "You have to believe me; I didn't do anything . . . I didn't do . . ."

It was about 2:00 P.M. when Glenn arrived. After discussing the situation with Perrault for a moment, he walked into the kitchen.

"What are you up to now?" he asked.

Glenn was disgusted with her. Not only had she taken off on him and bedded down with another man whose apartment he was right now standing in, but now she had the nerve to get him involved in their relationship. How pathetic. How heartless. Yet Glenn was a decent man, which was more than he could say for the two people who now stood before him. The only reason he had gone over to Perrault's in the first place was because of the kids.

"You have to believe me, Glenn; I didn't have anything to do with what they're saying. . . ."

Perrault just shrugged his shoulders.

"What?" Glenn asked.

"I didn't do anything. I didn't do anything," Kristen, getting louder, kept moaning.

Glenn then dialed up Kaiser Permanente, a local emergency health center.

"Can I get her any help without involving the police?"

"First, you should contact the police," the woman told him. "Then an ambulance, so they can take her to the hospital."

After a moment, Kristen got up off the kitchen floor and, astonishing Glenn and Perrault, began to walk around the apartment as if she were a real estate agent showing it to a newly married couple looking to move in.

Glenn and Perrault just looked at each other.

"It's a nice place, isn't it, Glenn?" Kristen asked.

Glenn put his head in his hands.

"We've got to get you to a hospital, Kris," Perrault said.

"Come on, Kristen. Let's go. You need help," Glenn added.

But she ran out the door.

So they followed.

Outside, in the parking lot, Kristen began kicking the driver's side door of Glenn's car. She was mad, she said, because Perrault had interfered and gotten Glenn involved.

The Easthampton Police arrived a few minutes later and gave Kristen two options: She could either get professional help or spend the afternoon in jail.

Kristen opted for admittance into the psychiatric ward of Holyoke Hospital.

Perrault stayed home. When Glenn arrived, Kristen was being processed in Admissions. She was "angry and uncooperative," yelling, and making a spectacle of herself. At one point, Glenn later recalled, she ran from the Admissions area and tried to "remove a doorstop from the floor to use against [him]."

"I did not 'intentionally' overdose," she kept telling the doctors. "As a nurse, I think I know the amount of pills I took would not be lethal!"

CHAPTER 42

Perrault visited Gilbert at the hospital on July 10. Not only did he want some answers, but he was concerned about her well being.

To his surprise, when he showed up, Gilbert was fine.

"She was happy; she was talking. Normal conversations," Perrault later said. "She didn't appear to be distraught or upset at all."

Hours later, while Glenn Gilbert was at home, Kristen called him.

"I want you to contact the investigators," Kristen said to Glenn. She was hyperventilating, crying, sobbing. "Hysterical," Glenn later remembered.

"What, Kristen? What's wrong with you?"

"Shut up and listen! I want to save the taxpayers of this state a lot of money. Call the IG, Glenn . . . I did it!"

"I don't want to hear this, Kris. I don't want to hear a confession. I don't want to be responsible for having that information . . . stop it now. Just stop it."

With that, Kristen changed her tune. She stopped crying and, with a direct, wry inflection, said, "Just kidding. Good-bye!" And hung up.

Glenn had started taking notes of the conversation when he realized what she was saying. He knew he would be called in front of the grand jury sooner or later, so he wanted to get it right.

After he finished writing down the conversation, Glenn made a mental note: *Go down to the court tomorrow and apply for a restraining order.*

Not shortly after Kristen phoned Glenn, she called Perrault.

Perrault, at this point, had been stewing about the events of the past day. He wanted to know what the hell was going on. What had she meant by "I didn't do anything"? After discussing their breakup and the stress she felt because the investigation had been focused exclusively on her, Perrault laid it on the line.

"Do you have anything to hide, Kris? Are you involved in this in any way?"

"No. Of course not!"

"I know you're under a lot of stress, but you seem [to be acting] more irrational than a person should be."

Gilbert began crying. Then, "I'm pregnant with your child."

"That's impossible. We haven't had sex in months, Kris." Perrault wanted to laugh. "Why would you say that?"

There was a pause. He could hear her whimpering.

A moment later, she snapped out of it, and, just like that, said, "I did it. I did it. You wanted to know. I injected those guys with a certain drug."

And then she hung up.

A half hour later, she called back, crying, begging Perrault to believe that she didn't mean what she had said.

"Are you mad at me?"

"Why did you say that?"

"I lied. I just wanted to make you mad. I wanted to get a reaction out of you, Jim."

"A reaction? You said *that* to get a reaction?"

"Can you tell the grand jury about the stress I'm under? Please don't tell them what I just said. I didn't mean to say that. I'm sorry; it was stupid of me."

"Of course I'm going to tell them, Kris."

With that, Gilbert became upset again.

"Think of my emotional state, Jim," she pleaded. "Tell them. Tell them the stress I'm under."

Doctors at Holyoke Hospital diagnosed Gilbert with Borderline Personality Disorder. It was even possible, they insisted, that she suffered from Narcissistic Personality Disorder and Anti-Social Personality Disorder.

Yet she refused any type of treatment.

In many respects, all three disorders, left untreated, render a person incapable of anticipating her own mental and social demise—like, for example, an exaggerated form of denial.

Dr. Sam Vaknin, author of *Malignant Self Love: Narcissism Revisited,* said that "narcissism cannot be treated." But the "side-effects and by-products" of it, however, "such as depressive episodes or obsessive-compulsive behaviors," both of which Gilbert suffered from, can.

"Pathological narcissism pervades every facet of the personality, every behavior, every cognition, and every emotion. Add to this the narcissist's unthinking and deeply-ingrained resistance to authority figures, such as therapists—and healing, or even mere behavior modification, are rendered unattainable. Pathological narcissism is often co-morbid with mood disorders, compulsive rituals, substance abuse, paraphilias, or reckless behavior patterns."

These are many of the same patterns of behavior Gilbert had displayed over the past year or more.

"Many narcissists," Vaknin went on to explain, "are also anti-social. Lacking empathy and convinced of their own magnificence, they feel that they are above social conventions and the law. The narcissist is both victimizer and victim. The essence of the narcissistic disorder is a breakdown of internal communication. The narcissist invents and nurtures a false self intended to elicit attention—positive or negative—from others and thus to fill [her] innermost void. [She] is so engrossed in securing narcissistic supply from [her] sources by putting on an energy-sapping show—that [she] fails to materialize [her] potential to have mature, adult relationships, to feel, and, in general, to enjoy life. To the narcissist, other people are never more than potential sources of supply with a useful 'shelf life.' The narcissist invariably ends up cruelly devaluing and discarding them, like dysfunctional objects. Little wonder that the narcissist—haughty, abrasive, exploitive, manipulative, untruthful—is universally held in contempt, derided, hated, persecuted, and cast out. But we should never forget that [she] pays a dear price for something which, essentially, is beyond [her] full control—i.e., for [her] illness."

CHAPTER 43

The phone call James Perrault received from Gilbert troubled him deeply. It had been the first time he'd heard her speak directly about the murder charges regarding being a prime suspect.

Doctors who treated Gilbert advised her not to leave the hospital; she needed help and wasn't able to control her own behavior. They could give her that help, of course—but only if she wanted it.

Late in the day on July 11, however, Gilbert signed herself out. As if falling into the hands of her diagnosis, later that night, she broke into Perrault's Parsons Street apartment, and he promptly had her arrested.

When she got out of jail the following morning, under the urging of Perrault, Gilbert was committed to the psychiatric ward of Arbour Hospital in Boston.

"I'll come up and see you, don't worry," Perrault told her.

Confused and perhaps even terrified now of what she was capable of, on July 12 Perrault obtained a ten-day restraining order against his former girlfriend. He didn't know what to believe anymore. She'd say one thing, then say she didn't mean it. She'd act bizarre, then later say she had no idea what she had done.

Feeling sorry for her, later that afternoon, Perrault kept his promise and made the two-hour trip to Arbour Hospital.

Gilbert apologized for saying "I did it."

"I'm sorry for that, Jim. I'm really, really sorry I said that."

"I'm going to have to tell the grand jury what you said, Kris. I thought you should know that."

Gilbert became upset.

"This is why you came up here to see me? I didn't do it," she said. "I *didn't* do it, Jimmy. Can you at least think about the position I was in when I said it?"

Before Perrault left, he said there was no way around it: He was obligated to tell the grand jury about the confession.

By July 15, Gilbert had convinced her doctors that there was nothing wrong with her.

"The patient," wrote one doctor, "does not have any symptoms of depression, self-destructive thoughts, no psychotic disorder, no delusions, and there [is] no need for the patient to be hospitalized."

Shortly before she was released, Gilbert phoned Perrault and begged him to give her a ride back to Easthampton.

Perrault lied. He said he had to work. There was no way he could do it.

The reality of the situation was that Perrault just didn't want to deal with Gilbert anymore. So he told her that Samantha Harris, her friend and neighbor, had mentioned to him earlier that day she would pick Gilbert up if she needed a ride home. Perrault said he'd go over and ask Samantha as soon they were finished talking.

Samantha Harris, her husband, *Phillip*, and their young son moved into 182 Northampton Street during the winter of 1995. They lived three doors down from Gilbert. But since the cold winter weather can sometimes keep people secluded in their homes, Harris and Gilbert never spoke at any length during the winter of 1995–96. They had passed each other in the parking lot once in a while, but hadn't really gotten to know each other until the spring of 1996. And since it hadn't been made public yet, Harris had no idea there was an investigation going on up at the VAMC.

At the time they met, Harris had one boy, *Ethan,* who was about the same age as Gilbert's oldest, Brian. As the children

grew closer, Gilbert and Harris began to spend more time together.

They got along great at first, swapping stories of their children, their families, and lost loves. But as time moved on,
Kristen came clean about Glenn, Perrault and how her affair
had broken up her seven-year marriage. She was in love with a
man she had met at work, Gilbert confessed to Harris. Although
Harris couldn't ever see herself in that same position, she knew
there were things in life that were sometimes out of a person's
control, and sympathized with Gilbert's predicament.
Marriages often became complacent. People went through the
motions, forgot to love each other, and one day it was over. She
assumed that Gilbert's marriage fell into the same category.

When Perrault finished telling Gilbert about his idea of
Harris picking her up, she said, "I don't want her asking all
sorts of questions. I don't want to talk about *anything.*"

"Okay, I'll tell her."

Perrault then drove over to Harris's, knocked on her door
and explained as best he could about what had gone on the past
few days.

Harris invited him in.

She was stunned right away by Perrault's appearance. He
was pale. Gaunt. Withdrawn. He had even developed stress-re-
lated sores on his face and picked at them nervously while he
talked.

Over the course of about a half hour, not once, though, did
Perrault mention there was a murder investigation going on. It
was more of a discussion about his unpredictable relationship
with Gilbert and how he felt bad about breaking up the relationship and her trying to kill herself. But what could he do?

"She's been acting crazy," Perrault said.

At the time, Harris had little sympathy for Perrault. She
liked Gilbert and felt sorry for her, viewing her as a struggling
single mother, with two beautiful kids, whom the system had
been beating up on. She had no idea Gilbert was being investigated for murder. Gilbert had been telling Harris that the VA
was fighting her workman's comp claim and making stuff up
about how to win that case.

Gilbert was slated to get out of Arbour Hospital that afternoon. Knowing that Perrault had refused to pick her up and that she didn't have a ride home, Harris had no trouble offering a ride.

After Perrault explained that Gilbert had been a bit hostile the last time he spoke to her regarding Harris's picking her up, and that she didn't want to talk about anything during the ride home, Harris said, "She can sleep in the backseat of the car for all I care. I don't need to know why she's in the hospital. I just want to make sure she gets home in one piece."

"All right," Perrault said. "Let me call her and ask."

When Perrault got Gilbert on the phone and told her that Harris had offered her a ride, Gilbert became incensed.

"I don't want a ride from anybody else. I don't want to talk to anybody. I don't want to explain everything,"

Perrault held his hand over the receiver and explained to Harris what Gilbert had said.

Harris motioned for Perrault to remove his hand from the receiver.

"She doesn't need a babysitter, or to be counseled by me. She just needs a damn ride," Harris said loud enough so Gilbert could hear.

Harris couldn't understand what the big deal was. It was just a ride home from a friend who cared about her.

After a bit more discussion, Gilbert agreed to let Harris go get her.

Hours later, as soon as Gilbert sat down in Harris's car, she started to go on and on about all the things she was so adamantly against talking about just a few hours ago.

"Do you know why I was in the hospital?"

"Yeah, I guess," Harris said. "I spoke to Jim, and he explained he had broken up with you and—"

Gilbert stopped her. "No. No. No," she said, shaking her head. "If Jim *ever* tried to break up with me, I'd just *stalk* him."

Harris looked at her and wondered what she was talking about. She had never heard Gilbert speak with such a resentful tone before.

"Stalk him, Kristen?"

"Now," Gilbert continued, "the real reason why I was in the hospital is because there's an investigation going on up at the VA. A lot of people have died."

"What?"

"More people than normally *should* die," Gilbert added.

"Are you kidding me?"

"Seventy-eight percent of the time they were on my shift," Gilbert said.

Harris was having trouble keeping track of what she was saying.

"You mean those people who died?"

"Yup."

"These people," Gilbert went on, "were killed with epi—do you know what epi is, Sami?"

"No. I mean, I might have heard the term on *ER*, but—" Gilbert cut her off again.

"When you give epi to somebody who is having a heart attack, it jump-starts their heart. But if you give it to somebody with a healthy heart, it'll send them into cardiac arrest."

Harris couldn't believe what she was hearing. The picture she had of Gilbert up until that point was of this young blonde who lived next door and had a good-looking boyfriend and struggled with the same mundane family issues that crop up in everyone else's life.

But epi, murder, when did that ever become part of the equation?

"What are you talking about, Kristen?"

"Well, they would never find it [epi] if they"—meaning medical examiners—"suspected foul play," Gilbert said.

"Why not?"

"Because, if the person was dying . . . if . . . I mean"—Gilbert began stumbling a bit now with her words, choosing them carefully—". . . once a person has a heart attack, you're going to give them epi, anyway."

"Could it be someone else in the hospital?" Harris asked. "Could someone you know be killing those patients?"

"No," Gilbert said. "I wouldn't suspect anybody."

CHAPTER 44

Grand jury day, Tuesday, July 16, 1996, was a beautiful New England summer afternoon. With the girls from Smith College gone until September, and the streets of Northampton filled with tourists, vendors and farmers' markets, the town takes on a wistful charm not comparable to any other part of New England.

For Kristen Gilbert, it was a day she had been dreading ever since she first heard about it from Perrault weeks ago.

Perrault's grand jury testimony was grueling. He was grilled by prosecutors about the codes he had responded to at the VAMC that Gilbert had participated in; about his romantic relationship with her; how she had been the one nurse to be present during most of the codes on her shift; and how, when Perrault asked her why there had been so many codes on her shift, she said that it was just a "coincidence," that most of the patients were "older and sicker" and there were always more codes during the winter months, anyway.

Then Ed Skwira's death was brought up.

Prosecutors asked Perrault about an ampoule of epinephrine that turned up missing while Skwira was in the middle of his code.

Gilbert, Perrault said, told him that "it would impossible to say who took [it]."

"Has Ms. Gilbert ever mentioned anything about the three

broken ampoules of epinephrine which were found in Skwira's room after the code?"

Gilbert's response to that, Perrault said, was that the VA was just making it up—that is, investigators were trying to scare people into thinking she had something to do with his death.

Then Perrault ended his testimony with perhaps the most startling piece of evidence against Gilbert to date: her confession.

Referencing that conversation he'd had with Gilbert over the phone, Perrault first explained, as he'd promised Gilbert he would, that she was hospitalized at the time and very stressed out.

But when it came time to explain the actual confession, Perrault remembered it a bit differently. In addition to telling the grand jury that Gilbert said, "I did it. I did it. I injected those guys with a certain drug," Perrault added that she had also said, "I killed those guys."

No matter how it was bottled, the grand jury took it as a confession nonetheless.

While Perrault was in Springfield testifying, Gilbert was at home, undoubtedly climbing the walls. By the end of the afternoon, she had allegedly taken sixty five-hundred-milligram aspirin tablets and was admitted to Cooley Dickson Hospital for yet another psychiatric evaluation. The admitting doctor, reviewing her prior admission to Holyoke Hospital, wrote that "there is some question about her truthfulness during [that admission] and some problems with manipulation of staff."

After he finished testifying, James Perrault went to work for his regular four P.M.-to-midnight shift. Later that night, while he was sitting at his desk, RN Karen Abderhalden called. For the past few months, Abderhalden had been asking Perrault about Gilbert and, being a friend, was concerned with her welfare.

A few minutes into the conversation, Abderhalden informed Perrault that Gilbert had been admitted to Cooley Dickinson while he was in Springfield.

"I spoke to her, Jimmy. She said to tell you that she needs a few things from your apartment, some clothes . . ."

"Jesus . . . all right. I'll go see her tomorrow."

"She told me they were transferring her back to Arbour tomorrow."

"I'll go to Cooley first thing, Karen."

"Thanks, Jimmy."

"Thank you, Karen. You've been a good friend to her."

Because the hospital really couldn't tell one way or the other if Gilbert had taken as many pills as she had claimed, she was put in the ICU for observation.

Perrault showed up the following morning.

As he approached her bed, Gilbert tried to jump up and lash out at him, but he was able to run out of the room before a problem occurred.

The hospital psychiatrist noted that Gilbert said she was "not intending to kill herself, but simply 'seeking attention.' The sort of attention she had in mind, [however], is not entirely definable. . . . She was quite eloquent in her desire not to be rehospitalized and offers a variety of assurances," the doctor wrote, that she will not attempt to try to kill herself again.

The doctor discharged Gilbert, under the pretense that she be committed to Arbour Hospital again for further evaluation.

His diagnosis?

"Axis II . . . rules out a personality disorder in Cluster II, possibly a borderline personality."

Axis II is a scale doctors use to describe a wide variety of personality disorders. In Gilbert's case, her personality traits fit into the scale as if it were designed specifically for her.

James Perrault visited Gilbert at Arbour Hospital almost every day she was there. On one occasion, he even brought Karen Abderhalden, her husband and their son. As a friend, Abderhalden mentioned that she thought it might be a good idea if Gilbert, when she was released, spent some time at Abderhalden's house. She lived out on the woods, away from everyone.

Gilbert agreed. Maybe the time away would do her some good.

On July 22, Perrault, by himself, went to see Gilbert again. They sat in the day room, near the visiting area.

"What happened in the grand jury?"

Perrault told her everything. Surprisingly, Gilbert accepted it all rather calmly.

"Why were they asking you those questions, Jim?"

"It's an investigation, Kris."

"How did they react to your testimony?"

Perrault changed the subject.

"You want me to pick you up tomorrow—aren't you supposed to be released?"

"Yes and yes!"

In his report, the attending psychiatrist at Arbour Hospital noted several characteristics about Gilbert that fell in line with a person who suffers from Narcissistic Personality Disorder. For one, he noted that ". . . [The] patient is trying to present herself healthier than what she might be. The most salient characteristics of patient's [score on a personality test she took] are elevation on Scale 5 (Masculinity/Feminity) and Scale 4 (Psychopathic Deviate scale). . . . Although overall she is trying to contain herself, the record reveals signs of impulsivity."

His diagnosis again included "Axis II Personality Disorder," with trends showing signs of "passive-aggressive, narcissistic [and] borderline."

The report went on to note that Gilbert was "an untrustworthy historian," that she only behaved "good" this time around because any bad behavior would "only tend to delay the discharge she was so earnestly seeking." He said she "had a strong tendency to minimize her difficulties and information that she was giving . . . about herself."

The picture that "emerged," the doctor wrote, was of a "long-standing pattern of telling untruths, even when confronted with conflicting data."

CHAPTER 45

As he said he would, Perrault picked up Gilbert at Arbour Hospital and drove her home. When they got to Gilbert's Easthampton apartment, however, Perrault noticed the front door was wide open. A break-in?

After they got out of his truck and approached the porch, Perrault saw SA Plante and Detective Murphy rummaging through Gilbert's living room.

"I suppose you have a search warrant?" Perrault asked.

Murphy handed Gilbert a copy of the search warrant.

"You can either stay here or leave. It's up to you."

Perrault suggested they go next door, to Samantha Harris's.

"You can call your attorney over there, Kris," he said.

"Let's go," Gilbert said, as she began to cry. "Why are they doing this to me?" she asked as they walked toward Harris's. "Why, Jim? What are they looking for? Why would they need to search my apartment?"

"Just calm down. Call your attorney when we get to Sami's."

At the urging of an attorney she had hired to handle her forthcoming divorce, Gilbert had hired noted criminal trial lawyer Harry Miles back in February, shortly after Wall, Rix and Walsh had turned her in.

A Dartmouth graduate with a flourishing partnership in downtown Northampton, Miles, at fifty-two, had more than two decades' worth of law experience when he first met Gilbert. He was no stranger to the type of high-profile client Gilbert would ultimately become. Nearly a year before he met Gilbert, Miles represented Richard Perry, a local man who was charged with and later found guilty of murdering a retarded Greenfield, Massachusetts, man named Billy Paige. Ironically, the judge who later heard the Perry case was none other than Judge William Welch, US attorney Bill Welch's father.

Gilbert conversed privately with Miles in Harris's kitchen, while Harris and Perrault stayed in the living room. Neither heard what she had said, and Gilbert, apparently under the urging of Miles, didn't talk about the short conversation afterward.

With Miles long gone, Perrault said he had to leave. It was a Tuesday. He had to go work.

"They're gone, Kristen," Harris said, looking out the window.

"I'll be back later tonight," Perrault told Gilbert. "We can talk about things then."

SA Plante's detailed affidavit to Federal District Court Judge Michael Ponsor left no stone unturned. Among the list of items Plante said he had hoped to find in Gilbert's apartment were medical or nursing textbooks, journals, manuals, any notes Gilbert might have made regarding acute medical care relating to cardiac illnesses and/or medication relating to cardiac illnesses; any cardiac medicines, including, but not limited to epinephrine; and any and all evidence relating to the Department of Veterans Affairs' investigation.

The thirty-page affidavit went into explicit detail concerning how the investigation was adding up. US attorney Bill Welch was right when he told Murphy to let Plante handle the report writing—because the man was as thorough as a CIA agent.

An important fact that stood out on the black-and-white document was that Plante found out that there were seventy-five ampoules of epinephrine missing from the VAMC between August 30, 1995 and February 21, 1996. Unaccounted for. Plante explained that no doctor had administered the drug during that same period.

* * *

When Perrault showed up at Gilbert's later that night, she was fuming over the search warrant.

"Why would they take my computer and answering machine?"

"I don't know."

"What use would they be to the investigation? And my notebooks . . . my notes . . . my medical textbooks?"

"What notebooks?" Perrault asked. He was curious.

"I was keeping a list . . . keeping track of the questions that were being asked of other employees and friends of mine."

Indeed, included in Plante and Murphy's find was a notebook with some of Perrault's handwriting inside of it. Back in June, Gilbert had asked Perrault to write down what the investigators had asked him about. Thinking nothing of it, he did. Now, he thought, it might appear as if he were helping her.

Plante and Murphy had also uncovered a piece of notebook paper with a list of names on it, and the heading explained it all: *Friendly and Unfriendly Witnesses.*

Another one of Gilbert's scorecards.

The first person on the list, under *Friendly Witnesses,* was Glenn Gilbert. Under Glenn's name was Perrault's. Then Carole Osman, David Rejniak and Karen Abderhalden.

Under the heading *Unfriendly Witnesses,* Kathy Rix's name topped the list.

"Because she was one of the ones that initiated the investigation," Gilbert told Perrault.

Next to Rix's name, of course, was John Wall. Lori Naumowitz was next. According to Perrault, Gilbert said she put Lori's name down only because "[Lori] was upset [that Perrault and Gilbert] were seeing each other and she felt that Lori was being loyal to [Glenn] instead of herself."

April Gougeon's name was next, right above Lisa Baronas's. On the second page, Beverly Scott, Jeff Begley and Frank Bertrand showed up—three nurses who, according to anyone who knew them, couldn't collectively hurt a fly, much less frame someone for murder.

Regarding Jeff Begley, who had been with Beverly Scott when Stanley Jagodowski coded, Gilbert later said he was "trying to frame her in order to get rid of her in order to get her slot."

When Plante and Murphy sat down to discuss what they had found at Gilbert's apartment, something became crystal clear: Any nurse who could place her at the scene of a death or code was on her list of potentially unfriendly witnesses.

Later, Perrault realized he had better come clean about what Gilbert had told him regarding the search. So he explained to Plante and Murphy one day that Gilbert was initially confused as to why her textbooks had been seized. Then she got extremely concerned, Perrault said, that at one time she had looked up the effects of epinephrine.

"My fingerprints are on that page, Jim! With my fingerprints on that page, the IG[O] will think that I looked it up prior to the deaths to see what would kill a patient."

"Well," Perrault asked, "why *did* you look it up, Kris?"

"I didn't know what the effects would be on a healthy person."

And . . . ?

Some time later, Perrault then explained, he and Gilbert had a second conversation about the effects of epinephrine.

"It would be difficult for investigators," Gilbert had told him, "to be able to trace epinephrine because, one, epinephrine is the first thing—or one of many things—used during a code to revive a patient, so it's put into the body. Secondly, epinephrine is a naturally occurring substance in the body. Third, epinephrine has such a short half-life—meaning that it breaks down [in the body] rather quickly—. . . the investigators would have a hard time trying to track it down."

CHAPTER 46

After all that he had heard, James Perrault still had mixed feelings regarding Gilbert's role in the deaths at the VAMC. On the one hand, he wanted to help Murphy and Plante, but on the other, he was still wrapped tight around Gilbert's finger. After the search warrant was issued on July 23, Perrault found himself, just like old times, spending more time with Gilbert.

They were an item again.

At the urging of Gilbert, one day while Perrault had some free time at work he decided to go through the VAMC security journals for the four-month period Plante and Murphy had been focusing on in their investigation. Particularly interested in the days he had been working, Perrault made a list of all the medical emergencies that had occurred: times, dates, patients' names, and the number of times security had responded, along with whom the security guard was.

Immediately, he saw he had been on duty for every single code. In fact, for the majority of them, he was the security guard who had responded to the code.

When he got home from work that night, he confronted Gilbert.

"Why were the two of us on for every single one of those codes?"

"It's just a coincidence, Jim."

* * *

The one person who still hadn't come forward to offer any more information than he had to was Glenn Gilbert. Here it was, the first week of August, and Glenn still wasn't convinced, even after his estranged wife had called and basically admitted her involvement.

But on August 15, something changed Glenn's mind—because he called Plante and told him to come over and search the pantry of his house right away.

Pantry? Plante wondered. *Why just the pantry?*

The following day, Plante and Murphy showed up. The pantry was right in front of them as they walked in the back door. It was a small space, like a walk-in closet, used for storing extra canned goods, a vacuum cleaner or whatever. Gilbert had taken over the area years ago and used it to store her sewing materials. Glenn had rarely entered the room, he explained, since she'd left the house almost nine months ago.

Glenn was an odd character, Murphy and Plante agreed. They couldn't understand, save for the kids, why the hell he was still protecting her. They knew there was a strong possibility she had tried to poison him back in November. One of Murphy's sources had said Glenn had admitted that "his sickness wasn't a medical condition," and Glenn had used the word "attempt" when he described the event to their source.

When Plante and Murphy sat down in Glenn's kitchen, Glenn explained why he wanted the pantry searched. And it all began to make sense.

Glenn had been away for the past week on vacation with the kids. Before he had left, Gilbert had been bugging him to come over. She wanted to get into the house for some reason, he said. Glenn kept telling her no. But she kept persisting.

Knowing she might break in while he was away, Glenn had his stepfather, Stanley Straub, come over and house-sit.

No sooner had Glenn made his way onto Interstate 91 than Kristen was trying to talk her way past Straub.

"I just need to get into the pantry," she told the old man. "Just let me in."

"No. Absolutely not, Kristen. Now get!"

When Glenn got home, Straub told him how adamant Kristen had been about getting into the house.

Later, Murphy and Plante went over and spoke to Glenn's next-door neighbor, who also confirmed that she had tried to gain access to the house while Glenn had been away.

By this point, Murphy had little patience left for Glenn Gilbert. He knew damn well Glenn was holding back. Murphy was caustic. He was as equally compassionate as Plante, but he did have a bite to him that scared people. He had no use for people who held back important information, especially when murder was involved. Here it was August, and Glenn was just now coming aboard.

"I take people . . . who will give me one hundred percent of their knowledge, and I'll treat them like gold," Murphy later recalled. "But those people who hold back a little bit . . . I don't know. At the end of every successful interview, whether you're interviewing a witness or a target, you have to ask some pretty hard questions. And a lot of times, when you ask people hard questions, they can feel the focus of the interview shift from gathering information to focusing on *them.* 'Where were you last night?' You know, when you ask somebody a simple question like that, they get pissed off, especially if they are totally innocent. If they're withholding information they don't want to give you . . . well, you can just tell at that point."

The first time Murphy, Plante and Bill Welch interviewed Glenn, he arrived at the US Attorney's Office with his lawyer. The interview became lax as it progressed and in a nonthreatening tone Welch and Plante were asking Glenn what he knew. Glenn started talking about the incident back in November when he believed Gilbert had tried to poison him. But he was beating around the bush, as if he were holding something back.

"They were patty-caking him," Murphy later recalled. "So I slapped a question on him, and everybody's hair stood up on the back of their necks."

Murphy, slamming his hand down on the table, looked directly into Glenn's eyes, and said, "Cut the *bullshit!* Is what you're telling us is that she tried to *kill* you? We need to *know* that stuff. You can't be holding onto to this."

Because of the countless murder investigations Murphy had been involved in, he knew people held on to things. "At some point in time," Murphy recalled later, "I am going to feel that you're full of shit. After I do, watch out."

As Plante spoke to Glenn in the kitchen, Murphy worked his way through the pantry. Tucked in back of a bunch of sewing material on the second to the last shelf, inside a satchel of some sort, Murphy located a book.

The Handbook of Poisoning was a five-hundred-page textbook dealing with the poisonous properties of various medications—including epinephrine. It also contained rather extensive narratives detailing all the different types of poisons, "the specific dosage necessary to be lethal, the symptoms of a lethal dose, and the recommended treatment for a lethal dose."

"Sweetheart," Murphy called out to Plante, who was still talking to Glenn, "can you come in here for a minute?"

"What's up?"

"Take a look at this."

Upon further examination, they could tell right away that the book, because of the stamp inside the front cover, had been taken from the ICU of the VAMC.

"I have never seen that before," Glenn said. Then explained that they had a separate area in their home, inside the bedroom, designated for child-rearing books, medical texts, and medical dictionaries. The bookcase had been placed in their room, Glenn explained, for easy access in case of an emergency.

Murphy opened up the book and began turning pages.

"Look at this," he whispered to Plante, who was standing over his shoulder.

Several pages in the book were dog-eared—in particular, pages explaining the drugs ketamine and cyanide, a poison "that is undetectable post-embalming," one of the more popular poisons chosen by killers.

"Perhaps it's time Dr. Baden began exhuming those bodies?" Murphy said, looking at Plante.

"Yeah, I guess so."

CHAPTER 47

Kristen was furious when she found out that Glenn had permitted Plante and Murphy to search the house. She told Perrault Glenn was "weak." Belittling him, she added, "Glenn's an idiot. He's stupid! What a pushover for allowing them to go into the house."

Besides Glenn's willingness to start cooperating with Plante and Murphy, however, Gilbert now had a bigger problem on her hands: How was she going to explain the book?

"What kind of book is it?" Perrault asked.

"It deals with poisons," Gilbert said. "I'm concerned, Jim. They might draw conclusions as to why I had the book."

Then she changed her story.

"But I'm not really sure exactly what book they're referring to."

"What do you mean?"

Then she changed her story again.

"It was in a bag of linens," she said. "Yes! That's it. Melodie [Turner] brought over a bag of linens one time, Jim. I *bet* it was in that bag."

A few days later, yet another story emerged.

"I recall taking the book from Ward C so I could look up poisonous plants we had in the house."

But Glenn was, at the same time, telling Plante and Murphy

that, because they had a cat, they never brought poisonous plants into the house.

"Cats like to chew on plants, so we never wanted the plants around," Glenn later recalled.

Gilbert's reaction to whatever piece of incriminating evidence had been found was becoming almost as predictable as her lies, and on August 19, 1996, she wasn't about to change her pattern.

After she called a friend and complained that she had, again, taken an overdose of Fiorinal, she was found "unresponsive" on the floor of her apartment by that same friend.

Paramedics showed up and inserted a "#18 catheter into her left wrist" to try to revive her.

But she didn't respond.

Quickly getting her into the back of their ambulance, para-medics found her to be in a state of "somnolence." She was in and out, sleepy and drunken.

Realizing Gilbert was likely suffering from an overdose, one of the paramedics began to insert a tube down her throat so she could breathe.

As he brought his finger close to her mouth, Gilbert bit it and abruptly sat up.

"I *do not* need to be intubated!" she shrieked. "And don't think about lavaging [pumping] my stomach . . . it's been way too long since I ingested those pills."

Shocked, the paramedics just looked at each other.

Now, inside the ER, the on-call doctor noted that upon ad-mission, Gilbert was "very lethargic, although apparently less lethargic than she was acting. She was initially completely un-responsive. . . ."

When asked why she took the pills in the first place, Gilbert indicated that she never intended to kill herself.

Doctors at Cooley Dickinson soon recommended that she be transferred to Arbour Hospital for further observation and treat-ment.

The following day, August 20, Gilbert found herself in the psychiatric ward of Arbour Hospital for the third time within a month.

In what had become a struggle to try to fool the doctors who were treating her, Gilbert denied any attempt at suicide.

"I am well aware that the lethal amount [of Fiorinal is] higher," Gilbert told the doctor.

The attending psychiatrist wrote, "[Kristen Gilbert] has a tendency to respond to any question that was asked and, according to the direction that she sees from you, she has a tendency of going back and correcting her response."

In other words, she kept changing her story to cover the lies she was telling.

CHAPTER 48

Perrault was forced, in many ways, to make two important decisions that would forever change the murder investigation that had centered around the woman he, at one time, was madly in love with: First, it was time to tell Gilbert how actively involved he had become over the past few weeks in the government's case against her. Second, even though they had reconciled weeks ago and things were seemingly okay between them, the relationship had to be terminated.

There was just too much going on.

These weren't easy decisions for the Persian Gulf War vet to make. He knew Gilbert well enough to know that once she found out he had been providing investigators with information behind her back, she would likely go berserk.

So, late in the day on September 9, Perrault picked up the phone and explained he would be meeting with Assistant US Attorney Bill Welch the following day to discuss the government's investigation into the "high number of suspicious deaths" at the VAMC, adding that the meeting was likely a follow-up to his grand jury testimony back on July 16.

"Don't go, Jim . . . please don't go," Gilbert begged.

Perrault was firm.

It's over. Period.

"The entire investigation is your fault!" Gilbert raged, her voice husky and forceful. "Please don't go to that meeting, Jim."

Perrault showed little reaction. Surely, some things *were* his fault. He wasn't denying that. But this was totally out of hand now.

In desperation, Gilbert started crying.

"I can't understand why they're trying to do this to me," she said, reminding him of the theory she had been trumpeting since day one: that John Wall, Kathy Rix and Renee Walsh were setting her up.

"Why don't you leave the area . . . get away from this town?" Perrault suggested. "It'll probably do you some good."

"No! I want everybody here to see that they're ruining my life."

On the morning of September 10, Perrault walked out of his Easthampton apartment a confused—yet determined—man. He was meeting with Joe Riggs, his attorney, and Bill Welch, in Springfield, at nine A.M. and there wasn't a damn thing Gilbert, or anybody else, could do to stop him.

When Perrault came out his door, he looked to the left and saw Gilbert's car parked up the street.

But he decided to ignore her.

Almost immediately, however, she pulled up and parked directly in back of him, preventing him from moving his car.

After a moment, she jumped out of her car and ran up to his window.

"Talk to me."

"What are you doing?" Perrault said, starting his car.

"Don't, Jim. Let's talk about this," Gilbert pleaded. She started whimpering. Begging. "Don't go. Please don't go. Do you have to go, Jimmy?"

"I'm going, Kris. Now get out of my way."

It wasn't that Perrault hadn't expected Gilbert to try something foolish, but it still incensed him that she would take it this far.

"I'm not letting you go," Gilbert said, becoming more serious in tone. "I'm not moving my car!"

Perrault bowed his head over the steering wheel and just sat there for a moment. He didn't want trouble. He didn't even really want to go. But there was no way he was going to let Gilbert prevent him from meeting his obligations.

So he laid on the horn.

"I'll keep it up," he said over the noise, "until one of my neighbors calls the cops."

Begging Perrault not to speak with the attorneys about a murder investigation was one thing, but blocking his car on the day he was scheduled to meet with them, in the eyes of the law, was obstruction of justice. Gilbert could be arrested. Thrown in jail. How would that look? If she wasn't guilty of anything, why was she trying so desperately to impede the investigation?

As Perrault continued to lay on his horn, Gilbert jumped into her car and took off.

The parking garage for the Federal Building in downtown Springfield is a narrow and dark maze of concrete tucked in the back of the building, standing in the shadows of I-91. Across the street, underneath the Tower Square Mall, is a second garage that handles the overflow.

Guards sit in tiny wooden kiosks and take money as people exit the parking garages. Although there is a government building attached to the garage and security is tight inside the building itself, both garages are public parking areas and have little security.

Perrault's head was spinning as he walked to his car following his meeting at the US Attorney's Office. The only good thing about the meeting was that it was finally over.

Walking alone in the dark recesses of the parking garage, Perrault was mortified by the thought of Gilbert's being responsible for what the investigators and, now, Bill Welch were saying. At the very least, they had ample evidence to warrant a grand jury investigation. That alone was frightening enough.

When Perrault finally reached his car, he found the right front tire flat. It wasn't sliced or cut; someone had let the air out of it.

So he walked around to the trunk, grabbed the spare, and proceeded to change the tire. While leaning over, he kept turning around, thinking Gilbert was, at any time, going to come screeching around the corner and run him down.

Within hours of being home, it was obvious that the tire incident was the start of something more sinister.

Later that night, Perrault found his vehicle covered with eggs. The following day, someone spray-painted the windshield with a high-gloss, black paint. If that weren't bad enough, both fenders had been keyed.

One morning not long after that, while he was sitting in a class he had been taking at Holyoke Community College, staring out the window, he saw a car identical to Gilbert's 1993 Olds pull into the parking lot and begin slowly circling around all the other cars. He thought about getting up and running out to see if it was, indeed, Gilbert, but decided against it. It just wasn't worth the hassle of yet another face-off.

After class, when he made it to his car, he saw that someone had demolished the license plates, twisting and turning them into corkscrews of metal.

The day after that, the phone calls started at his apartment—and never stopped.

During some, Gilbert would say she was sick and bedridden. She needed him to come over and care for her. He would, of course, refuse. After he failed to show up, she would call and hang up, sometimes three, four, five times a day.

Several days after the license plate event, Perrault confronted Gilbert. "I saw you pull into the parking lot."

"Yes. That was me. But I didn't do anything to your car."

When Perrault couldn't take any more of her lies and prank phone calls, he decided to get the Easthampton Police Department involved. By this time, around the second week of September, he was getting no fewer than five hang-ups a day. And if he wasn't home, his answering machine would record one call after the next of heavy breathing. The Easthampton Police put a trace and trap on his phone, and, as he expected, the prankster turned out to be Gilbert.

Further, there wasn't a person involved in the murder investigation, save for law enforcement, who hadn't had some type of vandalism done to his or her car throughout the summer of

1996. It was no secret who the culprit was, but no one could catch Gilbert in the act.

Many wondered now, however, how far would she take her threats? By this point, Gilbert had no one left. She was alone.

CHAPTER 49

By the middle of September, Samantha Harris had come to the horrifying conclusion that her next door neighbor was, possibly, a cold-blooded serial killer.

As she sat one day in her living room and put all she had seen throughout the summer into perspective, Harris became almost embarrassed by her naivety. How could she have been so blind? She remembered how Glenn had shown up after work one day and Kristen had attacked him in front of the kids, screaming obscenities.

What kind of mother would subject her kids to such animosity and bring them into the middle of a divorce?

It made more sense to Harris now.

A few days later, Glenn again came by to pick up the kids, and Kristen told him Brian hadn't been feeling well.

"He's had a headache all day," Kristen said. "I want to give him some medicine before you take him home, Glenn—"

"Absolutely not," Glenn snapped. "Don't give him anything! I'll take care of them myself."

A fight ensued. Kristen, clawing and kicking, went after Glenn while Harris huddled the kids together in the corner of the kitchen.

After a few moments, Harris calmed Kristen down enough so Glenn could gather the kids and leave. It was one of the last times Kristen had taken care of the children.

There were other times when Kristen would tease the children right before Glenn arrived. She would take things from them and taunt them. Gilbert's youngest was two years old at the time. Like Linus from "Charlie Brown," the boy had a favorite blue blanket he carried around with him. Harris couldn't believe it as she watched Kristen rip the blanket from his hands one afternoon, and, as he begged to have it back, she refused.

It was as if she were punishing the children because their father was talking to the investigators, Harris thought later.

By September, Harris was at her wit's end. Gilbert's behavior had become so unpredictable it was a crap shoot every day as to whom she would be. Harris had given her the benefit of the doubt throughout the summer. She still believed in Gilbert's innocence. She felt the system had been using Gilbert as a scapegoat, forcing its theory down the throats of her family, friends and coworkers until they agreed to believe it.

But here it was, the second week of September, and things were anything but normal. As Harris recalled different episodes throughout the past few months, she became convinced of Gilbert's guilt. As it was, Gilbert had been phoning Harris three and four times a day and stopping by unannounced whenever she had a chance. Now, Harris realized, the entire time Gilbert had been pumping her with misinformation—things she wanted only Harris to know.

As Harris began to put things together and discuss them with not only Perrault, but Gilbert's other friends and coworkers, she realized Gilbert had been playing her all along.

Three specific episodes stuck out in Harris's mind, chewing at the fabric of her perception enough to force her to go running to the Northampton DA's office seeking help.

First, there was the matter of a canoe Gilbert had given to Perrault for his twenty-sixth birthday back in May.

It seemed like an innocent gesture from a lonely woman in love. At that time, Harris was just getting to know Gilbert and Perrault. "Wow," she told herself, "what a wonderful gift. She must really love the guy."

It was a beautiful brand-new red canoe with hand-woven seats. There were several prime spots around the immediate area to go boating, and Perrault loved nothing better than to spend his day off soaking up the sunshine in the great New England outdoors. He and Gilbert had even taken the canoe out several times right after she had given it to him.

One day, however, as Glenn and his brother-in-law were driving by Gilbert's apartment, they noticed something odd: Perrault's car sitting in Gilbert's parking lot with Glenn's brother-in-law's canoe strapped to the top of it.

Someone had stolen the canoe out of Glenn's backyard a few weeks before. It had been locked and chained under a large oak tree. It was unimaginable to think that one person could break the lock's combination, carry a twenty-foot canoe up the slope, strap it to a car, and drive off without being seen.

Even more peculiar was that Kristen, at the time, had been wearing a sling because of the injury she had purportedly sustained on February 17.

Glenn confronted Kristen.

"What the hell is your boyfriend doing with my brother's canoe?" he asked.

"I bought that canoe for Jim for his birthday, Glenn."

"You stole the damn canoe and gave it to your boyfriend for his birthday? Are you kidding me? What the hell is wrong with you?"

Kristen denied it. She said she bought the canoe from a guy in Holyoke who sold outdoor sporting goods in his front yard.

"Do you have a receipt?"

"No," Gilbert said.

Glenn and his brother-in-law cut their losses and decided not to call the cops and press charges. There was enough going on already. It would have been hard to prove.

Perrault, on the other hand, felt ridiculed and embarrassed. He returned the canoe, and it was rarely ever discussed again.

When Glenn told Harris what had happened, she couldn't believe the story. Kristen, she insisted, because of her injury, was incapable picking up a handbag, much less a canoe.

So Harris wrote it off and, as Kristen had told her many times, assumed Glenn was upset that she had left him for another man. This was one of the ways he could get back at the both of them, Kristen said.

The canoe incident was usurped a couple of months later by

an event involving a pair of kittens Gilbert had taken in around the middle of July—an event that proved to Harris how most things in Gilbert's life were sketched around the way James Perrault felt about her.

"Attention," Harris would tell herself. "Everything Kristen did, she did under the guise of gaining attention."

It had something to do with Tara, Gilbert's younger sister, Harris believed. Gilbert didn't speak of Tara too often, but when she did, it was always in the realm of how much more attention Gilbert's father had given to Tara. One story was that the old man had built a tree house for Tara when they were kids, and Gilbert wasn't allowed in it. When Gilbert asked for one, the old man coldly refused.

The kittens Gilbert took in were beautiful females, about ten weeks old. Whenever Gilbert was confined to jail or the hospital, Harris and Perrault had made it a point to have keys to her apartment so one of them could feed the kittens in her absence. When Gilbert wasn't there, Perrault made sure always to enter her apartment with Harris, so Gilbert couldn't later accuse him of anything.

One day, out of the blue, Gilbert called Harris and said that one of the kittens had developed a bacterial infection and would be spending some time at the vet hospital.

It was the first time Harris had heard one of the kittens had been ill.

"She'll be okay," Harris promised Gilbert. "Don't worry about it. It's just an infection. It'll be okay, Kristen."

But a few days later, shortly after Harris had gotten home from work, Gilbert called a second time. She was hysterical.

"The kitten's dead. She's dead. I can't believe it . . ."

Thinking that it was the kitten Gilbert had taken to the vet a few days earlier, Harris rushed over to comfort her friend.

Gilbert was upstairs in the corner of her bedroom when Harris walked in: crying, moaning, visibly trembling, looking away from the kitten, but pointing at it as if she were scared to look.

As Harris approached the animal, she could see it curled up in a ball. It was barely breathing, with blood running out of its mouth. Its eyes were glossed over, a murky pus-colored yellow. But she could hear it making a faint wheezing sound.

"Kristen, *what* happened?"

"Well," Gilbert said. She wasn't looking at Harris or the kitten. She was looking off in the distance. "I came home, and it crawled out from underneath the bed . . . and . . . it . . . it had a seizure and just laid on the ground." Gilbert then began to get hyper, moving around, pacing. "So . . . I . . . I . . . I gave it mouth-to-mouth," she said, perking up, "and saved its life!"

The first thing Harris thought of was getting the kitten to the vet before it died in front of them.

"Kristen, we need to call the vet right away."

"Well, I *already* called Jim."

"No. No. No! We *need* to call the vet. *Right now!*"

Gilbert then went to the linen closet, got a towel, and wrapped up the kitten. As Harris watched, she couldn't believe how Gilbert, instead of comforting the thing, held it out in front of herself as if she were repulsed by the sight of it. As a mother, all Harris wanted to do was pick the animal up and cradle it in her arms.

Harris then called the vet.

"Can we bring it in right away? It's going to die at any time."

"Bring it in immediately."

"Kristen," Harris said, turning toward Gilbert and grabbing her by the shoulders, "listen to me. The vet said to bring it in right away."

Gilbert wouldn't look into Harris's eyes.

"Oh, no. I *have* to wait for Jim to come before I do anything."

"My God, Kristen, the kitten is going to die. Why in the world do you have to wait for Jim?"

"Because I called him, and he said he was on his way."

"Kristen, why don't you just take the kitten to the vet, and I'll wait here for Jim and send him down there when he gets here?"

"No! Absolutely not! I *have* to wait for Jim, Sami. Now that's the end of it!"

Gilbert put the cat down on the ground, walked away and sat down on the bed.

Harris was stunned by her lack of compassion. Gilbert had spent her entire adult life in nursing. Her job had been to care for people.

Luckily, while they were talking, Perrault arrived. He and Gilbert then brought the animal to the vet, and both kittens ended up being fine in a matter of a couple weeks.

The next day, Perrault went over to Harris's to thank her for what she had done.

"What the hell happened yesterday, Jim? I wish someone would explain it to me."

"I don't know, Sami. She's . . . she's . . . I don't know what to say."

"What the hell is wrong with her?"

Perrault then moved in closer as if he didn't want anyone else to hear what he was about to say.

"You know, Sami," he whispered, "just the other day, in the heat of an argument, I told her that I loved those kittens more than her. You know, just to hurt her feelings. Maybe this had something to do with that?"

"What?"

"And just last night we were watching one of those 'real video' shows on TV, and they showed a tape of this fireman who saved this cat's life by giving it mouth-to-mouth."

Harris just shook her head.

There was one more instance, even more horrifying, that finally sent Harris running to the DA's office.

In early September, Gilbert called Harris and started ranting and raving about the investigation and everyone who had turned their backs on her. It was same rhetoric Harris heard since the July car ride, when Gilbert had told her about the investigation. "I'll get them all," Gilbert would say. "They're all against me!" It had become casual conversation. All she ever talked about was the investigation.

Yet this particular morning, Gilbert said something that Harris didn't take as just another one of her informal threats. It gave her pause to wonder if Gilbert was planning on taking a grander step toward stopping the investigation.

"You know," Gilbert said over the phone, "that Karen Abderhalden better watch out."

"What do you mean?"

Harris liked Karen. She had only met her a few times, but

Gilbert, 27, in 1994, less than a year before she started her killing spree. *(Courtesy Rachel Webber)*

Kristen Gilbert living it up at a 1995 Halloween party. By this time, Gilbert had already killed one of her patients.

Kristen Strickland, 16, in her 1984 high-school yearbook photo.
(Courtesy Groton-Dunstable Regional High School yearbook)

Gilbert, 25, in 1992, looked every bit the "soccer mom."
(Courtesy Rachel Webber)

Since 1924, the 197-bed Veterans Affairs Medical Center (VAMC) in Leeds, Massachusetts, has served the needs of over 600,000 patients.

The back entrance to Building One, where Ward C was located.

Shortly before her killing spree began, Gilbert began an extramarital affair with VAMC security guard James Perrault

Perrault later realized his dream of becoming a "real" cop.
(Courtesy Hatfield Police Department Web site)

The Michael C. Curtain VFW in downtown Florence, Massachusetts, was a popular after-work hangout for the Ward C staff.

The Drewson Drive home in Florence, Massachusetts, where Kristen Gilbert lived with her husband, Glenn.

The Easthampton, Massachusetts, apartment where Gilbert moved after she left her husband was only two miles from her boyfriend James Perrault's apartment.

Inside Kristen Gilbert's apartment investigators found a book that clearly outlined adverse reactions to epinephrine.

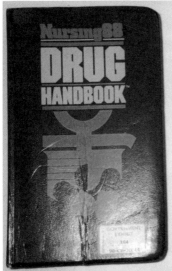

In the pantry of Kristen and Glenn Gilbert's home, investigators found this copy of the *Handbook of Poisoning*.

Epinephrine shocks the heart of a dying person back into a normal beating pattern, but to Kristen Gilbert it was the perfect poison.

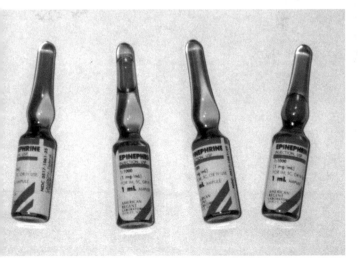

Gilbert's first victim, Stanley Jagodowski, in a tender moment with his grandchild. *(Courtesy Susan Lessard)*

Gilbert's second victim, thirty-five-year-old Air Force veteran Henry Hudon, succumbed to epinephrine poisoning on December 8, 1995. *(Courtesy U.S. Attorney's Office, Springfield, Mass.)*

Authorities believe Gilbert gave World War II veteran Francis "Buck" Marier a massive overdose of insulin just weeks after killing Henry Hudon. *(Courtesy U.S. Attorney's Office, Springfield, Mass.)*

Spent ampoules of epinephrine were found in Thomas "Tomcat" Callahan's room after his heart rate suddenly doubled on January 22, 1996. *(Courtesy U.S. Attorney's Office, Springfield, Mass.)*

Gilbert killed bedridden U.S. Army veteran Kenneth Cutting on February 2, 1996, so she could leave work early.
(Courtesy U.S. Attorney's Office, Springfield, Mass.)

Confined to a wheelchair and stricken with multiple sclerosis, Kenneth Cutting always had time for his children.
(Courtesy U.S. Attorney's Office, Springfield, Mass.)

Gilbert tried to kill Marine Corps veteran Angelo Vella, 68, right under the noses of several of her colleagues. (Courtesy U.S. Attorney's Office, Springfield, Mass.)

Gilbert's last known victim, Edward Skwira, loved fishing on the Connecticut River. (Courtesy U.S. Attorney's Office, Springfield, Mass.)

A proud father and dedicated husband, Edward Skwira gave away his daughter Marcia on her wedding day. (Courtesy U.S. Attorney's Office, Springfield, Mass.)

Special Agent Steve Plante, from the Northeast Field Office of the Veterans Affairs Office of Inspector General, in Bedford, Massachusetts, investigated and tracked Kristen Gilbert for five years.

With more than twenty-six years on the job, Massachusetts State Police Detective Kevin Murphy joined Steve Plante in the investigation of Kristen Gilbert in June 1996.

Dr. Michael Baden was asked by the Veterans Affairs Office of Inspector General to look at the medical files of VAMC patients who died during the seven years that Kristen Gilbert worked at the hospital. *(Courtesy Michael Baden)*

Arrested on July 11, 1996, for breaking and entering into boyfriend James Perrault's apartment, Kristen Gilbert was photographed by the Easthampton Police Department.
(Courtesy VA-Inspector General's Office, Bedford, Massachusetts)

Under a federal grand jury subpoena, Kristen Gilbert was photographed by Special Agent Steve Plante on September 5, 1996, shortly after submitting to handwriting samples and fingerprinting. *(Courtesy VA-Inspector General's Office, Bedford, Massachusetts)*

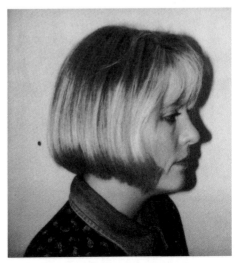

On November 24, 1998, for the first time in public,
U.S. Attorney William Welch announced the indictment
against Kristen Gilbert, which included three counts of murder.
(Courtesy Bruce Sackman)

United States Attorney
Ariane Vuono, co-council to
Bill Welsh, helped to convict
Kristen Gilbert.

Judge Michael Ponsor later
wrote that this case was
"the most complicated and
stressful thing [he'd] ever
done..." *(Courtesy U.S.
District Court of Mass.)*

Glenn Gilbert, ex-husband of convicted serial killer Kristen Gilbert, leaves the Federal Building in Springfield, Mass, after appearing at a hearing in U.S. District Court on March 16, 2001.
(AP/Wide World Photos)

In the spring of 2001, the people most responsible for bringing Kristen Gilbert to justice were honored with the Eagle Award by the Veterans Affairs Office of Inspector General. From left: Massachusetts State Police Detective Kevin Murphy, R.N. Renee Walsh-Skwirz, Special Agent Steve Plante, R.N. Kathy Rix, R.N. John Wall, and U.S. Attorney William Welch.

Edward Skwira's grave before his remains were exhumed
on November 27, 1997.
(Courtesy U.S. Attorney's Office, Springfield, Mass.)

The gravesite of Stanley Jagodowski shortly before
his body was exhumed on July 13, 1998.
(Courtesy U.S. Attorney's Office, Springfield, Mass.)

she had spoken to her over the phone on numerous occasions throughout the first few weeks of September. Abderhalden had a warm disposition. But like everyone else involved, she was petrified of Gilbert. And because Harris was so close to Gilbert, she became the epicenter of the investigation. Everyone involved was calling her at one time or another to see what Gilbert was up to. Most called out of fear, and actually believed Gilbert would follow through on her threats. It became a ritual. People would call Harris and, half-joking, half-serious, say, "Tell me: What kind of day am I going to have today, Sami?" Or maybe their car had been vandalized the previous day, and they would call to see if Gilbert was home at such-and-such a time.

Abderhalden lived with her parents in Ashfield, a rather spread-out, reclusive town just outside of Northampton, and had taken Gilbert in back in August. She had convinced her parents that Gilbert needed to be around friends. Everyone had turned their backs on her. She was having problems with Perrault, her husband had totally written her off, and the investigation was beginning to destroy her emotionally. Gilbert had attempted suicide several times, and Abderhalden just wanted to be there for her as a friend. Yet, in truth, Gilbert had played Abderhalden and her parents like a virtuoso, convincing them of her innocence and using them to further her agenda.

"Well, well, well," Gilbert said to Harris, "you know, Karen's house is so far out in the boondocks . . . if the whole family was killed, nobody would find them for a very long time."

This coming from a woman who had called Abderhalden eighty-six times between August thirtieth and early September to lean on her for support. The calls lasted anywhere from thirty seconds to more than an hour. During one call, Gilbert had told Abderhalden that "because Jimmy [Perrault] loved her cats so much, she intended to strike back at him by having them euphemized [sic] and was going to lay the cats at his doorstep."

Petrified by what she had just heard, Harris knew it was time to call the investigators.

CHAPTER 50

At 4:00 P.M., on September 11, 1996, Harris called the Northampton DA's office and requested an immediate meeting with investigators. She said James Perrault had given her the phone number. She said she had information that could help the investigation into the alleged murders up at the VAMC. She said she was eager to help. She had seen enough. She was scared to death for the welfare of her family. She said she wanted to disassociate herself from Gilbert right away—because if Gilbert ever found out that she had called the DA's office, the consequences, Harris believed, would be deadly.

"One of the most dangerous things you can do at this point," SA Plante warned Harris, "would be to end the relationship you have with Ms. Gilbert."

Plante's words sent a chill down Harris's spine. It was the last thing she wanted to hear. If she thought the past few weeks were scary, she knew now that the future was going to be ten times worse.

"Oh, my God," Harris said. "I lent her a bottle of ketchup the other day." She wasn't sure if anyone in the house had used it since Gilbert had returned it. "I'm confused. I don't know what to do anymore."

"Bring that ketchup bottle in with you when you come in," Plante said. "We'll want to have the lab take a look at it."

Regardless of how Harris felt, this was great news to Plante and Murphy. Having a source living right next door could add an element to the investigation that had been missing all along.

The DA's office was located right off Main, on Gothic Street, in downtown Northampton. A massive building by Northampton standards, the three-story, red brick structure housed some thirty lawyers. Whenever he had a break in the Gilbert case and needed to meet with Plante and Murphy, assistant US Attorney Bill Welch used the office as a remote location.

Plante and Murphy could tell right away that Harris wasn't fooling when she said over the phone the previous day that Gilbert had gotten under her skin—so much that every minute of every day was now spent worrying what Gilbert would do next.

"That's why I'm here. I have a child. A husband. I'm afraid for their lives. I pulled my boy out of school the other day because I thought she was going to grab him."

Of course, Murphy and Plante had seen witnesses like Harris their entire careers. Sometimes they panned out; other times they didn't. It was all part of the game.

They first convinced her that everything was going to be all right. Then Harris began to go through everything she had seen and heard over the past few months.

Plante and Murphy were particularly interested in the conversation Harris had had with Gilbert during the car ride home from the hospital back in July.

"Yeah, now that I think back on it," Harris said, "Kristen was actually trying to make me believe that it was impossible for you guys to ever catch her. She was filling me with information she thought would later help her. She was trying to manipulate me like everybody else."

After about an hour of discussing everything she could remember, Plante leaned back in his chair and made a suggestion.

"Listen, Ms. Harris. We appreciate you coming forward. You've given us a lot of quality information. Why don't you start keeping a diary of Gilbert's movements? You know, mark down times and notes regarding her comings and goings. You live right next door. You see a lot of things, I'm sure."

"Okay," Harris said.

"We think," Murphy added, "she's responsible for at least forty deaths."

"What?"

"Yes. And if she's killed as many people as we think she has, that makes your neighbor the most successful female serial killer in the history of the United States. We don't have to tell you that we need to put this person behind bars."

Plante and Murphy were a bit more optimistic after the meeting. They had been gathering facts and data for months now. But they were looking for that one tangible piece of evidence that might solidify an indictment.

CHAPTER 51

When Glenn Gilbert pulled into the driveway of his Drewson Drive home on September 15, 1996, he spied his estranged wife's Oldsmobile parked by the back door.

Glenn was furious. Back in June, he'd obtained a restraining order, prohibiting Kristen from coming anywhere near the house.

As Glenn entered, he saw Kristen in the kitchen and, startled, she turned around quickly.

"What are you doing here?" Glenn yelled.

"I . . . I . . . needed some things," Kristen said.

"You're not supposed to be in this house."

The kids, who were a few steps behind Glenn, walked in, and stood in the living room staring at their mother.

"I know," Kristen tried to say, "but—"

"Jesus, Kristen. Get out, or I'll call the cops!"

Kristen became enraged. She began yelling and screaming. Glenn couldn't even understand what she was saying. She was going on and on as if *he* had done something wrong.

"I want you out of here right now," he said as he picked up the phone to call the cops.

Shaken by the sound of their mother's screaming, the kids followed Glenn into the kitchen and stood behind him.

Kristen then ran toward Glenn and grabbed the base of the telephone and ripped it off the wall.

Glenn struggled with her for a moment, but then he stopped himself. After a moment, he stood back and calmly said, "Get out of my house."

By this point, Kristen had backed off and was standing about ten feet away. She looked dazed, but had apparently given up, and started walking toward the door.

Glenn turned around to comfort the children.

Kristen then turned back and charged at him. She had her car keys in her hand, with one key sticking out in between her middle and forefinger, like a knife.

Then, within a moment, as Glenn grabbed her by the arm, she went limp and began crying.

"Get the hell out," Glenn said. "Now!"

James Perrault, like almost everyone else who had anything to do with the VAMC murder investigation, had received sporadic prank phone calls throughout the entire summer of 1996. But by the beginning of September, they became more frequent.

There was no method to most of them. The caller wouldn't say much—just some melodramatic heavy breathing, similar to that in any low-budget "slasher" film. Other times, the caller would simply hang up as soon as Perrault answered the phone.

An even-tempered guy, Perrault felt no harm had been done after the first few calls. Every household on the planet received these types of calls once in a while.

By the middle of September, though, Perrault noticed a dramatic increase in the number of calls, along with a change in content.

Taking into account the events of the past year, and after receiving several calls within a short period of time, Perrault decided to put a trace on the calls to see what the hell was going on.

Like clockwork, the phone began to ring off the hook one night. Again, Perrault would pick it up, and the caller would hang up. After several calls in a row, he pressed the star fifty-seven function on his phone, which would normally log the number the person was calling from on his phone bill. Perrault could then order a copy of his phone records and check to see what number had been calling him.

Despite his ambitions of being a cop one day, Perrault's investigative efforts on this night proved fruitless—because the star fifty-seven function, he found out the following day, hadn't worked.

So he decided to call NYNEX and have it run a conventional trace. He knew damn well it was Gilbert, but he wanted hard evidence to confront her with.

NYNEX obliged.

Perrault soon learned that several of calls had been made from Gilbert's 182 Northampton Street telephone number. She had obsessively called his apartment on September 12, 15, 19, 20 and 21. And each time corresponded with the time he had gotten a hang-up or heavy breathing. Several of the calls were made from pay telephone booths around Easthampton and Northampton: the Tasty Top Ice Cream Shop, for one, which was about a quarter mile up the road from Gilbert's apartment; the Citgo Station, about a mile away; the phone booth in the parking lot of the *Hampshire Gazette* newspaper, about three miles away; and the phone booth just down the street from the VFW, in Florence.

It was then explained to Perrault that the reason he couldn't star fifty-seven Gilbert after she had hung up on him was that she had used the star sixty-seven function, which made it impossible to trace the calls.

A creature of habit, Glenn Gilbert got home from work on September 26 around 4:30, and he did what he had done every day: check his AT&T answering service for any phone messages.

Next saved message, received Thursday, September 26, at 3:34 P.M., the choppy computer voice stated.

"I just wanted to say good-bye for the last time—good-bye," a sullen, electronically altered voice chimed.

It was strange and, at first, frightened Glenn. It sounded as though it had been pre-recorded and played back at a slower speed to sound intimidating, maybe to add a sense of drama that wouldn't have been otherwise been there.

Glenn noticed immediately the odd familiarity of the tone of the voice. It sounded like Kristen, but it couldn't be—it was a male's voice. On top of that, whoever it was sounded anxious, hurt, shamed.

Ever since the investigation had began, like everyone else, Glenn had gotten bizarre calls from his estranged wife. For the most part, she'd use the kids as the reason behind the call. But after mentioning the kids only momentarily, she'd break into one of her "spousal immunity" rages, lecturing Glenn on the law.

Yet here was Kristen, on the verge of tears, speaking in an electronically altered voice, saying good-bye? It didn't add up. She had threatened to commit suicide all summer long, but never finished the job. Plante and Murphy had even found the infamous suicide "how to" book of the eighties, *Final Exit,* when they had searched Glenn's home for a second time.

After listening to the tape several times, Glenn decided to call Plante and Murphy.

"From what you're telling me, Glenn," Plante said, "I can say that it's probably her. I'll be over as soon as I can."

Plante showed up later that night. Glenn made it clear right away that he was still unsure who it was.

"Have you altered this tape in any way?" Plante asked as a formality, after they listened to the tape several times.

"No. Of course not."

CHAPTER 52

It was just after five o'clock on September 26, 1996, when James Perrault finished driving the VAMC grounds for his allotted two-hour tour of duty.

Gilbert had always made it a point to ask Perrault which rotation he was working. As recently as just a few days ago, she called and wanted to know if he had started his shift driving the grounds or at the security desk. To Perrault, it seemed to be just one more crazy request, part of a continuing hold she tried to maintain on her former place of employment and the people she'd worked with, so he obliged.

A few minutes after he returned from driving the grounds on September 26, Perrault sat down at the security desk to man the phones.

Perrault's colleague that night, Ron Shepard, a ten-year VAMC employee, then got into the SUV and began his two-hour tour of the grounds.

"I'll see you in a couple hours," Shepard told Perrault.

Perrault finished tidying up the desk and got comfortable in his chair. At 5:11 the security desk phone rang.

"Officer Perrault speaking. How may I help you?"

"This is a message for all Persian Gulf veterans who were exposed to chemical weapons," an odd-sounding voice stammered matter-of-factly before hanging up.

There was no doubt in Perrault's mind that the caller was

male, probably somewhere in the neighborhood of thirty to forty years old, he guessed. But something was wrong. The caller, for obvious reasons, had disguised his voice somehow. It was distorted and eerie. To the same extent, however, it was calm and well-pronounced. "Almost," Perrault later said, "like it had a mechanical ring to it."

As a first consideration, after the caller hung up, Perrault wrote it off as a prank. The high school was just down the street from the VAMC. Kids were always roaming around the grounds. Perhaps a dare had been set up? Perhaps Perrault had pissed off a few kids one time, maybe kicked them off the property, and they were getting even?

Eleven minutes later, however, at 5:22, the caller made it obvious that it wasn't an adolescent prank.

"There are three explosive devices in Building One. You have two hours," the caller stated and hung up.

It was the same haunting voice: electronic, deep, raspy—and male.

If it was the neighborhood pranksters, they were now teetering on doing some hard time in a federal pen.

Perrault called Bernie LeFlam, the evening clinical coordinator for nursing. With almost thirty years of federal service, ten of which LeFlam spent as a supervisor up at the Leeds VAMC, LeFlam was the "go to" man in a time of crisis. He knew VA protocol.

"Bernie, it's Jim in security. We have a situation."

Located near Admissions, on the ground level of Building One, LaFlam rushed over to security.

Perrault went over what had just happened. The threat was specifically directed to Building One, he explained. LeFlam, thinking fast, ordered a copy of the VAMC's "Medical Center Memorandum" from Admissions. Karen Abderhalden printed it out and got it to LaFlam as fast as she could.

It clearly outlined the procedure for bomb threats.

LeFlam then called Melodie Turner. He explained that the patients in Building One would have to be evacuated, but the decision as to when would be left up to the fire marshal, who, along with local police and fire personnel, were on their way.

Procedure dictated that it was the person's responsibility who had received the call to ask certain questions of the person phoning in the threat. Where is the bomb? Who are you? Where are you calling from?

But would a person phoning in a bomb threat actually respond to such absurd questions?

The rationale behind the questions wasn't necessarily to get the person to admit who he or she was; it was to keep him on the line as long as possible so a trace could be set up.

While LaFlam gathered all the supervisors together in Admissions and read from the memo, Perrault called Ron Shepard.

"Ronny," he said in a hurried tone, "come back here . . . we have a situation developing."

Around 5:30, Perrault stepped away from the security desk to explain the situation to a few of the nurses. Then he ran over to Medical Administration Services, located in a different building, and borrowed a device for tape recording incoming phone calls.

When Perrault returned, he noticed the cramped quarters of the security office were becoming a bit chaotic. Staff and senior personnel were scrambling around wondering what to do next. People were talking over one another. Theories were being thrown out. The patients had to be evacuated. Some were too weak to be moved. What was going to happen to them? Had anyone seen any weird packages lying around?

Then the phone rang again.

Ron Shepard was manning the phones. When Perrault heard the phone ring, he rushed over to Shepard and pressed the RECORD button on the recording device he had just finished hooking up.

Perrault pointed to Ron as if he were an actor.

"Go ahead."

"Security, Officer Shepard speaking."

"Nothing will compare as to what is going to happen tonight."

The caller said nothing more and hung up.

"That voice sounds distorted," Shepard said. "It was definitely not a person's normal speaking voice. It was like some kind of tape recorder . . . maybe even a computer . . . it was muffled, garbled."

Perrault nodded; they agreed it was the same person.

Moments before the call, two Northampton police cruisers and several fire trucks had arrived on the scene.

At 5:36, once again taking over the helm at the security desk phone, Perrault took another call.

"I want those patients out in time. Remember . . ."

"Sir . . ." Perrault said, trying to get him to say something. "Sir? You there?" But the line went dead.

The caller had been precise in his directions, Perrault thought. Not only that, but he had gone to great lengths to pronounce words slowly, accurately, and chose his words carefully. What was more, why would a self-proclaimed radical be concerned with the welfare of the people in the building he was about to bomb? Wasn't the point of blowing up the place to harm people?

At 5:40, the caller posed a question:

"Would you like to know where to locate the devices?"

"Sir," Perrault began to say . . . but again the line went dead.

A Northampton police officer then walked into the security office. Thus far, Perrault explained, they had received a total of five calls. He said he had written down what the caller had said earlier and was able to record one of the calls.

Two more calls came in at 5:45 and 5:50, but Perrault couldn't make out a word.

"You'll have to speak up, sir. I can't hear you," he said as the caller mumbled.

But there was no response.

Almost everyone agreed that the caller was using some sort of electronic device to disguise his voice. Perrault couldn't engage him in a conversation because his voice was being overridden by a recording. Exchanging dialogue would be impossible. Moreover, the hang-up calls were not hang-ups at all, but rather the caller's tape recorder malfunctioning.

The only background sounds Perrault could make out were from a small airplane. There were several small aircraft airports within a twenty-mile radius of the VAMC. It made sense to everyone that the caller was somewhere in the immediate area and was probably using a pay phone.

Security guard Timothy Reardon, after listening to the tape, said he thought he recognized the voice.

"It's John Noble," he said. "At least it sounds like him."

John Noble, a fifty-four-year-old ex-VAMC patient, lived in nearby Chesterfield. He had been the cause of some minor problems at the VAMC in years past. He was known as someone who would at times become angry while on the phone. He had issues with the government. It seemed logical to check him out.

One of the officers took down a description of Noble

A few minutes later, at 5:55, the caller decided to take a different approach.

"You sound dumb, or you would go see to . . . ," he said. But was cut off again when, as he spoke, the device began to malfunction.

"Hello . . . sir . . . ?" Perrault said. "Could you please speak up? I cannot hear you."

At 6:10, the caller became angry.

"You mustn't think this is very serious, just sitting in your office answering phones?"

Then, at 6:18: "If you're too stupid to find them, you deserve to die with them."

Another call came in at 6:25, but again, it was hard to understand. The sound of a horn, likely from a car, had drowned out the caller's low voice.

Nearly half an hour went by without another call. The small crowd that had gathered in the security office thought it was finally over. Many felt relieved. Some were shocked. Others just dumbfounded. What the hell was happening? Was the caller serious?

It was probably some disgruntled patient who had gotten drunk and decided to have a little fun, many speculated. Perhaps Reardon's assumptions were right: John Noble was up to his old tricks again.

Nevertheless, a bomb threat was a bomb threat. It was time to begin evacuating the patients.

NYNEX, meanwhile, had tried to trace the calls, but they were too short and happening with such rapidity that it was impossible. On top of that, the caller was likely moving from one location to the next to avoid being, as NYNEX termed it, "trapped."

Then, at 6:48, the phone rang again.

"You find this exciting, don't you, officer . . . ?"

"Sir, could you help me with this?" Perrault said sincerely, hoping to lure the caller into some sort of verbal showdown. "Sir, could *you* think about the patients?"

The caller quickly hung up.

Another call came in three minutes later. Plain and well-spoken, yet still on the chilling side, the caller made it perfectly clear what was going to happen within the next half hour: "This is my last call. In twenty-five minutes, I'll see you in hell!"

"Sir, could you think about . . ." Perrault tried saying as the caller hung up.

CHAPTER 53

Security went around and checked the pay phones in the immediate vicinity of the hospital and instructed staff to pay extra special attention to the phones inside the hospital. There was a chance the caller had made the calls from the grounds of the VAMC, or from one of the pay phones inside one of the buildings.

Around seven o'clock, Northampton Police Officer John McCarthy was ordered by his superiors to close off all access to the hospital.

As the process of evacuating patients began, state troopers, VAMC security, officers from the neighboring towns of Easthampton and Northampton, along with fire personnel, kept everyone calm as they directed patients and staff to safe areas. Things were getting hectic by the minute. People were scared. No one could say with any certainty that there wasn't a bomb in the building.

A small crowd had gathered by the main entrance on Route 9. Motorists driving by stopped to ask what was going on. Even if the threat turned out to be false, as almost everyone suspected, the caller had certainly done enough to make life at the VAMC, at least for this one night, a living hell—which was perhaps his only intention.

The parking lot of the Look Restaurant, a popular diner just fifty yards across the street from the VAMC's main entrance on Route 9, filled with onlookers and rubberneckers—among them, Kristen Gilbert, who later told a friend she stood a few feet from the pay telephone booth in the parking lot watching everything.

Then, at 7:07, amid the chaos that had erupted both in and outside the hospital as word about the threats began to spread, the security phone rang.

"It's your job to think about those patients," the caller said.

It was, in one sense, a belated reaction to Perrault's previous plea of "think about the patients."

This time, however, Perrault noticed that the caller sounded hurt, almost as if he were—or had been—crying.

After a moment of silence, "I *do* care," the caller said. "But the government needs a message."

Perrault tried reasoning with him.

"Yes, I care about the patients, sir. But I need help with working with them."

The caller abruptly hung up. It was obvious now that the calls had been pre-recorded. They were too one-sided. Too well planned. There was no interaction. The caller often talked right over Perrault's voice. Plus, if Perrault said something, the caller never addressed it immediately. It wouldn't be until the next call that he would make reference to the previous call. This led everyone to believe that the VA bomber was, in fact, recording his voice and playing it back.

By this time, staff were taking those patients who could walk on their own out of Building One. Patients confined to beds were rolled out. Those too weak or sick to walk were taken out on stretchers and wheelchairs. Some were extremely ill. Just moving them could be dangerous and life-threatening. The largest concern was for those patients with pneumonia and/or respiratory diseases and illnesses. Just exposing them to outside elements could worsen their conditions significantly.

In all, about fifty patients were moved without any serious problems.

After a careful sweep of the building, no suspicious objects were found, and it was soon determined that there were no bombs. As a precautionary measure, however, the evacuated patients, along with some of the staff, spent the night in Building Eleven and the Recreation Hall and were told they would be returned to their regular beds the following day.

Everyone was curious about the caller's identity. It was a Veterans Affairs Hospital, for God's sake. The caller had made no demands. He hadn't claimed to be part of some radical, extremist group.

What was the point?

CHAPTER 54

Samantha Harris had done a pretty good job throughout the final weeks of September of keeping a low profile—as far as running into Gilbert outside in the parking lot or taking her phone calls. The last thing Harris wanted to do was blow her cover. If Gilbert found out that she was literally tracking her every movement for the government, Harris feared the consequences would be fatal.

On the evening of September 26, Harris prepared to watch her favorite Thursday night television program, *ER*, when the sound of two cats fighting outside her window interrupted her.

Like most residents in town, Harris had no idea that the bomb scare at the VAMC was just winding down.

Around 8:00, she walked into the kitchen, grabbed a glass of water, went outside, and splashed the cats, hoping to drive them away.

While Harris was walking back up the cement walkway toward her apartment, she saw Gilbert barrel into the parking lot at high speed and pull her Olds into an open space in front of her apartment. At first, Gilbert didn't see Harris. She was too busy fidgeting with her house keys and looking in all directions.

Standing about a hundred yards from Harris, keys in hand, ready to open her door, Gilbert, in a surprised tone of voice, yelled, "What are *you* doing out here?"

Harris walked closer but didn't say anything.

"What. Are. You. Doing. Out. Here?"

Harris held up the empty glass of water and explained that the cats had been fighting. It was disrupting her show.

"Oh . . ." Gilbert said, somewhat relieved.

"Where are you coming from?" Harris asked.

"I'm . . . I'm . . . I'm just getting back from doing my laundry," Gilbert said, talking fast, looking around.

"Laundry?"

"I *have* to get inside, though. 'Must-see TV' is on tonight! You know how much I love that *ER*," Gilbert said. Then she paused for a moment to catch her breath. "See ya, Sami. I gots to go!"

The following day, one of the local newspapers ran a small article about the bomb threat the previous night.

That morning, while Harris was walking with her husband toward her car, Gilbert came running out of her apartment as if she had been waiting by the window for Harris to emerge.

"Take a look at this, Sami," Gilbert said, holding the newspaper open to the page where the article appeared, pointing to it. She was excited. Wound up.

"What am I looking at?" Harris asked.

"The article. The article. The bomb threat. See . . . it's right there!" Gilbert pointed to it. "I was at the Look Restaurant eating dinner when all of this happened," she said as though it had been some type of sporting event. "I watched the whole thing unfold."

Harris looked at Gilbert without saying anything.

Why the hell are you so preoccupied with this? And happy . . . this sort of thing makes you happy?

Gilbert, on the other hand, couldn't get her words out fast enough. She read the entire article aloud.

"I have a theory about who did it," Gilbert said after reading the article. "You want to hear it?"

"Sure, Kristen," Harris said, looking at her husband, who was rolling his eyes. "You're probably going to tell me anyway, right?"

"It was probably a former patient at the VA who wanted to

sit by and watch. Some nut who wanted to see all the action. He probably called in the threat from right there at the Look Restaurant pay phone."

"Could be," Harris said.

In a frenzy, Gilbert continued to explain how she had seen fire trucks and police swarming the area around the VAMC. At one point, Harris had to tell her to chill out.

"Take your time."

Then, as Harris and her husband got into their car and Gilbert went back inside her apartment, Harris recalled the conversation she'd had with Gilbert less than twelve hours before.

If she had been doing her laundry, like she claimed, Harris thought, *wouldn't she have, at the least, had a basket of clothes with her?*

But there was one more thing: Why hadn't Gilbert mentioned the bomb threat incident the previous night? *If it had that much of an impact on her, why the hell didn't she say anything about it?*

The following day, Gilbert knocked on Harris's door. She said she needed to talk to someone. There had been more coverage in the newspapers about the bomb threat. Gilbert said she sensed that investigators would try to pin it on her. They had blamed her for everything else. Why not this, too?

"Do you remember what happened at the Olympics when they were in Atlanta?" Gilbert asked.

"No. But I'm sure you're going to tell me."

"That guy who got blamed for the bombing. You don't remember?"

Gilbert was referring to security guard Richard Jewell, whom the FBI named as an early suspect in the bombing of a Centennial Olympic Park tent during the 1996 Atlanta games. Someone at the FBI had leaked Jewell's name to the press, and a feeding frenzy ensued. Jewell was later found to be innocent. But the press had already tarred and feathered him.

"Yeah," Harris said. "I think I remember something about that now."

"Well, I know exactly how he feels, Sami," Gilbert said.

"Why is that? No one's accused you of anything, Kristen."

"I bet they rented an apartment across the way," Gilbert said. Then she got up off the couch and went to the window. She pointed at the apartment directly across from Harris's. "They're watching me. They're spying on me all the time. I can fucking feel it."

In fact, Gilbert's sensibilities were accurate. But they weren't in an apartment across the way; they were in a black surveillance van on the other side of Route 10. It wasn't anything out of a spy novel, just a trooper inside the van who watched Gilbert come and go. When the trooper felt Gilbert went to bed for the night, the surveillance ended. If there was an available officer the following day, the surveillance continued.

"You know what, Kristen?" Harris asked. "I bet you're right. I bet they're watching your every move."

Gilbert looked at her and smiled.

"Bridget Fonda!" she said, waving her finger at Harris.

"What, Kristen?"

"The movie—I want Bridget Fonda to play me."

"What are you talking about now? You want Bridget Fonda to play you? What in God's name are—"

"When they make a movie of my life, she'd be perfect. Don't you think?"

CHAPTER 55

Assistant US Attorney Bill Welch had plenty of reason to believe Gilbert was responsible for both the bomb threat and the murders up at the VAMC, but he didn't yet have enough evidence to indict her on federal felony murder charges or even consider an arrest warrant for the bomb threat.

He needed proof, not speculation.

In the eyes of the law, the two crimes were separate. Yet it was impossible to believe they weren't connected in some bizarre way.

Concerning the deaths at the VAMC between the summer of 1995 and the winter of 1996, Plante was convinced of Gilbert's guilt. He had been embroiled in the murder investigation since June and knew the particulars of the case better than anyone—and had been telling some of his sources that Gilbert could be responsible for as many as forty deaths.

After hearing threads of the false bomb threat from various sources at the Northampton DA's office, SA Plante phoned Timothy Reardon and asked him for his take on what happened. The two men discussed the calls in detail. Reardon said they had made several tapes. "Whoever it was," Reardon noted, "had used some sort of electronically altered device to disguise his voice. A tape recorder or something. It was the strangest thing."

"Great," Plante said. "We'll come up and listen to the tapes."

Satisfied with what Reardon had told him, Plante and Detective Thomas Soutier then drove to the Northampton Police Department to interview the officers who had responded to the scene. After that, they decided to stop in town for a little shopping trip before continuing up to the VAMC.

But something kept gnawing at Plante as they drove from one place to the next trying to piece together the previous night's events: the call Glenn Gilbert had received from his estranged wife the previous day, September 26. So Plante made a mental note: The call she had made to Glenn was just an hour and a half *before* the first threatening call had been made to the VAMC. *Electronically altered device,* Plante kept repeating to himself.

After spending about an hour at the NPD, Plante and Soutier took a walk around downtown Northampton, stopping in various electronic shops, hoping they could dig up some sort of electronic device Gilbert might have used.

They went in and out of several stores, asking questions, looking at several different devices. But nothing stood out.

When the shopping trip failed, Plante and Soutier went back up to the VAMC to see if they had missed something earlier.

Plante spoke with Perrault first.

The two men knew each other well by this point. Plante had been in and out of the VAMC during the past six months hunting down leads in the murder investigation. Perrault, he knew, could be helpful. He was cocky and sometimes difficult, but professional and cooperative, nonetheless.

"I'll be honest with you, Jim. I have a hunch it's her," Plante said.

"It sounds like her," Perrault agreed, nodding his head. "But it can't be," he added. "It was a man's voice."

"Do you know where she was yesterday?"

"I think . . . I think she went to the Holyoke Mall—some sort of Internet place . . . the Worldwide Café . . . something like that. I guess she logged on to the Internet for some reason. Who knows?"

"Thanks," Plante said. "That could help us out."

* * *

It was late Friday afternoon. Bill Welch had already left earlier that day to be with his family for the weekend, and Murphy had been working another case and was nowhere to be found. Plante wanted to be on the Mass Pike with a hot cup of coffee in his hand traveling back to Bedford for a long weekend with his wife and kids. Fridays were precious. All he thought about was seeing his wife and children.

But Plante was a doer. He couldn't leave things unfinished. Having an open lead on his desk all weekend would ruin the little time he had with his family. There was nothing worse than figuring something out, but being ninety miles away from the case when it hit.

So he decided, on September 27, to visit the Holyoke Mall and see what he could uncover. There was something there. He could sense it. What Perrault said bothered him. Gilbert wouldn't go to the mall unless she had something in mind.

The Holyoke Mall at Ingleside was a fifteen-minute drive from Gilbert's Easthampton apartment. The town of Holyoke sits just below the mall to the east. The famous Mount Tom ski resort, where teenagers and families flock to by the bus loads during winter months, overlooks the mall to the north. A look to the south, and Springfield rises out of the mountains as if it were Emerald City.

Plante visited the Worldwide Café first, which was located on the main level. He asked the manager if it was possible to search the computers to see who had logged on to the Internet the previous day.

"Sure," the manager said. "That'll be easy."

They searched to see if Gilbert had been stupid enough to use her own name when she had logged on.

Not a chance.

Then Plante had him try Gilbert's maiden name.

"Strickland," he said. "Try Kristen Strickland."

But again, nothing.

Plante then pulled out a current picture of Gilbert.

"You recognize this woman?"

"No, sir. Sorry."

Another dead end.

Plante was hoping to track Gilbert's movements via her surf through cyberspace, but she had obviously used a bogus name.

He was curious as to why she had browsed the Internet in the first place. *What role did the Internet play in all of this?* Although he believed it was definitely Gilbert who had made the threat, Plante didn't believe she had actually planted a bomb inside the building. She was all about making threats; not carrying them out. Her kind of criminal, Plante had learned from experience, rarely went through with threats. The thrill was in the threat itself. Like poking an animal in a cage to see what kind of reaction she would get, Gilbert prodded and pushed people and then ran away to watch their reaction.

Walking out of the café, Plante had a thought as he stopped for a moment and looked across the walkway.

Why not check all the stores in the mall that sell electronic devices?

Directly across the aisle from the Worldwide Café was Service Merchandise. But after a careful search through the electronics department, he came up empty-handed.

Then it was on to Sears. But again, nothing. Then Brookstones.

Nothing.

By the time he reached KB-Toys, Plante realized he was probably on some sort of wild-goose chase. But maybe, he thought, he had been looking at it from the wrong angle all along? He had to try to piece together what Gilbert was thinking at the time she was at the mall.

While he was in KB-Toys, Plante found a device that could change the tone of a person's voice, but it was more of a microphone-type of device, similar to a karaoke machine. It was too big and bulky. There was no way Gilbert could have toted it around.

But KB-Toys opened the floodgates: *Toys. She had used a kid's toy.* Then he remembered Toys-R-Us was right around the corner from the Worldwide Café, back up on the main level.

The manager of Toys-R-Us, Ann Millett, was all ears when Plante flashed his badge and asked her the question that perhaps blew the entire bomb-threat investigation wide open.

"Do you sell a device that can change the tone of a person's voice?"

"Sure," Millett said. "Come right over here, and I'll show it to you."

Millett then lead Plante to the electronics department. There was a wide array of devices to choose from: everything from karaoke machines to tape recorders to large robot-type machines that a child could record different sounds on. It was overwhelming at first. But Plante realized he had hit the jackpot. Somewhere within this pile of toys was what he had been looking for all day.

As he stood for a moment in deep thought, scanning each toy, Millett pointed out something specific.

"It's called a Talkgirl. It's the most popular of all these types of toys," she said.

Plante looked at it and smiled.

"Is it possible to find out if someone purchased one of these toys yesterday?"

"Certainly. We can check the sku number on the package itself."

"Can you do that right now?"

"No problem."

"How 'bout credit card receipts? Is there any way we can see if someone purchased a toy like this"—Plante held it up like a trophy—"with a credit card?"

"Most certainly."

On September 5, at the request of a grand jury subpoena, Gilbert was ordered to give "handwriting exemplars" to the Northampton DA's office, which she did without incident. That same day, Plante fingerprinted her and took several photos. It would be piece of cake to match her fingerprints and her handwriting with any evidence culled from Ann Millett's search.

Within a few minutes, Millett plucked a receipt from a pile, lifting it up in the air as if she had found a lost lottery ticket, and said, "Here it is right here."

Sure enough, Gilbert had used her VISA card to purchase a Talkgirl toy at two P.M. on the afternoon of September 26—the day of the bomb threat.

CHAPTER 56

While Plante made his way east on the Mass Pike to go home for the weekend, his new toy sitting securely in a bag next to him on the front seat, James Perrault was finishing up making his first two-hour sweep of the VAMC grounds. It was Friday night. For Perrault, the work week would be over in about six hours.

When he finally sat down at the security desk to man the phones, it was just after five o'clock. Perrault was tired. It had been an emotionally draining couple of days.

As soon as he got comfortable in his chair, the phone rang.

This time, Perrault was prepared. NYNEX had been informed there might be more calls, so it was waiting to run a trace.

"VA Officer Perrault speaking. How may I help you?"

"You did very well during last night's trial run," the caller said, and hung up.

There was no doubt in Perrault's mind it was the same caller as the previous night. But this time he heard something familiar in the voice that hadn't really dawned on him the day before. Earlier that morning, he had come to the conclusion it was probably Gilbert who had made the calls. Who else could it have been? Still, there was that one problem: It was a man's voice. If it had been Gilbert, he figured, she had to have been using some sort of device that changed the tone of her very distinctive voice.

At 6:38, one more call came in: "The next time you won't get so long," the caller threatened.

Perrault phoned NYNEX to see if someone had been successful in "trapping" the call.

"Sorry," the operator said. The calls weren't long enough.

When Perrault returned to work on Monday afternoon, after having the weekend off, he wasn't surprised to learn that the VAMC hadn't received one strange phone call in his absence.

Over the weekend, a kid playing with his friends out in the center courtyard of 182 Northampton Street kicked his ball into the bushes, reached down to grab it, and noticed a familiar-looking toy just sitting there.

It was a voice-changing device—a pink Talkgirl—just like the one Plante had bought at Toys-R-Us.

Samantha Harris, when she later found out that the kid had found the toy, asked him where.

"Over there," the kid said, pointing to the bushes.

Gilbert's window was directly above where the kid was pointing.

A day later, something clicked in Harris's mind. So she went to the boy's mother and told her to call Plante or Murphy. "It could mean something," she said. "Kristen's window is right above where he found it."

The woman said she didn't want to get involved. It was a kid's toy. What kind of trouble could Gilbert get herself into with a child's toy?

Harris decided to call Plante and Murphy herself, just to make sure the toy didn't hold any significance.

The day the kid found the toy, he played with it, but couldn't get it to work. It kept malfunctioning.

On Monday morning, the boy took it to school and showed it off to some friends. They were impressed. They passed it around all morning—that is, until the teacher took it away because it was disrupting her class.

She, in turn, handed it over to the principal.

By the time Harris had gotten hold of Plante and Murphy and they tracked down the boy's mother and went to the school, the Talkgirl had gone through so many different hands that it was impossible to extract any fingerprints from it.

On Monday night, September 30, around six o'clock, Gilbert returned to the Holyoke Mall and walked into the Toys-R-Us for the second time in four days.

Combing the aisles, she found what she was looking for within minutes and headed up to the cash register.

"Will you take a check?" Gilbert asked the clerk, Stephanie Lussier, as she placed her one item, this time a Talkboy, Jr., on the counter.

The only noticeable differences between the Talkgirl and Talkboy are the size and color: The Talkboy is about the size of a paperback book and comes in more masculine colors of gray and blue; the Talkgirl, a little bit bigger than a pack of cigarettes, comes in pink and lavender.

"As long as you have some ID," Lussier said.

"I'm concerned about the size of the batteries this thing takes," Gilbert said. "What size batteries do I need?"

The box clearly stated that the toy took four double-A batteries. Gilbert, undoubtedly worried that she might purchase the wrong size batteries and waste time returning them, asked Lussier to open the box to make sure. She wanted the toy to be in working condition the minute she walked out of the store.

While she tore open the box, Lussier turned the carton over and pointed out to Gilbert that the toy took four double-A batteries.

"See," she said. "Right there. It says four double-A batteries. Those you have in your hand will do the job."

"Are you sure? I don't want to get home and find out they don't fit," Gilbert said. She seemed frustrated. "Open it and make sure."

"They'll fit, ma'am. I'm positive."

Lussier then placed the batteries in the toy.

"See."

"Nice toy, huh?" Gilbert said, holding it up in the air, staring at it. She was a bit more relaxed now that she knew the toy was in working condition.

"Sure is," Lussier said politely, placing it in a bag.

"You know . . . it's a gift for my nephew," Gilbert offered, smiling.

"I'm sure he'll love it, ma'am," Lussier said as Gilbert left.

For some reason, Gilbert felt the need to lie; she didn't have a nephew.

An hour or so later, when Gilbert stopped at her apartment for a moment, she ran into Samantha Harris, who was sitting outside watching her son play with some of the other children who lived nearby.

Harris didn't even want to bump into Gilbert anymore. And she didn't feel like participating in Plante and Murphy's version of *Murder, She Wrote* much longer. It was dangerous. Gilbert was still calling her three and four times a day, and showing up at her door unannounced. Sooner or later, she was going to catch on to what Harris had been doing.

"Hello," Harris said as Gilbert walked up to her. She seemed to be in a really good mood, Harris noticed. It was odd.

"You'll never guess where I was today," Gilbert said.

"I give up. Where, Kristen?"

"I went to the Holyoke Mall. You know they have an Internet coffee shop up there now?" Smiling, she seemed thrilled at the prospect. Harris, on the other hand, was unimpressed. She just wanted Gilbert to go away.

"So I've heard," Harris said, nodding her head.

"The Internet is amazing. I mean, do you know how easy it was for me to download a bomb recipe?"

"That's nice, Kristen," Harris said. "But I have to go inside and get dinner started."

"I'll call you later then."

Later that same night, after Harris had readied her son for bed and began to wind down herself, Gilbert made good on her promise. And as soon as Harris picked up the phone, she knew immediately something had happened.

"Did Jim call? Did he check up on me today?" Gilbert asked.

It had been the second time that day Gilbert had asked the same question. She was forever preoccupied with Perrault's inquiries as to where she was and what she was doing.

"It was almost as if she wasn't able to function," Harris later recalled, "without knowing that Jim had inquired about her." But at the same time, because she was following him around and vandalizing his car so much, she was also worried that Perrault might have seen her and told Harris and her husband what she had done.

"Not that I know of," Harris said.

"Well, ask Phillip," Gilbert insisted.

Harris's husband had indeed spoken to Perrault earlier that day. Perrault told him that his car had been damaged again, and he knew Gilbert had done it.

The reason Perrault had called right after he found out about the vandalism was because he wanted to know if Phillip had seen Gilbert or her car. "No," Phillip told him.

Harris held her hand over the receiver so Gilbert couldn't hear what was being said. She debated for a moment if she should lie and tell her that Perrault hadn't called, or just tell her the truth. Her choices weren't exactly welcoming: Either Gilbert was going to catch Harris in a lie or realize that Perrault had lied to her and that Phillip was covering for him. It was obvious Perrault had called Gilbert already and given her hell for vandalizing his car. Besides, Perrault and Harris had decided not to let Gilbert know that they were conferring with each other.

To avoid any fuss, Harris said, *"Yes,* Jim *did* call! He asked Phillip where you were. What time you had gone out and what time you got home."

Gilbert didn't say anything.

"Kristen, you there?"

After a moment, Gilbert dropped her voice down real low and said, "Twit . . . fucking twit!"

"What did you say, Kristen?"

"Okay . . . okay . . . Sami, I have to go."

Harris went into her bedroom, and made the day's entry in her diary. The following morning, she woke to find her car had been vandalized.

"I guess it was my payback," she later said, "for talking to Jim."

CHAPTER 57

Karen Abderhalden was sitting at the VAMC Admissions desk at 6:40 P.M., on Monday, September 30, 1996, when the phone rang.

Using the same disguise, the caller said, "Pay close attention to this message. . . ."

"Excuse me?" Abderhalden said.

"Remember the bomb scare a week ago?" the caller asked.

"Yes!" Abderhalden answered.

The caller hung up.

By this time, there wasn't anyone at the VAMC who didn't think it was Gilbert making the calls. In fact, Abderhalden recognized the voice immediately as being Gilbert's because she knew it so well. The two had recently lived together for three weeks. Gilbert would phone Abderhalden every day and ask her what was going on at the hospital. "Are people talking about me? What are they saying? Are the investigators asking a lot of questions?" One time, Gilbert even put the blame on her old boss, Melodie Turner, telling Abderhalden, "I think they ought to investigate Melodie."

Now, though, with the caller using a disguise, something else occurred to Abderhalden when she heard the voice for the first time.

She had a fourteen-year-old son who had a tiny tape recorder he used to go around the house and tape everyone with. She

also owned the movie *Home Alone II* and had seen it more times
than she wanted to admit. When she heard the caller's voice, it
immediately reminded her of the movie and her son's zany an-
tics.

So Abderhalden called Perrault after the caller hung up on
her and explained to him what had just happened.

"Thanks, Karen," he said. "It'll probably continue . . . just
let me know if you receive any more calls."

Shortly after hanging up with Abderhalden, at 6:44, the security desk phone rang.

"Officer Perrault speaking . . ."

There was silence. Then the caller hung up.

A few moments later, however, the caller called back.

"Is this Officer Perrault?" the caller asked.

"Yes, this is Officer Perrault."

"I've been watching you, boy." This time it sounded like a
woman trying desperately to disguise her voice as a man's.

"Sir, uh . . ." Perrault tried explaining before the line went
dead.

It occurred to Perrault that beside the fact that he was being
addressed now by name, there was something noticeably different about the caller's voice from the previous times. Whoever it
was had gotten pretty comfortable with what he or she was saying. The only difference Perrault noticed tonight was that the
caller had tried, as Perrault later described it, to put a "Southern
drawl" into his speech and sounded as if he was drunk.

Gilbert's imitation of a drunken Southerner, however, failed.
Perrault, the first time he heard the new voice, did everything he
could not to laugh.

Ironically, not a minute after Gilbert, posing as the mysterious caller, called and hung up, the security phone rang once
again. Perrault thought for sure it was going to be another
threatening call.

But it wasn't. Instead, it was Gilbert calling as herself. She
was curious about something.

"What do you think about the bomb threats?" Gilbert asked.
She explained that she had read about them in the newspaper.

"I don't know, Kris. I'm real busy right now."

"What about those newspaper articles? They said there were
only four calls."

"Yeah . . . so?"

"Hadn't there been more calls than that?"

"I can't talk about it, Kris. I have to go now," Perrault said before hanging up.

About a half hour went by without another call. Then, at 7:42, the phone rang again at Karen Abderhalden's desk.

"Don't transfer this call. I was paid by a police officer a week ago, in Northampton, to make the threatening call," Gilbert said, sounding halfheartedly distressed, in the same drunken Southern drawl, referring to the calls on September 26 and 27.

Almost immediately afterward, the Ward C nurse's station upstairs took a call.

"Hello, I met a police officer in a bar last Saturday night, and he paid me fifty dollars to make the bomb threat."

Two hours later, Perrault picked up the phone at the security desk, and the caller simply said, "Officer Perrault?"

"Yes?"

Silence.

"Hello . . . ?"

Then she breathed heavily and hung up.

Ten minutes later: "VA Police Officer Perrault speaking, how may I help you?"

"What makes you think my problem is personal?" Gilbert asked in her Southern voice.

Perrault heard some clicking in the background. It sounded to him as if someone were pounding on a computer keyboard, as if maybe Gilbert were taking notes as they spoke.

"Well, sir," Perrault said, "you seem to be directing it toward me, sir. I don't know if it's personal or not. I'm a Gulf War veteran, and you used my name, so I tend to think you're directing it toward me."

There was a long pause.

"What do you think?" Perrault asked when he got no response.

"Do you think that I am stupid?" Gilbert said, her voice bellowing a long, drawn-out Southern drawl as if she were speaking in slow motion.

"No, I don't think you're stupid, sir. I just think that we have a problem that we have to work out."

Another long pause.

"Are you there?"

The line was dead.

For the remainder of his shift, Perrault and the VAMC staff waited, anticipating more calls. By this time, he had been schooled by Plante and Murphy enough to know that he somehow had to keep Gilbert on the line if they were going to prove it was, in fact, her making the calls. They wanted her to reveal something substantial. Maybe a town. A street sign. A piece of information that only someone who had worked at the VAMC could have known—a smoking gun: Gilbert, on tape, admitting it had been her the entire time. They thought that if Perrault provoked her enough, she might become enraged, drop the Talkboy, and lash out at him in real time, in her own voice. Besides, there was still that sixty-four-thousand-dollar question that nearly everyone wanted an answer to: "If you're innocent of the crimes you're being investigated for, why, then, are you phoning bomb threats into a federal institution?"

Gilbert must have sensed they were on to her, because after the "Do you think that I am stupid?" call, she didn't call back.

CHAPTER 58

Monday, September 30, had been a long day—and even longer night—for James Perrault and most of the VAMC staff involved in the bomb-threat debacle. They had been through several days of what amounted to terrifying phone calls from someone they now presumed might also be a murderer.

It was no secret that the events were, in everyone's assessment, escalating. If Gilbert was capable of killing her own patients, and truly believed the entire VAMC staff was "out to get her," what was she capable of doing to get even?

After the end of his shift on September 30, James Perrault found solace the same way he had on many nights: at the VAMC Rec Hall gym. Three or four times a week, Perrault went to the Rec Hall and lifted weights. Lately, though, spending time in the Rec Hall was twofold. The time and energy he burnt working out not only benefited his appearance and physical strength, but also took his mind off the utter chaos that had been going on around him.

As he often did after working out, Perrault stopped at the Michael C. Curtain VFW on Meadow Street, just down the street from the VAMC. It was a convenient place to stop and unwind after a night of work. Beers were cheap. Talk was casual. Playing pool helped kill some time and take his mind off things.

It had been a rough summer. Hell, the last year had been anything but normal. Going down to the bar after work and discussing things with colleagues and locals over a few cold ones seemed to take a little bit of the sting out of the events.

Plante and Murphy had been telling Perrault right along that it was possible Gilbert had murdered forty patients during her seven-year tenure at the VAMC. It was an unthinkable crime. Perrault couldn't fathom how a person could do such a thing. The thought of Gilbert's killing someone during her shift and Perrault's bedding down with her the same night made him sick to his stomach.

But that was only the half of it. As almost everyone knew, Perrault's dream was to become a cop one day. He talked about it all the time. Regardless of what anybody said, he knew his track record during this investigation would unquestionably have something to do with his future in law enforcement. He had to forget about Gilbert and focus on helping Murphy and Plante. He had no other choice.

Around 11:55, after a quick workout and shower, Perrault flung the solid oak VFW bar door open, walked up to the bar, and sat down.

"Whatcha havin' tonight, Jimmy?" Jane Moran, the nighttime VFW barmaid, said in a flinty, nice-to-see-ya voice. It was comforting to Perrault.

"Same thing, Janey."

Sipping his beer, Perrault ran his hand through his military-cropped haircut and stared blankly at the projection television at the bar.

Earlier that day, he had received an odd letter from Gilbert.

Gilbert wrote that while she was out driving one night she just happened to be going by the VFW and, wouldn't you know it, she spied Perrault's car out in the front parking lot. She said she "couldn't help herself," so she pulled in. Instead of going in and saying hi, however, she said she stood outside the window, just watching him as he threw darts. After a while, she left. Seeing him like that and not being part of his life, she said, was just too much to bear.

Perrault shook his head. He was appalled. "I never lied to you about loving you," Gilbert's letter ended.

"Hey, Jimmy, you got a phone call," Janey yelled.

It was a few minutes past midnight.

Perrault motioned that he would take the call in the lobby. It was odd, he thought, someone phoning him at the bar at this hour. The only person he knew to have done that in the past was Gilbert. And there was certainly no reason for her to be calling him at the bar, especially since she didn't even know where he was.

"Yeah . . . hello?"

"You think you have a problem? Just wait and see what I have planned for you."

It was that same cold, eerie voice. Same speech pattern. Same angry, threatening tone. Same phony Southern drawl, along with the same articulate pronunciation of words and syllables.

Yet something else struck Perrault as he stared out the window, holding the buzzing phone receiver in his hand: It was obvious to him now that Gilbert could have been the only person to know where he was at that exact moment. The timing of the call was too perfect.

"Janey," Perrault quickly yelled from the foyer, "star fifty-seven the call I just got."

"Hold on."

It didn't work. Gilbert had again blocked the call.

But Perrault had heard enough. It was time to do something about Gilbert before she did something about him.

CHAPTER 59

October 1, 1996 dawned crisp and cool in Hampshire County. With fall came that cold Canadian air from the north that enveloped the Northeast every year. Within weeks, the leaves on the gigantic maples around town would be bursting a fiery collage of blood red, pumpkin orange, coppery-bronze and sun yellow. Tourists would be swirling around, settling in to rooms at local inns, and clogging local restaurants. All here to take in the breathtaking view of the foliage.

Perrault had scheduled a meeting at the Northampton DA's office before his shift. Gilbert was out of control, he told Plante on the phone earlier that day. Her behavior was turning vindictive, violent. If letting the air out of Perrault's tires and keying the cars of just about everyone who had ever been involved in the case weren't enough, now she was following him around.

What would she do next?

When Perrault introduced himself to the secretary in the DA's office, she phoned Detective Thomas Soutier, and let him know Perrault had shown up a bit early.

"Send him to my office," Soutier said.

Detective Soutier knew why Perrault was there, and he wanted to make him feel comfortable while he waited for Murphy and Plante.

"How's your job search going?" Soutier asked. "I understand you're applying at several local police departments."

The detective seemed excited. They had something in common. A bit of small talk might do them both some good and maybe loosen Perrault up a bit. It was obvious he was uncomfortable about going to the DA's office.

"It's slow," Perrault said, regarding his search for a job in law enforcement. "I'm concerned that my involvement in the murder investigation will taint my possibilities of *ever* being a cop."

"If there ever comes a point in time that anyone questions your part in the murder investigation, Jim," Detective Soutier said sincerely, "feel free to have them call me, and I will explain everything."

"Thanks. I appreciate that."

Soutier, Murphy and Plante considered Perrault to be a professional. He acted mature, and they agreed between themselves that he would probably make a fine cop one day. He was a good man who had made a few bad choices and was trying his best to clean up the mess.

An hour before Perrault showed up for the meeting, Plante had one of the female clerks in the office make a recording into the Talkgirl Plante had purchased at the Toys-R-Us just days ago—one of the calls—verbatim—that the VAMC had received. Before that, Plante had his wife record her own voice into the Talkgirl. He wanted to be sure it was possible to change a woman's voice into a man's.

The experiment had worked perfectly.

Detectives Murphy and Soutier, along with Bill Welch and Plante, agreed they wouldn't tell Perrault they had made a recording of the clerk. They would simply play the tape and see what Perrault's reaction was. It was a bit devious, perhaps. But it would certainly produce an unbiased opinion of what they believed to be the truth—that there was absolutely no way in hell James Perrault could mistake Kristen Gilbert's voice for somebody else's, disguise or no disguise. Perrault knew her possibly better than anyone.

After listening to the tape, Perrault identified the "distortion and background noise" as being similar to that in the calls he had received, but there was a problem recognizing the caller's voice. It sounded similar, he said, meaning "metallicky" and "mechanical sounding," but he could tell from the tone and inflections that it was definitely not Gilbert.

It wasn't necessarily something they could use as evidence in court, but at least it told the detectives that Perrault could discriminate between Gilbert's voice and somebody else's.

"We figure Gilbert made the calls from the phone booth at the Look Restaurant across the street," Plante, who had just walked into the room, said. "The traffic sounds are what lead us to believe that. What do you think, Jim?"

"I'll buy that," Perrault answered.

"We need you to do something," Murphy, who had also come in with Plante, then suggested. "When you get to work today, after you make your usual rounds, we want you to call her."

Perrault agreed.

Murphy then explained that he would conduct surveillance around the immediate area of Gilbert's apartment—especially the pay telephone booths, both north and south of where she lived. Easthampton was farming country. Beside the fast-food restaurants, gas stations and car dealerships found in any town, there really wasn't much to it. There was only one main road, Route 10, which ran perpendicular through town in a north-south direction. Telephone booths were spotty. Putting a cop at one for the evening would be a piece of cake. And if Gilbert was dumb enough to be making the mistakes she had been making up until that point, being fingered wasn't something Plante or Murphy had to worry about.

Plante would be on the other side of town, driving back and forth between several phone booths, but concentrating mainly on the one in the parking lot of the *Daily Hampshire Gazette*.

Before the surveillance, Plante had driven by every pay phone in the area and jotted down their numbers. It had been agreed that when a call came in, someone would get hold of NYNEX, who was now working closely with them, to see if a trace turned up a match to any one of the numbers Plante had written down. NYNEX had already placed a pen register, at the request of Plante and Murphy, on Gilbert's home phone. If, for some reason, she decided to make calls from her apartment, the pen register, in real time, would tell the investigators whom she was calling.

It wasn't rocket science—just good, solid police work.

At 5:12, as he said he would, Perrault called Gilbert's apartment. She wasn't home—or wasn't answering the phone. So he left a message on her answering machine.

"I'll be at the security desk until seven o'clock. Call me."

Around 5:30, the security desk phone rang. As luck would have it, it was the mysterious VAMC bomber.

Gilbert didn't say much of anything that Perrault could understand during the first call; her words were garbled and inaudible, as if the recording device she was using had once again malfunctioned. But if everyone's assumptions were correct, she wouldn't stop there. It was a game to her now, an obsession. Murphy and Plante had investigated criminals similar to Gilbert in the past. As they saw it, like an active alcoholic, there was no way she could just stop.

Between 5:40 and 6:30, Gilbert made several more calls. Most were brief and rather indiscernible. Yet she began to reveal an entirely different side of herself that no one had anticipated.

In the first call, disguising her voice once again in a thick and slow Southern drawl, she asked, "What can I do to make you understand what's going on here . . . ?"

"Well," Perrault said, "you can talk to me and tell me what's going on. I mean, I'm—"

"—Oh, man, her pussy taste so sweet," Gilbert said, cutting in on Perrault, before she hung up.

A few moments later, "I'm going to fuck your bitch, Perrault."

"Why would you want to do that?"

There was a pause. Then, ". . . until she begs . . ." before the line went dead.

A minute later, "Officer Perrault speaking, how may I . . ."

"I really enjoy looking in the window of Apartment D, James Perrault. She looks mighty fine today in those . . ."

Perrault tried interrupting, but his voice was squelched by Gilbert's.

"Well, she is available," Perrault tried insisting. "If you want to go out with her, you can call her up."

When he realized that it was useless to try to interact with a recording, Perrault stopped talking and let it finish.

". . . I got a hard one just thinking about it. I been following her . . ."

Perrault couldn't help himself, thinking maybe Gilbert was listening somehow. So he said, "Why don't you talk to her and see about doing something?"

"I been seeing her around, James Perrault . . . I know where she's been today."

"Where *has* she been today?"

The line went dead.

A minute later, Perrault picked up the phone again.

At first, all he heard was a loud buzzing sound. So he tried to get things going. It was possible that Gilbert was just hanging on the line, waiting for the right time to press the PLAY button on the Talkboy.

"Sir, do you have a problem with me?" Perrault asked. "I mean, I know you happen to like my ex-girlfriend. And from what I understand, you happen to like me. . . . I personally am not into that. But if you would like to talk to me, I'll see what we could arrange. You know, give me a call, talk to me face to face . . . do something."

Perrault seemed to be letting the calls get the best of him by this point. His tone kept rising as he spoke. He was getting frustrated.

"I'm tired . . . tired of the little threats," he said, "so . . . so . . . why don't you *do somethin'?*"

There was a sigh—then a long, heavy breath.

"Well," Perrault said, "breathing sounds nice." He could hear someone tapping on a computer keyboard in the background. "Hello . . . is anybody there?"

Gilbert hung up.

Shortly after that, the phone rang again.

"This is . . . so . . . I can go in and *fuck* her brains out," Gilbert said, again disguising her voice as the Southern black man.

Surprisingly, around 5:50, Gilbert phoned the security office.

"Hi, it's Kristen," she said in a soft and innocent voice.

When Perrault asked her why she was calling, Gilbert said she had received several "sexually graphic" phone calls the previous night, September 30, and into the early morning hours of

October 1, from the same person who, she believed, had been calling the VAMC. She thought Perrault needed to know.

"The calls," Gilbert said, "were very demeaning to you, Jim. That's why I'm calling you."

Confused, or perhaps overwhelmed by her gall, Perrault demanded an explanation.

"Well, the caller said he has given you so much information about himself that he can't believe you haven't caught him by now. He said you couldn't police a 7-Eleven . . . that you're nothing but a rent-a-cop."

"Is that right?" Perrault asked sarcastically. "What did the caller sound like? How many calls did you receive?"

"About five. He sounded like . . . like a Southern black male."

"Listen, Kris, why don't you star fifty-seven the calls? Maybe you can trace them back and find out who it is . . . you know, where he's calling from? I mean, if you're that scared—"

Gilbert cut him off. "I can't do that," she said.

"Why not?"

"Well . . . I don't want to be dragged into the investigation. Let's just keep this between you and me, Jimmy. Okay?"

"You *can* help, though . . ."

"Actually," Gilbert said, interrupting Perrault, "if you really want me to, I'll try that star fifty-seven thing."

After a bit more small talk, Perrault said he had to go.

CHAPTER 60

At 6:30 P.M., on October 1, Murphy pulled into the Tasty Top Ice Cream Stand and drove his blue Crown Victoria toward the back of the empty lot. After carefully assessing the situation, he parked where he had a good view of several pay telephone booths in the area.

He then lit a cigarette, reclined back in his seat, and waited to see if Gilbert would make a move.

Across town, about four miles away, Plante sat in the parking lot of the *Daily Hampshire Gazette* newspaper on Conz Street. He was running the same type of surveillance at a phone booth NYNEX had earlier confirmed could have been used to make some of the earlier calls.

The Tasty Top was a popular summer stop for area families, located smack dab in the middle of town on Route 10, just a half mile down the street from Gilbert's apartment.

From where he sat in his car, Murphy was confident that if Gilbert decided to use any one of five phone booths around him, he would have no problem seeing her. Just fifty feet to his left there was a booth straddling Route 10, on the north side of the street, directly to the right of Tasty Top's walk-up counter. It was one of the newer booths, open on all sides, with two small panels fanning out from each end like an old wicker chair. Across the street, at a BP gas station, there was a standing booth. Next door to the Tasty Top was a Burger King. Along the side of the building was yet another booth. Looking south, Murphy could see Gilbert's apartment complex down below the crest of the hill.

It was a waiting game now.

Murphy was a practical man. With twenty-six years on the job, there wasn't too much he hadn't seen. But for the life of him, he had never witnessed a suspect he was investigating commit a crime right in front of his face.

As he put out his first cigarette and prepared to light another, the veteran homicide detective looked up and couldn't believe his eyes: there was Gilbert's 1993 Oldsmobile Cutlass pulling into the parking lot.

She had taken a left off Route 10 and made a U-turn into the parking lot, nearly clipping Murphy's cruiser in the process, yet she hadn't even seen him.

"You've *got* to be kidding me," Murphy said to himself. "Will you get a load of this shit?"

Gilbert parked right in front of his car. He could have spit on her back windshield from where he was sitting. With the tail end of Gilbert's car facing him, Murphy verified her license plate number with dispatch. Gilbert, wearing a pair of blue jeans and an outdoor-type winter jacket, her blond hair blowing in the slight wind, got out of her car, looked around, and walked up to the phone booth.

It was 6:35 P.M.

Murphy quickly picked up his radio and called his lieutenant to see if Plante was within radio range.

"Steve is not going to believe this," Murphy said. He was almost laughing.

Plante had since moved on to the Look Restaurant, about five miles away, which was just across the street from the VAMC. They had learned earlier that day that Gilbert had used the Look Restaurant phone booth on several occasions. So he had been roaming back and forth, between Conz Street and the Look Restaurant.

"Plante, you there?" Murphy whispered into his radio, his eyes glued on Gilbert.

"Go ahead, Murph . . ."

"You're not going to believe this. She just pulled in and . . . she's using the phone booth right in front of me."

"No way?"

"No shit. I'm serious."

"I'll call the VA to see if Jimmy received any calls."

Plante called Perrault at the VAMC.

"Anything going on over there, Jim?"

"I just took a call," Perrault said. "I could hear a lot of traffic in the background. The caller breathed heavy and hung up."

As Murphy sat in his cruiser watching Gilbert use the phone, he faced several problems. First of all, knowing what he knew, should he arrest her, or just let her go and secure the scene? Or maybe he should follow her? Murphy worked for the state police. This was a federal crime. Did he have jurisdiction? Murphy and Plante, working closely with Bill Welch, had taken careful steps not to cross paths between federal and state law.

Gilbert was at the Tasty Top telephone booth for twenty-five seconds, which was just enough time to make one call, hang up, and get back in her car.

NYNEX was contacted to make sure the call Perrault had received had, in fact, come from the Tasty Top phone booth. It was a match; the number NYNEX traced was the same as one of those SA Plante had earlier written down.

As Gilbert backed out, she turned her car to the right and ended up directly facing Murphy's cruiser. He did everything he could not to mock her with a sarcastic smile and a wave of his hand. But Murphy didn't say or do anything, deciding instead to let her leave.

Gilbert must have driven directly from the Tasty Top straight to her apartment, which, Plante had already timed, was a mere sixty-second ride. At 6:42, she called Perrault at the security office for the second time that night.

"He called again!" Gilbert said, referring to the Southern male. She was out of breath. "He's making fun of my anatomy, Jimmy. He left messages on my answering machine."

She was frantic, babbling, on the verge of tears.

"Hold on. Hold on," Perrault said, trying to calm her down. "Save those messages."

"I won't. I'm going to erase them!" she said before hanging up.

Then she called back five minutes later.

"Can you help me do something about the calls, Jimmy? I'm

really concerned. I think he's following me around. Help me." She was panicking, talking fast. "Please help me . . ."

As clearly as he could, Perrault said no. Then he paused for a moment, perhaps to add a bit more weight to his next suggestion, and added, "Call the Easthampton Police if you want help."

It was now near seven o'clock. Perrault had to leave his post at the security desk for a while to attend to other matters.

At 7:35, an officer filling in for Perrault took a call. The voice was "distorted, male-sounding, and strange," he later told Plante and Murphy.

During the interim, NYNEX confirmed that the previous calls—the sexually graphic ones—were made from the Condor Citgo gas station, which was about four miles from Gilbert's apartment, and the *Daily Hampshire Gazette* parking lot phone booth.

Gilbert had obviously thought she was smart, running from phone booth to phone booth, hoping to avoid any chance of a trap.

Murphy, meanwhile, had secured the Tasty Top phone booth as a crime scene. Detective Soutier showed up shortly afterward, with Plante not far behind.

Soutier arranged for the Massachusetts State Police Crime Scene Services to dust the phone booth for fingerprints.

In the meantime, several other troopers were called in to do various tasks. The most important, seeing that Gilbert had without question seen Murphy as she was driving out of the parking lot, was to put an unmarked cruiser in the area of her apartment. While Plante and Bill Welch applied for a search warrant, they wanted to be sure Gilbert wouldn't run. Things were moving at a feverish pace now. They had to act fast. Every decision was critical.

About a half hour went by. Agents confirmed that one of the prints pulled from the Tasty Top telephone receiver was that of Gilbert's right index finger.

Welch, who had been maintaining a careful watch on the situation from the DA's office, and Plante then took off for the town of Amherst, about ten miles away, where they were to meet with Judge Michael Ponsor at the Amherst Police Department.

At 9:10, Judge Ponsor signed a search warrant filed by Plante. It was for a search and seizure of any and all pieces of evidence used in making a false bomb threat to the VAMC on September 26 that might be found inside Gilbert's Easthampton apartment or her Oldsmobile Cutlass.

"I find reasonable cause to initiate and conduct the search after ten P.M.," Judge Ponsor wrote.

He went on to state his reason for issuing a search warrant at such an ungodly hour: to "preserve evidence" immediately.

It was clear from Plante's filing that Gilbert had gone to great lengths within the past few days to block phone calls, obstruct justice, and hinder different parts of both the murder and bomb-threat investigations. They certainly wouldn't put it past her to get rid of evidence if she thought the heat was on. Time was crucial.

So, while Welch and Plante made certain all the paperwork was in order, a posse of state troopers, local police and special agents converged on 182 Northampton Street, Apartment D.

CHAPTER 61

A tough-looking cop at five-eight, one hundred and ninety pounds, Massachusetts State Police Lieutenant Thomas Soutier knocked on Kristen Gilbert's front door at eight P.M. Several of his colleagues, including Detective Murphy, stood behind him—one of whom was carrying a video camera. Welch and Plante were still trying to obtain a copy of the search warrant.

As Soutier and Murphy, along with the rest of the crew, waited patiently on the front steps for Gilbert to come to the door, above them, on the second floor, they heard the squeal of a window being pushed open.

Pushing her face up against the screen, Gilbert shouted, "What do *you* want?"

"Ma'am, we need to come inside now. You need to come to the door," Soutier said.

To preserve the integrity of any search, an "entrance 'in-and-out' video" is shot upon first entering a residence, car, or any area where a search will later be conducted. It is designed to preserve the exact layout of a location before investigators disturb the scene while conducting the actual search. It was important for Welch's team in this case, because they didn't have the search warrant in their hands yet. They wanted to be sure there were no screw-ups. Not now. They were too close to having Gilbert where they wanted her.

After a few moments, Gilbert thumped her way down the

stairs and opened the door. She had been in her child's room—or the room, rather, that her kids had slept in when Glenn used to allow them to visit. It had been almost six weeks since she had lost joint custody. She hadn't seen the children since she entered Glenn's house without permission and attacked him back on September 15, three weeks ago.

After letting everyone in, Gilbert asked what they were looking for.

"We are looking for a *recording device* used to make calls to the VA. We'll be here for a while. You can either stay here or leave, Ms. Gilbert. It's up to you," Soutier said.

Murphy was a bit more impersonal. With his rough and overpowering voice, "We're seizing the house," he said, pushing his way toward Gilbert. "We have a warrant for your car, too. You can leave, but don't touch anything!"

Gilbert went for her pocketbook and began heading for the door.

Murphy took a step to his right, blocking her from going any farther. "No. No. No. That stays here," he said, placing his hand on Gilbert's purse.

A female trooper, Sue Cronin, then rushed over. "That stays with us, ma'am," she said. "But you're welcome to get your house keys out of it."

So Gilbert grabbed her keys and walked out the door. There were a few troopers standing outside, and they watched her as she headed straight for Samantha Harris's apartment.

"Perfect," Murphy said after one of the young troopers came in and told him where she had gone.

While they waited for a copy of the search warrant, one of the troopers made a video recording of the entire apartment. Murphy noticed right away that the light in the children's bedroom upstairs wasn't working. So he ordered a floodlight so they could have some light while they filmed and, later, searched. A video would be made at the end, also, to preserve the aftereffects of the search. This way, while they applied for an arrest warrant, Gilbert, who would be free to come back into the apartment, couldn't accuse them of ransacking the place or, even worse, planting evidence.

Downstairs, just inside the front door, was the living room.

The walls were bare. It was unusual for a woman not to decorate her home. Most women, even single women, made it a priority to pepper their walls, end tables and coffee tables with knick-knacks and pictures. But not Gilbert. Except for one picture, her apartment was empty, as if she had used the place only to sleep in.

Strangely enough, the one picture Gilbert kept in her home was that of her sister Tara. It had been blown up, framed, and hung on the wall above the sofa as if it were some type of homage to her younger sibling.

Even more unusual, however, was that there weren't any pictures of Gilbert's children in the house.

After the entrance video was made and Plante and Bill Welch showed up with the search warrant, the crew snapped on their latex gloves and got to work.

Plante went upstairs, while Soutier took the living room, and Murphy the kitchen.

In the living room, Soutier picked up a notebook that was sitting on the coffee table in plain sight. As soon as he opened it, he knew it was going to be a good night.

"He wishes—he thinks he's a real cop. He's nothing but a rent-a-cop," was scrawled across the inside page, alongside a few obscenities that Soutier guessed were in reference to Perrault, too.

Participating in dozens of searches throughout his twenty-six-year career, Murphy knew exactly where to start in the kitchen: the garbage can. Digging like a possum in a Dumpster, he hit the jackpot right away: three empty packages of Energizer batteries, two batteries and a receipt from Thrifty's Health & Beauty. A quick look at the receipt told him Gilbert had purchased the batteries just days ago.

Sometime later, Soutier, now upstairs in the child's bedroom where Gilbert had been when they showed up, standing inside the closet, buried knee-deep in clothes and toys and boxes, waded through several items and finally reached into a cardboard box and pulled out a Talkboy, Jr.

He then walked into the master bedroom, where Plante was rummaging through Gilbert's closet.

"Whata ya got?"

Soutier smiled. "Take a look at this."

They rewound the tape and listened. But it was mostly static, blank.

Plante placed the Talkboy on the dresser and pointed to several items he had found lying on Gilbert's bed: a book, pen, a few letters, telephone, a copy of the September 27, 1996, edition of the *Daily Hampshire Gazette,* and the jacket she had been wearing when Murphy fingered her at the Tasty Top just a few hours ago.

"What do you make of this stuff?" Plante asked Soutier.

"Check inside the jacket."

In the lefthand pocket, Plante pulled out the operating instructions for the Talkboy.

Next to the jacket, an issue of the *Daily Hampshire Gazette* piqued Plante's attention next. It was soft and worn. He could tell it had been read through several times. There was a headline on page A-3 that immediately stuck out:

BOMB THREATS AT VA PROBED

As Murphy, Plante and Soutier continued the search, Gilbert was at Samantha Harris's apartment climbing the walls.

"Why are they doing this to me? I have done nothing wrong," Gilbert said as she walked through the door.

"Relax," Harris said. "Let me get you a glass of water."

"They say they're looking for a voice-changing device or something. A kid's toy. You know . . . you can change your voice up high, like a chipmunk, or down low like a man," Gilbert said. "It's probably in the kids' room, but there's probably no tape in it . . . it's probably been erased or the batteries are dead or there's no batteries in it."

She was talking in quick-fire repetition. Looking toward the door. Fidgeting with her house keys. Pacing.

What Harris didn't know at the time, but would soon find out, was that Soutier or Murphy never told Gilbert they were looking for a "child's toy." They simply secured the apartment, said they were looking for a "recording device," and told her she could stay or leave.

CHAPTER 62

While Welch and his crew continued with the search, Gilbert called Harry Miles from Harris's apartment and told him what was going on.

Some time later, the tall, balding, gray-haired defense attorney with glasses barged through Harris's front door without even knocking.

"Where is my client?" Miles demanded to know.

Harris was sitting in the living room. Startled, she could think of nothing more to say other than, "Excuse me?"

With his rumpled suit, loud voice and forceful manner, Miles repeated himself: "Where is my client?"

Hesitantly, Harris got up and began to speak. "I think you should have at least—"

Paying no mind to what she was trying to say, Miles cut her off and walked into the kitchen where Gilbert was sitting.

Harris thought it best to stay put. There was no need for her to know what they were talking about. It would mean only more explaining on her part when everything was said and done.

After spending about ten minutes with Gilbert, Miles rushed out of the house without saying a word.

"Come in here," Gilbert yelled from the kitchen.

Harris walked in and sat down. "I don't want to know what your lawyer said to you, Kristen. It's none of my business."

"Don't worry . . . it was . . . nothing." Gilbert was acting strange, Harris noticed.

In what had become one of Gilbert's signatures, her entire mood changed in the blink of an eye. With her arms folded, she was now rocking back and forth in her chair, trembling like a junkie. Every so often, she would stop rocking, run her hands through her hair, and mumble something. She began to sweat and speak in broken sentences. Harris had seen her like this before, but never as bad as she was tonight.

Yet whenever Gilbert wanted to make a point, she would snap out of her trance and speak flawlessly.

In an eerie whisper, she looked at Harris one time and said, "I want you to bring me to the bank, then to the pharmacy . . . and . . . and . . . a hotel."

My God, she's planning on killing herself, Harris thought.

"Why are they doing this to me?" Gilbert asked again. "I haven't *done* anything."

"Come on," Harris said, grabbing Gilbert by the arm. "Let's go."

It was well after eleven now.

As they drove to the ATM machine down the street, Gilbert continued to talk. She wanted Harris to know she was grateful for all she had done. She wanted Harris to understand she wasn't a bad person. "I haven't done anything wrong," she kept repeating. It was everyone else's fault. The VA was out to get her. Perrault was lying. Her coworkers were setting her up.

Gilbert then said she was thankful most of all for the fact that Harris had kept her mouth shut and had never spoken to the investigators.

At that point, Harris just looked at her. *If you only knew. You freakin' lunatic. If you only knew what I've been up to.*

"Listen," Gilbert said. "I want you to bring me into Northampton now." They had already stopped at the ATM machine and pharmacy. Gilbert had plenty of money and a bag of pills.

"I thought you wanted me to bring you to a hotel."

"No!" Gilbert said, getting louder. "Bring me to the bus station!"

"The bus station? Come on, Kristen. I can't do that."

"No. Listen to me. I don't want you to know where I'm going. This way you won't feel obligated to tell them *anything* when they come around asking questions. I mean, they know I came over your house. So you're the first person they're going to when they can't find me."

When Harris pulled into the bus station, Gilbert got out of the car and stopped just short of shutting the door.

"I feel like I can't trust *anyone* anymore," she said.

"You know, Kristen, you probably can't trust anyone."

Gilbert closed the door and walked away.

For Samantha Harris, the night was just beginning.

CHAPTER 63

About an hour after Harris got home, she called Gilbert's apartment and left a message on the answering machine.

"Hi, Kristen . . . just checking up on you to see what's going on. Call me."

A few minutes later, Plante showed up at her door.

"Very funny," he said.

"Come in."

"I suppose that was a signal to come over?"

Harris smiled.

Plante explained that he only had a few minutes. They were meticulously going through everything in Gilbert's apartment, and he had to get back to work as soon as possible.

"I think you'll want to sit down for a minute and hear me out," Harris said.

She brought him up to date and told him everything that had just happened.

"Thanks, Sami. You've been a big help. You know that, don't you?"

It certainly felt good to hear Plante say she had done the right thing by dropping Gilbert off at the bus depot. Harris had felt funny about it up until that point, as if she had been an accomplice in helping Gilbert escape.

Everything was about subterfuge with her, Harris thought as she walked up the stairs toward her bedroom. It was now near midnight, and she had to get up at five A.M. to start her bus route. *She was always trying to lead people in the wrong direction.*

"They're going to arrest her any day now, Phillip," Harris told her husband. He was watching television upstairs. "I can feel it. They're over there digging through her apartment . . . they're going to find something."

"Go to sleep," Phillip said. "It's late. I'll be in bed soon."

An hour later, after Harris and her husband had fallen asleep, the telephone rang. When she picked it up, she could hear someone moaning on the other end of the line.

Here we go . . .

Gilbert sounded groggy and tired, even drugged, Harris thought as she listened.

"Sami . . . is that you?" Gilbert mumbled. "Sami . . . you there?"

"Kristen?"

"I don't feel so . . . good . . . Sami. I feel like—"

It sounded to Harris as if Gilbert had dropped the phone.

"Are you there?" Harris yelled.

There was silence, followed by what sounded like the phone being picked up and dropped.

"You need to call 911, Kristen," Harris said. She was frightened. "Where are you?"

Silence. Then breathing. Then moaning.

"I'm. Going. To. Hang. Up. Now," Harris said slowly, as if she were speaking to a child, "and you're going to call 911."

They went back and forth a few times. Gilbert would mumble something and then drop the phone. Harris would say she was going to hang up, and Gilbert would quickly pick up the phone and, as sober as a doorknob, snap out of it and say, "I'm here. I'm here."

After several more calls, Harris concluded that Gilbert's latest suicide attempt, like all the others, was merely another attempt to put the spotlight on herself. She sounded as if she were play-acting. Harris didn't believe for one minute that the same woman who had falsely attempted suicide time and again throughout the summer was tonight suddenly on the verge of dying.

"I'm hanging up now," Harris said at one point.

"No, don't hang up. I wanted to leave my parents' phone number with you, Sami," Gilbert said.

"Why, Kristen?"

"Call them in the morning and tell them I'm dead." Then she dropped the phone and started moaning.

Jesus, Kristen, could you make it any more obvious?

After a pause, Harris snapped. "Damnitall, Kristen!" she said. "Are you there? Tell me where you are? I'm hanging up now, so you can call 911."

As soon as she heard that, Gilbert picked up the phone again. "I can't deal with this shit anymore. I just can't do it."

Harris hung up.

Gilbert called back.

"Kristen," Harris said in a more relaxed, pleading tone. "You need to call 911. I have no idea where you are. It's late. I have to get up in a few hours and go to work. . . . I'm hanging up now. I have no—"

Gilbert dropped the phone.

Harris hung up.

Two minutes later, Gilbert called back.

"Don't hang up on me, please. . . ." She was crying and slurring her speech.

"You need to call 911! I cannot do anything for you." Harris heard the phone drop. "I'm hanging up. . . ."

"Wait," Gilbert said as she picked the phone back up. "Just wait a minute."

"Kristen, where are you? I'll call Jim or Glenn. One of them can come and get you."

There was a long pause. But Gilbert hadn't dropped the phone this time. Harris could tell she was just holding it, thinking.

"Glenn is not such an intellectual firecracker now, is he?" Gilbert finally said. She began to laugh. "He's stupid, isn't he?"

"Call 911, Kristen. I'm hanging up."

Gilbert called at least another ten times before Harris decided to turn off the ringer and get some sleep.

When Gilbert realized Harris wasn't going to pick up her phone any more, she turned her attention toward her new friend, Carole Osman.

Osman, a divorced mother of two grown daughters, was easy prey for Gilbert. Osman enjoyed living in Northampton and being around the artsy, well-educated class of people Gilbert had fooled everyone into thinking she fit in with. In her late forties, Osman kept few friends and hadn't become friendly with Gilbert until after the murder investigation had been initiated. Some considered Osman to be "weird" and on the "eccentric" side. Gilbert used to belittle her when they worked together, making fun of her around colleagues whenever she saw the opportunity. Some said Osman was perhaps in the midst of a midlife crisis at the time she went to work at the VAMC. She had been a florist for most of her adult life and, late into her forties, decided to go to nursing school. One VAMC nurse, who had worked with Osman for many years, said she was the most incompetent nurse she had ever seen in some twenty years on the job.

Gilbert must have known that a call to Carole Osman would mean she'd be tracked down—because Osman had two separate phone lines installed in her home, and Gilbert had been over there plenty enough times to know that. But she still called Osman and gave her the same sob story she had just given to Samantha Harris.

Unlike Harris, Carole Osman fell for it hook, line and sinker. She later told Harris that she felt as if Gilbert was "at the end of her rope and near death that night." She felt sorry for her.

Working Osman like a piece of clay, Gilbert carried on and on about her problems and her need to kill herself.

Osman, scared for her life, told Gilbert to hold on for a moment. She had something on the stove she needed to check on before it burnt the house down.

When Gilbert agreed, Osman rushed over to the second phone line and dialed up the Northampton Police Department so they could trace the call.

Osman kept Gilbert on the line while the police learned she was calling from just a few miles down the road—at the local Days Inn, in Northampton.

When the police got to the hotel, Gilbert appeared to be shaken, desolate, and in distress.

But close to death? Not a chance.

Officers from the NPD determined that Gilbert would need psychiatric evaluating and brought her to Cooley Dickinson Hospital.

CHAPTER 64

Confined to the psych ward of Cooley Dickinson, on the morning of October 2, Gilbert decided to retaliate against the one person she saw as being responsible for everything that had just happened—James Perrault—by using the only weapon she had at her disposal: the telephone.

During the first couple of messages she left on Perrault's answering machine, Gilbert said she had suspected for the past month or so that he had been supplying investigators with information about her.

"You fucking prick," Gilbert said into Perrault's answering machine in a deep, threatening tone. "I *know* you're the one behind the search warrant."

It wasn't such a stretch to think that Perrault had something to do with the search warrant. What other choice did he have? Plante and Murphy were telling him that his ex-girlfriend, a woman he had been sleeping with for the past ten months, had possibly killed as many as forty of her patients, maybe even more. What was he supposed to do?

Gilbert went on to say she knew he had broken into her apartment when she wasn't home.

Perrault did have keys to Gilbert's apartment. She had given them to him herself. But what Gilbert didn't know was that every time Perrault had entered her apartment, he had taken

Samantha Harris along with him as a witness for that very reason.

"I will press breaking-and-entering charges against you," she rambled on. "Your police career will be ruined! Do you think that the investigators have any keys to your getting a job? How 'bout when you have a police record . . . huh?"

After Gilbert hung up, she called Samantha Harris.

"I want my fucking keys back, Sami." She sounded different. It wasn't the same person Harris had dropped off at the bus station the night before, or the suicidal victim Harris had spoken to on the phone later on.

Harris wanted to laugh. *You crazy bitch. It's all over for you now.* But she kept her composure.

"You don't need keys to my apartment," Gilbert continued. "I want my fucking keys back."

"I don't have your keys, Kristen."

The psychiatric ward of area hospitals had become a second home to Gilbert by this point. She had been admitted nearly a half-dozen times throughout the summer. Plante and Murphy speculated that it had been Harry Miles putting Gilbert up to all the hospital admissions: telling her that it would help her case if it ever went to court. Regardless, here she was, close to being arrested, doing the same thing she had done all summer along: threatening people from the telephone.

The same day Gilbert called Perrault and Harris, she called her old friend, Rachel Webber.

Webber and her husband had moved to Albany, New York, in late 1994, to raise a family and begin new careers. Gilbert had always stayed in touch, making sure to call Webber once a week and fill her in on all that was going on back in Northampton— that is, the things she wanted Webber to know. But as far as the murder investigation, her affair with Perrault and the end of her marriage were concerned, Gilbert never confided in Webber much more than to dispel rumor.

When Webber first heard about the investigation back in February, she presumed it was a witch hunt. She had a hard time believing what people were saying about her friend. But now, hearing stories from other nurses and reading newspaper accounts, Webber was having second thoughts about Gilbert's innocence. Gilbert had been calling her throughout the summer, yet she would tell her only bits and pieces of what was happening. Gilbert always maintained that Webber was one of her only "true" friends left and would often joke over the phone about the entire situation.

One day, shortly after word had spread that Gilbert was the main suspect in the bomb threat, she called Webber. Laughing, as if nothing were wrong, she said, "This is going to make a good movie someday, huh, Rachel?"

She then went through a list of actors she had handpicked for everyone involved. Still believing Gilbert was being railroaded, Webber laughed with her about it.

Gilbert always kept the juicy details of her real life to herself. Webber would find out from other nurses what was really going on and call Gilbert on it the next time they spoke. Gilbert would explain it all away, and Webber would buy it.

It wasn't a shock to Webber when Gilbert phoned the day after the search and confessed she was once again in the hospital.

"I heard, Kristen. Are you okay?" Webber asked.

"Oh, I'm fine. They thought I did something to myself. They strapped me down and put a tube down my nose. You should have seen them try to fight with me," Gilbert said, laughing.

It occurred to Webber that if there were tubes and stomach pumps involved, well, it must have been serious. *They're pumping her stomach, and she's making light of the situation?* she said to herself as Gilbert continued to mock the doctors.

"What did you do, Kristen?"

"Oh, you know, they thought I took something."

It was a game, Webber told herself after hanging up. Gilbert looked at it as though it were some sort of "me against them" battle she was winning.

As Assistant US Attorney Bill Welch sat in his office during the first week of October, he mulled over his options. Gilbert was, at least for the time being, out of everyone's hair. But Welch hardly had his suspect where he wanted her: confined to a cold, eight-by-ten-foot jail cell on the fourth floor of the Federal Building, in Springfield, just one floor above his office.

With Gilbert in the hospital, he could at least monitor her movements and keep an eye on her comings and goings. If she so much as sneezed on someone, Murphy and Plante would be on her like a shadow.

Welch had to act fast if he was going to secure an arrest warrant. Ideally, he wanted to transport Gilbert from her hospital bed at Cooley Dickinson to a metal bunk in Springfield. He knew she would never plead guilty to any of the charges he was preparing to file, and she would likely fight down to the wire, so his case had to be solid. No frills. No holes. No problems with evidence. The trick was to think long term. Nothing short of an air-tight case would suffice. The US Magistrate Judge who would ultimately review the arrest warrant didn't want hearsay evidence and shoddy police work; he wanted Welch to prove on paper that Gilbert was the only person who could have made those calls to the VAMC. It didn't matter that she was being investigated for murder. That was a separate case.

Further confusing the situation, there were several safety concerns that took precedence over everything else. After listening to the messages Gilbert had left at Perrault's apartment, and speaking with Samantha Harris, Welch felt Gilbert would retaliate against Perrault's property as soon as she had the opportunity and likely confront Harris the minute she got out of the hospital. He had to think about protecting his witnesses.

He also had to make sure Gilbert didn't get wind of what he was doing. Every legal maneuver he made would have to be sealed. Reporters from the *Union-News* and *Daily Hampshire Gazette* would be scouring the area like buzzards waiting for a break in the murder case. Welch couldn't take any chances and endanger all the work his office had done up until that point.

Then there was the possibility Gilbert would sign herself out of the hospital and split. Her parents lived in Long Island and, as far as Welch was concerned, they couldn't be trusted. The last thing he needed was Gilbert on the loose, running around Long Island causing trouble. With an open warrant for her arrest, witnesses would be hard-pressed to say anything.

Filing an arrest complaint was not as easy as filling out paperwork and handing it over to a judge to sign. It took time. Judges demanded rock-solid evidence.

A few things were certain, but Welch wanted to point them out to Plante and Murphy so there would be no disagreement as to the goal at hand. Welch, Murphy and Plante had butted heads before on issues regarding the murder case. All good teams disagreed from time to time. It was a natural part of discovering the absolute truth. But now was not the time to be arguing a point. It was time to act. Speculation and hindsight wouldn't cut it. Welch was too smart an attorney to talk himself into believing that. They needed proof. Stick to "this case," Welch urged. He wanted hard facts to back up his hypothesis that Gilbert had called in the bomb threat. Period. They would nail her on murder charges later.

While Gilbert stewed like a caged animal at Cooley Dickinson, continually calling people and threatening them, Welch sat in the board room down the hall from his office with Plante and Murphy devising their plan.

"Let's send out the check and credit card receipts she used to purchase the Talkboy and Talkgirl to the VA Criminalistics Lab for handwriting comparison," Welch suggested, looking at Plante and Murphy. "Agreed?"

"Right," Murphy said.

"We'll have to issue subpoenas for her bank records and credit card statements," Welch added. "Make a note of that."

Murphy and Plante understood why, of course. But they agreed it would take some time to do that. What was the significance of doing that now, anyway? Didn't they have enough?

"We want to show she had been paying her credit card bills and that she never reported her credit card stolen or lost."

They feared Gilbert, as conniving and calculating as she had proved herself to be, would say her credit card had been stolen and someone else had used the card to charge the Talkgirl.

"Let's put ourselves in the position of the defense," Welch urged, raising his eyebrows. "You follow me?"

CHAPTER 65

As it turned out, Gilbert had paid her credit card bill, and she never made a formal complaint about the card ever being stolen.

Just like that, step one was complete.

But there was still one major problem, maybe even the most pressing of the moment: How could Bill Welch be sure Gilbert wouldn't sign herself out of the hospital and take off? After all, she hadn't been arrested yet. She was free to do what she pleased.

On October 3, while Plante and Murphy continued to gather evidence and conduct follow-up interviews, Welch obtained a court order to have Gilbert transferred to Baystate Medical Center. Legally speaking, it was a simple "psychiatric evaluation transfer" request. Welch argued that Cooley Dickinson didn't have a full-time psychiatric unit and Baystate Medical did. He wanted her evaluated as soon as possible.

The judge agreed.

It was explained to the staff at Baystate before she arrived that she was likely going to be arrested within the week. "Keep an eye on her," Plante and Murphy advised hospital staff. Welch wanted to know everything she was doing, and, most important, he wanted doctors to assess her psychologically.

* * *

For the first time under a court order, several psychiatrists began to evaluate Gilbert. Two things became clear: For one, she was never going to admit to having any psychiatric problems; and, two, she was going to try her best to manipulate anyone who said she did.

Fooling a few friends whom she had worked with for the past seven years and a security guard she had been sleeping with was one thing, but a doctor trained to pick out this kind of behavior was quite another.

After assessing her condition, the attending psychiatrist at Baystate Medical said that she "cannot be trusted to tell accurate information about herself or what was going on. We had information from the patient's father that she, in fact, lies and has lied about her own past psychiatric history."

Indeed, Gilbert's father, Richard Strickland, told doctors when Gilbert was getting into trouble in high school that she was a "habitual liar." He said one time Gilbert claimed that her mother was a raging drunk and, at times, even abusive.

Gilbert's hatred for her mother wasn't something she discussed openly. But from time to time, she would give subtle hints about what she thought of her. Once, Gilbert confided in Rachel Webber. They were talking about Gilbert's mother being an elementary school teacher.

"You know," Gilbert said, "it always surprised me [that she was a teacher], because my mother really didn't like kids."

Webber was curious. She had never heard Gilbert, in the five years she had known her, even mention her parents.

"Why?" Webber asked.

Gilbert became quiet.

"Kristen . . . you there? Kristen?"

"I don't know why she's a teacher—she doesn't like kids." Then Gilbert changed the subject and refused to talk about it anymore.

Further evaluating her mental condition at the time of her admission at Baystate, one of the doctors who interviewed Gilbert finished his report by noting that "she apparently had overdoses in her early twenties which she denied to us. She has given contradictory statements to various people about her intentions—particularly around suicide."

He also went on to say that an unnamed friend of Gilbert's

reported that most of Gilbert's friends "appear frightened of her because so many strange things appear to be happening in her life and she is unpredictable."

It was then determined that Gilbert suffered from three disorders: Narcissistic Personality Disorder, Obsessive Compulsive Personality Traits and Antisocial Personality Disorder.

The first step in fixing any one of these problems is for the patient to stop denying there is, in fact, a problem.

Something Gilbert was just not ready to do.

Later, as more doctors weighed in, it became obvious to Welch and his team that Gilbert fit into the mold of a female serial killer rather well and that most "angels of death" suffer from similar personality disorders.

Regarding how Gilbert fared on a "Psychopathic Deviate Scale" test, her psychiatrist wrote:

This clinical profile has marginal validity because the client attempted to place herself in an overly positive light by minimizing faults and denying psychological problems. This defensive stance is characteristic of individuals who are trying to maintain the appearance of adequacy and self-control. . . . The clinical profile may be an underestimate of the client's psychological problems.

In other words, Gilbert wasn't a willing participant; therefore, since she was manipulating her own diagnosis, her doctors couldn't rely on what she was saying to be true.

On a second test, one designed to check masculine and feminine traits in females, a second doctor had this to say:

The clinical scale prototype used in the development of this narrative included evaluations on Pd [the Psychopathic Deviate Scale]. Individuals with this MMPI-2 clinical profile are not admitting to many psychological symptoms or problems. The client's profile is within normal range, suggesting that she views her present adjustment as adequate. However, she reported some personality characteristics, such as pleasure seeking, impulsivity, proneness to rule infractions, and high-risk behavior, that may make her vulnerable to clashes with authority at times. . . . The client has a wide range of interests. Women who score high on MF [the Masculinity/Feminity Scale test] are somewhat unusual compared to other women. They endorse item content that is typically seen as representing extreme masculine interests.

CHAPTER 66

While Glenn Gilbert was rummaging through his kitchen cabinets one evening in early October, he found a plastic bag stuffed inside an old pill box. Looking at it, Glenn noticed it was lined with an acrid-smelling white powder he could not immediately identify.

So he called SA Plante.

After taking the bag to the Massachusetts State Police Crime Laboratory for testing, Plante learned that it was Acepromazine, a common tranquilizer used in veterinary medicine to prepare animals for anesthesia.

Gilbert, Plante surmised, must have ground the tablets into a fine powder after she stole them from an area veterinary clinic. So he had Murphy visit every vet in the area. Murphy found out that Gilbert had made seven visits to the Northampton Veterinary Clinic back in 1995. On several occasions, Murphy had personally observed Acepromazine left out in the open. Stealing it, as they thought Gilbert had done, would be easier than lifting a pack of gum from a supermarket.

But as Murphy began to look deeper into this new direction, he uncovered even more. Talking to Glenn one day about all the pets he and Kristen had kept as a couple, Murphy learned that every dog or cat they had ever owned had "mysteriously died." The last dog, Glenn explained, had been sick for quite a while during the latter part of 1995. He remembered Kristen had taken it to the vet one night and returned home empty-handed.

"They had to put it to sleep," she told him.

But when Murphy and Plante went back to talk to the vet, he said he had no record of Gilbert's ever bringing the dog in during that time frame. So they visited other veterinarians. Again, there was no record of Gilbert's having brought the dog to a vet in the area.

Murphy then looked for the dog's body in every animal graveyard and vet hospital in the immediate and surrounding areas, but his search turned up nothing.

"We were prepared to exhume the dog's body if it came down to it."

After a series of dead ends, Murphy looked at Plante one day and said, "She probably zipped the dog and dumped it somewhere in the woods . . . we'll never find it."

On October 7, Gilbert made one last-ditch effort to cover her tracks for the night Murphy had observed her making a call to the VAMC in the parking lot of the Tasty Top Ice Cream Stand.

Early that morning, Perrault received a phone call from Gilbert. She said she had something to say regarding the events of a week ago.

"I placed several phone calls from different phone booths that day, Jim."

"You did what?"

"I stopped at the Tasty Top to call my apartment so I could check my messages to see if you had called."

Perrault couldn't believe what he was hearing.

"I used the pay phone in front of the *Gazette* and the Condor Citgo pay phone, too."

October 8, 1996 was a day Plante, Murphy and Bill Welch had been waiting for all summer long.

"She's going to be released from the hospital at two this afternoon," Bill Welch said over the phone to Murphy. "I want you to be there when she gets out."

There was one small problem that haunted Murphy as he prepared to go: Plante was out of town on family business. With Plante gone, Murphy felt terrible about having to make the arrest without him.

Nevertheless, they wanted Gilbert behind bars. As Welch suggested, Murphy would have to set aside for the moment his brotherly code of respect and get the job done. Plante would have to understand. There would be plenty of time in the coming weeks for Plante's hands-on involvement. One way or another, Gilbert was going to be released from the hospital. This could be their only chance.

"Kevin," Welch said over the phone. "Go get her . . . now."

"Okay, Bill. I'm on my way."

Murphy and John Stevens, a federal marshal, showed up at the Baystate Medical Center about five minutes before two o'-clock and waited in the lobby.

Ten minutes later, Gilbert came waltzing through the elevator doors and stopped dead in her tracks when she saw Murphy standing there staring at her.

"Ms. Gilbert," he said. "Would you please follow us?"

Gilbert didn't resist.

She appeared to be unmoved, Murphy later remembered, as if to say, "What took you so long?" There was no dramatic, last-minute declaration of innocence. No remorse. No apologies. She simply invoked her Miranda rights and chose not to speak.

Several hours after she was booked, bound by shackles, Gilbert clanked her way into Judge Nieman's courtroom.

Harry Miles stood a few inches from his client, resting his arm on her shoulder. Because Gilbert had been out of work for so long and barely had enough money even to take care of herself, the court appointed Harry Miles as her attorney, seeing that she'd already had dealings with him.

Judge Nieman acquainted Gilbert with her rights and told her what she was being charged with.

"I will set a date for your arraignment where you can formally plead guilty or not guilty," he concluded. "Do you understand these charges?"

"Yes, Your Honor."

Gilbert was then locked up at the Hamden County House of Corrections.

Days later, she was brought back in front of Judge Neiman for an arraignment. After she pled not guilty, the judge ordered her released into the custody of her parents to await trial on the bomb-threat charge, which could take upward of a year. She would have to be fitted for an electronic anklet monitoring device, which would restrict her movements once she got to Long Island. And while waiting for that to happen, the judge said, she would be moved to Hampshire County Jail in Amherst.

After Gilbert made several threatening phone calls to several witnesses throughout the next few days from a pay phone in the jail, Judge Neiman brought Gilbert back in his courtroom for violating her conditions for release. He ordered a restraining order prohibiting her from making any calls to anyone in Massachusetts.

With no one in town left to call, Gilbert turned to the one person whom she felt she could still confide in: her old friend Rachel Webber. With Webber living in upstate New York, still completely detached from the Northampton scene, Gilbert used Webber as a go-between, someone who could fill her in on what was happening in town.

During that first call Webber received from Gilbert, she questioned her.

"Kristen," she said, *"what* is going on?"

"The investigators found some sort of voice-changer thing in the bushes outside my house."

"Okay," Webber said, "continue."

"They think I called this bomb threat into the hospital, Rachel."

It sounded to Webber as if it weren't that big of a deal to Gilbert. She even made light of the threat, Webber thought, in the tone she had used. Webber didn't know then, but it had never been made public that a Talkgirl had been found in the bushes outside Gilbert's apartment.

"Yeah, well, maybe, Kristen . . . I think you did it!" Webber confessed.

"You and my grandmother," Gilbert said defiantly, "you both think I did it."

"I do, Krissy. I think you snapped. I think you did it, and I think you snapped."

A silence followed Webber's statement.

"Krissy . . . you there?"

After a long pause, Gilbert dropped her voice down low, Webber imagined, so no one in the jail could hear her.

In a whisper, she said, "All I can tell you is that people do strange things when they're under a lot of stress."

"Well, Krissy, we've all done dumb things—but, thankfully, I haven't done anything *that* dumb."

"You'll come visit me in jail, won't you?" Gilbert asked.

"Of course, Krissy. Of course, I will."

From that moment on, Webber never doubted for a moment that Gilbert had committed the bomb threat. But she still wasn't convinced of Gilbert's role in the murders. Calling in a bomb threat under the emotional stress of losing a husband and a boyfriend, along with being investigated for murder, was one thing, but actually murdering people was another. There would have to be some hard evidence, Webber told herself, for her to believe that a woman whom she saw as a good nurse, a good mother, a good wife, someone who had even taken care of Webber's kids, was a serial killer.

During another phone call later that same week, Gilbert asked Webber if her husband, Steven, would mind if she moved to upstate New York to be near her after the bomb threat trial was over.

"I have to start a new life somewhere. You think Steven would mind if I moved near you guys?"

"No, not at all."

Later that night, Webber shared the conversation with her husband.

"There's no way in hell she's involved in those murders. I don't care what the statistics show; she *did not* kill anybody! She'll get through this and get on with her life."

Steven wasn't buying it.

"If she gets out of jail, she's *not* coming here."

Prior to her release from Hamden County Jail on October 15, Gilbert was ordered by the court to live in Setauket, Long Island, New York, with her parents. She was warned not to set foot on Massachusetts soil or call anyone involved in the murder or bomb-threat cases. While in New York, Gilbert was to continue the therapy she had started. And if she didn't like it, well, there was a bunk waiting for her in Springfield where she could easily wait for her trial to begin.

CHAPTER 67

To Kristen Gilbert, being confined to her parents' home two hundred miles away from Northampton was the same as being locked up. The telephone had become both her weapon and source of information. Yet here she was now ordered by a judge not to use it.

For the past seven or so years, Richard and Claudia Strickland lived in a modest, middle-class neighborhood in Setauket, a rustic, homey community in Suffolk County situated halfway between Manhattan and Montauk, on the eastern tip of Long Island.

Gilbert was prohibited by law from leaving the house. If she stepped out of her boundary, the anklet would trip a circuit, which would alert the local federal officers monitoring her actions.

She was livid. Bored. And beginning slowly to self-destruct.

With no one left to talk to, she phoned Rachel Webber weekly. Webber had still been in contact with several people from Northampton, and she was beginning to see things differently.

By early November, Welch and his team were back on track with both the murder investigation and the bomb-threat investigation. He wasn't worried too much about getting a conviction on the bomb-threat charge, but there was still a lot of work to be done on the murder case.

Local newspapers in Northampton began running a variety of stories, most of which were based on rumor and speculation. Welch had done a good job keeping most of the records sealed. Nevertheless, the "leaked" stories fed the public's growing need to find out what had been going on up at the VAMC for the past several years.

As if there were going to be some sort of lottery, nurses were jogging their memories and drumming up all kinds of totals regarding the number of people Gilbert could have killed. Some said thirty, maybe forty; one even said it was closer to seventy-five or eighty.

Any patient on Ward C who had died while Gilbert had worked there suddenly became one of her victims.

For Rachel Webber, one thought kept haunting her as she read the newspapers and talked to her former coworkers: *Whenever Kristen was on duty, we'd have a code.* She couldn't get the thought out of her mind. The busier the night was, Webber recalled, the more codes they'd have.

"What are the newspapers saying about me?" Gilbert asked Webber one night over the phone.

"Oh, Kristen. The same old stuff, you know."

"What have you heard?"

"I haven't heard anything. How are you?"

"Ah, I don't know. I'm going to therapy. At least it gets me out of the house once a week."

During another call, Webber voiced her concern about something she had heard just days before.

"Kristen, I read an article—or someone told me, I can't recall which—that you had a 'psych background.' You know, something in your past. Is that true?"

"Mom," Gilbert yelled into another room in her parents' house, "do I have any psychiatric problems?"

Gilbert held the phone out so Webber could hear her mother shout, "Nope!"

"Kristen, this is serious."

"You heard her, Rachel," she said, laughing. "No psychiatric problems here."

Under house arrest, facing serious time behind bars, a murder investigation under way, and it was still all just a joke to Kristen Gilbert.

With the bomb-threat investigation just about wrapped up, Plante and Murphy began a vigorous interviewing schedule involving the nurses on Ward C. They would sit down and go through entries in medical files, being sure to get a clear picture of the notes each nurse had made. Each potential victim of Gilbert's was treated as a separate case. So sometimes Plante and Murphy would have to talk to the same witness several times regarding several different victims.

Rachel Webber had left the area shortly before everything blew up. But still, Plante and Murphy thought she might know something.

When they showed up at Webber's New York home, their presence negated any denial Webber might have still clung to at that point and helped her focus on the side of Gilbert she perhaps didn't know.

"We think," Plante said as he sat down in the Webbers' living room, "she is one of the most dangerous criminals we have ever come in contact with. It's possible she's killed forty, even forty-five of her patients."

Murphy nodded his head in agreement and Webber's jaw dropped.

"We think she killed her cats and dogs, too," Plante said.

"What?"

"We think she tried to poison Glenn."

For about an hour, they filled Webber in on whatever they could legally. Webber just sat, listened, and added whatever she could. Plante said it was unlikely, from what Webber had told them, that she would be dragged into court to testify.

"But who knows?" Murphy said.

Plante, before they left, wanted to know one last thing.

"Ms. Webber, your phone has been ringing off the hook since we've been here. That's Gilbert calling, isn't it?"

Webber explained she had told Gilbert when they were coming.

"We'll be in touch," Plante said. "Thanks for your time. Listen, the more you talk to her, the more you're going to become involved. We could end up calling you into court."

Webber was mortified. Here were two investigators who had traveled more than one hundred and fifty miles to confirm rumors she had heard for the past few months. It wasn't phone gossip and newspaper propaganda anymore. It was fact.

Her phone didn't stop ringing after Plante and Murphy left. So she picked it up and, at first, didn't say anything.

"They got to you, didn't they?" Gilbert snapped.

After a brief pause, "Yes, Kristen, they did."

"That's real nice of them to take away my only friend."

"Kristen, there is a mountain of evidence against you."

"You know, you're the only one I have left—that was real nice of them to do that."

"I really, really want . . . I want . . . to believe you, Kristen. But—"

They both began to cry.

"I just want you to know something, Rachel. I never killed anybody."

"I really want to believe you. It's just that I can't keep supporting you anymore. I can't keep doing this."

"You know, I understand," Gilbert said. She was weeping. "Kristen . . ."

"I understand, and you'll always be my friend," Gilbert said before she hung up.

CHAPTER 68

Gilbert was indicted on November 2, 1996, on felony charges of falsely phoning in a bomb threat to a federal institution. She was ordered to spend the next year under house arrest at her parents' Long Island home while waiting to tell her side of what happened on the night of September 26, 1996, and the trial was set for January 1998.

Rumors circulating around town had it that Gilbert was going to pin the bomb-threat call on her old beau, James Perrault. The story was that he had set her up because he wanted her out of the picture, and, in doing so, it would make him look good during his bid to become a "real" cop.

Laying out the dish on her old boyfriend, or even preparing for the bomb-threat trial, however, weren't Gilbert's biggest problems. Because three and a half weeks after the bomb-threat indictment was handed down, on November 27, 1996, Bill Welch, under the urging of forensic pathologist Dr. Michael Baden, got permission from the family of Ed Skwira to exhume his body, conduct an autopsy, and run the appropriate toxicology tests.

Depending on what was found in Skwira's body, more bodies might have to be exhumed in the coming weeks and months—maybe even years.

* * *

Burying a family member once is hard enough. Yet the thought of doing it twice is horrifying to most people. The Skwira family was hesitant at first, but later agreed that it was for the good of the case to have Skwira's body exhumed. After all, if he had been murdered, they wanted some answers.

Plante and Murphy promised the Skwiras that his body would go back in the ground the exact same way it came out, they would see to it personally. Neither Plante nor Murphy had ever been present at an exhumation, but Welch wanted them both there, from the time the first shovelful of dirt was unearthed to the time the last shovelful was replaced.

Murphy, of course, was no stranger to autopsies. He had seen dead bodies in many different forms throughout his career. As he explained to Plante one day shortly before the Skwira exhumation, "There is a lot to be learned from the viewing of a corpse."

Each body, Murphy explained, whether during an autopsy or at a crime scene, has an "individual horror attached to it—but also, more important, some teaching value." Humor, he said, was one of the things that saved him from losing it over the years during an autopsy or arriving on the scene where he had to conduct his business in the presence of a child's naked, mutilated body.

"If you don't find a way to vent the horror of what you see, you will be back on the Interstate with the radar gun watching the years pass you by."

The last place Plante and Murphy wanted to be on Monday, November 25, 1996, was six feet underground, giving hand signals to a backhoe operator. But here they were, standing in Ed Skwira's grave, wrapping a leather strap around his casket so it could be hoisted out of the ground and into the medical examiner's van.

As Plante pushed Skwira's casket into the medical examiner's van and watched it drive away, he had only one thing to say to his partner, as they stood there watching.

"What the hell are we going to find when we open up that box?"

"Hopefully, sweetheart," Murphy said, squishing his cigarette butt with the heel of his shoe into the ground, "some answers."

* * *

"Exhumation," Dr. Baden wrote in his book *Dead Reckoning,* "is a painstaking process that begins with the very ground in which the person is buried." An "important first step" is taking "soil samples" of the ground around the gravesite to "ensure that elements in the earth, such as arsenic, can be identified, so that any minerals seeping into the body are not mistaken for a cause of death."

One of the main reasons Ed Skwira had been selected for exhumation was that he'd had, Baden noticed, an "unanticipated sudden cardiac arrest with a rapid heart beat and there were three broken vials of epinephrine . . . found broken and used i. the bucket . . . after [his] code. . . ."

When they opened Skwira's casket, there was a thick, cottonlike substance covering his face, similar to mold that grows on an orange as it rots. Although the fungus looked bad, it actually helped to preserve the body, absorbing any water that might seep into the casket.

Lifting Skwira from his casket to the table, Murphy and Plante went to great pains not to disrupt the integrity of his body. Anything they found, be it incriminating or exculpatory, would be brought into evidence during trial proceedings. They had to be careful. Undressing Skwira, Murphy, who had been around countless corpses in his time, tried to lighten the mood for Plante, who was seeing this sort of thing for the first time.

As the video camera rolled, Dr. Baden, who had done thousands of autopsies during his forty years of practice, began to look at Skwira's internal organs. Immediately, he learned Skwira had not died of a heart attack. He did have heart disease, but that was not the cause of his death. His heart, Baden suggested, just gave out. What made it do that, however, was something he couldn't tell right away. It would take months before the toxicology tests came back.

While they waited for the results of the toxicology tests, Welch still had several things to do to cinch the bomb-threat case: matching Gilbert's handwriting samples, matching her fingerprints, finding credit card and check receipts, and interviewing potential witnesses.

And as the weeks progressed, the paper evidence began to convince Welch that a conviction was imminent; Gilbert was facing some hard time behind bars for making a false bomb threat. Maybe, Welch wondered, when Gilbert and Harry Miles had a chance to weigh the evidence he now had, she would save everyone the trouble of a long and tedious trial and change her plea?

PART THREE

I may be a murderer. Felony.
Oh, but worse. There's a law beyond the law,
and a justice beyond human justice.
Damnation is my only highway.

—Douglas Clegg, The Halloween Man

CHAPTER 69

It was Sunday, January 4, 1998, and William Welch sat at his desk inside the Federal Building and contemplated the week ahead.

The bomb-threat trial was finally here.

He felt confident about a conviction. After all, the proof was sitting right in front of him on his desk: Gilbert's own voice on tape.

As he went over his opening statement one final time, Welch decided to listen again to the tapes Perrault had made on the nights in question.

Welch agreed with Perrault that the tones and inflections in Gilbert's voice were all there. But the question remained: Would a jury buy the theory that she had slowed her voice down to make it sound like a man's?

They might, but it would be far better if Welch could somehow mine Gilbert's actual voice from the tapes.

So he began to think that if the toy could slow a voice down, there had to be a way to speed it back up to its natural state.

After fumbling through the office and coming up with a Dictaphone, putting the tape in and fiddling with the knobs, thus reversing the process Gilbert had used to disguise her voice in the first place, there it was: Gilbert's normal voice.

Of course, Welch thought, *it was so damn simple.*

On Monday, January 5, Glenn Gilbert came into the US Attorney's Office and confirmed Gilbert's voice on the new and improved tape.

Harry Miles was informed on Tuesday.

Miles, of course, wasn't happy about Welch's eleventh-hour discovery. But either way he looked at it, it was a destructive blow to his defense.

Giving the situation some prudent thought, Miles said he was prepared to talk about a plea bargain. "If you're offering probation, we can settle this thing right now."

"Eighteen months. No less," Welch said.

"Probation?"

"Are you kidding me? Eighteen months in *prison!*"

Miles walked out of the room.

At fifty-one, Judge Michael Ponsor, a soft-spoken man with a reputation for putting up with nothing above a whisper in his courtroom, had been sitting on the US District Court in Springfield since 1994. Before that, the six-foot-two, slenderly built judge spent ten years as a magistrate. After receiving his bachelor's degree from Harvard, in 1969, Ponsor went on to earn a second bachelor's degree, along with a master's, from Oxford, where he was also named a Rhodes Scholar. Like many area judges and attorneys, Ponsor received his law degree from Yale Law School.

Judge Ponsor addressed the Springfield US District Court in the *Government vs. Kristen Gilbert* case early Wednesday morning, January 7, 1998.

There had been so many pre-trial hearings regarding which pieces of evidence would be allowed and which wouldn't, many wondered if Gilbert would *ever* stand trial. But here they were, about sixteen months after the crime itself had been committed, on the fifth floor of the Federal Building, ready to make a go of it.

The main argument wasn't if any of the evidence collected during the course of the murder investigation would be allowed into the bomb-threat trial, but rather would Bill Welch be able even to *mention* there was a murder investigation going on. Not being able to talk about the murder investigation would be a severe blow to his case—if not for its effect on the jury, then for the evidence that lent itself to Gilbert's demeanor at the time she made the threatening call. Without knowing about the murder investigation, jurors might wonder, *What motive did she have for making the bomb-threat call?*

Harry Miles argued that the two matters were separate and should be treated as such. The jury, he worried, would form a judgment against his client based on the murder investigation, not the false bomb-threat allegation.

It was a good, solid argument, and Miles sounded sincere. In theory, a defendant—any defendant—is presumed innocent until proven otherwise.

But as some of the witnesses in both the murder and bomb-threat cases could acknowledge, however, Harry Miles wasn't the gentle soul he was making himself out to be in front of Judge Ponsor's court. Just days before the trial, Miles hired a private investigator to knock on the door of every single one of Samantha Harris's neighbors.

"Have you ever seen Ms. Harris using drugs? Does she cheat on her husband? How does she treat her kid?"

It was the oldest trick in the book. Miles wanted the dish on Harris—who he, undoubtedly, knew was going to bury his client when it came time for her testimony.

The same PI had also called Renee Walsh on one occasion and started asking questions about her relationship with Gilbert. Walsh said she wasn't interested in talking; she had been working with the US Attorney's Office. A day later, the PI showed up at her house. Her ten-year-old son answered the door.

"Is your mother home?" he asked.

"Nope."

"Do you mind if I come in for a few minutes?"

"No, I don't think so," Walsh's son said.

Judge Ponsor, after listening to both attorneys argue the matter without the jury present, made his decision.

". . . I'm going to allow the government to put into evidence the fact that there was [a murder] investigation going on."

With that, it was time to put the gloves on and get it on.

CHAPTER 70

In his dark blue, Hart Shaffner & Marx suit, Assistant U.S. Attorney Bill Welch stood up from his seat on the afternoon of January 7, 1998, and walked slowly toward the podium to deliver his opening statement.

In the front row of the courtroom, SA Plante and Detective Murphy sat directly in back of Welch. The reason for their presence was threefold: for support, of course; to be ready to testify whenever Welch needed them to; and because Welch had a gut feeling that Gilbert's father, Richard Strickland, who was himself sitting in the front row behind Gilbert, only a few feet from Welch, would lash out at him at some point during the trial. They had crossed paths several times in the hallway, and Strickland would just stare Welch down, like a boxer during the weigh-in before a big fight. Welch took it as a *How dare you accuse my daughter?* type of reaction to the charges he had lodged against Gilbert.

"On September 26, 1996, Kristen Gilbert decided to get even," Welch said, pointing at Gilbert. "In short, this case is about revenge, payback—about getting even with people you're not happy with."

From there, Welch, piece by piece, laid out the government's case.

* * *

"Studies have shown," Harry Miles said as he walked toward the podium an hour later, "that after the openings, jurors tend to start to form opinions." He paused and let the thought linger for a moment. "Therefore, I ask you to pay specific and very close attention to the court's instruction to you not to form any opinion or even begin to form one.

"The evidence gathered was gathered," Miles claimed at one point, "with blinders on, ignoring other potential evidence that would have exculpated the defendant, or the investigation was simply incompetent."

It was an outrageous claim. Between Murphy, Plante and Detective Thomas Soutier, there was over sixty years of collective police experience working the Gilbert case on any given day. Furthermore, Murphy had never lost one of the more than one hundred murder cases he had investigated throughout his twenty-six-year career. If Murphy was a shoddy investigator, pressuring people for information and evidence, overlooking possible suspects, a jury would have seen through it long ago.

Then came the assault on James Perrault.

"Does he have another motive for what he does?" Miles asked jurors. James Perrault "[suddenly] decides, oops, the inflections [in Gilbert's voice when she called in the threats] are the same[.]

"Well, you're going to hear that Mr. Perrault is a police officer . . . at the VAMC [and . . .] that he wanted to be a police officer, a real police officer, a town police officer, a state police officer."

Moments later, Miles said, "I'd submit to you that you also need to consider as we go though this case, was Mr. Perrault helped by that phone call? Did he, in fact, gain a professional advantage because he was now able to participate in this investigation?

"The government's case is one of character assassination in which they tell you that Kristen Gilbert is a terrible person and is guilty."

Miles sat down as the bell rang for round one.

Welch's first witness was Ann Millett, the manager of Toys-R-Us. She was on the stand for one reason—and Welch wasted no time getting it out of her.

After Millett explained that she had experimented with the

Talkboy, Welch asked her what kind of affect the toy had on her voice.

"It made my voice sound like a man's voice," she said.

"Objection! Move to strike," Miles interjected.

But it didn't matter. Millett had already said it; the jury had already heard it.

"I'm going to overrule it," Judge Ponsor, staring at Welch, said.

Gilbert shook her head. They were less than an hour into her trial, and she was getting buried. Gilbert's mother, sitting emotionless next to her impatient husband, hadn't moved a muscle. "Claudia Strickland was stoic, as if she were a ghost," someone later recalled.

After a short recess for lunch, through Stephanie Lussier, the Toys-R-Us cashier who had waited on Gilbert, Welch brought out the fact that Gilbert mentioned that she was purchasing the toy for a nephew.

By the time Stephen Fortenberry, the director of the forensic lab with the Department of VA-IGO, in Washington, DC, who had studied Gilbert's handwriting samples and compared them to the VISA receipt SA Plante had confiscated from Toys-R-Us, and Michelle Lawrence, a Bank of Boston detail operator specialist, were finished, it was clear that it was Gilbert—and no one else—who had purchased the Talkboy toys.

Then came one of Welch's star witnesses: Glenn Gilbert.

The room was quiet as Glenn worked his way from the double doors at the back of the courtroom to the witness stand. At five-ten, one hundred and eighty pounds, wearing a brown tweed jacket and a fabric tie to match, with his brown hair parted in the middle and slicked back, Glenn looked every bit as innocent and naïve as he was.

Gilbert didn't react one way or the other toward her former husband.

After getting Glenn to talk about his and Gilbert's children for a moment, Welch had him establish that he had a half-brother, Alan Clemente, who, more important, *didn't* have any children. Then he asked Glenn if Kristen's sister, Tara, had any children.

"No."

Just like that, the jury understood that there were no male

children on either Glenn or Kristen's side of the family. To say that she had purchased the toy as a gift for a nephew was a lie. Gilbert didn't have any nephews.

Welch asked Glenn when his wife filed for divorce. December 20, 1995, he said. One of Glenn's Christmas presents that year consisted of a sheriff showing up at his door on Christmas Eve to serve him divorce papers. The divorce, Glenn added, went through two years later, in December 1997.

Then Welch moved on to the calls Glenn had gotten from Gilbert throughout the summer of 1996. For the most part, she was calling, Glenn explained, to urge him not to speak to investigators about the "other" investigation. He noted that the annoying calls—hang-ups, heavy breathing—didn't begin until *after* Kristen learned he was helping investigators.

Glenn said she was "angry" and "nervous" most of the time.

"What else would she say?"

"Again, reminding me of the fact that I didn't have to speak with anyone."

Welch wanted the jury to realize the time of the year it was. Because just about everyone involved in Gilbert's life began receiving similar calls around that same period.

"When was that, Mr. Gilbert?"

"Toward the end of spring, 1996."

Glenn next brought jurors back to September 15, 1996, the day he came home from work early, found Gilbert inside their Drewson Drive home, and she attacked him with her car keys.

"And during that argument, did you see an emotional reaction? Did you physically see that—"

"Yes."

"—in her?" Welch said, finishing the question anyway.

"Would you describe that?"

"Anger followed by crying," Glenn said.

Patterns. Glenn had seen his wife act like that plenty enough times to recall an episode at will. It had all fit into what he described as his ex-wife's being "scared" and worried about being "singled out" in regard to the murder investigation.

Then it was on to the day in question—September 26, 1996. Welch asked Glenn if he received any strange messages on his answering machine that day.

"Yes."

I just wanted to say good-bye for the last time—good-bye!

"Your reaction to that message?"

"It frightened me."

"Why?"

"Because the sound of the voice . . ."

"How would you describe the sound of the voice that was on the message?"

"It sounded to me like an altered voice in a very deep, almost haunting tone."

And with that, Welch made the connection that he would later tie to SA Plante's theory that Gilbert made *both* calls.

Miles didn't have much for Glenn. He had to be careful. The last thing he wanted to do was badger the ex-husband who had been duped by his wife and her boyfriend. It would come across to the jury the wrong way—as if Kristen was the victim and Glenn was up there trying to get back at her. The jury wouldn't buy it. They liked Glenn. He was the harmless husband who had gotten screwed. The guy next door who cut his lawn on Saturday and took the family to church on Sunday. There wasn't a person in Northampton who had a bad word to say about him. The jury wasn't going to appreciate some crass criminal lawyer from uptown who made more money in the course of a morning than most of them made all week, trying to pin the blame on the innocent ex-husband. It would backfire horribly.

After asking a few personal questions about the marriage, Miles looked directly at Glenn and proceeded to bombard him for about half an hour with questions about Glenn's archenemy, James Perrault: How Perrault and Glenn met? When? Where? Did Glenn like him? Did he have any "feeling" for him?

At one point, Welch decided he'd heard enough and objected. "Relevance?" He was looking at Miles.

"I'll overrule it."

So Miles began asking about the kinds of toys Glenn and Kristen kept around the house, but carefully slithered his way back into Glenn and Perrault's relationship.

Realizing he wasn't getting the answers he'd hoped for, Miles threw his hands in the air, shook his head, and quickly concluded his cross-examination.

On redirect, Welch, without moving from his seat, had only two questions, the most important being, "In respect to obtain-

ing sole custody of your children, when did that occur, as well
as having custody during the days *and* evenings?"

"Again, around August '96," Glenn answered.

Welch wanted to clear up any confusion the jury might have
regarding whether Gilbert's children were staying with her at
the time investigators found the Talkboy in her apartment. They
were not. She hadn't seen the kids for weeks.

CHAPTER 71

By Friday, January 9, word had spread that Welch's next witness was James Perrault.

The previous day, Bernie LaFlam, the evening clinical coordinator at the VAMC who had directed emergency procedures during the bomb-threat calls, told the jury how chaotic that night had been.

Besides Samantha Harris, who was going to testify to dates and times, along with Gilbert's erratic behavior on the night of September 26, Perrault was the show. Since Perrault had answered most of the calls, Welch first had the soft-spoken security guard go through each call and tell the jury how the calls made him feel.

Perrault said he felt the caller was "taunting . . . [and] provocative towards" him. Then Welch asked about the "In twenty-five minutes, I'll see you all in hell" call. That specific call, Perrault said, left him with the thought that the caller was "cold [and] lacking in feeling."

Then it was time for the jury to hear why Perrault felt so sure it was his ex-girlfriend making the calls.

The tones and inflections in her voice, Perrault said. The first call ". . . sounded familiar to me."

"When was it that you decided it was the defendant?"

"I believe it was probably maybe that evening . . ."

"And who was the person you associated with the tones?"

"Because the pronunciation was very precise and Kris likes to pronounce everything very precisely. A lot of the tones were very familiar to the ones I heard during arguments with her where she would leave messages on my machine or call me up . . . upset with myself."

Perrault was nervous. He was fumbling some of his words and leaving sentences unfinished. But it didn't change their meaning or power.

"What *tones?*" Welch asked.

"The coldness . . . the lack of feeling. Upset. . . . [H]urt."

Next Welch wanted to make sure the jury clearly understood why Gilbert had purchased a Talkboy a few days after she bought a Talkgirl.

"Did you notice anything about the message at the time [September 27], other than the voice that you've described?"

"It sounded like that whatever [it] was being played on . . . it was malfunctioning and the tape was being eaten."

With that, Welch had given the jury an explanation as to why Gilbert purchased a second toy. She had probably broken the first toy in the process of using it.

After nearly talking the jury to sleep describing his adventures with several NYNEX operators, Perrault explained how preoccupied Gilbert became with the bomb threat. He said she would call and want to discuss the newspaper articles written about it—that she wanted to be involved in the investigation.

Welch asked him about October 7, 1996, the day before Gilbert was arrested, and how she had tried to cover her tracks.

"You mentioned that she told you that she stopped at the Tasty Top to check on her messages. Her messages where . . . at her home? And do you know from your own personal knowledge the distance between the Tasty Top and her home?"

"Approximately a half mile."

"Did she tell you anything that occurred at the Tasty Top during this conversation?"

"Yes."

"What did she tell you?"

"She felt she had observed a state trooper, and she felt that he was following her around. . . ."

"I have nothing further, Your Honor," Welch said.

"Good morning, Mr. Perrault," Miles offered comfortingly after Welch sat down.

That said, Gilbert's gray-haired attorney first went after Perrault's background in the military and how he should have known, because of his time in the military, how to keep better records. In particular, Miles insisted, Perrault's "report writing" and "investigative" skills as a security guard, making the assumption that on the night of September 26, Perrault should have written "tighter" reports. He made the point that Perrault, professionally speaking, was a cop wannabe, a security guard who tried, but failed to become a cop.

Using Perrault's job record as a launching pad, noting that he had applied to several area police departments but had been turned down by every last one of them, Miles began to lay out one of his theories.

"Has anyone ever told you that they would give you a recommendation for the state police . . . ?"

"Yes."

"And who told you that . . . ?"

"Trooper Soutier."

"Detective Lieutenant Soutier?"

"Yes."

"When did Detective Soutier tell you that he would recommend you to the state police?"

"I believe it was October [1996]."

"That would be after these incidents . . . occurred?"

"No. It was while we were investigating them."

"So while you were investigating this bomb threat, Detective Soutier told you that he would like to give you a recommendation to the state police?"

"Yes."

Miles rubbed his chin. This was the cusp of his defense: that Perrault had made all of this up to get a job with a "real" police force and get the woman he wanted nothing to do with anymore off his back for good.

"Is that when you were asked to report telephone calls from Kristen Gilbert?"

"It was before."

"And how long before you were requested to report telephone calls from Kristen Gilbert did Detective Soutier tell you that he would . . . recommend you for a position with the state police?"

"Maybe ten minutes."

Miles then had Perrault talk about several cards Perrault had received from Gilbert and when he received them, suggesting that Perrault and Gilbert had been romantically linked for longer than Perrault wanted to admit.

Getting nowhere, Miles brought Glenn into the picture, asking Perrault whether he wanted Kristen and her husband to get back together. Perrault said he "encouraged" Kristen back in the fall of 1995, and the winter of 1996 to reconcile with Glenn. He said he told Kristen she should go to counseling with Glenn.

"And you're still having a sexual relationship with her at the time?" Miles asked.

"Yes."

Then he wanted to know if Perrault had suspected Gilbert, at that time, of doing "it," killing her patients.

"Not at that time."

"Do you suspect it today?"

"Yes."

"And you suspect it today because it helps you to testify against her. Isn't that correct?"

"No. It doesn't."

"Isn't it true, sir, that the reasons you're saying some of these things against Kristen Gilbert is because it helps you in your career and it justifies your dumping her?"

"No. It doesn't, sir."

"You don't think it does?"

"No, *sir.*"

Miles kept throwing dates at Perrault like darts, hoping to confuse him. But it didn't work. More confident now than ever, Perrault stayed sharp.

For the next half an hour, Miles went through several turbulent episodes during the affair, hoping to convince the jury that Perrault had reasons to want Gilbert out of his life.

"Did she [ever] physically threaten you [. . .]?"

"Physically without words, yes."

"Did she hit you?"

"Yes."

"Did you hit her back?"

"No."

"Did you report it?"

"No."

"Did you make any notes of it?"

"No. I did not."

"Did you tell her that you wanted to go to counseling with her?"

"No."

"Did she ask you if you wanted to go to counseling?"

"I don't recall."

"And when she hit you, would it be just a punch or a slap . . . ?"

"She's punched me twice in the testicles."

That one statement put a damper on Miles's momentum. Perhaps he shouldn't pry anymore? There was a chance Perrault knew something else.

As Perrault's testimony wore on, it became remarkably clear that after the initial courtship, the affair he had with Gilbert was a rocky road of emotional instability that continued to escalate as the pressure surrounding the murder investigation began to wear Gilbert down. Her life was becoming more unmanageable by the day, and she was bringing all that baggage into the relationship. What was clear—and Miles probably didn't want it to come out this way, but it did—was that as soon as Perrault got a whiff of what kind of woman he had been shacking up with, he quickly made the decision that there wasn't a piece of ass in the world worth that much trouble.

CHAPTER 72

The *Daily Hampshire Gazette,* which had been covering the trial from gavel to gavel, ran a front-page headline over the weekend that hit Bill Welch like a sucker punch:

NURSE'S CO-WORKER SAYS INVESTIGATORS THREATENED HIS JOB

Many who were in the courtroom the previous week, however, didn't quite see it that way. The *Gazette* article rallied many on the side of Gilbert, saying Perrault had said that a "VA investigator offered him help with a job search" if he helped in the murder investigation or he could "face losing his job" at the VAMC.

But to a lot of the people who were in Ponsor's courtroom during Perrault's testimony, it never happened that way.

Nevertheless, if any of the jurors had seen the weekend paper, there was a good chance they were questioning the very testimony they had just witnessed.

It was a prosecutor's worst nightmare.

On Monday, January 12, Miles indicated he had only a few more questions for Perrault. Perrault had been on the stand for about three days. He looked tired. Drained. He was ready to call it a day.

But before Perrault took the stand, Miles and Welch argued about the testimony of Welch's next witness, Bruce Koenig, a former FBI expert who specialized in analyzing voice and tape. Miles said he was informed months ago that Koenig wasn't going to be used as an "expert" witness.

"I was hoping . . . I would have a little more time to ponder it. . . ." Ponsor said after hearing out Welch and Miles, but "I would say that it's very likely I am going to permit the government to put on [Mr. Koenig]. . . ."

With that out of the way, the coast was clear for Perrault to return.

After asking him a few questions about the trap NYNEX had installed on the VAMC phone line on September 26, Miles turned his attention toward Gilbert's home phone.

"On [September] twenty-seventh, were any of the calls [you received at the VAMC] traced to Kristen Gilbert's apartment?"

"I don't believe any of them were. . . ."

"I'm sorry?"

"None of them were traced to Kristen's apartment!"

"So, did you know how many calls were made by this person you identify as the caller?"

"Between twenty and thirty maybe."

"So twenty or thirty calls were made by this individual and none of them were traced to [Gilbert's] apartment; is that correct?"

"No, they weren't. That is correct."

"I have no further questions."

On redirect, Welch established that even before Perrault had met Gilbert and became romantically involved, he had been applying for law-enforcement jobs. There was little need to go over the obvious: that phone calls from Gilbert's apartment had little, if anything, to do with the case. The government had never claimed Gilbert had made the calls from her home.

Miles stood back up.

"Do you remember being asked on redirect examination . . . if you would manufacture a bomb threat in the case?"

"Yes."

"And if you would have manufactured a bomb threat, would you tell us that?"

"I wouldn't manufacture a bomb threat."

"If you had, would you tell us that?"

"I wouldn't make a bomb threat, so therefore I wouldn't have to."

"And do you recall being asked if you manufactured a bomb threat to get rid of Kristen Gilbert?"

"Yes, I recall that."

"And would you tell us that if you had?"

"I hadn't made one, so therefore I wouldn't have to worry about that."

Perrault was tough.

"Is it fair to say, sir, that with respect to the actual threatening telephone call, the one that mentioned an explosive device, you're the only person who heard that?"

"Yes."

"In order to believe that that occurred, we have to believe your testimony?"

"Yes."

It hadn't been a good start to the new week for Harry Miles and Kristen Gilbert. With Ponsor ruling against a motion Miles had filed, seeking to stop several witnesses from testifying that the voice on one of the tapes was, in fact, Gilbert's, it appeared Miles's claim of bias on the part of the government had some credence—if only in the way things looked.

There was, though, little he could do about it at this point besides plan an appeal if Gilbert was found guilty—because Welch was calling retired FBI voice expert Bruce Koenig, who had eliminated most of the distortion on the sped-up tape Welch had discovered before trial, and there wasn't much Miles could do about it. Although Koenig couldn't make the determination that the voice on the tape was Gilbert's, Welch won the argument earlier that morning and said he would be bringing in witnesses who could.

* * *

While the court waited for Detective Kevin Murphy to make his way to the witness stand, Miles walked over to Welch and said something with regard to how the case was proceeding.

Seizing the moment, Welch said, "You just keep a leash on Gilbert's father, Mr. Strickland. I don't want him lashing out at me during the proceedings."

Miles took a look over to where Mr. Strickland was sitting, and paused for a moment. "Yes," he said, "he's been acting a bit strange lately. . . . He requires a lot of maintenance."

Earlier that morning, Strickland had once again made Welch feel uncomfortable with the way he had stared at him. They were in the hall outside the courtroom, and the old man gave Welch one of his how-dare-you-do-this-to-my-daughter stares that had become part of his daily regimen.

"He's coming over that railing one of these days," Welch had said half-jokingly to Murphy as they entered the courtroom.

Welch felt Strickland wasn't the type to whip out a knife or gun and "go postal." But he wasn't putting it past the old man to do something irrational if he thought his daughter was going to prison.

With his neighborly charm, Detective Kevin Murphy took a seat in the witness stand. He looked every bit like the seasoned pro he was.

Welch had him first describe his role in the bomb-threat investigation and then had him give the jury a blow-by-blow account of the night he watched Gilbert make a call from the Tasty Top Ice Cream Stand public telephone. But beyond that, there really wasn't much more the detective could offer as far as evidence was concerned.

On January 13, the following morning, Miles tore right into Murphy, questioning just about every aspect of his investigation. Yet, in the end, Murphy stood his ground and offered Miles absolutely nothing he could build upon.

He was a cop doing his job. Period. Miles couldn't get out of him what wasn't there.

By the end of the day, Welch brought in FBI expert Bruce Koenig and had him make the point that it was highly possible

that the person who had made the calls to the VAMC on
September 26 used a Talkboy toy. The clicking sounds in the
background were a dead giveaway, Koenig explained. There
was no other conclusion he could come to.

CHAPTER 73

Days before the start of the second week of proceedings in the Gilbert bomb threat trial, the world's most famous serial bomber, Theodore "Ted" Kaczynski, the Unabomber, was in the midst of the start of his trial three thousand miles away.

The Gilbert trial hadn't quite lived up to the same dramatics as the Unabomber's, nor had it garnered the same mass television coverage, but one thing was certain by the time January 13 rolled around: Harry Miles was feeling the walls of the government's case closing in around him. He needed to do something—and quick.

Earlier that morning, Miles argued that his voice identification "expert" witness, Christopher Ryan, would be leaving for California at 12:15 that day, and he needed either to get him on the stand right away, or, as they had previously discussed, have the court videotape his testimony.

On top of that, Miles said that Ryan would testify on the mechanics of the Talkboy and how it was mechanically impossible for a person to record her voice and keep rolling the tape as another person—meaning Perrault—spoke over it, and then play another message.

Welch was raging mad at Miles for his eleventh-hour proclamations.

Judge Ponsor, after listening to both attorneys for several

minutes, said he would allow Ryan to testify as an "expert" and the jury was returned to the courtroom.

Living up to the image of the crowd he ran with, Christopher Ryan wore his hair long, in a pony tail, and had that hard-edged look most musicians succumb to after years on the road. He wasn't quite Willie Nelson, but thirty years down the road, well, he might just be able pull it off.

After he sat down in the witness chair, Ryan said good morning.

"If you could lean forward a little bit," Miles said, "so your voice would be amplified for the jury, I'd appreciate it."

Here was a man who was supposed to be a "sound expert," a sound technician and recording engineer being told to speak into the microphone so he could be heard. Welch couldn't have scripted a better start.

Miles first asked Ryan what he did for a living.

"I am a full-time musician, master engineer and record producer."

"What is a master engineer?"

"A master engineer is someone who tweaks and puts the icing on the final product of a record or CD for production or mass-producing of records."

After a few more questions, Miles asked Ryan who he had worked with.

". . . Def Leppard, John Mellencamp, Billy Cobin . . . Phil Collins, Whitney Houston."

And then—after Ryan explained how he had listened to the tapes—came the question of the hour.

"And as you were listening to the tape, and later with your examination of the Talkboy, did you come to any conclusion as to whether that conversation was taking place in real time?"

"I definitely thought that the conversation was in real time."

"I have no further questions."

The main reason why Ryan was testifying, Welch knew as he stared at his notes before beginning his cross-examination, was to counter Bruce Koenig's claim that the phone calls Perrault had received were pre-recorded.

So Welch stood and, immediately, put Ryan's qualifications and credentials into perspective.

"Is it fair to say you don't have any sort of graduate degree in engineering, phonetics, linguistics, or anything like that?"

"That is true."

"Nor do you have any sort of graduate degree in those fields—is that right?"

"True."

"Do you have a high school degree?"

"Yes, I do."

"As far as training and listening to tapes, are you familiar with, for example, the FBI's, or the Internal Association for Identification's two-year apprenticeship program?"

"No, I'm not."

"In fact, everything you have done is with respect to music, is that correct?"

"Yes, it is."

"Specifically with replicating drum sounds, is that right?"

"True."

"Which on occasion are quite loud, is that right?"

"Yes."

Soon Ryan admitted that he hadn't had an ear exam in quite some time and that he couldn't tell the court how good his hearing was. He was a drummer. He had been around loud music his entire life. One didn't have to be an ear specialist to draw the conclusion that his hearing probably wasn't the same as a person who hadn't.

"You certainly haven't been formally certified by anybody, either an entity or an individual, in doing tape comparisons or tape analysis, is that right?"

"Correct."

On January 14 the government got back on track.

The next phase of Welch's case involved time: Did Gilbert have the opportunity that night to commit the bomb threat? Welch wanted to make sure the jury knew Gilbert was out and about between the hours of the threat. And if there was any doubt in the jury's mind that she didn't have the opportunity to commit the crime, Welch's next witness, Samantha Harris, would clear it up.

As Harris entered the courtroom, Gilbert took a long, hard

look at her and shook her head. The most grueling part of testifying, many of the witnesses agreed, was having to sit only a few feet from Gilbert. The witness box was directly in front of the defense table, where Gilbert could stare down each one of her old friends.

Harris was the government's fourteenth witness in what was amounting to the end of its case.

She first explained how she and Gilbert had met back in the spring of 1996. Then Welch had her recall the conversation she had with Gilbert the day she picked her up at the hospital in Boston. It was the same day Harris had learned for the first time there was a murder investigation going on at the VAMC, and Gilbert was the main focus of it.

Welch had to be careful. If Harris blurted out "murder investigation" and "Gilbert" in the same breath, Ponsor would have Welch's ass served up on a silver platter.

A smart attorney, Welch didn't bother trying to slip in anything he knew he couldn't get away with. He kept to Ponsor's earlier instructions and, it was clear, had coached Harris rather well.

"During the course of this car ride, did the issue of Ms. Gilbert and Mr. Perrault's relationship come up?"

". . . Kristen asked me if I knew why she was in the hospital, and I told her that Jim had told me that she was having trouble with the breakup."

Welch then had Harris work in the fact that during that same car trip, Gilbert told her she would "stalk" Perrault if he ever "dumped her."

Next Harris made it clear how and why she decided to contact the DA's office in late September 1996, which opened up an opportunity for Welch to bring in the diary Harris had began keeping after she initially met with Murphy, Soutier and Plante.

Miles, who most likely wanted to suppress as much of what was in that diary as possible, kept objecting, saying again and again that it was all "hearsay." But Ponsor kept allowing the testimony.

As Welch continued, he zeroed in on Gilbert's need to know where Perrault was all the time, and how she continually called Harris's house to check if Perrault had called while she was out.

Using the diary to help her recall exactly what had happened on a particular day, Harris painted a dark picture of an "angry" woman with a "very controlled" and "very deep-pitched voice" on a day she had called and, after Harris had confirmed that Perrault had inquired about her whereabouts, told Harris that Perrault was a "fucking twit."

"Now, on the twenty-sixth [of September], did you know when Ms. Gilbert left her apartment?" Welch asked.

Harris told jurors how Gilbert left at five P.M. and didn't return until eight, which placed her out of the house at the time of the calls.

In addition, she said Gilbert was "jumpy" and "agitated" when she returned at eight o'clock. Welch got her to describe how Gilbert said she had been out doing laundry, but didn't have anything—much less a laundry basket—in her hands when she returned.

Before Welch finished, Harris brought the jury back to the morning of September 27 (the day after the bomb threat), and asked her if Gilbert had a hypothesis about the bomb threat.

"She told me . . . it was probably a patient who wanted to sit by and watch the action," Harris said. "She said she was at the Look Restaurant across the street and watched the police cars and fire trucks show up."

"Nothing further . . ."

From his first question, Miles tried tripping Harris up on dates, but she kept saying she didn't recall the exact date. Beyond that, there really wasn't much more Miles could pry into. It was best sometimes to leave well enough alone. There was no telling what else Harris knew that Welch hadn't gotten out of her.

As she left the courtroom, Harris couldn't help but think how Gilbert hadn't flinched one bit or showed any emotion while she had been on the stand.

"Maybe she was in denial," Harris later recalled. "Or maybe she just didn't give a damn about anything."

CHAPTER 74

Before testimony was over on Wednesday, January 14, Karen Abderhalden—who at one time considered Gilbert to be one of her closest friends—explained to the jury that Gilbert had stayed with her and her family for about three weeks during late August 1996, and how upset Gilbert was by the investigation.

Within moments, Abderhalden admitted that Gilbert's hatred and frustration over the "other" investigation didn't stop at just her coworkers and friends; it went right to the top—particularly her nursing supervisor, Melodie Turner, who, by a stroke of luck, was at the VAMC the night of the bomb threat, even though she wasn't supposed to be.

"Did Ms. Gilbert ever talk about Melodie Turner with you during the summer of 1996?"

"Yeah. She didn't really care for Melodie. They had some problems—working relations. She had been upset with Melodie."

"Did she ever make a comment to you about Melodie Turner during this period of time . . . ?"

"Well, one comment I recall . . . in her anger with Melodie . . . is that she believed maybe they ought to investigate Melodie."

"Did she specifically mention which people she was upset with?"

"In particular, Kathy Rix and John Wall."

"And were they working up at the VA Medical Center in Ward C on the evening shift in September 1996 . . .?"

"Yes."

By the time she finished, Abderhalden had made a reference to the movie *Home Alone II,* describing how her son had watched the movie several times and how familiar she was with the Talkboy toy, which, literally, gave the jury an image of Gilbert making the bomb-threat call. Because all Welch needed was for one of the twelve jurors to have seen the movie, where Macaulay Culkin's character, Kevin, had used a Talkboy, Jr. to reserve a room at the Plaza Hotel in New York. It was even possible Gilbert had devised the bomb-threat plan while watching the movie with Abderhalden's son.

Harry Miles began his cross-examination of Abderhalden by trying to refocus the jury on Gilbert's "good girl" status. Referring to his client as a "good nurse," Miles had Abderhalden explain how Gilbert used to set up a Secret Santa during the holidays as well as help out at Jessie's House, a homeless shelter in the Northampton area.

Would it work? It was anybody's guess.

Welch next called Detective Thomas Soutier, who had found the Talkboy in Gilbert's closet. Soutier was on the stand to try and clarify a conversation he'd had with James Perrault regarding Perrault's future plans for employment.

"Did there come a point in time around the time of the bomb threat investigation when you saw [James Perrault] at the DA's office?" Welch asked.

"Yes," Soutier said, "numerous times."

"And did there come a point in time when you had a conversation with him about his job search?"

"Yes, sir."

"Can you explain first the context of how that [conversation] arose?"

Soutier said that Perrault had been in the office that day for a scheduled meeting with SA Plante. Perrault had shown up early. Waiting, he looked bored, Soutier said. So he invited him into his office to kill some time.

"Did you have a conversation with him there?"

"Yes . . . I did."

"And what was the nature of that conversation?"

"It was a casual conversation. I asked him how his job search was going."

"Did you know about his job search?"

"Yes, sir. I did."

"How did you know that?"

Soutier said he had found out through checking Perrault's phone records as part of "the other" investigation. Someone— he assumed Perrault—had been calling various police stations in the area from Perrault's phone.

"Did he make any comment back to you when you asked him how his job search was going?"

"Well, he said it was slow. That he was concerned that his involvement in the 'other investigation' would taint his possibilities."

It was nothing more than informal, unplanned conversation, Soutier opined.

"When he made that response to you, did you have a further conversation with him?"

"I told him that if there ever came a point in time that anyone questioned his part in the 'other investigation,' he could feel free to have them call me, and I would explain it."

Miles then began questioning Soutier about the kind of relationship he and Perrault had shared. Looking to show the jury that Soutier had crossed the line in promising Perrault a job if he cooperated with investigators, Miles wanted to know if their friendship was more than just casual.

But it failed. Soutier was as smooth as a desktop. He answered each one of Miles's questions in a pleasing, reassuring tone. If the jury couldn't believe a detective with more than twenty-six years on the job and not one blemish on his record, whom could be believed?

Late in the day on January 15, Special Agent Steve Plante, dressed to a tee, sauntered into the courtroom as though he had just walked out of the pages of *GQ* magazine. His full shock of hair was perfectly styled and trimmed. At just a hair over five feet, Plante certainly wasn't the tallest man in the courtroom, but if what he had to say was half of what people had been speculating, he would leave the stand with the distinction of having been the most compelling player in Gilbert's trial to date.

Plante first established that Gilbert had become the target of a probe into several suspicious deaths up at the VAMC in February 1996. Then he said the investigation he was conducting for the IGO became "very active" during the end of the summer in 1996.

But in the end, however, Plante hadn't offered the definitive final nail in Gilbert's coffin that many thought he would, but more or less just reminded the jury of everything it had heard for the past two weeks.

CHAPTER 75

The biggest story in the nation on Tuesday, January 20, 1998, wasn't that a Nor'easter had pummeled most of New England with a blanket of fresh packed powder and delayed the Gilbert trial by four days, or that the trial had taken up banner headlines in the *Daily Hampshire Gazette* for the past two weeks. It was a certain White House intern who had claimed to have sexual relations with President Bill Clinton.

But the president's infidelity and the major snowstorm made little difference to Kristen Gilbert. All she could do was sit in her cell and wonder what the hell had been going on in the courtroom for the last twelve days. A narcissist, the attention the trial had brought Gilbert was more than she could have ever imagined. Reporters were constantly sticking microphones and cameras in her face as she was escorted away from the courtroom, and, as she would tell a friend later that week, she "loved every minute of it."

"Can you believe that [TV news anchor] was chasing me down like that?" Gilbert, laughing, told a friend over the phone one day.

Harry Miles, on the other hand, had his hands full with trying to defend his client. The evidence Welch had presented was devastating. Gilbert looked guilty as hell.

Miles's cross of Plante on the morning of January 20 turned out to be a bust. It hadn't yielded much of anything that would

sway the jury one way or the other if, in fact, one or more of
them were sitting on the fence.

After Plante left the stand, Welch indicated that he had one
more witness: Glenn Gilbert. Glenn had already testified. But
since he was the only one who had "confirmed" Gilbert's voice
on the now infamous "sped-up" tape Welch had made in his office on the Sunday before the trial, Welch needed him back to
explain it to the jury. Judge Ponsor had stated earlier that Glenn
couldn't testify about the tape until after Bruce Koenig testified.

So here he was.

As the tape played, a chill went through the courtroom. Here
was Gilbert's voice, crystal clear, for everyone to hear.

While it was playing, Plante happened to look over at the
Stricklands. Gilbert's father's jaw dropped when he heard her
voice ring out in the room, while her mother just put her head in
her hands and began shaking it, slowly, back and forth.

Miles had said back at the start of the trial he was going to
prove the government had overlooked two possible suspects and
targeted his client from day one. He said it was a substandard
investigation from the start, and he promised he would fill many
holes in the government's case with the truth.

Well, here was his chance.

Miles's witnesses consisted of three police officers who had
been summoned to the scene on September 26, 1996, along
with VAMC Chief of Security, Timothy O'Donnell. They were
there to back up his theory that there had been two additional
suspects the government had failed to investigate. Northampton
PD Officer Carlos Lebron testified that one suspect was John
Noble, a former VAMC patient who had been involved in an incident at the hospital some time ago and had made threats toward hospital staff. Northampton Detective Peter Fappiano
testified that the other suspect was a jogger he'd spotted along
Route 9, near the hospital, who was using a pay telephone right
around the time the bomb threat was called in.

Indeed, the two stories would give the jury a second and
third theory to chew on during deliberations. But the case ultimately came down to one vital question: Was it—or was it

not—Kristen Gilbert on those tapes the jury had heard in court the past few weeks?

Closing arguments began on Wednesday, January 21.

Welch addressed the jury at 1:05 P.M. Before he sat down an hour later, he had made it clear to the jury that Gilbert's "problem was personal." She chose to phone in the bomb threat to get back at those people who were helping investigators in the murder investigation, thus turning their backs on her.

It was just after two P.M. when Welch finished. After a five-minute recess, Miles stood and walked toward the jury.

"Kristen Gilbert was a nurse," Miles said, "who ran the Sunshine Club . . . who organized the Christmas festivities for the staff . . . a nurse who took care of patients." Then, in a whisper, Gilbert was "a good nurse," he said.

Reading part of a letter Gilbert had written to Perrault, where she described how she had watched him one night at the VFW throwing darts, Miles posed a question: "Are these the words of a techno terrorist—or the words of a plaintive woman who loved Jim Perrault?"

Then he broke into his attack on Perrault.

"This is a man who told you that he was a cop wannabe." He called Perrault and Gilbert's relationship a "paragon of immorality," questioning Perrault's integrity, motives, and his believability under oath.

"He's an individual without honor, morality, and who's governed by self-interest."

After that, Miles shifted his focus and laid into SA Plante's desire to find someone responsible for the crimes he had been investigating—because, according to Miles, Plante was "frustrated" that the murder investigation wasn't going anywhere.

"Did they ever try to determine whether Mr. Perrault set this whole thing up with a confidant?"

Welch smiled and shook his head.

By 2:30, Miles was finished.

Judge Ponsor told Welch he had fifteen minutes for his rebuttal.

"Timing was everything," Welch offered. Plante, he explained, had to make decisions fast. Wherever the leads took him, was where he went. It was like being pulled by a team of horses.

"That's why it's important to look at *all* the evidence . . . build it brick by brick and see how . . . *she*"— he raised his voice and pointed at Gilbert—"could have been the *only* person to have made that call on September 26, 1996, at 5:22 P.M."

As Welch turned to walk back toward his table, a final thought occurred to him.

"Don't forget this one iota of evidence," he shouted. "That Melodie Turner was working on the twenty-sixth and she normally didn't work the evening shift. But on the very day that the bomb threat comes in, Melodie Turner happens to be working . . . *wow* . . . that's a coincidence." He threw up his hands in disgust. "The one person that she"—he pointed again at Gilbert, who now had her head bowed as if she were being scolded by a parent—"wants the IGO to investigate is there!

"I'll submit to you that there are two sides to this person. There's the side that her attorney wants to tell you about"—he lowered his voice—"and the side that the evidence told you about."

CHAPTER 76

Judge Michael Ponsor handed the case over to the jury at 3:01 P.M., on Tuesday, January 20, 1998. Three days later, the jury weighed in.

At 10:17, on January 23, Ponsor addressed the courtroom. He said he didn't want any jubilation at the reading of the verdict. "Act," he said, "in a dignified manner."

Gilbert's parents held hands as the foreperson stood.

"Guilty."

After each member of the jury was polled, Ponsor excused them.

With the jury gone, Ponsor said that there was a pressing matter at hand.

"[T]here are a couple of . . . issues that have come up—very serious issues—with regard to the defendant's conditions of release given the guilty finding, and we're going to have to take up those issues . . . [after] I have a chance to talk to the jury."

He ordered Gilbert to remain seated.

Fifteen minutes later, after personally thanking each member of the jury, Ponsor was back on the bench, ready to do battle with Welch and Miles concerning where Gilbert would spend her days and nights pending her sentencing.

"I have concern in two areas," Ponsor began. "One of them relates to a complaint or report that has been placed on your desk from Alan Chipman, who is the home confinement specialist for this court."

With the exception of the attorneys, this was news to almost everyone in the courtroom. According to the report, Gilbert, while under house arrest at her parents' home in Long Island, had "tampered" with her electronic anklet, a thick rubber band-like apparatus, similar-looking to a donut, that slides over a defendant's ankle.

On Monday, January 5, the first official day of the trial, Gilbert's anklet had been removed. But as the officer removed the anklet, she noticed something strange. It looked as though it had been picked at with some type of sharp object. So it was sent off to the New York Office of Pretrial Services for examination.

On January 22 it was confirmed that the anklet showed "clear signs of an attempt of tampering, including a penny that had been taped to the inside of [it]."

The only conclusion that could be made from the evidence was that Gilbert had tried to pry the anklet off and, worried she might have broken the copper wire that runs through the center of it keeping a continuous electrical current, taped a penny to the inside of it to try to maintain the current. The Uniondale, New York, office responsible for monitoring Gilbert while she was at her parents' home, confirmed it had "frequent problems maintaining monitoring of the defendant . . ."

This new problem, coupled with the fact that Gilbert's "emotional fragility" was an issue throughout the entire trial, worried the judge, he said.

". . . I'm concerned that she receives proper evaluation and care pending sentencing and pending the commencement of what may even be an even more stressful period in her life." Furthermore, Ponsor added, he worried what she might do now that her fate for the bomb threat had been sealed.

Any thoughts?

Welch argued that Gilbert's crime was a crime of violence. She should be "mandatorily detained," he said. "My argument is that she . . . [be] placed on suicide watch, and that she does receive [a] psychiatric evaluation . . ."

Welch was frightened for the safety of his witnesses, particularly Samantha Harris and James Perrault. He was afraid of what Gilbert might do now that she had heard Perrault and Harris testify against her. Welch added that he had presented to the court a history of violence by Gilbert "towards ex-boyfriends." He told the story of what Gilbert had said to Karen Abderhalden back in August 1996, regarding Perrault loving her cats more than her and how she would have them put to sleep and placed on his doorstep.

"You had to spell it out as clearly as you possibly could that when you meant she would have no contact with anyone, that meant no telephone contact, that meant no contact by mail—*that meant no contact with anyone*," Welch, raising his voice, insisted.

Judge Ponsor, after hearing arguments from both sides, decided to detain Gilbert at the Hampshire County Jail while she awaited sentencing.

Nearly a year and a half after she'd committed the bomb-threat crime, Gilbert was brought for sentencing before Judge Ponsor on April 20, 1998.

For most of the day, Welch and Miles argued back and forth on many issues, ranging from Gilbert's sanity at the time of the bomb threat to her mental decline throughout the entire ordeal.

"Your Honor," Miles interjected at one point, "Mr. Strickland requests permission to speak to the Court with the Court's permission?"

"All right," Ponsor said. "Will we be hearing from the defendant, [too]?"

"Yes, we will. Briefly," Miles said.

The room was abuzz. Gilbert, who had uttered publicly only two words since the day she was arrested—"Not guilty"—would finally say something.

But it was Daddy's turn first.

Overweight and noticeably stressed, Richard Strickland stared at Bill Welch the entire time he got up and walked from his seat to the chair on the witness stand.

"We're law-abiding citizens," Strickland said after offering his appreciation to the judge. "I don't think anyone in our family has ever had anything more than a speeding ticket in forty or fifty years, so we don't condone my daughter's actions. . . ."

Next he went through his family's ties to government throughout the centuries, while Welch sat and wondered what the hell any of it had to do with Gilbert's sentencing.

Strickland then spoke of Tara, Gilbert's sister, and her "aspirations" of joining the FBI.

"I will say that the recent experience in the family has soured her on the federal justice system"—he was looking directly at Welch—"for a variety of reasons, and she's taken another path in her career."

Strickland said his daughter's behavior was "bizarre over a period . . . but [it started only when] she walked out and split with her husband. [H]e refused to participate in [marriage] counseling, and only after she walked out was *he* willing to change. We tried to get her to move into our home perhaps in late spring '96 because we knew she was out of control.

"There were a few other facts that never came into evidence during the course of [the] proceeding, and . . . I don't know the rules of evidence, but I understand that there are rules, but the stresses were even more."

He was referring to the testimony of Dr. Ronald Winfield, the director of the Greater Lowell Psychiatric Services and a defense witness Miles had brought in earlier, during sentencing arguments. Dr. Winfield testified that Gilbert suffered from Post-Traumatic Stress Syndrome and committed the bomb threat under the influence of that disorder.

After that, Strickland explained how Gilbert's disability insurance had been suddenly cut off in the middle of July 1996, and she stopped receiving disability payments shortly thereafter.

". . . [S]he couldn't get her disability attorney, and to this day can't get the federal government to answer why. They won't even answer her phone calls or letters. It seems suspicious, to be honest, and I think it was induced to put stress on her."

Welch was having a ball listening to Strickland blame him and his office for just about everything that had happened in Gilbert's life. The fact of the matter was, Gilbert's disability payments had been cut off because she could not return to work, and the VA was left with nowhere to place her.

"I think a lot of this was circumstances beyond her control," Strickland said shortly before he was finished. "I'm not saying that she was guiltless—certainly not. And I'm not trying to make an excuse for that. But the circumstances, unlike what Mr. Welch has said, that this is a lifelong history of behavior. . . . This person is anything but a lifelong criminal."

With that, Gilbert stood and bowed her head. Crying, she said, "I'd just like to say that I'm very sorry for what happened. And as Dr. Winfield testified, I really don't have a very clear memory of that particular time period and, actually, that's sort of growing over time.

"I don't really have a very clear memory except bits and pieces of really that whole summer, patches here and there. It was a very stressful, hectic time of my life. Sometimes, it seems the mind chooses to block out things we don't want to remember. A lot of what I remember is what people have told me about my own behavior, and my own behavior was very erratic and whatever.

"I would never intentionally hurt anyone. And I have no animosity towards anybody that testified here or anybody involved in the case at all.

"I would really just like to move on with my life and see my children, and remind the court that in addition to my fifteen-month confinement, that you had also ordered therapy during that time, and I went every week. I never missed an appointment, and I utilized it.

"I think it's . . . you know—" She stopped talking to catch her breath. "I'm a little nervous right now, but I think it's certainly helped me deal with everything that was happening at that time, and I just hope you take all that into consideration."

"Thank you," Judge Ponsor said. "If you have any final words, Mr. Welch, I will hear from you now?"

"I do not."

So it was: Richard Strickland's accusations that the government had had it out for his daughter from the start, Gilbert's own testimony that she was under such severe emotional distress at the time of the bomb threat that she had no idea what she was doing, nor Harry Miles's weak argument that Welch and his bandits had railroaded his client did little to sway Judge Ponsor—because he imposed a sentence of fifteen months.

"It is customary to stand during sentencing, but I'm going to make a couple of remarks, and then I'm going to formally impose the sentence," Ponsor said.

Now it was the judge's turn to speak.

Ponsor first told the court that he didn't "consider this in any sense a light sentence at all." He recommended that Gilbert be placed in the Bureau of Prisons mental health program. It would allow her to, he said, continue "to make progress" with the therapeutic work she had been doing ever since she became part of the justice system back in 1996.

"There are aspects of this case which, frankly, from the beginning have mystified me more than any case I could think of. There are certain parts of the case that I simply don't understand. A judge is always riding along the tip of an iceberg and never is completely sure of what's going on underneath the water. But in this case there seems to have been more going on beneath the water than I could acknowledge.

"I don't understand what's going on in Ms. Gilbert's background or what happened here. I *do* know that the defendant was proved guilty beyond a reasonable doubt and that the evidence at trial was overwhelming on that point.

"Only one or two realities is possible, and one is that the defendant is, despite having been proved guilty beyond a reasonable doubt, the victim of the most extraordinary series of coincidences that I've ever heard of in my life or in fiction because the evidence was certainly there."

That line received a few laughs from the packed courtroom.

"The other possibility is that the defendant is, in fact, guilty and did make those phone calls. And if the defendant is, in fact, guilty . . . it absolutely mystifies me that there was no plea or formal acceptance of responsibility and the possibility of a better shot at showing aberrant behavior which would have lowered the potential sentence. So there's an aspect of this case which is an utter mystery to me.

"I do not understand how the case ended up in the format that it did, but in any event, it did. And I'm very satisfied in my own mind that the defendant committed the crimes that she's

harged with and was certainly properly found guilty beyond a
reasonable doubt of those crimes."

The first phase of Gilbert's criminal life was over. The second phase, however, was just heating up.

Yet as Welch, Murphy and Plante would find out in the coming months, Gilbert would be hard-pressed to stay out of trouble—even while confined to her cell at the Danbury,
Connecticut, Federal Prison that would be her home for the next
fifteen months.

CHAPTER 77

The long list of indictments the US Attorney's Office was putting together against Gilbert was beginning to overwhelm Bill Welch, who had been on the case since June 1996.

As Gilbert did her time for the bomb threat, the murder investigation moved forward. In reaction to the growing number of witnesses and new evidence, including the Kenny Cutting and Stanley Jagodowski exhumations, Welch went to his boss, supervising US attorney Kevin O'Regan, and said he wanted another prosecutor who could share equally in the workload.

The court had already appointed defense attorney David Hoose back in December 1997 to represent Gilbert in any future matters. Hoose had been recommended by trial judge David Bruck, who was in charge of coordinating public defenders for federal defendants in capital cases.

At forty-five, Hoose was a Northampton resident and partner in Katz, Sasson, Hoose and Turnbull, with offices in Springfield and Northampton. Welch had seen Hoose in court and he knew the tall, slick and bald defense attorney was going to be tough to go up against. Hoose had a reputation for being a hard hitter, both on and off the field. Shortly before taking the Gilbert case, Hoose had defended Alex Rankin, who was later convicted of killing a South Hadley dentist, Robert D'Amour, in 1993.

Under federal law, a person accused of capital felony murder is entitled to two lawyers, and one of them must have death penalty case experience. Hoose had worked on appeals in capital punishment cases before. Since Harry Miles had already been dealing with Gilbert for a number of years, Hoose quickly announced Miles would act as his co-counsel.

After some prudent thought, Miles and Hoose decided to ask the court if they could bring in another attorney. Judge Ponsor heard their argument and agreed.

Hoose and Miles chose Paul Weinberg, who, in over twenty years of practicing law, had never tried a criminal case. Weinberg was a malpractice attorney. Hoose and Miles had chosen him because of his obvious expertise in medical records. Later, Weinberg told a reporter for the *Hampshire Gazette* he was "reluctant to get aboard" what he called "the train from hell. . . . Because once you buy your ticket, the doors close . . . and you're off, and there is nothing you can do about it."

Welch's first choice for co-counsel was Ariane Vuono, a former Northwestern assistant district attorney who had been sworn in as a US Attorney in July 1995. Not only did Vuono have trial experience, but she could bring a female perspective to the case, something Welch was looking for.

She was the "perfect fit," Welch later said. "Extremely talented." She could bring to the team insight they didn't have, and, hopefully, answer the one question Plante, Murphy and Welch had been asking themselves for well over two years now: What made Gilbert tick?

Back in 1995, Vuono went to work under Jeffrey Kinder, the assistant US attorney in charge of the Springfield office at the time. She had been brought in by Kinder to take on the large-scale drug-dealing cases and corruption cases the Springfield US Attorney's Office prosecuted. She was chosen, Kinder later said, because of her trial experience and appellate work in Northampton.

Around the office, the soft-spoken Vuono came across to most of her new colleagues as laid-back and nonthreatening. Strikingly attractive, rather small and petite, just under five feet, maybe one hundred pounds, an avid runner, at forty-one Vuono was in the incredible shape of a healthy twenty-year-old.

Prior to her appointment as a US Attorney, Vuono had

worked as an A.D.A. in the Northwestern District Attorney's Office for seven years. She graduated from Yale University, received a master's degree in Italian Language and Literature from Middlebury College, and a law degree from the University of Connecticut.

She was married to a well-respected chair of the Italian Literature department at Smith College, Alfonse Procaccini. Only months before Vuono had been sworn in as an assistant US attorney, she prosecuted Sandra Dotsie, a twenty-eight-year-old nurse who had smothered her stepson to death over resentment of child-support payments and the time her husband had spent with the child. With a child of her own from a previous relationship and two stepchildren, Vuono had a unique point of view to bring to the Dotsie case, for which she ultimately obtained a conviction.

One day shortly before the bomb-threat trial concluded, Welch walked about twenty yards from his corner office, sat down in Vuono's office, and just stared at her.

"What is it, Bill?"

"I need you to come aboard," Welch said. "Would you be willing to do the murder investigation and prosecute Gilbert?"

There had been another prosecutor working with Welch at the time, David Gier, and Vuono wanted to know where she fit in. Three prosecutors? She didn't like the sound of it.

"In what capacity would you need me, Bill, if you already have David?"

"Just you and me, Ariane. David won't be part of this."

Gier was certainly a competent attorney in his own right. He was working for the Northampton DA's office, and he had just taken on more responsibility in the office. Welch knew he wasn't going to have the time. Plus, it was a federal case. Local law enforcement would be helping, sure, but it was a government case all the way.

Vuono was still a bit skeptical, however.

"Is it going to be fifty-fifty, Bill?"

"I heard David is withdrawing from the case, anyway," Welch said. Vuono could tell by the look in Welch's eyes he was serious. "Yes, of course. Fifty-fifty. You and me!"

Vuono turned out to be exactly what Welch needed. Not only was she talented, but Vuono was the only attorney in the US Attorney's Office at the time to have tried a murder case.

As the evidence continued to pour in, the case against Gilbert was amounting to the biggest thing to roll through Western Massachusetts in decades. Bill Welch needed the best. By his estimation, he now had it.

CHAPTER 78

The first few months of the new year, 1998, had been difficult for Special Agent Steve Plante. With pressure mounting to secure an indictment, Plante and Murphy had been meeting with one family member after the next to inform them of the bad news: there was a good chance their son, brother, father or husband had not died of natural causes as they had once believed, but Kristen Gilbert had murdered them. In the midst of breaking the dreadful news to family members, Plante had just gotten word that his father had been diagnosed with cancer and had only six months left to live, which made it only that much more difficult for Plante to face each family member.

On the first warm spring afternoon in May 1998, Plante was exactly where he wanted to be: at home, in Bedford, taking a stress-relieving jog through the neighborhood where he lived. He had just visited with his father, who wasn't doing so well. Running helped Plante deal with what was turning out to be one of the worst years he could recall. In addition to watching his father die a slow and painful death, Plante had been involved in the Gilbert investigation now for nearly two years, and they still hadn't secured enough evidence, Welch kept telling him, to indict her.

That, of course, could all change when the toxicology results from Ed Skwira's exhumation came in. But, like any good cop, Plante knew they couldn't depend on it.

As he came up on a hill about a mile from his house, Plante's pager went off.

"George Jackson?" he said to himself looking down at the number. "Why the hell is George calling?"

A forensic toxicologist, Jackson was employed by National Medical Services, one of the leading toxicology companies in the private sector. The IGO had retained the services of NMS to test the tissue samples from Ed Skwira and Henry Hudon. Hudon's body had been cremated, but because the medical examiner couldn't find a natural cause of death at the time he conducted an autopsy, he saved tissue samples.

Plante jogged to the nearest pay phone and dialed up Jackson.

"What's up, George? I haven't spoken to you in a long time."

"Steve, listen," Jackson said. "We found ketamine in your guy, Ed Skwira."

"Ketamine?" Plante had never heard of the drug.

"Yeah, Steve. Ketamine!"

"What the hell is ketamine, George?"

"Well, it's a veterinarian type of drug. Kids on the street call it 'Special K.' "

"What? You've *got* to be kidding me."

At first, Plante stood in the phone booth and just thought about the depth of the case. Every time he turned around, there was another path to follow. Yet, as soon as he started to become overwhelmed, the alarm bells went off.

"It all began making sense after I thought about it," Plante later recalled: the seven trips Gilbert had made to area veterinarians throughout August 1995 and June 1996, all of Gilbert's pets mysteriously dying throughout the years, the story Samantha Harris had told him about Gilbert's cats, and, possibly, Glenn Gilbert's deteriorating health throughout the fall of 1995.

Ketamine!

When Plante got home, he called Murphy right away.

"Now, sweetheart," Murphy said, "all we have to do is find out where she got it."

*   *   *

Ketamine wasn't a controlled substance in 1996, so anyone could order the drug through the mail if he or she wanted. Kristen Gilbert had been telling a story for the past two years that she and Glenn had always ordered drugs for their pets through catalogue companies so they could save money. But Glenn, of course, later denied it.

There was one more interesting fact that made much more sense to Plante and Murphy now: The VAMC had never purchased or stocked ketamine, but Baystate, along with many other area hospitals—including all the veterinarian clinics in the area—had.

Perhaps Gilbert had stolen the drug?

They soon developed the theory that Gilbert had ordered several different drugs for several different reasons, one of which was to poison people. They surmised that she had tried to kill Skwira with epinephrine, but when it failed, she took a ride with him to Baystate and somewhere along the way tried to "zip" him with ketamine. That would explain why Skwira suddenly began having hallucinations once he got to Baystate, and later at the VAMC, shortly before he died.

After a laborious search, they couldn't locate a canceled check or money order in Gilbert's name, thus tying her directly to mail-ordering ketamine. At best, it was a longshot, anyway. Gilbert had made mistakes in the past, sure. But using her own name to order a potential murder weapon, nearly everyone agreed, was not something she would have likely done.

It turned out to be another dead end.

On September 22, Steve Plante got the news he had been dreading ever since the beginning of the year: His father had passed away.

After returning from the funeral a few days later, Plante learned that Mary Vella, Angelo Vella's daughter, was going to be informed that day that Gilbert had attempted to kill her father. Vella had died of natural causes only a short time before, but Plante knew Mary well enough to know that the news of Gilbert's poisoning attempt was going to devastate her.

"Let me tell her," Plante insisted.

As he walked Mary out of the US Attorney's Office after

breaking the news, she broke down in his arms and began crying. So Plante comforted her.

"It's going to be okay, Mary," he said.

As he stood there, everything just hit Plante all at once: his father dying, the funeral, the years of the investigation piling up, and the ripple effect on the lives Gilbert had ruined. He was mad at himself for being pulled away from his father by the investigation. He had wanted to go to his father, who had been following the Gilbert case right along, one day and tell him before he died that she had been found guilty. But now he realized that day would never come.

For a few minutes, Plante and Mary Vella didn't speak; they just stood, rocking back and forth, embracing each other and crying.

For perhaps the first time, Plante realized how much of an impact Gilbert's narcissistic behavior had on the people involved, not to mention how many lives she had affected. The killing had stopped up at the VAMC years ago, but the aftereffects were still being felt years later. *It was time*, Plante thought, *Gilbert paid for that.*

CHAPTER 79

November 24, 1998 was a dreary day in Springfield. Temperatures hovered around sixty degrees, which was a pleasant relief from all of the cold weather lately, but it had been raining on and off all day long.

Kristen Gilbert was confined to her six-by-eight-foot cell in Danbury, Connecticut. For her, the gloominess of the day would pale in comparison to what was about to happen.

With Kevin Murphy and Steve Plante standing like bodyguards behind him, Bill Welch, Massachusetts US Attorney Donald Stern, and Ariane Vuono called a press conference for late afternoon. It was no secret around town that the time had finally come for the feds to announce the long list of indictments against former VAMC registered nurse Kristen Gilbert.

One might have expected the attorneys to be gloating, a look of triumph in their eyes. But Stern, Welch and Vuono were stoic, as if it had been a long night of deep reflection. After all, they weren't only there to announce the government was going ahead with its serial murder case against a former nurse, but to solidify to the public that, from their view, several people had been murdered while under Gilbert's care. When the facts about the case emerged, the public was going to be outraged.

Donald Stern stepped up to the podium, while print reporters sat captivated and television cameras focused on him sharply. They waited to hear what the government had on Gilbert.

With his normally soft-spoken voice now emotional, Stern called the government's case against Gilbert "deeply disturbing." Looking from side to side and blinking continuously as cameras flashed around him, Stern said, "The fact that a nurse, expected and obliged to care for patients who were in an intensive care facility at the VA [hospital], would murder them in their vulnerable condition while they lie in their beds, is shocking and un*think*able."

Stern didn't want to give away the government's case, so he quickly announced that he wouldn't be addressing what the government thought was Gilbert's motive for the killings. Yet he assured everyone in the room that the deaths were *not* mercy killings.

"These men did not want to die," he said. "This was not a mercy killing by any stretch of the imagination."

WWLP, TV-20, one of the local television news stations that had been covering the Gilbert case since her bomb-threat trial, headlined the day's events later that night by beginning its newscast with: "She was supposed to be an angel of mercy; instead, she was an angel of death."

Gilbert was indicted on three counts of murder for the deaths of Henry Hudon, Ed Skwira and Kenny Cutting; two counts of attempted murder for Angelo Vella and Thomas Callahan; and obstruction of justice for, among many other things, blocking James Perrault's car back on September 10, 1996 while he was en route to the US Attorney's Office. Six months later, two more indictments were added: one for the murder of Stanley Jagodowski and another for the attempted murder of Francis Marier.

After the official announcement, talk around town quickly shifted from shock and disbelief to whether the government would pursue the death penalty.

US Attorney Donald Stern said he wasn't sure if his office was going forward with the death penalty, stating that he first wanted to speak to family members of the victims and see how they felt about it.

Christine Duquette, Henry Hudon's sister, was later interviewed by a local television station and said she wasn't quite sure how she felt regarding the death penalty.

"Now, my parents, on the other hand," she said, ". . . that's their baby, even though he was thirty-five. That was their son. I honestly think they're going to look at this, especially as the trial goes on in the months to come . . . as, you know, an eye for an eye."

No matter what any of the families felt, however, the decision to prosecute Gilbert under the death penalty was in the hands of one person: US Attorney General Janet Reno. Her office would have the final say.

CHAPTER 80

While Gilbert was in Danbury Federal Prison finishing up her sentence for the false bomb threat and awaiting the start of her murder trial, Bill Welch insisted that Murphy and Plante keep a close watch on any phone calls she made from the jail.

"I want you guys to get a list of her phone calls every week and go through them. See who she's been calling. Once a month, I want you down there listening to the tapes."

It was a painstaking process, but one Murphy and Plante knew could yield new leads.

Most of the calls Gilbert made were quick, only one or two minutes. Being in prison, it took at least that long to make a call, so at first Murphy and Plante focused their attention on the longer, ten- to fifteen-minute calls. The prison would fax a list of the calls Gilbert had made throughout a week-long period to the US Attorney's Office. If Plante and Murphy saw something exciting, they'd make the two-hour trip to Danbury, sit in a stuffy little room, and listen to the tapes.

"I don't care how long a call is," Welch blasted them one day. "I want you to listen to *every* call."

Gilbert spent most of her phone time talking to her parents. Yet once in a while she'd call an old friend in Connecticut, or a former colleague in Northampton. For the most part, the calls didn't amount to much. But one phone number, Murphy and

Plante noticed, kept showing up week after week: that of Carole Osman.

Osman had befriended Gilbert back in 1996, after the investigation had begun. Ever since then, Plante and Murphy had kept a close eye on her movements. She wasn't under any type of surveillance, but they still wanted to know what she was up to.

"Here's a few calls," Murphy said one day, "to Carole. They're quite long."

On December 2, Plante and Murphy got down to Danbury at about one P.M. As they listened to several calls made to several different people, nothing out of the ordinary struck a chord with them right off the bat. But when they got to one particular call Gilbert had made to Carole Osman, the two investigators, sitting slouched in their chairs drinking coffee, nearly spit up.

Osman, at one point during the call, asked Gilbert what she had been doing with all the free time she'd had.

Gilbert said she had been working on a novel that "drew on some life experiences."

Plante and Murphy perked right up, looked at each other, and smiled.

"I bet we're in it," Plante said, as they laughed.

Plante called Welch with the news.

"Get yourself a hotel. I'll initiate a search warrant for her cell."

Murphy spent the night writing up an affidavit. The following day, along with the search warrant he had gotten from Welch, Murphy drove down to the Bridgeport Federal Court, in Bridgeport, Connecticut, and saw the judge whose federal court held jurisdiction over the Danbury prison. The judge needed to sign the warrant before Plante and Murphy could legally enter Gilbert's cell.

After taking a look at the affidavit, shaking his head, the judge said, "This is the most incredible case I have *ever* seen. Good luck to you."

Murphy smiled.

Gilbert was to be in a scheduled counseling session at four o'clock. Her counselor had wanted to explain the gravity of the charges that had just been brought against her in the indictments and discuss how Gilbert felt about them.

As soon as Gilbert left her cell for the meeting, Plante and Murphy entered it.

Within minutes, Murphy had in his hands twenty-five pages of a novel, handwritten by Gilbert, along with a three-page outline, detailing every character in the book, along with how the remainder of the book, which hadn't been written yet, would play out.

After confiscating the book, Plante met with Gilbert and explained what they had done, and then handed her a "return," which was a receipt of items they had taken from her cell.

With her jaw nearly rubbing against the floor, she just took the receipt and walked away without a word.

It didn't take a literary scholar to see that not only had Gilbert based the novel on her life, but her plan was, according to the "outline," to write a detailed account of the past two years.

"Looks like we'll be doing some reading tonight, sweetheart," Murphy said when they got into the car.

Plante looked at the book and just shook his head.

"I couldn't believe it," Plante later recalled. "Our biggest mistake, at least that day, may have been not letting her finish the book."

Gilbert's fictional account of her life opened as a jury foreperson stood in front of her main character and read a "guilty" verdict. From there, it backtracked, telling the story of a married woman with two kids who worked at a government agency. The woman, in the book's opening pages, was thinking about initiating an affair with a security guard, "Clive," who also worked at the same agency.

As the book moved on, and, as Gilbert wrote in her outline, the "torrid" affair between Clive and the married woman progressed, a second security guard at the fictional government agency was murdered. All eyes, of course, focused on the married woman. Her co-workers "shun" her as "the pressure is placed on them to cooperate" with the authorities.

The most telling part of the book for Plante and Murphy, upon first look, was the married woman's name: "Heather

Morgan." Gilbert's middle name is Heather and her grand-mother's maiden name is "Morgan."

"Can you believe this shit?" Murphy said aloud while reading.

As the pressure of the investigation began to get to Heather, Gilbert wrote, Heather tried to commit suicide, failed, and was hospitalized. Her husband, "James," who had been behind her ever since the beginning of the accusations, saw the suicide attempt as "a sign of guilt" and ended up taking the children away from Heather.

Then Clive dumped her and began to emotionally abuse her. Clive "resents" her, seeing her as a "threat" to his job.

Then the government agency receives a "handwritten" letter from Heather, threatening "grievous harm and destruction." Yet Heather has no memory of writing it.

Every major player in Gilbert's real life was outlined in the book, from Melodie Turner to Kathy Rix to Bill Welch to Samantha Harris to Gilbert's new friends at the Federal Prison in Danbury.

Perhaps the most telling section of the book proposal was an author's note at the top of the outline page. The outline itself was sketched out to look like a Mafia family tree designed by the FBI.

Gilbert wrote that the "following work is fiction." She mentioned that although the main character, Heather, was "loosely" based on herself, "none of the events" were "real." She made a point to write that "no other character" was dreamed up with the notion of a "real person" in mind.

"Any similarities," she concluded, "are purely coincidental."

Many later wondered why Gilbert would do such a thing.

"A jail term is a useless deterrent," Dr. Sam Vaknin, author of *Malignant Self Love: Narcissism Revisited,* explained, "if it only serves to focus attention on the narcissist. Being infamous is second best to being famous—and far preferable to being ignored. The only way to effectively punish a narcissist is to withhold narcissistic supply from [her], to prevent [her] from becoming a notorious celebrity. Given a sufficient amount of media exposure, book contracts, talk shows, lectures, and public attention, the narcissist may even consider the whole grisly affair to be emotionally rewarding. To the narcissist, freedom, wealth, social status, family, vocation are all means to an end. And the end is *attention*. If [she] can secure attention by being the big bad wolf—the narcissist will unhesitatingly transform [herself] into one."

"In many respects," Dr. Vaknin continued, "narcissists are children. Like children, they engage in magical thinking."

CHAPTER 81

Gilbert was transferred from her cell in Danbury on February 15, 1999, after serving ten months out of her fifteen-month bomb-threat sentence, to the Hamden County House of Correction for Women, in Ludlow, Massachusetts. Since she'd been denied bail, Hamden County would be her new home until the murder trial was over.

She had been scheduled to be released from Danbury in November 1998, so she could serve the rest of her time at a halfway house nearby. But the US Attorney's Office intervened at the eleventh hour, offering the court a strong opinion as to why she should be kept behind bars. Welch wasn't sure at the time that they were going to indict her, so he sent a letter to the Bureau of Prisons (BOP) stating that she was suspected in a "number of murders . . . was very dangerous, and they would be putting people at risk" if they allowed her release.

The BOP, once it heard the facts from Welch, changed its mind.

Later, Welch heard through the grapevine that when Gilbert and her father got wind of what he had done, they went "ballistic," preaching to anyone who would listen that Welch had some sort of personal "vendetta" against her.

They were groundless accusations, of course. Welch was only, he later said, protecting the public from someone he viewed as a vicious sociopath capable of God knows what.

Meanwhile, as Gilbert got comfortable in her new sur-
roundings, word that the US Attorney's Office was going to
seek the death penalty began to spread through Western
Massachusetts. Some residents were outraged; others were
quick to judge, pegging Gilbert as a sadistic serial killer who
deserved nothing less than death. To make matters worse, an
earlier poll, taken by the Northeastern University College of
Criminal Justice, reflected the unbalance Western Massachusetts residents were feeling.

In 1994, Northeastern found that out of six hundred and
three Massachusetts residents, seventy-four percent favored the
death penalty for a first-degree murder conviction. Yet, when
these same people were asked to choose between the death
penalty and life without parole, only thirty-eight percent opted
for death, and fifty-four percent chose life without parole.

Nevertheless, on May 13, 1999, U.S. Attorney General Janet
Reno weighed in with the government's decision: Bill Welch
and his team had the green light. Ironically, if Gilbert were convicted and sentenced to death, she would die in the same manner as she had killed: by lethal injection.

It was an unprecedented move on the government's part—
because the last time a criminal had been executed in
Massachusetts was more than fifty years ago. On May 9, 1947,
thirty-four-year-old Edward Gertson and his thirty-two-year-
old partner, Phillip Billeno, convicted in the murder of Robert
Williams, were electrocuted.

Nearly two weeks after the government announced its plan
to go forward with the death penalty, Gilbert was brought before Judge Michael Ponsor. If she ever wanted to save the taxpayers of the state of Massachusetts any money, as she had once
told her then-husband, Glenn Gilbert, back in 1996, well, here
was her opportunity.

Although she had gained some weight, Gilbert hadn't really
changed much since she'd been incarcerated. She was still rather
attractive, considering the life she had led for the past two years.

Looking down the entire time, Gilbert stood before the soft-
spoken judge and calmly pled not guilty.

CHAPTER 82

For the next year, defense attorneys David Hoose, Harry Miles and Paul Weinberg filed one motion after another, while Bill Welch and Ariane Vuono countered with their own. Each motion filed by Gilbert's defense was flavored with the same mantra Hoose and Miles had been trumpeting ever since they had taken on the Gilbert case: The government's shoddy scientific evidence and heap of circumstantial evidence pointed to their client only because it had no one else to pin the deaths on. The government was on a "witchhunt," they insisted—and Kristen Gilbert had been its target since day one!

By March 2000, after several hearings on routine matters, the central theme of Gilbert's defense began to emerge as Hoose and Miles, opposing just about every motion filed by the government, continued to maintain that the patients in question had died of natural causes. There were no murders.

With a deadline of June 15 for all motions looming, Judge Ponsor was now faced with the decision of which pieces of evidence to allow into the trial.

Right away, Hoose went after what he thought was the government's most damning evidence: the toxicology tests done on Skwira, Jagodowski, Cutting and Hudon. Hoose called it "junk science," and said that the specific type of testing done in this case actually disguised the natural cause of the death.

Dr. Fredric Rieders, the laboratory director of National Medical Services in Pennsylvania, where the testing in question had been done, took the stand during a hearing in late March to discuss his methods for testing tissue samples. Rieders had testified in several prominent murder cases throughout the years. In the OJ Simpson case, for example, he brought out the fact for Simpson's defense that blood on the socks found at Simpson's house and the back gate of Nicole Brown's condominium both contained EDTA, a blood preservative used in police labs.

Rieders would be saying that it was massive amounts of epinephrine that killed Gilbert's patients, not natural causes, as Hoose and Miles continued to claim.

He also said he was going to testify that Skwira, Jagodowski, Cutting and Hudon all had high levels of epinephrine in their tissue—much higher levels than are naturally occurring. This was consistent, Rieders claimed, with epinephrine poisoning—especially in the case of Cutting and Skwira, patients who hadn't received any injections of epinephrine during their codes.

For most of the day, Welch and Hoose grilled Rieders about his testing methods.

Then Hoose brought in his own experts to quash Rieders's theory that his method of testing was first-rate science. If the jury was allowed to hear Rieders's testimony, Hoose argued, it would mislead them.

At the end of the day, Judge Ponsor said he would take both arguments under consideration and make a decision as soon as he could.

Throughout the next few weeks and months, Ponsor began to crack his whip and show just how tight a leash he was going to keep on the Gilbert trial. The government's charges of obstruction of justice and retaliating against a witness, Ponsor ruled on Tuesday, April 11, 2000, would not be part of the murder trial. Gilbert, he said, would have to be tried separately on those charges.

By June, Ponsor had made a decision regarding Dr. Rieders's testimony.

"A jury should be permitted to consider—and accept or reject—this evidence," Ponsor ruled.

The government had won a key ruling.

Then Ponsor shot down a motion by Hoose and Miles to challenge the death penalty. Ponsor said most of the defense's death penalty arguments had already been turned down by the US Supreme Court years ago in other cases, and as to those that hadn't, well, Hoose's arguments, according to the judge, were "unpersuasive."

As one decision after the next came in from Judge Ponsor, Hoose and Miles were flippant about how one-sided the judge appeared to be in his rulings.

But two key motions eventually fell in Gilbert's favor, the most important being whether the jury would end up hearing from Glenn Gilbert that his then-wife had tried to murder him with an injection of potassium back in November 1995.

Ponsor barred any testimony about the incident saying it would "create unfair prejudice."

The second ruling regarded the statistical evidence SA Plante had obtained back in 1996 from Stephen Gehlbach, dean of the School of Public Health at the University of Massachusetts. Gehlbach had run the numbers for Plante and, among many things, concluded that there was less than a one in one million chance it could have been a coincidence that Gilbert had been on duty for so many codes and medical emergencies. Ponsor made a point that there was no room in his courtroom for such evidence. It would only taint the jury's belief that the defendant was innocent until proven guilty. Along those same lines, Ponsor also ruled that Gilbert's colleagues were barred from testifying "that the death rate at the hospital increased during Gilbert's shifts."

Things were, apparently, evening out.

The government sent out about seventeen hundred jury summonses during the first week of July, setting the stage for what was amounting to one of the largest jury pools the state of Massachusetts had even amassed.

In his jury proposal, Ponsor wrote that he would not sequester the jury, and that he was also considering keeping a scrapbook of newspaper articles about the case to give to each juror after the trial was over in hope of stifling any temptation on their part during the trial to read the coverage.

Each side had until August 11 to submit replies to Ponsor's proposal. After that, the process of picking a jury would begin.

CHAPTER 83

The trial was expected to begin on Monday, November 20, 2000. It took weeks, but by the beginning of November a jury was chosen: nine women and three men. Their ages ranged from sixty-nine-year-old Olga Flynn, the oldest, to Scott Stetz, a twenty-year-old UPS worker from way upstate, in Lenox, the youngest. Among them was a nurse, a homemaker, a high school special needs teacher, a female lumber store worker, a dental assistant, a machine designer, along with a gamut of other professions. If Hoose and Miles wanted a jury of their client's peers, they had certainly scored one for the home team—because not only did the females outnumber the males by three-to-one, but there were mothers on the jury, something any defense attorney would want.

As the trial approached, the enormity of the task ahead began to take a toll on Judge Ponsor, who had never presided over a death penalty case in his decades of sitting on the bench.

Ponsor received a call one night a few days before opening arguments from a friend and colleague who had known first-hand how demanding a trial of such magnitude could be on a judge. He told Ponsor to keep an eye on the "level of stress [he] would be facing" in the coming months. The judge's reasoning? He, too, had sat on a death penalty case years ago and, shortly after it was all over, suffered a massive heart attack.

It was good advice for the tall and slender judge who considered himself to be in good physical shape and health. So Ponsor pledged to get twenty minutes of exercise each day and suggested that the defense, prosecution and jury members do the same.

Still, there loomed the anxiety of what was ahead.

Days before trial, Ponsor began having nightmares. In each dream, he was either the person facing execution or the executioner himself, preparing to dole out the punishment. Ponsor would see himself "walking down a hall, breathless with terror as to [the] imminence of death" with prison guards slowly shuffling alongside him. There, at the end of the hall, he would see a "vaguely recognizable man" staring back at him, "partly concealing [an] ax in the folds of his long black robe."

Without the luxury of a hair salon, an L.L Bean catalogue to order clothes from, or even the freedom to eat what she wanted when she wanted, Kristen Gilbert had gone through a physical transformation like no one could have imagined since her arraignment on murder charges in 1998. A glutton for the spotlight at one time, here she was now on the first day of her murder trial—Monday, November 20, 2000—seated next to her lawyers, more than one hundred people packed into the courtroom behind her, severely overweight, with her normally shoulder-length, bleached-blond hair grown out into its natural auburn color, falling halfway down her back. Dressed in a purple blouse, dress pants and black pumps, Gilbert tried desperately to carry herself like the young woman she was, having just turned thirty-three on November 13. But as she sat in a courtroom with the possibly of a death sentence hanging over her head, Gilbert's face told a different story. Bloated and unrecognizable, she looked nothing like the trim and fit strawberry blonde of just three short years ago.

"Can you believe that's her?" echoed throughout the courtroom as spectators and reporters saw Gilbert for the first time in years.

"This is the case of the *United States vs. Kristen Gilbert. . . .*" the clerk read aloud, looking down at her ticket. It was 9:53 A.M.

With all that had happened during the past four and a half years, it all came down to two simple words and a seven-digit number: Criminal Action 98-30044.

Ever since Welch had gotten involved in the Gilbert case, he'd promised the victims' families he would give their loved ones a voice if the case ever made it to trial. And as Welch and Vuono learned the particulars of how each veteran had died, the case came down to two very important—yet simple—medical issues: sudden cardiac death versus death.

As he worked on his opening statement over a four-week period, Welch knew that beyond making the point that the victims were common people the same as the jurors, the aim of the speech had to drive home one significant point: No matter how sick a person is, no matter what ailment they suffer from, rarely will they just die suddenly one day—and, if they do, there has to be a specific reason as to why.

That reason, the government maintained, was epinephrine poisoning at the hands of the defendant. Why? To impress her then-boyfriend, James Perrault, and to get him to come up to the ward for the medical emergencies so she could flirt with him. It sounded ridiculous. But according to the government, over the next several months, one witness after the next would walk through the stained-glass oak courtroom doors on the fifth floor of the Springfield Federal Building, past Gilbert's parents, past all the reporters, past Steven Plante and Kevin Murphy, past the victims' family members, raise his or her right hand, and tell one story after the next that lent itself to that theory.

Detective Kevin Murphy and Special Agent Steve Plante would play the part of courtroom watcher now, sitting behind Vuono and Welch, scanning the jury for reactions, taking note of anything they could. Downstairs, in the U.S. Attorney's Office on the third floor, they would offer moral support to the witnesses who were preparing to testify.

Although many of the government's witnesses were headstrong, wanting nothing more than to get up on the stand and explain what they knew, others were terrified. To every single witness, Murphy and Plante said something they had told themselves over and over throughout the years they had worked the case: "The truth has a way of standing there all by itself. Just explain to the jury what you know."

Each witness held one piece of information that, coupled together with the next witness, would chronologically tell the story from day one.

To Murphy and Plante, it was simple.

"This is the nugget that you hold," they would tell witnesses, "and we need you to deliver it."

Years before the Gilbert trial, Bill Welch and fellow U.S. Attorney Kevin O'Regan had prosecuted a bank fraud case that consisted of thousands of pages of documents they had to get the jury to understand. For the first time in Springfield, Welch and O'Regan had used a Power Point presentation during what became known as the "paperless trial." Incorporating several video monitors and laptop computers spread about the courtroom, each side could orally present its case along with pictures and videos. All the documents had been scanned into a computer beforehand, and several video presentations were created. The system turned out to be such a time-saving device that the same technology was used in just about every major trial at the Federal Building.

With the Gilbert case centered on the condition of the heart before and after death, this breakthrough technology, Welch knew, would prove itself priceless and, in a sense, allow the jury to feel as if they were sitting in their living room watching a documentary film about the case.

"I don't like it," Ariane Vuono, a self-proclaimed technophobe, said when she first heard about it. "I am totally against it!"

But within weeks of incorporating the Power Point technology into the Gilbert case, Vuono was not only won over, but she was overwhelmed at how innovative the system actually was. As they used multi-colored, three-dimensional images similar to a heart echogram and ultrasound, when the jury was finished listening to—and watching—the trial, each juror, Welch and Vuono knew, would walk out of the courtroom with a lesson in medical anatomy they had never seen before.

* * *

When Bill Welch and Ariane Vuono showed up for the first
day of proceedings, they looked exhausted. Both had been up
for a better part of the previous night preparing the appropriate
responses to dozens of motions David Hoose had filed during
the last week before trial.

It was an underhanded move on Hoose's part. Judge Ponsor
had set June 15, 2000, as a deadline for turning in all motions.
The judge said that date would give both sides enough time to
prepare arguments.

Raging mad, Ponsor blasted Hoose. "This is the last thing I
need to deal with right now!"

But Ponsor was in a jam. If he refused to hear the motions,
his decision would be undoubtedly reversed on appeal. So he
gave Hoose hell, and let Welch and Vuono have all the time they
needed to answer the arguments.

During his two-hour opening statement, Assistant US
Attorney Bill Welch pointed at Gilbert several times, raising his
voice, accusing her of causing great pain to each veteran she
had killed.

". . . [T]hese seven victims had to go through a most horrible
experience. In many cases feeling the burn or the pain of the epinephrine as it flowed into their IV lines and directly into their
veins. Their hearts raced wildly until almost beating and bursting out of their chests, the feeling of the impending doom as
death quickly approached."

Reporters vigorously scratched on their notebooks. People
looked at one another with alarm, shock, bemusement.

Regarding Gilbert's coworkers not realizing Gilbert had
been killing for so long, Welch wanted to address the subject
right away.

"[E]veryone on Ward C . . . was in a state of denial," Welch
blasted before he went through each of the victims' stories,
while photographs hovered in the background on the video
monitors. As he spoke of war heroes, alcoholics and diabetics,
grandfathers, husbands and brothers, their family members in
the courtroom sobbed in remembrance. One by one, Welch ex-

plained how Gilbert had taken the life of each victim for no other reason than to leave work early to meet her boyfriend, James Perrault, or just to get him upstairs so she could see him.

"[T]here was not a single code," Welch said, "[between October 1, 1996 and February 17, 1996] on a night when James Perrault was off duty." A few minutes later, pointing to Gilbert once again, ripping a hole in what Welch presumed would be one of Hoose's main arguments: "It's kind of like lightning striking not *once,* not *twice,* but several times in the *same* month, in the *same* hospital, on the *same* ward—all following this defendant."

At one point, Welch compared Gilbert to a firebug—an arsonist—calling her a "codebug" who staged medical emergencies to impress Perrault.

"In the end . . . this case is about . . . a defendant who took advantage of a system that places its trust in the hands of its caregivers—a system in which patients placed their trust in the hands of its caregivers! This defendant used that *trust"*—he stopped for a moment, using silence to build suspense— "against the patients and the system to commit acts of cold-blooded murder and attempted murder."

Welch scanned each member of the jury with his eyes for a moment.

"Thank you."

Suave and professional-looking, David Hoose centered his one-hour-and-thirty-five minute speech on the defense's "witch-hunt" theory, proclaiming that Gilbert was a fit mother, a good nurse, and that she and her then-husband, Glenn, were "blessed with two beautiful boys who became the center of their lives." But working opposite shifts, Hoose said, was ". . . enough to put a strain on any marriage."

For the defense, this was a good strategy. Because when it came down to it, to the jurors who had most likely never laid eyes on Gilbert before, she didn't look any different from their next-door neighbors. If they expected to see a one-eyed, one-toothed, snarling monster in an orange jumpsuit and shackles they could identify as being a serial killer, they were disappointed. Most people equated serial killers with John Wayne Gacy in a clown suit, Ted Bundy cruising the countryside in a

Volkswagon, Jeffrey Dahmer stowing his victims in a refrigerator and later cooking and eating their flesh, or Charles Manson waving his arms while shouting Nazi propaganda.

But an overweight woman in a purple blazer who had lived and worked in Northampton, Massachusetts? No way.

Indeed, no matter what picture Welch had painted in his opening statement, Hoose would have to make the jury believe they were looking at themselves, or someone they had perhaps worked with, when they stared at Gilbert.

Hoose made sure the jury knew that Gilbert was, at one time, nothing more than a quiet, professional mother of two living in a small house, with two cars in the driveway and a boat in the garage. She was a nurse. A soccer mom. For crying out loud, she helped the needy.

It was all a conspiracy arranged by her coworkers.

"The day she left, the rumors began flying. The rumor mill pushed her to a psychiatric bed," Hoose snarled.

What about all those missing ampoules of epinephrine? Hoose had a theory.

"Epinephrine is a drug," he said, then, using his hands like a politician to help move his point along, "and like any other drug it can be abused, and the people most likely to abuse it are other drug users."

He then attacked Bonnie Bledsoe and John Wall, saying *they* could have been responsible for the missing drugs. He called Bledsoe an "asthmatic with a hundred-dollar-a-day crack habit."

By the time he was finished, Hoose already had given the jurors plenty of reasons to doubt. He suggested that the toxicological evidence against his client was taken under erroneous circumstances, that perhaps Dr. Michael Baden and Dr. Fredrick Rieders were involved in a cover-up.

It was a compelling speech, one that had spectators on the edge of their seats the entire time.

For Vuono and Welch, however, it was a folly. They knew when the jury had a chance to see the autopsy photos of Kenny Cutting, Ed Skwira and Stanley Jagodowski, whose flesh had rotted and peeled back like paint chips in the years hence, reality would set in rather quickly. Hoose's theatrics and conspiracy theories would be long forgotten. It didn't matter that Gilbert was a "good nurse," "a good mother," and did good deeds for the needy. Or that Bonnie Bledsoe and John Wall were drug addicts who could have stolen ampoules of epinephrine. The fact was Gilbert had killed these helpless veterans to impress a man with whom she was having an adulterous affair—and the autopsy photos, together with all the other evidence, would present the end result of those crimes in a way that no one had ever seen before.

CHAPTER 84

Beverly Scott, Stanley Jagodowski's nurse on the night he coded, took the stand and explained to the jury that Jagodowski had not been scheduled to receive any injectable medications on the night he died, and that Gilbert had walked into his room with a syringe in hand. Susan Lessard, Jagodowski's daughter, was next, and she recalled her memories of that night.

Then the government called Dr. Thomas Rocco, the head of cardiology at the VAMC in West Roxbury, Massachusetts.

Dr. Rocco's long list of credentials—Cornell and Harvard Medical School, the UMASS Medical Center, Massachusetts General Hospital in Boston—made it clear that if there was one person in that courtroom who knew about the condition of the patients' hearts in question, it was Dr. Rocco. He had studied the medical records of all the victims for months and came to the conclusion that their deaths were consistent with epinephrine poisoning. Using the Power Point presentation technology to describe in detail the science of the heart and how it is affected by cardiac arrest, Rocco told the jury that coronary artery disease accounted for more than three quarters of the number of the cardiac arrests in the country. Then, after carefully explaining how he had analyzed each of the victims' medical records, including notations made by all of the nurses and doctors involved, their autopsy reports, and any other data he could find, he said that none of the veterans had died of coronary artery disease.

Hoose took notes as Rocco explained how he had used seventy-percent blockage of an artery as a threshold for diagnosing death by coronary artery disease.

Back after a break for the Thanksgiving holiday, Rocco took the stand for a second day, Monday, November 27. Throughout the day, he further illustrated how the heart works, how it becomes diseased, and how it can, unexpectedly, stop. Welch had him go through each of the victims' codes and explain in detail how he thought each patient had died from sudden cardiac death, not cardiac arrest.

There are basically two forms of death, Rocco explained: natural death and sudden cardiac death. Natural death occurs in someone who is ill with, say, pneumonia or kidney failure. There's a serious illness in the body that is "not directly related to the heart, and essentially the cause of death is *that* problem. The body dies, and the heart follows," Rocco said.

But sudden cardiac death, as one might assume, comes on without warning.

"It's naturally occurring death or a natural sudden cardiac death, but the heart is the problem; something happens to the heart directly, and *that* causes the death of the body."

Referring to Kenny Cutting's code, Rocco said, "The sudden cardiac arrest described here was not normal."

Although Thomas Callahan and Angelo Vella had respiratory diseases, Rocco insisted that those particular afflictions did not "trigger" their cardiac events.

Welch had been scheduled to conclude his direct examination of Dr. Rocco later that day, with Paul Weinberg set to begin the defense's cross-examination soon thereafter. But David Hoose had called Welch over the weekend and said that Weinberg had been taken to Baystate Medical and wouldn't be available until perhaps Wednesday.

"Why?" Welch asked.

Hoose began laughing. "Well, Bill, Paul had some chest pain last night. He was dizzy, sweating . . ." In other words, he had an anxiety attack.

On Tuesday, Hoose argued in front of Judge Ponsor that his team could not continue without Weinberg. Ponsor agreed, and gave them the remainder of the day off, but said they would be back in court on Wednesday—with or without Paul Weinberg.

So with Weinberg still not available, Welch agreed to bring in several more witnesses, among them, respiratory therapist Michael Krason and RN Mary O'Hanlon.

Krason and O'Hanlon went on to bolster the government's theory that Gilbert had lied on several occasions by compromising the medical records of certain patients. Like many of the witnesses, O'Hanlon hadn't seen Gilbert in four and a half years.

"Do you see Ms. Gilbert in the courtroom today?" Assistant U.S. Attorney Ariane Vuono asked O'Hanlon. Then, after a brief moment of silence, as O'Hanlon looked around the room, Vuono said, "If you do not recognize Ms. Gilbert, you can state that for the record, Mrs. O'Hanlon."

"I'm having trouble recognizing her," O'Hanlon reiterated.

Michael Krason brought to the trial its first taste of melodrama when he told the jury he had watched as Gilbert wiped the sweat off of James Perrault's brow during a code one night.

On November 30, Dr. Rocco returned. Welch had him discuss how many of the symptoms Thomas Callahan suffered prior to his cardiac event were consistent with an injection of epinephrine. Regarding Callahan's heart rate nearly doubling after he coughed, Rocco said, "This was a striking biological event."

When asked about Callahan singing "Ave Maria" at the top of his lungs before his code, Rocco stated that Callahan was "improved to the point where he could sing."

Watching the proceedings closely, with what many would later say was an "evil" gaze, Gilbert wrote dozens of Post-It notes and handed them to Hoose and Miles as Rocco described one code after the next, giving various reasons why he thought they were not natural events.

Rocco made a point to explain why some of the veterans hadn't gone into cardiac arrest immediately after Gilbert had injected them with epinephrine directly, as opposed to when she injected the drug into their IV lines.

Epinephrine injected into the arm—as in Stanley Jagodowski's case—or into the muscle tissue, Rocco said, is not only painful, but it takes longer to reach the heart and cause damage, which explained why, when Beverly Scott later asked Stanley Jagodowski if he was feeling okay, he said that besides the pain in his arm, he was fine.

By Friday, December 1, anyone sitting in the courtroom for the past week now understood completely the difference between sudden cardiac death, cardiac arrest, and death by natural causes. Entirely composed, Rocco had come across on the stand as if testifying in high-profile cases was a full-time job. Many of the jurors had scribbled notes while Rocco spoke, while others sat captivated by his obvious expertise.

Before Welch handed Rocco over to Hoose—who had since decided to take over the cross-examination from Weinberg—at about noon, he fired off his final few questions.

"... [A]re you a salaried employee for the VA Medical Center?" Welch asked.

"Yes, I am," Rocco said.

"Are you receiving any extra compensation for the time, both in preparation for your testimony and your testimony in court?"

"No, I'm not."

"Can you tell the jury whether you've ever testified before?"

"No, I have not."

After trying to get Dr. Rocco to admit he had gotten involved in the Gilbert case with a bias toward a criminal investigation, and that his opinion had been tainted from the beginning by Dr. Michael Baden and Assistant U.S. Attorney Bill Welch, Hoose went right after the seventy-percent threshold the doctor had put on his diagnosing coronary artery disease.

Rocco admitted that although he chose seventy-percent blockage of an artery as the bar, most doctors chose fifty percent. But still, by his estimation, all of the victims in question had not been at risk from dying of sudden cardiac arrest, which could have been, Hoose insisted, brought on by coronary artery disease.

What about Ed Skwira?

Rocco admitted that Skwira *had* suffered from coronary artery disease and hypertension, two ailments that could have led to his cardiac events.

After the weekend, Hoose continued grilling Rocco about his methods of diagnosing coronary artery disease and why he had drawn the conclusions he had. But it was beginning to sound as if Hoose was just repeating himself. The jury looked restless. Bored. They had heard enough from Dr. Rocco. It was December 5, time to move on.

CHAPTER 85

Continuing with the chronology of the events and deaths, Ariane Vuono called several witnesses who explained thirty-five-year-old Air Force veteran Henry Hudon's death. None offered a definitive smoking gun. But it was clear—especially when one took into context Dr. Rocco's earlier testimony—that Henry Hudon, a man who, other than waging a fifteen-year battle with schizophrenia, was as healthy as an ox and, for no reason anyone could entirely explain, died of sudden cardiac death.

Special Agent Donna Neves, who had gone to the scene in late February 1996, shortly after John Wall, Kathy Rix and Renee Walsh had first turned Gilbert in, testified how she had helped locate several e-mails between Perrault and Gilbert that had been written on the night Hudon died. It was one of the first glimpses the jury got into the sexual affair that the government claimed had initiated Gilbert's killing spree.

Since Gilbert was defended by public defenders Hoose, Miles and Weinberg, the buzz around the courtroom during the fourth week of trial was that any grandiose claims of coming from a wealthy family Gilbert had made in the past to her former colleagues had been dismantled by the testimony of her former friends and coworkers, not to mention the lack of moral support by her own family. Many thought it odd that Gilbert's parents, Richard and Claudia Strickland, who had pledged their loyal support from day one, hadn't been in the courtroom since the second day of proceedings.

When the trial resumed on December 11, RN Elizabeth Corey finished giving her rendition of Henry Hudon's admittance into the VAMC on December 8, 1995, while Dr. Gregory Blackman, who followed Corey, explained how he had responded to each of Hudon's four codes.

Next, Massachusetts state medical examiner Dr. Loren Mednick, who had conducted Henry Hudon's autopsy, shocked the courtroom by saying he could find no natural cause of death for the thirty-five-year-old vet.

"It's not very often I run into a case where I don't have an answer—or even a hint of an answer."

On December 13, being questioned by Bill Welch, Julia Hudon brought tears to the room as she recalled Henry's final words to her as he was being wheeled into the elevator on December 8, 1995, the last time she saw her son alive.

"He said, 'I don't want to die, Momma,' " Julia Hudon explained, fighting back tears.

More than three years after Francis Marier had suffered a cardiac arrest that nearly killed him, looking pasty and weak, he was interviewed via videotape by Assistant U.S. Attorney Bill Welch. Because Marier's health was in such a rapid decline, Welch wanted to document the Army vet's rather extensive knowledge of diabetes, along with how the seventy-two-year-old knew what to do when his blood sugar was low.

The video was part of Dr. Margo Denke's testimony on the afternoon of December 13. Denke was the government's diabetes expert, having run a clinic for diabetics at a Dallas VAMC. Denke couldn't explain, she said, Marier's bout with low blood sugar levels on the night he coded. There was no natural cause for it, she insisted.

When further pressed by Vuono for more detail, Denke said, "The only explanation is a very large dose of long-acting insulin."

Exactly what Vuono wanted to hear.

Pressed even further to explain why Marier's blood sugar level, for eight hours, had hovered in the forties on that same night, Denke could only say that "there must have been something that was soaking up the blood sugar and utilizing it."

To clear up any misconception the jury might have regarding a connection between low blood sugar and cardiac arrest, Vuono asked the doctor if it was possible one could cause the other.

"There is absolutely no proven relationship between a low blood sugar level and a cardiopulmonary arrest. It *does not* happen."

After Denke left the stand, a gruff-looking, heavyset man walked through the double doors and, after being sworn in, took a seat in the witness box just in front of Gilbert.

Frank Bertrand first said he owed Gilbert for the life he now had with his wife of many years, because Gilbert had been the one to set them up on a date.

But Bertrand, who had lived in nearby Goshen all his life and worked at the VAMC for the past twelve years, had always been an honest man, and today was no exception. He was there to explain what had happened to Angelo Vella on February 4, 1996, and whatever Gilbert had done for him in the past had nothing to do with that.

As the government's seventeenth witness, Frank Bertrand said that when he heard Vella scream out in pain, he rushed into his room only to find Gilbert standing by his side, syringe in hand.

Bertrand told the jury that Vella screamed out, "She did it."

The courtroom went silent.

She did it.

Gilbert, staring at anything else in the room besides Bertrand, kept writing notes and handing them to Hoose and Miles as Bertrand continued to implicate her further in Vella's code.

CHAPTER 86

Because a winter storm had arrived in Springfield on Thursday, December 14, court proceedings were canceled for the day. When things picked back up on Friday, Frank Bertrand finished David Hoose's cross-examination and Ariane Vuono's redirect examination. For perhaps the first time during the trial, a witness had placed Gilbert in a patient's room as he went into cardiac arrest. It wasn't eye-witness testimony to murder, but the closest thing to it Welch and Vuono had to offer thus far.

After Bertrand, it was up to former Ward C nursing manager Melodie Turner to give jurors a glimpse into life on Ward C both before Gilbert had been under suspicion for murder and afterward. Since the investigation had begun in 1996, Turner had been ousted from her managerial position and placed in the outpatient clinic at the hospital as a registered nurse. It was a political move all the way. Turner hadn't been qualified for the job as nursing manger in the first place. But her superiors, of course, had told her she was. Yet a nurse who had never even participated in a code taking a job in which she would have to supervise those who did, it was surely something that would now, as soon as Hoose got hold of her, come into question and fall on her shoulders.

First thing Monday morning, December 18, with Turner still on the stand, Welch wasted no time bringing into the record her history of letting the nurses know how important it was to document a patient's vital signs and staple various sections of a patient's heart monitor rhythm strips to his chart.

"Did you make [this] known to all of your nursing staff?"

"Yes."

"Did you leave signs or messages within the ICU or out on Ward C with respect to rhythm strips and charting?"

"I had things under the glass blotters. I had blank medication sheets posted right in front of the nurse's station and the same setup in the ICU under the glass top blotter. . . ."

Turner was explaining to the jury one of the government's main theories: that Gilbert knew VAMC policy and procedure, yet failed to document the condition of her patients the same as the other nurses on the ward had been doing. There were many times throughout Turner's testimony where Welch brought into the record a chart from a patient that, with the exception of Gilbert, had been documented accurately. It showed one of two things: that Gilbert had either failed to follow procedure or that she chose not to include information that might later implicate her in something that had happened to a particular patient.

For the next few hours, Welch had Turner testify as to the different types of epinephrine the VAMC stocked (1:10,000 bristo-jet plungers and the 1:1000 glass ampoules), several tour sheets that placed Gilbert at work on the nights in question, how Gilbert had lost weight, how her appearance changed drastically, becoming, according to Turner, "flamboyant" and "provocative looking," how she started wearing makeup to work where she previously hadn't, how she had gotten a "layered kind of tossing hairdo," and how Gilbert had left her husband after she started a relationship with Perrault.

By the time Welch finished, he had brought twenty-two pieces of evidence into the record, mostly memos and letters from the Labor Board describing Gilbert's work-related injuries over the years.

Before lunch, Paul Weinberg got his shot at Turner. Since she'd had *The Handbook of Poisoning* in front of her already, Weinberg decided to take a stab at trying to convince jurors that the book was mainly used for preventative methods, not as a murderer's how-to manual. Welch had already established that Turner had never given the book to Gilbert or placed it in her sewing bag, as Gilbert had once claimed.

"Is it fair to say that this book is aimed at prevention, diagnoses and treatment of poisoning?" Weinberg asked.

"That is what it says on the back of the jacket."

"It wouldn't be fair to describe that book as a 'how-to' manual of poisoning, would it?"

"I don't think I could make that decision one way or another. I think it tells you what poisonings are."

When Weinberg realized he wasn't getting anywhere, he moved on to another subject: the fact that Turner's mother and husband had worked for the VA. Then another: that Turner had perhaps "developed a sort of affection for [Gilbert]." Then another: that maybe Turner, because of the position she had held, had been preventing certain employees from moving up the professional ladder.

"Now, during the time that you were working with Ms. Gilbert, it's true that you never saw her engage in any obvious inappropriate behavior or actions that could be interpreted as harmful to a patient, isn't that correct?"

Either Turner didn't understand the question, or she didn't want to respond.

"You want me to rephrase the question?" Weinberg asked after waiting a few moments.

"Yes."

"During the time you worked with Ms. Gilbert, you *never* saw her do anything you thought was done intentionally to hurt a patient, *did* you?"

"No, I never saw her do anything intentionally to a patient."

Paul Weinberg may have been a lawyer who had never before tried a criminal case in his professional career. But here he was now, standing in front of the podium like a peacock, firing off questions as if he were an old pro.

At one point near the end of his cross-examination, Weinberg got Turner to admit she had initiated prior investigations when she found out that drugs had become missing. He was laying the groundwork for one of the defense's key arguments: that there were several other people who had worked at the VAMC in 1996 who could have, for their own selfish reasons, stolen the missing ampoules of epinephrine.

*   *   *

With the Christmas and New Year holiday seasons approaching, it was obvious to anyone who had been keeping score that Hoose and his team were getting beat up by each new witness the government presented. Although Weinberg had scored a few points with Melodie Turner, by December 19, with James Perrault and Glenn Gilbert still waiting in the wings, the defense needed to find some sort of life raft they could cling to. Because when Gilbert's two former lovers came into the courtroom and spoke of the confessions she had made, Gilbert's boat was likely going to take a plunge into an abyss with a very deep and dark bottom.

Indeed, it would be hard for her to recover—especially if she wasn't going to take the stand herself.

David Hoose was a professional, however, with a reputation for being a crack lawyer who knew the ropes better than most of his peers. He knew John Wall and Bonnie Bledsoe's past drug use would cast doubt on the government's case and suppress any momentum that was building.

The years immediately after the investigation had begun hadn't been good to Bonnie Bledsoe. Her drug use, as Hoose would soon get his chance to expose during his cross-examination, had escalated to a point higher than it had ever been.

In fact, in October 1999, Bledsoe crashed and burned. After a binge, she collapsed on the floor of her home, stopped breathing, and went into cardiac arrest. From there, she was put on a respirator for twelve days and ended up staying in the hospital for six weeks. It was the last time she had used drugs.

On Tuesday, December 19, 2000, when she took the stand under an offer of immunity from the U.S. Attorney's Office, Bledsoe had been clean for well over a year. She wore a red winter scarf and a black dress. She looked anxious, but no more so than any other witness. She had family members sitting in the third row for moral support alongside her attorney.

The previous day had been taken up with arguments without the jury present. Welch wanted restrictions put on Hoose's questioning of Bledsoe's history of drug abuse. Hoose, of course, wanted to go up one side of her and down the other. He said he had evidence that she stole money from John Wall and her parents' bank accounts to support her drug habit.

"It's important for the jury to understand the depth of her problem. She repeatedly lies about her drug use."

Ponsor decided to let Hoose question Bledsoe at will. She was going to say some incriminating things against the defendant; it was only fair that the jury knew the kind of person who was making those accusations. Weinberg had already established through Melodie Turner that the defense was going after Bledsoe's drug use with full force, asking Turner if she knew Bledsoe, who had worked for her all those years, had also been using crack cocaine and heroin while employed at the VAMC.

Turner had said she didn't have a clue.

Welch was an experienced trial attorney. He knew how to work things in gradually, hoping to lessen the sting of the more potent problems Bledsoe had had.

But Bonnie Bledsoe was a reformed drug addict; there was no way of getting around it.

Welch established immediately that Bledsoe and Wall had dated on and off from 1991 until 1999, and that between October 1991 and March 1996, they had lived together. Regarding Gilbert's performance as a nurse, Bledsoe, like many of Welch's previous witnesses, admitted she thought Gilbert was a "good nurse," kind and intelligent.

Bledsoe explained she had been asthmatic all her life, often taking shots of epinephrine to control the more severe bouts with the disease. "It worked very well," she said of the drug. But at the same time, she added, it made her heart race.

Then Welch had her describe the one reason why she was on the stand: Michael Cascone's several codes on January 28, 1996.

During Cascone's third code, Bledsoe said she told Gilbert that if she had to run over to Building One, where Cascone was, to respond to another code, she was going to start "wheezing."

That was when, Bledsoe testified, Gilbert had reached into her pocket and pulled out "a vial of something" and asked, "Do you want some epi, Bonnie?"

Whispers were heard throughout the courtroom. It hadn't mattered at that moment that a former drug addict had said it; what mattered was that Gilbert had been carrying ampoules of epinephrine around the ward with her.

Then came the hardball questions.

"I want to ask you," Welch said, "whether or not there came a time in late 1994 when you began using heroin?"

"Yes."

"Do you remember when you first started using heroin?"

"Around the fall of '94."

"For approximately how long did you use heroin after the fall of 1994?"

"Until April of '95."

After Bledsoe indicated she had detoxed herself off the drug on April Fool's Day 1995, Welch asked if she thought that she was addicted to the drug.

"Yes, I did."

"Approximately how much heroin were you using as of, say, February or March of 1995?"

"Between five and ten bags a day."

"Can you indicate to the members of the jury whether or not there were occasions when you would use at work?"

"Yes, there was."

Welch then asked if Bledsoe thought her drug use affected her performance while at work.

"No, it did not."

To reinforce Bledsoe's claim that a five-to-ten-bag-a-day drug habit had nothing to do with her job performance, Welch admitted into evidence several work performance evaluations backing up her earlier testimony.

She hadn't a blemish on her record.

"Did there come a point . . . in 1995 when you began using another controlled substance?"

"Yes, there was."

While Bledsoe answered Welch's questions, she looked nervously around the room, sizing up the jury, looking toward her parents and, finally, staring down Gilbert, who never once looked back.

"And what controlled substance was that?"

"Crack cocaine."

He asked when.

"Late summer, fall of '95."

"For how long did you continue to use crack cocaine?"

"On and off until 1999."

Welch then toned it down a bit, getting Bledsoe to acknowledge that her addiction to crack had caused her to miss long periods of time from work. Then he questioned her about John Wall, and how she had stolen money from him to support her habit.

"During this time frame [1996–1997], were you on occasion using with Mr. Wall?"

"Yes, I was."

Establishing the fact that she had begun using both heroin *and* crack cocaine during the same period, and that it had put a huge strain on her asthma, which put her in and out of area hospitals on many different occasions, Welch wanted again to know how much of each drug she had been using.

"A day?" Bledsoe asked.

"A day."

"A hundred dollars of heroin a day, a couple of hundred dollars of crack a day."

"How were you financing that sort of habit?"

"Selling things I owned. I sold most of my furniture, sold most of John's [Wall] furniture. When I left the [VAMC] the year before, I took my thrift savings plan, spent all that. We had sold John's house in May of 1999, so we had a lot of money left over from that."

"How much money was that?"

"Two hundred and fifty thousand dollars."

It got worse.

"And by the end of 1999," Welch asked, "what happened to all that money?"

"I'm sorry?"

"By the end of 1999, *what happened* to all that money?"

"It was gone."

In less than a year, Bledsoe and Wall had used a quarter of a million dollars worth of cocaine and heroin.

"As your resources dwindled, did you have to begin to steal things in order to support your habit?"

"Yes, I did."

"What did you do?"

"I would go to Home Depot and shoplift items and return them for cash."

Then Welch got into the cardiac episode that, according to Bledsoe, changed her life and sent her running for treatment.

Finishing up, Welch had her admit she was now a card-carrying member of Narcotics Anonymous.

"Do you also chair and teach [at] such meetings?"

"Yes, I do."

"My last question to you, Ms. Bledsoe, is whether or not you were the only person to blame for your drug addiction?"

"Yes, I was."

CHAPTER 87

"Ms. Bledsoe, my name is David Hoose. I think you know me, don't you?"

"Yes, I do."

That was the last time anything pleasant would come from David Hoose's mouth, as far as Bonnie Bledsoe was concerned. He had a job to do. He had a witness accusing his client of having in her possession an ampoule of the drug that the government was claiming she had killed patients with. It wasn't time to exchange pleasantries; it was time to let the jury know exactly who Bonnie Bledsoe was.

"[W]hen you're using drugs to the level you were using them, you learn a lot about deceptive behavior, don't you?" Hoose asked.

"Yes, you do."

"You learn a lot about how to manipulate people and things, don't you?"

"Yes, you do."

"And you *certainly* learn how to lie a lot, don't you?"

". . . I didn't learn how to lie. No."

"Well, when you were using drugs you told a lot of lies, didn't you?"

"Yes, I did."

After several more questions regarding Bledsoe's reasoning

ehind not telling people she had used drugs, Hoose's voice
etting louder with each word, he said, "And a couple of people
at you particularly didn't want to know about your drug use
istory was Mr. Welch and Ms. Vuono, isn't that correct?"

"I figured they knew about it."

"All right. That wasn't my question. You didn't want them to
now, did you?"

"At one point, no."

"All right. Now, what about Agent Plante, you didn't want
im to know either, did you?"

"At one point, no."

"Trooper Murphy, you didn't want him to know at one point
ither, did you?"

"At one point, no."

"All right. And, in fact, you had met with all those people
vithout telling them anything about your drug history, isn't that
orrect?"

"It was never asked of me."

Hoose continued along these lines for quite a while, hoping
o break Bledsoe down and get her to keep repeating that she
ad held back information. However, when it came down to it,
he lies she had told had nothing to do with what she saw while
vorking with Gilbert that cold night in January 1996. They
vere two separate issues. And Welch had been solid in his ques-
ioning, making sure to bring up the later dates, 1997, 1998,
1999, when Bledsoe's drug addiction was at its peak.

Bledsoe had an uncanny way of smiling while Hoose ques-
ioned her.

"Is this humorous to you? I notice you smiling a lot."

"No, it's not."

By the end of the day, Hoose wanted to convince the jury
hat what Bledsoe had said she saw on the night Michael
Cascone coded was not at all what had happened.

"You can't be sure it was epinephrine, can you?"

"No . . ." Bledsoe answered, looking down toward the floor.

By the following day, December 20, word around the courthouse had it that David Hoose was just getting started with
Bonnie Bledsoe. Today he was really going to get to the core of
her credibility.

First thing in the morning, Hoose made sure the jury knew Bledsoe didn't just decide one day to quit her job at the VAMC as Welch had suggested during his direct examination. Rather she had been written up so many times for missing work because of her addiction to drugs that she was forced to leave

But that was about it. Hoose didn't have much more.

Nonetheless, by the time Bledsoe left the stand, Hoose had planted in the jury's minds the theory that she and Wall lifted several ampoules of epinephrine from the VAMC at around the same period Gilbert was said to have used them to kill Jagodowski, Hudon, Cutting and Skwira.

When Hoose subpoenaed Wall and Bledsoe's medical records, he noticed that on several different occasions Bledsoe had asked to have a shot of epinephrine for her asthma. Yet on a few occasions, Hoose noted, Bledsoe had told the hospital or clinic that she had already taken a shot at home before coming in.

Who gave her the shot?

John Wall.

Hoose wanted to know if John Wall had stolen the epinephrine that he had given to her from the VAMC?

"No! He most certainly did not."

Then he wanted to know if Bledsoe had.

"No, I did not."

As April Gougeon began to testify later that same day, it was clear where Welch and Vuono were bringing the government's case against Gilbert next.

Gougeon told the jury about a phone call she had received one night from Gilbert where she talked about getting a new garter belt. During a code the next night, Gougeon explained, she saw Gilbert straddling a patient, like a horse, showing that same garter belt off to James Perrault, who was participating in the code.

She then talked about the night in November 1995 when Gilbert had come into the VAMC on her night off to get some potassium out of the medical supply closet. Gilbert claimed it was for her husband. On several occasions throughout her testimony, Gougeon praised Gilbert's nursing skills, claiming she outdid just about everybody else on the ward when it came to code work.

Most of the testimony now was geared toward one destination: the affair Gilbert had had with James Perrault. A clear picture of Gilbert and Perrault's burgeoning relationship during the fall of 1995 was beginning to develop, with the jury getting intimate glimpses into how the relationship heated up over the summer and fall.

While her coworkers filed up to the stand and spoke about how they viewed Gilbert during those crucial months of 1995 and the first months of 1996, Gilbert never once looked at any of them.

The jury, on the other hand, was heading into the holiday break with an earful of circumstantial evidence to chew on for the next twelve days. When they came back, things were going to get even more interesting. Kathy Rix, James Perrault, John Wall, Glenn Gilbert and, finally, Dr. Michael Baden were set, along with several other material witnesses, to finish out the government's case.

On Tuesday, January 2, 2001, court resumed. After Lori Naumowitz and Carl Broughear concluded their testimony, the government called one of its key witnesses: Kathleen Rix. If there was ever a doubt in the jury's mind at this point whether Gilbert had been responsible for the deaths at the VAMC, Welch and Vuono were confident Rix's testimony would wash it away.

However compelling Kathy Rix's narrative of finding broken ampoules of epinephrine might be, the government had been dealt a brutal setback over the holiday break. On a trip to Pennsylvania to visit Dr. Rieders to see how he was coming along with the toxicology tests he was conducting on the tissue samples, Welch and Vuono learned that the doctor had miscalculated some of his figures and made several mathematical errors.

Rieders's laboratory was said to be one of the only labs in the U.S. with the proper equipment to detect epinephrine in

418

M. William Phelps

human tissue. Even so, a simple mathematical error tainted the entire batch of evidence. Rieders would get hammered for making the mistake, and the rest of his testimony would be suspect. Welch and Vuono realized they couldn't use it—which meant their entire case now relied on circumstantial evidence.

A hard-nosed, straight-to-the-point woman who held little back, Kathy Rix had not changed much since 1996. She was still the good-looking cop's wife from Westfield who had held on to perhaps one of the most important "nuggets" of information in the trial.

Rix may have broken down during those first few meetings with the HCI inspectors who had first arrived on the scene years ago, but she'd had several years to think about what she was going to say when she got on the stand.

"How long have you been a registered nurse?"

"Twenty-five years."

For the next fifteen minutes, Welch had Rix run through her rather impressive credentials. By the time she was finished, spectators were asking themselves if there was anything Rix *hadn't* done within the medical community.

"How would you describe [the defendant's] professional skills as a nurse?"

Rix looked over at Gilbert, yet Gilbert kept her head down.

"Kristen was an excellent nurse. She had very good clinical skills, assessment skills."

"What was her knowledge with respect to medications? Was it up to par?"

"Excellent."

Short, quick responses. Rix said only what she had to, no more.

While Hoose continually objected to Welch's next line of questioning, Welch got Rix to talk about Gilbert's "bedside manner." Rix said it was normal. But that was it. When Welch asked if it was better than anyone else's, Rix simply said "no," over an objection by Hoose.

"What do you know about epinephrine and its effects?" Welch asked next.

"Epinephrine is a very powerful cardiac drug. It's an emer-

gency drug. It causes the blood vessels in the periphery of the
arms and legs to constrict and bring the blood flow to the torso
and head. It raises a person's blood pressure and their pulse and
helps, hopefully, to revive a person when used in an emergency."

Next, Welch had Rix explain where ampoules of epinephrine
were stocked, and which form the drug came in. He established
through Rix that the Ward C nurses had full access to the drug
and knew where the key to the satellite pharmacy was kept.

"During the time you worked at the VAMC . . . did you ever
know the 1:1000 epinephrine [ampoules] to be used on Ward C
or in the ICU?"

"No."

Welch asked her if she had ever—in her ten years as a nurse
at the VAMC—personally used the 1:1000 ampoules of epinephrine.

"Once."

But it was after the fact, in 1998. And as Rix continued to
tell the jury when and why she used it, Hoose objected to any
further testimony.

But Ponsor continued to let Rix tell her story.

For the following half hour, Welch and Rix talked about
Francis Marier. She went through Marier's vital signs—"stable,
normal"—his mental status—"alert and orientated"—and how
his blood sugar level continued to drop, even after he received
several ampoules of D-50. At one point, Welch got Rix to confirm Gilbert had given Marier his shot of insulin at five P.M., but
still, eight hours later, his body was consuming the D-50 at levels like she had never seen.

Then it was on to how Gilbert had changed throughout the
summer and fall of 1995. As Rix answered his questions, Welch
kept an eye on the time. With the end of the day approaching, he
had a plan.

By the time court broke at four o'clock, Welch had Rix drop
a bombshell.

"When you looked in the medicine cabinet area of the ICU
[in Thomas Callahan's room], into the round disposal needle
bucket, what did you see?"

"I saw epinephrine vials broken and used."

"How were you able to see these epinephrine broken vials?"

"You can look sort of in the half-moon hole, sort of shake i
around and look."

"When you saw the broken epinephrine vials, what was you
reaction?"

"I was stunned."

CHAPTER 88

When court resumed the following day, Kathy Rix continued on the pace Welch had set when they broke the previous day. Following Ed Skwira's code, several weeks after Thomas Callahan's, Rix told the jury she had searched the medicine supply cabinet and noticed that the ampoules of epinephrine she had counted earlier that day were gone.

"I opened the drawer and there was no epinephrine. It was awful," Rix said, looking jurors square in the eyes. "It made me sick."

Then she told the story of how she, Renee Walsh and John Wall had gotten together sometime later and decided to turn Gilbert in.

"Thank you," Welch said.

David Hoose had listened closely to every word. There were holes in Rix's story. But he didn't attack her account of finding the spent ampoules of epinephrine right away. Instead, he wanted to first bring into the record one of his theories: that because several nurses had a problem with Gilbert and Perrault's adulterous relationship, all these stories were somehow dreamed up to get back at her.

Rix gladly told jurors she felt Gilbert and Perrault's affair was wrong.

Hoose then asked Rix about her decision to forgo reporting what she had found in Thomas Callahan's room. He wanted to know why she hadn't told anyone beside John Wall about the discovery.

Rix said she was afraid Gilbert would find out.

When Hoose pressed, Rix said she was concerned with Timothy O'Donnell, the Chief of Security. She thought he would likely go running to Perrault, and then Gilbert would find out.

"Kristen could be very vindictive," Rix said. "It was very likely that Jim would find out who was bringing the investigation."

"Why didn't you take the used ampoules of epinephrine?" Hoose asked.

"What was the point?"

"To get the evidence that is *not* in front of the jury!" Hoose screamed.

It was a cheap shot. Rix, along with the rest of the nurses on Ward C, did not go to work every day looking for evidence of murder; they went to work to save lives. At the moment Rix found those spent ampoules of epinephrine, she didn't consider them to be "evidence" in the sense of the law. She viewed them as internal evidence that a friend and colleague had been killing patients.

After Kathy Rix came Carol McCarthy, a material witness, and Nancy Cutting, Kenny Cutting's wife. But all eyes weren't on Nancy's recollections of Kenny's life and death—the buzz in the room was that Gilbert's old beau, James Perrault, was set to take the stand as soon as Nancy finished.

Sure enough, with the end of the day approaching, Assistant U.S. Attorney Ariane Vuono called James Perrault.

Wearing a suit that looked a bit out of place on the muscular security guard's large frame, Perrault walked into the courtroom the same way he walked into any room: cocky, smug, full of himself. Having been in his twenties when he dated Gilbert, Perrault, now at thirty, had put on a little weight, but it was nothing that made him appear to be out of shape.

Gilbert didn't look at Perrault as he made his way through the aisle and onto the witness stand. She knew what Perrault had to say was going be devastating to her defense. He just had too many stories to tell that implicated her.

Vuono spent what little time she had left in the day going through Perrault's background, then setting the atmosphere of the medical emergencies he had participated in with Gilbert.

"It [the mood in the room] became more charged. There was more excitement in the air when we were working on a patient," Perrault said before they broke for the day.

First thing the next morning, Vuono questioned Perrault about his relationship with Gilbert, along with her suicide attempts throughout the summer of 1996. Then it was on to what everyone in the room had been waiting for: Had Gilbert said anything to Perrault about her involvement in the deaths at the VAMC when he asked her about it?

"What was her response to your—"

Perrault couldn't even wait until Vuono finished the question.

"Initially, she was denying it. And I asked her . . . and her response—she became very upset at me and she stated, 'I did it. I did it. I injected those guys with a certain drug.' "

"What did she say after that?"

"She hung up the phone."

There really wasn't anything more powerful James Perrault could offer the government than Gilbert's confession. After Vuono got it out of him, Perrault went through his entire relationship with Gilbert, all the times he had broken up with her, the night they had first made love, the drinking they had done at the VFW and his lack of concern for dating a married woman.

After a recess at 2:45, Vuono had only a few more questions for the brawny security guard, who was holding up rather well despite the fact that Hoose had sat the entire time directly in front of the witness stand, staring at Perrault, licking his chops.

Vuono wanted the jury to understand that Gilbert had gone over to her former home in Florence to try to retrieve "something"—meaning the *The Handbook of Poisoning*—while Glenn and the kids were on vacation.

"What did she tell you [about that incident]?"

"She stated that . . . she had tried to go into the house . . . [and] that her father-in-law would not allow her into the house . . ."

"Did she tell you why she was attempting to enter the home at that time?"

"She stated that she needed to retrieve 'something,' but she didn't identify it."

"I have no further questions."

Hoose stood and walked, sluggishly, toward the podium. He looked tired and weak, as if he had aged ten years during the past two months. With large circles under his eyes, he was much thinner since the start of the trial.

One man later said Hoose reminded him of "Ichabod Crane" at that point of the trial.

With all due respect, David Hoose had carried the load. Weinberg and Miles did a lot of sitting while Hoose did a lot of the questioning.

He immediately questioned Perrault's integrity, insinuating that although he knew he was dating a married woman, he still did it without reservation. Perrault answered Hoose's questions with short "yes-no" answers, not elaborating too much.

As the day moved on, Hoose led Perrault down a path of the defense's good-cop, bad-cop theory.

"They told you Kristen Gilbert is going down and you're going down with her, and that's going to be the end of your career [as a cop], is that right?"

"That was implied."

Hoose plugged Perrault for hours, trying to get him to admit the reason why Gilbert had been so "charged" during all those codes was perhaps because she had been thrilled about the new relationship she was getting involved in.

"Is it a fair statement to say that by the end of October the two of you were, if not in love . . . pretty infatuated with each other?"

"We were attracted, yes."

"And it was fun, wasn't it?"

"Yes."

"It was exciting, wasn't it?"

"Yes, it was."

"And Kristen seemed excited by the attention that you were giving her, didn't she?"

"Yes, she did."

"And she seemed to enjoy it, didn't she?"

"Yes."

"She got a new haircut, didn't she?"

"I don't recall . . ."

"She began to lose weight, is that correct?"

"I don't recall . . ."

"Did she begin dressing differently?"

"Yes."

"She began dressing more sexy, is that correct?"

"Yes."

"You liked that, didn't you?"

"Yes."

"You encouraged it, didn't you?"

"Yes."

"You have no recollection of her losing about thirty pounds and getting her hair cut?"

"No . . ."

"If you ever get married, you better notice those things. . . ." Hoose said, as the courtroom broke out in laughter.

Before court recessed, Perrault told the jury Gilbert had been under a tremendous amount of stress back in January 1996 because of her grandfather's death, her pending divorce, and an "abnormal pap smear" she'd had that month.

On Monday, January 8, Perrault was back on the stand.

"You indicated something to Ms. Vuono along the lines of whether . . . [Ms. Gilbert's] husband was abusing her. Do you recall that?"

"Yes."

"Isn't it true that you asked Ms. Gilbert all the time if Glenn was physically abusing her?"

"During our conversation she admitted that he had been abusive and we discussed that."

"Isn't it true, *sir,* that she told you that he only ever touched her once and that it wasn't a big deal?"

"No . . ."

"And isn't it true that every time she would see Glenn and be upset that you would say, 'Is he physically abusing you'?"

"No, that's not true."

Hoose realized he wasn't getting anywhere and moved on to how "upset" and "distressed" Gilbert was about the investigation during the beginning of March, April and May. When he didn't get anywhere with that, he asked Perrault about his military training and his desire to become a bonafide cop, hoping to get the jury to believe that everything Perrault had done after that point was done with the mindset that he wanted to make an impression on the local cops.

For the first time during the trial, Hoose then brought into light the possibility of a second suspect.

"Did you know Jeff Begley?"

"Yes."

"He was a nurse on Ward C?"

"Yes, he was."

'And would you agree with me that Mr. Begley was a pretty weird guy?"

"Objection, Your Honor," Ariane Vuono lashed out.

Ponsor told Hoose to rephrase the question.

"Well, was Mr. Begley someone that you knew to be having problems with other people on the ward?"

"He seemed to be, yes."

"In fact, were you aware that other people were refusing to work with him?"

"No, I wasn't."

"Objection!" This time Vuono stood up, threw up her hands, and rolled her eyes.

"Overruled."

"In any event, had you heard any rumors about the investigation initially, in the early stages, focusing on Mr. Begley?"

"Not that I recall."

After several more questions, trying unsuccessfully to get Perrault to indict Jeff Begley, Hoose moved on. He tried, almost desperately at times, to poke holes into the theory that it could have been someone else and that Gilbert hadn't done anything out of the ordinary, but it failed time and again.

Then Hoose brought up Perrault's testimony during the grand jury investigation, and how what he had said was different from what he had said just days ago in court.

"[Do] you remember being asked specifically [during the grand jury] what Ms. Gilbert had said to you . . . ?"

"Yes."

"And did you say that 'she called back . . .' stating that . . . 'I did it. I did it. You wanted to know. I killed all those guys . . .' "

"Yes."

"Is that what you told the grand jury . . . ?"

"Yes."

No matter how it was sliced, James Perrault had brought to the table some pretty solid evidence that Kristen Gilbert had admitted to her part in the crimes she was on trial for. How she chose to put that confession into words was irrelevant.

CHAPTER 89

When John Wall took the stand, he looked as if he had not slept in weeks. At one time, Wall was a good-looking man with movie star-like features. He had a promising career ahead of him in nursing. But as Ariane Vuono began to question Wall now, five years later, it became utterly apparent that the past few years had been the worst of his life.

After corroborating incriminating testimony from several other witnesses, Wall, the government's thirtieth witness, went through each victim and the role he thought Gilbert played in their deaths.

"I suspected that Ms. Gilbert might be sabotaging my patients because she was angry at me," Wall said at one point. Regarding Francis Marier, he said he was "stunned" to find out that Marier had had a cardiac arrest while under Gilbert's watch shortly after Wall had gone home.

Stopping every once in a while to take a sip of water, Wall told the jury he developed a severe addiction to heroin in 1998. He said he was now taking methadone. He said he was involved in a drug treatment program. He said his drug addiction had no adverse effect on his memory of the events at the VAMC in 1996.

By January 10, Vuono was finished. That afternoon, after getting the okay from Judge Ponsor to question Wall at length about his drug use, David Hoose began firing away.

Wall said he used drugs while working at the VAMC, beginning in 1994.

Since Wall had begun taking methadone, Hoose wanted to know if he had stopped using heroin.

"No," Wall admitted.

Then Hoose got him to admit that, like his former girlfriend, Bonnie Bledsoe, Wall had kept his drug use hidden from the U.S. attorneys throughout most of the investigation.

"You have chosen to deliberately tell lies, isn't that true, Mr. Wall?"

Wall bowed his head.

"Yes . . ."

Hampshire Gazette staff writer Judith Cameron, who had been covering the trial from day one, ended a piece she wrote that week by saying that "Phillip Cass, a private investigator" who had been hired by Hoose and Miles, had "uncovered Wall's history of drug use and addiction." Further, Gilbert's defense had maintained throughout the trial that Bill Welch and Ariane Vuono hadn't known about Bonnie Bledsoe and John Wall's drug use until a few days before trial.

But the government saw it differently.

Under the rules of discovery, the U.S. Attorney's Office was obligated to provide the defense with any impeachment evidence it had on potential witnesses. But it didn't have to turn over the evidence until no later than three weeks before trial, even if the government knew about it months or years before. Impeachment evidence is the ugly stuff prosecutors want more than anything to keep out of the courtroom: prior convictions, mental health history, drug use, alcoholism, bias, etc.

Back in July, David Hoose had improperly (and, the government claimed, illegally) subpoenaed John Wall and Bonnie Bledsoe's personal medical records and found out about their subsequent drug problems in the course of studying those records. In turn, it was thought that the U.S. Attorney's Office had been blindsided by Wall and Bledsoe—that Wall and Bledsoe had hidden the drug abuse from them. But Welch and Vuono, it turned out, were only waiting for the three-week period to come up before submitting the evidence.

Under the law, Hoose was supposed to notify John Wall and

Bonnie Bledsoe he was subpoenaing their medical records. But
he never did.

Welch and Vuono were incensed. Hoose and his team were
officers of the court who knew the law.

But what was done was done. When Ponsor found out, he really couldn't do much more than give Gilbert's defense a slap
on the wrist and continue on with the trial.

On January 10 and 11, David Hoose finished drilling John
Wall about his drug use, his addiction, how he had lied to his
family, friends, coworkers and drug counselors, and how he had
refused on several occasions to take a urine test for the defense.

Then, "It can only be described as a deeply disturbing development in the case," Judge Ponsor said on Friday, January 12,
when he heard that the government wouldn't be using Dr.
Fredrick Rieders's toxicological evidence.

In April 2000, there had been a rather long hearing about
whether Rieders's evidence would be allowed. Hoose had called
it "junk science," and now it was turning out to be just that.

Hoose said he was going to seek a dismissal of the indictments. If Rieders's tests were inconclusive, then any future testimony from Dr. Baden or Dr. Thomas Grayboys, a cardiac
specialist, shouldn't be allowed, he argued, because the doctors
were basing part of their testimony on what Rieders had found.

Judge Ponsor, fuming at Vuono and Welch, said he would
make a decision on Hoose's motions by month's end.

Over the next two weeks, there were several witnesses who
kept adding to the incriminating evidence the government was
building brick by brick.

Each nurse and doctor had his or her own stories to tell insofar as Gilbert and missing ampoules of epinephrine were concerned.

Judge Ponsor was seen one day with a copy of the
Hampshire Gazette folded under his arm and, for a second time,
lashed out at Gilbert's defense team for violating a gag order he
had put on the trial.

His reason? Hoose, Miles and Weinberg had not only spent the weekend talking to the *Gazette* about the "toll of defending Gilbert," but their pictures were plastered all around the article.

Later that week, Ponsor ruled against the motions Hoose had filed regarding government witnesses Grayboys and Baden. It was back to business as usual.

Renee Walsh took the stand on January 18. Sitting directly in front of Walsh, in the pew behind the government's table, was her fiancé, George Edward Skwirz, a scholarly-looking local accountant who had met Walsh in May 2000 following her second divorce.

As the clerk announced Walsh's name, Edward Skwirz noticed that Gilbert, who had been actively participating in her defense as many of the expert witnesses took the stand, sat back in her chair, slouched her shoulders, put her hands in her lap, and fell silent, never once looking at Walsh. Gilbert, Skwirz noticed, seemed to react differently to each witness. While an expert witness would get her full attention, a former colleague or friend wouldn't even get a passing glimpse.

Other than referring to the March 6, 1996, phone call, when Gilbert had expressed her concerns to Walsh about being called the "angel of death" by her coworkers, Walsh didn't present anything that was extremely damaging. More or less, she was called as a witness to corroborate previous testimony by Kathy Rix and John Wall that the three of them had gotten together in February 1996 and decided to blow the whistle on Gilbert.

On January 23, dressed in a tweed suit, with his head hung low, Glenn Gilbert entered the courtroom to a muffled silence of stares and whispers. He looked gaunt, tired, and worn down with worry.

Like James Perrault, Glenn Gilbert was sitting on the witness stand for one reason: to tell the jury that Kristen had confessed to the murders.

As he spoke, Welch and Judge Ponsor continually had to ask Glenn to speak up. Earlier, Ponsor had ruled that Glenn wouldn't be allowed to tell the jury about his wife's alleged poisoning attempt on his life.

Welch had a way of letting each witness he questioned tell a story that was similar to those of each of the previous witnesses. Glenn spoke of his then-wife's metamorphosis from soccer mom to single mom; from never going out after work to going out every night; from wearing conservative clothes to something out of an MTV video.

It was obvious Glenn was still shaken by the events, even five years later.

Kristen never once looked at her ex-husband. She kept her head down and doodled on a notepad.

At the end of Welch's direct, Glenn laid it all out.

"On the evening of July 10, 1996, did there come a point in time when Ms. Gilbert called you from Holyoke Hospital and discussed the investigation with you?"

"Yes."

"What was her demeanor when she had this conversation with you, initially?"

"She was in hysterics: crying, sobbing, and sounding like she was hyperventilating."

". . . [D]id she then begin to make some statements about the investigation?"

"Yes."

"What did she say?"

"She had said to me that she was calling to tell me to contact the investigators. She wanted to save the taxpayers a lot of money for this investigation. She was basically confessing."

Harry Miles, who would conduct the cross-examination, turned red as he stood up and shouted, *"Objection,* move to strike."

Ponsor agreed. He said he wanted Glenn to "relate the precise words" he heard from the defendant that night.

"She had mentioned specifically that she wanted me to call the IG [Inspector General's Office], that she wanted to save the taxpayers a lot of money. That she *did it.*"

There was lots of sidebar discussion after Glenn had incriminated his ex-wife. Miles wanted a mistrial. Welch laughed. Ponsor agreed to not let Welch go any further down the hearsay path.

But in the end, Glenn Gilbert had told the jury that his then-

wife had confessed to killing the patients she was being investigated for. There was no silver lining on the testimony; it was,
simply, one man's word against a defendant who, at this point,
still wasn't scheduled to testify on her own behalf.

During the next week and a half, several more nurses and
doctors took the stand and added more weight to the testimony
that preceded them. On February 1, however, Gilbert's defense
was blasted by Judge Ponsor for a last-minute request to show a
controversial videotape of Ed Skwira's autopsy.

David Hoose argued that some of the government's investigators were overheard during the video saying they needed to
find epinephrine in Skwira's tissue. Hoose said Dr. Michael
Baden could be heard saying, "We've got to beat up on [Dr.]
Rieders . . . to find something."

Ponsor denied the motion, but the left the door open to show
the tape later.

With that out of the way, SA Plante took the stand and tied
together all the testimony up until that point. Any question that
hadn't been previously answered was put to Plante, and he carefully filled in the blanks.

Next, Plante's partner, Detective Kevin Murphy, sat down in
the witness chair and assistant U.S Attorney Ariane Vuono pep-
pered him with the same questions Plante had just been asked
by Welch: Why? Where? When? How?

After about a half hour, Vuono said, "Thank you, I have
nothing further," and passed her witness over to Hoose.

With the jury out of the room, David Hoose asked Judge
Ponsor if he could now play the video. It would impeach the
government's witness, he said. Detective Murphy, Hoose argued, at one point during the tape, said, "We ought to put a little
epi in there," while leaning over Ed Skwira's open chest cavity.

Ponsor then went into his chambers and viewed the tape.

"I don't know why on earth I had not been given this yesterday," Ponsor lashed out when he returned. "It's absolutely
ridiculous to put me in a position in the middle of a trial to be
seeing this for the first time." He paused. "I can't believe you
did this to me."

Ponsor then said that the tape could have a "lurid and emotional impact" on the jury if it were allowed to see it. At one point, someone is seen, Ponsor said, holding Skwira's heart "like it's something you pick up at a grocery store."

Then Vuono weighed in.

"They want to discredit an investigation that took years by pulling out twelve lines of a three-and-a-half-hour videotape. . . ."

"The government started with a suspect, they started with a drug they were looking for, and, *by God,* they were going to find it," Hoose maintained.

Ponsor ruled that Hoose could cross-examine Detective Murphy without the tape.

After a series of questions regarding where and how Murphy located *The Handbook of Poisoning* in Glenn Gilbert's pantry, Hoose then got right into the Skwira autopsy.

He asked Murphy if he knew the videotape recorder was recording audio. Murphy said he wasn't sure. Then Hoose insinuated that, because there was no audio in any of the latter autopsy tapes, Murphy, Baden and the rest of those participating in the autopsy might be saying things they didn't want anyone else to hear.

Then Hoose asked Murphy if he could be heard during Skwira's autopsy saying that someone "ought to put a little EPI in there"?

"Yes," Murphy said.

And that was it. Hoose wasn't going to get anything else about the matter out of the thirty-year veteran of the Massachusetts State Police.

After several more government witnesses testified, rumor around the courthouse on Friday, February 2, had it that Dr. Michael Baden would be taking the stand when court resumed after the weekend.

Welch told reporters outside the courthouse that following Baden there would be a few more key medical witnesses, but that would be it. The government would rest its case.

CHAPTER 90

Dr. Michael Baden brought to the courtroom its first taste of national celebrity. Having testified in numerous high-profile cases throughout his forty years of practicing forensic medicine, and basking in the success of his first book, *Unnatural Death: Confessions of a Medical Examiner*—a book Harry Miles had been seen reading—Baden was sure to bring with him to the stand a profound appreciation and understanding for how the justice system worked.

Ariane Vuono spent the first forty-five minutes having Baden go through his rather stellar list of credentials. By the time he was finished, it was understood that there wasn't much Baden hadn't done.

Then he began to talk about what he had found when he autopsied Ed Skwira, Kenny Cutting, and Stanley Jagodowski.

Regarding Skwira, Baden said that ". . . there was evidence of an old heart attack that may have occurred many years ago, but there was no fresh or recent heart attack."

". . . [O]n the basis of your autopsy, what is your opinion with respect to the death certificate's statement that chronic alcoholism led to Mr. Skwira's death?"

"A number of answers to that question. One is [that] chronic alcoholism did not have anything to do with his death, did not lead to his death. There was no damage from alcoholism that caused or contributed to his death."

Baden went on to say that although Skwira had drunk alcohol daily for fifty years, "his liver, which is often the target organ for alcohol injury, was in very good condition."

Vuono then asked if Skwira's cardiac event on February 15, 1996, could have been caused by what Baden had explained was a pre-existing heart condition, or heart disease.

"No. He did not have any finding that could cause sudden death. There is [sic] just a few things that can cause sudden death, like a blood clot, pulmonary embolism, massive myocardial infarc[tion]. He did not have any evidence that . . . he had an infarc. No fresh infarc. He did not have a dissecting aortic aneurysm. . . ."

After a break in the trial because of a winter storm, Baden returned on February 7 and confirmed that he found ketamine in Ed Skwira's tissue. Then it was on to the comments he made about Dr. Rieders during the videotape.

"Doctor, what did you mean when you said that you have to 'beat up on Rieders and that he's got to find something'?"

"What I meant was that I know, from past dealings with Dr. Rieders, that he has many distractions and other cases . . . I wanted to make the point that it's important to keep after Dr. Rieders to do his studies . . . to get those tests done in a timely fashion, we had to keep calling him up and making sure that progress was being made. . . ."

One by one, Baden went through each victim's death and responded with the same conclusion: Based on his extensive study of medical records and the autopsies he performed, all the victims had died of acute epinephrine poisoning.

Vuono wanted to be sure she covered every base. Regarding Dr. Rieders's toxicology tests being inconclusive and withdrawn because of the mathematical errors he had made, she had one final question for Baden.

"With respect to your opinions that you have given to the court and jury here . . . did you rely at all upon the test results that Dr. Rieders had provided to you earlier regarding the presence or nonpresence of epinephrine in the tissue samples obtained during the autopsies that you preformed?"

"No, I did not."

Vuono conferred with Bill Welch for a moment.

"Thank you, Doctor. I have no further questions."

With David Hoose carrying the load for the defense throughout the last ten weeks of trial, it was time for Harry Miles to stand up and show Gilbert and the government what he was made of.

It would get ugly right away.

A few minutes into his cross-examination, Miles asked Baden about his grand jury testimony, where he alluded to the fact that Ed Skwira had a "normal" aorta.

"Did you say that Mr. Skwira's aorta was perfectly normal. Are those the words you used?"

"Those are the words I used, that's right. I refer to it as my senile moment."

"Did you also say there was no dissecting aneurysm?"

"Yes."

"And you said there was no abnormality of any kind in the aorta, is that correct?"

"Yes."

"And all of those were senile moments, were they?"

"No . . . no . . . there was no dissecting aneurysm—and the aorta was perfectly normal as far as any abnormality that would lead to a dissecting aneurysm—"

"Was Dr. Joann Richmond, excuse me, if I might—"

"Can I finish?"

Miles was trying to get Baden to admit that a second medical examiner—Dr. Joann Richmond—who took part in Ed Skwira's autopsy disagreed with what Baden had found and that the two doctors had discussed it at one point.

But Baden stuck by his words and finished what he had started to say: that he could find no other cause of death.

"And, initially, doctor, after the autopsy, if you had found no other competing cause of death, would you have had to conclude that it was a bad heart that caused Mr. Skwira's death?"

"If the only information I knew was the autopsy findings and there was no obvious competing cause of death, yes."

For the next hour or so, Harry Miles tried to get the jury to believe that Dr. Baden's findings had been significantly influenced by the toxicological tests Dr. Rieders had performed. Using several letters Baden had written to Assistant U.S. Attorney Bill Welch over the past few years, Miles proved his point rather well: that Baden had relied not only on his findings but the fact that Rieders had found in several of the victims an overabundance of metanephrine, which is a "breakdown product" of epinephrine.

Baden kept mixing up the dates of his meetings with Bill Welch, always sure to correct himself by saying it was "one of [his] senile moments."

As late afternoon approached, Miles broke out the infamous autopsy videotape and, having received permission from Judge Ponsor, popped it in and played a small portion where Baden could be clearly heard saying that "we gotta beat up on Rieders . . . he's gotta find something."

"You didn't say we have to track him to make sure he gets out his results in a timely way, did you?"

Baden looked tired. He had been on the stand for two full days.

"No, I didn't use those words."

"And you refer to—you didn't refer to pushing to get Dr. Rieders to get out prompt results, did you?"

Still sharp, despite being fatigued, Baden said, "That's what I meant!"

"But you didn't say that, did you?"

"I said . . . I used different words, but that's what I had intended to convey: that we have to push Rieders."

Miles moved on to another portion of the tape; he asked Baden if Dr. Rieders had told a joke during the course of the Skwira autopsy.

"He told a lot of things that he thought were jokes in the course of that autopsy to lighten things up."

Miles then asked the judge if he could play another section of the videotape. Ponsor indicated that he was going to end the day's proceedings after the jury got a chance to see the tape.

Before they broke after watching the video tape, Ponsor agreed to let Miles pose a few more questions to Dr. Baden.

"You didn't tell Dr. Rieders that . . . he should find what is there and not what people what him to find, did you?" Miles asked.

"One, I didn't have to tell him that; and, two, there was nothng that we wanted him to find. We wanted to know if there *was* or *wasn't* epinephrine or its breakdown products present, and Dr. Rieders knows that. He doesn't make things up."

On February 8, Miles continued his cross-examination of Dr. Michael Baden, delivering a diatribe regarding Kenny Cutting's condition at the time of his death. However, Baden fired back a series of answers that emphasized that Cutting could not have died from anything else besides sudden cardiac death.

After noting that Baden had written a book, Miles got into Baden's reason for becoming a forensic pathologist.

"And the reason you became a forensic pathologist, sir, was because you like the public side of it, is that correct?"

"No, that's not the reason for it."

"Didn't you say, sir, in your book that you like the public side of being a forensic pathologist . . . ?"

"Yes, that's not the reason I became a . . . but in my early youth . . . I found that very exciting."

"And you liked the reporters and the television cameras?"

"At the time, yes. We're talking about *1965!* I've outgrown that phase."

For the next thirty minutes, Miles questioned Baden about a medical examiner's bias toward the establishment he or she works for, and concluded by asking Baden how much he had charged the government for the work he had done in the Gilbert case—about eighteen thousand dollars thus far.

Ariane Vuono had a few questions on redirect examination, getting Baden to reaffirm his opinion that each victim had died from *one* cause of death: epinephrine poisoning.

After Baden stepped down from the stand, the government rested its case.

CHAPTER 91

On November 17, 2000, David Hoose had told Judge Ponsor that he wasn't sure his client was going to testify. Under federal law, defense attorneys can call their client to the stand at any time during a trial. But here they were nearly three months later, after the prosecution had called fifty-two witnesses, and Gilbert's defense team was ready to present its case. But a quick look at its witness list revealed that Hoose still hadn't decided whether Gilbert would take the stand. With all that going on in the courtroom the past few months, many were speculating that it was the only chance the former VA nurse had left.

When Judge Ponsor turned the trial over to the defense on Tuesday, February 8, 2001, the first thing David Hoose did was file a motion to acquit Gilbert on all charges.

Judge Ponsor denied the request.

The defense's first witness, Dr. Thomas Aretz, the director of cardiovascular pathology at Massachusetts General Hospital, took the stand and repeatedly disputed prior testimony by government witnesses who had claimed the veterans died of epinephrine poisoning.

Under cross-examination by Ariane Vuono, however, Aretz contradicted himself, telling the jury that a determination of death by epinephrine poisoning is complicated science.

"That makes epinephrine a pretty good poisoning [then], doesn't it, doctor?" Vuono asked.

"I can't answer that."

On Friday, Dell Levy, the policy and procedure inspector from the HCI in Washington, DC, was among three witnesses called. Hoose questioned Levy about her preliminary investigation and how she initially noted that, in her early opinion, no crimes had been committed. Using reports, medical records and interviews she had conducted with some forty VAMC employees, Hoose made it clear to the jury that Levy never viewed the deaths as suspicious.

But under cross-examination, Vuono got Levy to admit that her job was to generate a "clinical"—not a "criminal"—report, and that her first draft was rewritten by her supervisors, who, she said, removed incriminating information.

Late in the afternoon, Judge Ponsor held a hearing without the jury present regarding whether a convicted drug dealer, Khalil "O-Dog" White, would be allowed to testify that Bonnie Bledsoe and John Wall stole a bag of medication from the VAMC so they could use it to barter for street drugs. White, himself in the middle of an eighteen-month sentence for marijuana possession, said he met Wall one day, and Wall had a paper bag full of medicines he had apparently taken from the VAMC.

Hoose theorized that the bag was full of epinephrine. But White admitted he didn't know what was in the bag, because he never looked inside of it.

After listening to White testify, Ponsor said he would "review case law" before making a decision whether the jury should hear the testimony.

When the trial resumed on Monday, Dell Levy was followed by David Rejniak, Gilbert's former friend and colleague.

As Rejniak made his way to the witness stand, Gilbert seemed to perk up a bit, as if she were happy to see him.

Rejniak testified that Gilbert had summoned him to the ICU on Feb. 2, 1996, mainly because Kenny Cutting wasn't looking so good. Then he said, "She seemed a little bit upset. She didn't want to be alone with him when he died."

Under cross-examination, however, Welch got Rejniak to admit that Cutting had been stable when Rejniak relieved Gilbert, and that he didn't expect Cutting to die less than an hour after Gilbert took her break.

Dr. Graham R. Jones, the director of a toxicology lab in Edmonton, Alberta, told the jury on February 13 that tests by National Medical Services showing that ketamine was found in one of the victims should be considered "inconsistent and unreliable."

Jones, the sixth witness for the defense, said that because NMS had made mistakes in its epinephrine tests, it shouldn't be trusted to test for ketamine.

When Vuono got a crack at the doctor, she asked him several questions about his qualifications, then whether he had ever tested tissue samples from embalmed and exhumed bodies for the presence of metanephrine or norepinepherine, breakdown products of epinephrine.

"No, I have not," Jones said.

It was easy to tell by the fourth day of defense testimony that the *Government vs. Kristen Gilbert* was turning into *Kristen Gilbert vs. Bonnie Bledsoe and John Wall*. Just about every witness Hoose, Miles and Weinberg had put on the stand so far had something to offer that would give the jury a reason to believe the missing ampoules of epinephrine had been stolen by John Wall and Bonnie Bledsoe.

Maybe Hoose saw it as his only option?

Nevertheless, when respiratory therapists James Kolodziej and William Gibb took the stand on February 13, they testified that medicine cabinets on Ward C where ampoules of epinephrine were kept had sometimes been left wide open and unattended. Anyone, from the janitor to the director of the VAMC, could walk up and grab an ampoule of epinephrine.

But by the end of the day, Judge Ponsor had heard enough.

During a hearing, Ponsor said he wasn't sure he was going to let the defense continue asking witnesses about Bonnie Bledsoe's life. It was, as he had earlier suspected, getting out hand.

"I'm concerned about to what extent this should become a trial of 'Is Bonnie Bledsoe a good nurse?' " Ponsor said.

He had a point.

Hoose said the government had put a bull's-eye on Gilbert's back from day one, pinning the missing ampoules of epinephrine on her, and refused to look at any other suspects.

Also a good point.

"What we've attempted to do is demonstrate that there was an opportunity to steal medications available not only to nurses but to respiratory therapists."

Hoose paused.

Then, loudly, he said, "Bonnie Bledsoe [had] a *motive.*"

Later during the same hearing, Ponsor ruled that the defense could not call convicted drug dealer O-Dog White to testify that Bledsoe and Wall wanted to trade hospital drugs for crack cocaine. There just wasn't enough evidence to the fact.

Vuono, at one point, argued that White's testimony was just another attempt to disgrace Wall and Bledsoe.

"They've had their shot at Bonnie Bledsoe and Mr. Wall," Vuono shouted.

Judge Ponsor ultimately agreed.

Dr. William Boutelle, chief of the medical staff at the VAMC, testified on Wednesday, February 14 that, at first, the allegations brought by John Wall, Kathy Rix and Renee Walsh contained no evidence of any crimes. Boutelle had come under fire for not closing Ward C after the nurses had come forward. Many said he should have immediately closed the ward and started a thorough investigation that day. But on the stand, he said that his staff's initial findings—made in early March 1996—indicated there wasn't a pressing need to relocate staff and lock up the ward.

At one point during his testimony, Boutelle, perhaps unknowingly, tightened the noose around Gilbert's neck by suggesting that since the spike in medical emergencies and deaths dramatically declined after February 17—the day Gilbert left—there was no need, after that, to look any further.

Ignoring Judge Ponsor's suggestion, thus continuing with its bashing of Bonnie Bledsoe, the defense called George Ponte, who, in 1995 and 1996, supervised respiratory therapists at the VAMC.

Ponte, a short man, balding on top with a ponytail snaking down his back, had been a professor at Springfield Technical

Community College when he met Bonnie Bledsoe in the late eighties.

In March 1991, when Ponte was hired by the VAMC, he was disappointed to learn that Bledsoe was also working there. They hadn't really parted on good terms back at STCC, and Ponte testified that he and Bledsoe carried that animosity into their new relationship at the VAMC.

Ponte told the jury he had heard that John Wall had given Bledsoe a shot of epinephrine as late as the spring of 1995.

After telling jurors that Bledsoe deliberately began to avoid him when the two began working together, he said he found out in February 1995 that she and Wall had been using heroin and crack, and, by late October, initiated steps to terminate her employment because of that discovery.

Paul Weinberg wanted to know how Ponte knew they were abusing drugs.

"She told me she had snorted heroin and smoked crack at work."

Ending his direct examination, Weinberg asked, "Finally, Mr. Ponte, what is your opinion of the reputation of Bonnie Bledsoe for truthfulness?"

"I think she was a liar. I think that was a known fact amongst the people that she worked with. She was a manipulatative person. . . ."

"Thank you."

On cross-examination, Ariane Vuono had Ponte establish right away that Bledsoe was only eighteen or nineteen years old at the time they had met at STCC. Then she had him describe Bledsoe's asthmatic condition, how it was treated with shots of epinephrine, and that it was no secret.

Using a report filed on May 1, 1996, only months after the investigation had started, Vuono pointed out that Ponte didn't know Bledsoe had a drug problem years before, as he had claimed on direct examination, because there simply wasn't any documentation of it. Since he was her boss, part of Ponte's job would have been to write her up if he suspected drug use, Vuono suggested. But he waited. Vuono wanted to know why.

Ponte admitted that although he suspected her of abusing drugs as early as the fall of 1994, he had indeed waited until the spring of 1996 to write a "Medical Certification alert" about it. But he gave no specific reason for his decision to wait.

At 11:30, Ponsor recessed for a much-needed break.

Back in court twenty minutes later, Vuono grilled Ponte about the relationship he'd had with Bledsoe prior to the time they had begun working together, and asked him if he had a "history" with Bledsoe?

"Could you define 'history'?"

"Well, you had been her professor at STCC, is that right?"

"That's correct."

"She was eighteen or nineteen at the time?"

"That's correct."

"And it was also during that time when you had a sexual encounter with Ms. Bledsoe, didn't you?"

"No . . ."

"Did you have sexual intercourse with Ms. Bledsoe?"

"No!"

"You were Ms. Bledsoe's professor when she was a student at STCC, is that right?"

"That's correct."

"And are you telling this court *and* jury that during the time that you were her professor and she was your student, you *didn't* have sexual intercourse with her?"

"That's right."

"Object, Your Honor," Weinberg shouted. "It's been asked already."

"I'm going to overrule. . . . The answer is in evidence."

Vuono was confused. She knew Ponte had slept with Bledsoe.

"Did the event happen shortly after her graduation?"

"Maybe a year or more."

"So she was maybe nineteen or twenty years old at the time?"

Ponte then made a point to say that he wasn't married at the time, and that the relationship between him and Bledsoe "wasn't serious."

"In fact, it was a one-time encounter, wasn't it?" Vuono wanted to know.

"Exactly!"

"And was in your car?"

"I believe it was."

By the end of his testimony, Ponte admitted that Bledsoe had filed a sexual harassment suit against him while they were working at the VAMC, and that she had expressed her concern over the harassment to fellow employees, but the suit was later dropped.

Vuono then wanted to bring Ponte (and the jury) up to date on Bledsoe's new life.

"Did you know that she has been sober for the past year and that she was back to working as a respiratory therapist again?"

Ponte said he did not.

Ann French, Gilbert's former coworker and new friend, testified next that Gilbert had been shaken over the deaths at the VAMC and that, in her opinion, some of the patients in question could have died of natural causes.

Regarding Ed Skwira, French said, "I didn't expect him to survive the evening—never mind the night," adding that "his color was terrible. He just didn't look good. He was gray, almost like cement color."

CHAPTER 92

First thing the next morning, Dr. James Kirchhoffer, chief cardiologist at Baystate Medical Center, began painting a significantly different picture of how Kenny Cutting, Stanley Jagodowski, Henry Hudon and Ed Skwira died. The government had already put on its expert, Dr. Thomas Rocco, who had, some said, given a very convincing argument as to how the men had died of sudden cardiac death. But now it was Gilbert's defense team's turn at presenting its version of the deaths, using its own cardiology expert.

After going through his extensive list of credentials, Kirchhoffer, who had acquired his degree in medicine during the late seventies, told the jury that his specialty included cardiac eletrophysiology, which is "the study of abnormal heart rhythms and diagnosis and treatment of patients who have abnormal heart rhythms and symptoms that go along with that."

Then he broke into his theories about epinephrine, which contradicted completely Dr. Rocco's, Dr. Grayboys's and Dr. Baden's previous opinions.

"Have you . . . become familiar with the literature on epinephrine and its effects on the human body?" David Hoose asked the doctor.

"Yes."

"We've been through this with other physicians. So . . . based on your experience, what is the normal time that it takes for epinephrine to have an effect on the body when it's injected intravenously?"

"It depends on how close the IV line is to the heart. But generally, if it's a central IV, close—where the veins are actually close to the heart—you can see epinephrine effect within fifteen or thirty seconds. If it's a vein that's . . . in the arm someplace, it may take thirty to forty-five seconds, even a minute, before you can start to see the epinephrine effect."

"And how long does the epinephrine effect last?"

"Epinephrine effect usually lasts—it peaks at two to three minutes and lasts around five minutes."

Kirchhoffer, who sat in the courtroom's front row and took notes while Dr. Rocco testified nearly three months before, explained to the jury that he believed the cause of death of the patients in question had nothing to do with epinephrine, but was more of a combination of the ailments each victim had suffered from and the drugs each had been on while at the VAMC.

By the end of the morning, after Kirchhoffer made a compelling argument as to how Stanley Jagodowski had died of natural causes, Hoose got to the core of why he had the doctor on the stand.

"Let me ask you one final set of questions with regard to Mr. Jagodowski, doctor, and I'm going to put it in the form of a hypothetical. Let's assume . . . that an LPN saw someone, an RN, go into Jagodowski's room with a needle and syringe, that the LPN said that she heard Mr. Jagodowski say, 'Ow, you're hurting me,' or, 'You're killing me,' that immediately thereafter . . . the LPN went into the room, asked Mr. Jagodowski if he was all right, that she spent four to five minutes with him, that she left the room and that fifteen minutes later . . . a code was called as a result of Mr. Jagodowski's cardiac arrest. . . . [D]o you have an opinion as to whether epinephrine could have caused that event?"

"Yes."

"And what is that opinion?"

"That's not something that epinephrine would do. Epinephrine is a rapidly acting and rapidly disappearing medication. I would expect its effect to be gone within five minutes. This time course is much too long for epinephrine."

Judge Ponsor broke for lunch.

When court resumed an hour later, Hoose wanted to clear up an error, he said, in Kirchhoffer's earlier testimony. The doctor had testified that he was being paid one hundred and fifty dollars an hour for his work in the case, but it was, Hoose told the court, two hundred dollars an hour.

As Kirchhoffer went through each of the victims' medical charts, he continually repeated his theory that each vet had died of natural causes, not epinephrine poisoning. Even those patients with healthy hearts, Kirchhoffer opined, could have died of sudden cardiac death, mainly, he said, because of the medications they were on at the time of their deaths. He cited alcohol abuse, smoking and a poor diet as major factors in all of the deaths. But not an overdose of epinephrine.

It was a solid argument from someone who, like Dr. Rocco, appeared to know what he was talking about. Still, for the jury the bottom line was, who was the more credible witness?

Bill Welch was about to answer that question.

Several days before Welch knew he was going to cross-examine Dr. Kirchhoffer, he decided, for the hell of it, to key Kirchhoffer's name into an Internet search engine. A minute later, Welch was shocked to discover Kirchhoffer had received some type of "letter of reprimand" from the FDA regarding one of his clinical trials, a study he had conducted at Baystate Medical Center in 1995.

Welch, of course, was curious.

To obtain a copy of the letter, the Web site said, "send a check for fifty dollars."

So Welch went one better: He sent the check, along with a subpoena for the entire file.

On the morning of February 16, Welch first questioned how Kirchhoffer had come to his conclusions regarding the deaths in question.

Kirchhoffer admitted that, in determining causes of death for the patients, he never considered that Gilbert had been one of the nurses giving out medicines. Welch contended that some of the patients may have died from the medications they were on—but it was the *defendant* who had administered the meds.

Welch then wanted to know how Kirchhoffer could have come to a definitive conclusion as to how Thomas Callahan had died if he hadn't taken into account all the factors involved in his death. Further, Welch suggested, Kirchhoffer had based his findings on medical records that contained entries made by Gilbert herself, but didn't take into account that she had either falsified some of the records or failed to include relevant information.

"But is it fair to say that . . . you're relying upon something," Welch asked in a sarcastic tone, flipping through Callahan's medical file, "in this particular progress note written by the defendant, isn't that correct?"

"That's correct," Kirchhoffer said.

"And it's also accurate that we don't see the conversation [between Gilbert and Callahan] anywhere in this particular progress note, isn't that true?"

"That's true."

"We don't get to see what the rhythm was before [his medical emergency] and whether it truly converted or how it evolved, isn't that correct?"

"That's correct."

"My recollection of your testimony with respect to Mr. Callahan was that this particular chart offered you very little significance, is that true?"

"That's correct."

Throughout the morning, Welch continued to hammer Kirchhoffer about how he had reviewed the medical records of the victims with blinders on. For example, how he failed time and again to take into account all of the evidence from all of the doctors involved, but instead based his findings on only certain sections of the medical records. It had been well documented that Callahan had shouted, "I think I'm going to die" shortly before his code, but Kirchhoffer said he didn't find any importance in that declaration.

"Regarding Callahan's episode, were you advised that three 1:1000 epinephrine ampoules were found in his—in the needle disposal bucket in the ICU sometime after this event?"

"I've heard rumors to that effect."

"But you have not received any direct information to that effect?"

"No, that's not in the medical chart."

At 12:57, Ponsor let the jury have a break. They looked tired, moving around and slouching in their seats while Kirchhoffer testified. It was clear many of them had heard enough from the doctor. As his testimony dragged on, one juror later said Kirchhoffer began to sound like he was "full of shit." He kept trying to give the impression that he knew more than he did.

It had been a long three months since opening arguments, and many of the jurors had changed remarkably. Scott Stetz, at twenty, the youngest juror, had gained nearly fifty pounds since the start of the trial, and others were beginning to complain about how grueling the whole process had become.

By two o'clock, everyone was back in court listening to Welch as he continued with his grilling of Dr. Kirchhoffer.

He first outlined the many reasons why Kenny Cutting should have lived.

"And Mr. Cutting had a normal heart?"

"That's correct."

After a few more medical questions regarding Cutting's condition at the time of his death, Welch walked over to where Ariane Vuono was sitting, leaned down, and whispered, "What do you think . . . now?"

"Go for it," Vuono said.

"Doctor, during the course of your direct examination, you were [asked] about a peer review function that you performed, is that right?"

"Yes."

"And you were also asked about quality assurance tasks that you performed, correct?"

Obviously uncomfortable, Kirchhoffer began to shift in his seat.

"Yes," he said after a brief pause.

"And you indicated that you approached this case in somewhat of the same way, sort of doing a peer review of these medical files, correct?"

"Yes."

Welch had come from the old school of law where litigation

was all about information—possessing it, controlling it, managing it, and using it effectively.

It turned out that Kirchhoffer had been in charge of a government-funded study involving the use of pacemakers, but had received a letter from the FDA in 1995 warning him about "his failure to thoroughly document [the study]." One of his patients involved in the study, Welch found out through the subpoena, had died, and Kirchhoffer never knew about it because he wasn't keeping tabs on the study the way he was supposed to. He had also been reprimanded for putting the wrong pacemaker into a patient, for pre-recording the results of tests into charts, and for not having the appropriate documentation—like rhythm strips, for example—to support some of his data.

"Did there come a point in time in the fall of 1995 when you received an FDA warning letter concerning poor documentation of your cardiovascular studies"

"Yes."

David Hoose began to slouch in his chair as if someone had let the air out of him. Kirchhoffer put his head down for a moment, looked up at Welch, and began shaking his head, slowly.

"And you were criticized by the FDA for not documenting the death of a patient in one of your studies, isn't that correct?"

"No. I was *criticized* for not sending a copy of the documentation to the IRB. I had sent a copy directly to the coordinating center, and the copy that was supposed to go to the IRB didn't go."

"And when you say 'IRB,' that is the Institutional Research Board of the Baystate Medical Center?"

"Yes."

"So you had no time frame at Baystate . . . via documentation that a patient had died in one of your cardiovascular studies?"

"That's correct."

"The FDA warning letter," Welch continued, "wasn't limited solely to not documenting the death of the patient, isn't that correct?"

"You know," Kirchhoffer said mockingly, "I don't have the FDA warning letter in front of me, and I don't have it memorized."

"Well," Welch said, smiling, "let me see if I can help you. It

also had to do with not documenting the accidental implanta-
tion of an experimental pacemaker in a patient and then subsequent explanation?"

Kirchhoffer became incensed. He said it had to do with the
wiring, *not* the pacemaker itself.

For the next few minutes, in a heated exchange, Welch went
toe-to-toe with Kirchhoffer over the lack of control Kirchhoffer
had over the study, along with his not following up on patients
to see how they were doing. Then Welch tried to tie together
how Kirchhoffer's negligence in the pacemaker study could
have had an ill effect on his testimony in court.

"It's your testimony that [Ed] Skwira, I believe, had an acute
myocardial infarction on the morning of February 15, correct?"

"That was my opinion."

During his redirect examination, David Hoose asked
Kirchhoffer if he had anything further he wanted to add. After
briefly explaining the letter, Kirchhoffer said, "No one has a
perfect study."

CHAPTER 93

After questioning a jury consultant it had hired—Anita Sarro—Kristen Gilbert's defense rested its case on Tuesday, February 20. The government then brought in two rebuttal witnesses, DEA agent Clarence Shuler, and the former head of the Springfield Police Department's Narcotics Unit, Officer John Delaney. Welch had worked on a case in 1995 with Delaney involving the distribution of approximately one-hundred-and-fifty kilograms of cocaine.

Both cops were there to explain to the jury that in all their years of narcotics investigation they had never heard of crack cocaine and heroin users mixing epinephrine with street drugs. Another misguided claim by Gilbert's defense.

With that, Ponsor said closing arguments would begin in two days.

The previous weekend, Ariane Vuono had labored for three days, trying to come up with the right words to describe to jurors what they had heard for the past four months. She began early Saturday morning and, except for breaking to sleep and eat, didn't stop writing until late Sunday night. Knowing that it would the biggest day of her professional career, on Tuesday, Vuono practiced the speech before her colleagues in the US Attorney's Office.

"It's perfect," they agreed after she was done.

As she began in court, Vuono thanked the jury for the time they had spent away from their families, then quickly explained the crux of the government's case—that Gilbert murdered Stanley Jagodowski, Henry Hudon, Kenny Cutting and Ed Skwira, and she "assaulted with the intent to murder Francis Marier, Thomas Callahan, and Angelo Vella," simply to impress her new boyfriend, James Perrault.

Pointing at Gilbert, Vuono raised her voice and lashed out, "These seven victims, ladies and gentlemen, were veterans. They protected our country during war and peace. They were vulnerable, due to their physical and mental illnesses. Some were seriously ill. And some had no family. And because of that, ladies and gentlemen, they were the *perfect* victims. And when Kristen Gilbert decided to kill them or assault in attempt to kill them, she used the *perfect* poison."

Gilbert sat with her head bowed, showing no sign of emotion. Not since day one and two of the trial had her parents been in the courtroom, but now they sat staring at Ariane Vuono as she accused their daughter of the unthinkable.

"This small vial of 1:1000 epinephrine," Vuono said, holding an ampoule in her hand as if she were a magician doing tricks with a coin, "can be a life-saving drug. . . . On the other hand, if this is used maliciously, it can cause death. And don't think for one minute this defendant, Kristen Gilbert, didn't know exactly what epinephrine would do when she used it, because everybody will agree that this woman was a bright nurse."

For the next hour and a half, Vuono meticulously went through and explained each victim's death and how each witness implicated Gilbert in that death.

At 11:36, she began her timeline argument, explaining how Gilbert had killed Stanley Jagodowski, Henry Hudon, Kenny Cutting and, finally, Ed Skwira.

"She confessed from her own words. She corroborated all the medical evidence in this case . . . she admitted her guilt," Vuono said.

At one point, Vuono argued how, during a conversation the defendant had with Glenn Gilbert, she confessed she was "the world's best con artist."

Vuono next wanted the jury to understand why Gilbert's co-workers hadn't come forward sooner.

"They were working elbow to elbow with a person who was killing patients—they were afraid!"

Blasting Dr. Kirchhoffer, Vuono asked jurors if they wanted to rely on the testimony of a doctor who implanted an experimental wire in pacemaker patients during a study without letting them know.

"Do you know how Dr. Kirchhoffer got involved in this case?" Vuono asked, throwing up her hands. "He had a prior case with attorney Weinberg. They were friendly. And now [Dr. Kirchhoffer] is *forty* thousand dollars richer! Those are sufficient reasons to discount his testimony.

"Let me just say, quickly, that with respect to Dr. Kirchhoffer, anything is possible. . . . Dr. Grayboys told you, 'A chair could levitate across the room, too, but it's not likely to happen.' "

After describing what each victim should have been able to do in his life if Gilbert hadn't cut it short, Vuono concluded by saying, "Ed Skwira, he should have been able to celebrate his sobriety with his family. And instead, his family had to make a decision to let him die."

Since day one, David Hoose had perhaps the most difficult job out of anyone in the courtroom: putting together a defense for a defendant who failed to provide him with any tangible evidence he could put his arms around. Besides saying that she didn't do it, and remaining steadfast in her claim throughout the trial, Gilbert hadn't given Hoose answers to some of the government's most damaging questions. One witness after the other had placed Gilbert at the scene of each death and given a believable reason as to how and why she could have done it. But the only explanation Gilbert offered was that there was a vendetta against her, and Bonnie Bledsoe and John Wall were stealing epinephrine to support their own heroin and cocaine habits.

Still, Hoose had to give it his best shot.

After explaining to the jury that he wasn't going to wow them with charts and graphics during his closing, like Vuono had, Hoose said he appreciated the time the jurors had taken out of their lives to participate in such a long and taxing trial.

Then he broke into the only real argument he had at his disposal.

"You must understand this fundamental principle, ladies and gentlemen, to understand why this prosecution was fatally and irretrievably flawed from the outset. We had a suspect before we even knew if there had been a crime committed. And everything that the government did on this case was distorted by that perception.

"There really were only four possible proofs," Hoose said. "First there is pathology, which never existed. Then there is toxicology, which was not produced. The last two are medicine and circumstantial evidence. We've already got two legs of the table cut off. It is being supported by two others: circumstantial evidence and medicine.

"The government has this notion that you can pinpoint the exact moment and cause of death. They're doctors, not God. Alcohol, weight, cholesterol, tobacco, diabetes—all of them [the patients] had problems with those things. Is everything our family physicians have been telling us all our lives completely irrelevant?

"You have to look for the most obvious cause of death. That is something no government witness did. They *looked* for epinephrine *first*," Hoose shouted. "If you start out looking at cases with sinister eyes and suspicions that something is wrong, then you'll find it."

For the next forty-five minutes, Hoose tried to discredit several of the government's key witnesses, mainly John Wall and Bonnie Bledsoe, who had reasons, he insisted, to try to frame his client.

"[T]o divert attention from themselves, their own drug use and their own probable thefts of epinephrine. Once you have drug addicts like John Wall and Bonnie Bledsoe in the middle of something like this, all bets are off. You cannot believe anything they say or do."

He talked about a coup, suggesting that some of the nurses had gotten together with Wall and Bledsoe because they disapproved of the affair Gilbert was having with Perrault.

After two and a half hours, Hoose finished his argument

with a simple plea: "You may, in your lifetimes, ladies and gentlemen, you may never have the opportunity to take a stand as
important as the one that you can take tomorrow. It is important
for you to do justice in this case and to stand up and to hold on
to principle and to hold on to everything that you believe in and
to stick to your guns and to not be overwhelmed by an enormous government effort by a technically masterful presentation, but one that is devoid of substance of the type necessary
for you to vote for a conviction.

"I ask you to go to the jury room tomorrow and to do what is
long overdue in this case: acquit Kristen Gilbert of these horrendous charges that have been levied against her."

Those who knew Hoose's work said it was one of the best
closing arguments of his career.

With the first word of his twenty-minute rebuttal, Assistant
US Attorney Bill Welch summed up how the government felt
about Hoose's continued claims that it had started with a suspect and built a case around her.

"Baloney!" Welch screamed as he stood and walked toward
the podium. "That's what I say, that the government started with
a suspect and then forced the facts to fit that theory. I was
drowning in a river of analogies for two and a half hours, but in
these twenty minutes, I would like to tell you what the *facts* are
in this case. In this case, a witness took the stand and said this:
Time is a great test of humility. Well, I say that time is a great
test of whether or not you have the right suspect, because in this
case every fact that was developed after February 1996 continued to point to that defendant.

"She took the *trust* and *faith* the profession put in her hands
and *abused* it in the most horrible way. . . . [W]hen you take all
the facts of this case and you put them together, it forms a compelling wall of guilt. In the end, she is guilty of first-degree
murder. She is guilty of assaulting with intent to kill, and the
reason she is guilty is because"—and here Welch kicked the
volume up a notch—*"she did it.* Thank you."

plea. You may, in your lifetimes, ladies and gen-

CHAPTER 94

"Now I can say to you," Judge Ponsor admonished the jury while looking over the bridge of his glasses, "you can begin to discuss the case."

Late into the day on February 23, 2001, deliberations were finally under way in the *Government vs. Kristen Gilbert,* a case that with more than seventy witnesses and two hundred pieces of evidence was heading into its fifth month.

Judge Ponsor decided to split up the jury, sending the twelve regulars off to one room and the five alternates to another. The separation of the two groups, Ponsor said, was "a poignant moment [and] a bit of a tug of heart" for him, but, in the end, something he thought he had to do.

He then explained that he wouldn't be sequestering the jury, and that they would retain regular hours—nine-to-five—during deliberations.

Putting on his serious face, Ponsor then gave the jury his last bit of advice.

"You must not allow any possible punishment which may be imposed upon the defendant to—*in any way*—influence your verdict or enter into your deliberations."

During the trial, a few of the jurors had been pumping another juror, a nurse, for information, asking her questions about some of the more complex testimony—a situation that could have potentially been grounds for a mistrial.

Judge Ponsor was informed. After carefully weighing his options, he decided the trial hadn't been compromised in any way.

The episode, however, caused some friction among several jurors, and that turmoil spilled over into the first day of deliberations.

For four hours, jurors talked in circles, breaking off into groups of three to discuss not one or two of the alleged murders, but throwing out bits and pieces of the trial they thought were most meaningful. Ponsor had let them takes notes during the proceedings, and most did. But the first few hours were nothing short of a free-for-all as jurors tore through their notes and started spitting out all sorts of scenarios and halfhearted claims.

On Tuesday, the second day, Howard Darnley, a sixty-two-year-old machine designer, stood up and, frustrated, decided to take control of a situation he saw was getting out of hand. With Hilda Colon, a human resources worker, Darnley walked over to the blackboard and wrote down Stanley Jagodowski's name and listed the pros and cons of the case insofar as Jagodowski was concerned.

One by one, jurors began to toss out bits of information, and within a short time, a rather telling picture of Jagodowski's death, entirely based on the medical evidence offered in the case, emerged.

The following day, after briefly discussing Jagodowski's death, one of the jurors suggested they take a paper ballot to see where they stood.

Connie Berneche, a stay-at-home mom from Chicopee, helped the foreperson tally the votes.

When Berneche got to the last ballot, she began to weep. Then she ran into the bathroom and vomited. Soon, the other eight women began to cry, with a few others retreating to the bathroom to vomit. Scott Stetz, Howard Darnley and Gerald Murphy, the only males in the group, looked at one another, wondering what the hell they should do.

"It was emotional," one juror remembered, "because once we had a guilty verdict, we knew we would ultimately be deciding on the death penalty. At that point, it became all too real."

Letting the women have the time they needed to compose themselves, Darnley suggested they curtail deliberations for the rest of the day.

Judge Ponsor agreed, and let them leave early.

Because Jagodowski was Gilbert's first victim, the jury decided she was trying to figure out how to kill. They felt she didn't intend to kill Jagodowski, but it just happened. So, even though Judge Ponsor had warned them not to discuss the penalty Gilbert could ultimately receive, after discussing it they agreed to convict her of second-degree murder instead of first-degree, which carried the death penalty.

As the days wore on, they took each victim separately, discussed the evidence, and decided that Gilbert had, without a doubt, intended to murder Ed Skwira, Kenny Cutting and Henry Hudon.

They would find her guilty of first-degree murder on those counts.

When it came down to it, most of the jurors didn't put as much thought into Bonnie Bledsoe and John Wall's testimony as David Hoose and his team had perhaps hoped.

"I may not have gotten along with them as people," Scott Stetz later recalled, "but I didn't think they were lying. Bonnie Bledsoe may have had a checkered past and made some mistakes in her life, but I just couldn't see her coming into a federal court and lying about it. It's one thing to start rumors about someone at work and bad-mouth them. But to take it all the way to federal court is a different story."

For the most part, coworker testimony, as the deliberations wore on, rarely came into play. The jurors put most of their focus on the medical records.

"People can lie," one juror later said, "but documents cannot."

At one point, a heated exchange took place as several jurors began discussing whether Kathy Rix could have seen the broken ampoules of epinephrine in the needle-disposal bucket. In the deliberations room, they took the bucket, placed some ampoules in it, and began to re-enact what Rix had seen that day.

Many claimed there was no way she could have seen the broken ampoules. It was just too dark at the bottom of the bucket, and the ampoules weren't clearly marked.

Howard Darnley just sat, listening intently. As he watched the re-enactment, he felt the jurors were beating up on Rix, discounting her state of mind at the time she had found the ampoules.

"Hey! Hey!" Darnley said, standing up. "Don't you remember how you felt when we first voted on Stanley Jagodowski? You all cried. When Kathy Rix saw those vials, that was her guilty verdict! For crissakes, how do you *think* she felt?"

On Friday, March 2, Judge Ponsor brought up something during the morning's proceedings that was bothering him. The *Boston Globe* ran a story the previous day stating that one of the jurors had been seen giving a thumbs-up to Gilbert as the jury walked out of the courtroom. Ponsor wanted to know if anyone else had seen the gesture.

No one admitted they had.

In chambers, Ponsor blasted the *Globe*. He said he had been "very disappointed" in its coverage of the entire trial. "The *[Globe]* . . . has really emphasized the lurid and flamboyant sides of the case and has had an almost *National Enquirer* tone at times . . ."

Yet, after further discussing it with counsel, Ponsor told the jury that the Court had concluded that the gesture never took place—that the reporter was seeing something no else had.

It was time to get back to deliberating.

CHAPTER 95

By the afternoon of March 14, after almost two weeks of deliberations, the jury submitted word to the court that it had reached a verdict on all counts.

"Before we walked in, I looked in the mirror and realized I was crying and didn't even know it," Scott Stetz later recalled. "I'm twenty years old, and here I am deciding the fate of this woman. It was a remarkable feeling."

As the jury filed into the courtroom, the anxiety Stetz had felt in the deliberations room stayed with him as he took his seat, which was about twenty yards from Gilbert. He couldn't look at her, or the attorneys, or anyone. He felt as if his heart were going to stop as the foreperson handed in the verdicts.

Gilbert, sitting nervously, moving around in her chair, hung her head and began to sob as the packed courtroom learned of her fate for the first time.

On three counts—involving Skwira, Cutting and Hudon—she was found guilty of first-degree murder. On one count—Jagodowski's death—she was found guilty of second-degree murder. In the deaths of Angelo Vella and Thomas Callahan, Gilbert was found guilty of attempted murder.

But the jury acquitted her of the death of Francis Marier.

"At that point," one juror later recalled, "it didn't matter. A conviction on the Francis Marier count wouldn't have added

anything to her sentence. We had doubts that she did it, so we
chose to acquit."

The only thing left now for Kristen Gilbert was to learn
whether she was going to die for her crimes. The jury would sit
once again, and hear testimony as the government argued why
she should die and Gilbert's defense team argued why she
should live. Emotions would run high. Rumor around the court
was that Glenn Gilbert was going to testify that in 1995 his
then-wife had tried to poison him. In addition, the jury would
finally hear about the false bomb threat Gilbert had been convicted of back in 1998, along with her extensive history of violence toward the men in her life.

For US attorneys Ariane Vuono and Bill Welch, their day
had come. They could present to the jury, finally, a complete
portrait of Kristen Gilbert.

Thursday, March 15, at a hearing to set the ground rules for
the sentencing, Bill Welch informed Judge Ponsor that the government, on the one hand, wanted to call Glenn Gilbert to testify during the sentencing phase. On the other, it was having
second thoughts because it placed Glenn and his family "in an
extremely difficult position."

Sensing that Glenn was going to testify against her, Gilbert
refused to show up in court on Friday, and signed a waiver allowing her attorneys to handle her affairs. Ponsor, however,
wouldn't hear of it. He demanded that she be there, if for nothing else, to avoid a mistrial.

By Monday, March 19, Welch and Vuono decided to with-
draw Glenn from their witness list after giving the matter some
prudent thought. Welch and Vuono later said they could have
made Glenn testify, but Welch explained that Glenn was totally
against being part of putting the mother of his children to death.

The decision had little to do with the job Bill Welch had
been sworn to do as a public servant, and it wouldn't change the
tongue-lashing he was about to unleash on Gilbert.

During his opening statement, Welch said the killings were

"morally repugnant and deserve death." They were "so dark, so unfathomable," Welch argued, that "the circumstances of these murders show that no humanity exists behind the mask. Behind that face, it is dark, it is empty. It is evil!"

Harry Miles asked jurors not to use their "God-like" powers. "Kristen Gilbert is in your hands, and I can only ask that they be merciful."

Miles then wanted the jury to understand that his client never intended to kill anyone. For the first time, Gilbert's defense team actually admitted that she had perhaps done something wrong.

"Her aim," Miles said sincerely, "was to cause medical emergencies so she could be a hero."

By Wednesday, March 21, the courtroom was filled with relatives of the victims, Gilbert's parents, a few of her relatives, and a throng of reporters and spectators.

Using family photographs displayed over the monitors in the courtroom, Welch and Vuono had relatives of the victims on the stand explain how their losses had affected their daily lives.

Ed Skwira's daughter, Marsha Yarrows, said, "There is not a day that goes by that I don't think about him. It's a big loss. You don't have him for advice. You don't have him there for holidays."

Kenny Cutting's father said, "He made me a better man."

Then it was Nancy Cutting's turn. Then Julia Hudon. One after the other, family members of the victims brought tears to the eyes of some of the jurors as they explained the true nature of their losses.

"I felt a connection there between the family members and the person they had lost," one juror later recalled. "When [Kristen Gilbert's] father was on the stand, I felt like he was reading from a checklist he had written beforehand. There was no emotion."

Richard Strickland finally got his chance to explain how deeply the loss of his daughter would be felt if she were to be killed by lethal injection. With Harry Miles at the podium, a photo of Gilbert as a newborn appeared on screens throughout the room as Strickland explained how he had not been there when Gilbert was born.

Next, as Gilbert began to cry, Strickland began on page one and described where Gilbert had grown up, her accomplishments in high school, and how gifted a child she was.

When Miles asked him how his daughter's death might affect the family, Strickland said, "I only have two daughters. . . How else can one describe the love of a daughter?"

Then he explained how his wife might not be able to survive Gilbert's execution. He shocked the room by saying that Gilbert's mother had been in Springfield for the past five weeks but couldn't bring herself to sit in the courtroom. He said she was depressed and suffered from high blood pressure and glaucoma.

"She couldn't deal with it emotionally."

"All her father did," Scott Stetz later said, "was talk about himself. It was all about him and his wife. His spiel had nothing to do with his daughter. Anyone sitting in that room could have seen that!"

Glenn Gilbert finally spoke on Friday, March 23, through Cynthia Monahon, the director of an outpatient clinic where Gilbert's two children were being treated.

Not surprising anyone, Glenn was speaking on behalf of his former wife, hoping the jury would spare her life for the sake of the kids.

"He believes the execution of Kristen Gilbert," Monahon read, "will have a . . . profoundly detrimental impact on his children and their well-being." Glenn Gilbert believes, she added, that it is "critically important for his two sons to have their mother as they grow older."

Welch and Vuono chose not to cross-examine Monahan.

The jury room during the death penalty phase was a somber, gloom-filled atmosphere of bewilderment and concern. Jurors decided there would be no discussion. They would take a vote, and that would be it. Gilbert's fate would be decided.

"The fact that she was a good mother, a good nurse, and did all these things for the needy was great," Scott Stetz later recalled. "But it didn't give her a license to kill!"

Stetz was adamant. He wanted to see Gilbert die.

At noon, on Monday, March 26, after the jury failed to reach a unanimous decision, by a vote of eight to four, Gilbert's life had been spared. When Judge Ponsor read the jury's decision, Gilbert and her attorneys wept.

But it still wasn't over.

Now it was up to Judge Michael Ponsor to decide on Gilbert's punishment.

After her lawyers indicated that she had nothing to say, Ponsor, his voice quiet and unyielding, sentenced Gilbert to four consecutive life terms.

"This should be the beginning of a better day for the relatives of her victims. . . ." Ponsor said, looking out into the galley of spectators, reporters, and anyone else at the courthouse who could find an open space to sit and listen.

In May 2001, Kristen Heather Strickland Gilbert was transferred from a federal prison for women in Framingham, Massachusetts, to a federal prison for women in Carswell, Texas, where she has remained ever since.

By June, the Court had tallied the cost of Gilbert's defense: approximately one million, eight hundred thousand dollars, with Harry Miles receiving the bulk of it—six hundred and fifty-four thousand, nine hundred and eighty-nine dollars.

Then the government's cost of prosecuting the case was released: about seven hundred and fifty thousand dollars, merely half of what the defense had amassed in expenses.

What was the cost of one ampoule of 1:1000 strength epinephrine, which was enough to kill either Ed Skwira, Henry Hudon, Kenny Cutting or Stanley Jagodowski?

Twenty-two cents.

EPILOGUE

As of the date of this writing, Kristen Gilbert has filed "a notice of appeal." A legal brief, spelling out her reasons why the convictions should be overturned, was due in February 2003, but there has been no ruling on the appeal or brief.

I made several attempts to contact Gilbert and her former lawyers, David Hoose and Harry Miles. They never returned my phone calls or letters. A letter was sent to Charles Rankin, a lawyer from Boston who is now handling Gilbert's affairs, shortly before this book went to press, offering him an opportunity to make a statement, but I have not heard back from him.

According to Springfield's *Union-News*, Carole Osman and Ann French continue to cultivate a close relationship with Gilbert, corresponding via telephone and mail. Gilbert has said through Osman and French that she misses her children and spends a lot of her "free" time reading novels Osman sends her. An "avid sewer," Ann French told the *Union-News,* Gilbert has been making quilts for premature babies. Doing this, French claims, helps Gilbert forget about "being branded a serial killer."

Ann French went on to say that Gilbert is "very embarrassed by the whole situation"; and she can't stand the fact that some people have compared her to the likes of Timothy McVeigh and Manual Noriega.

Glenn Gilbert, who still resides in Florence, refuses any contact with the media.

James Perrault, along with several of Gilbert's former co-workers, still works at the Leeds VAMC. Fulfilling a life-long dream, Perrault is now a part-time cop for the town of Hatfield, Massachusetts.

John Wall, Renee Walsh, Kathy Rix, Dr. Michael Baden, Special Agent Steve Plante, Detective Kevin Murphy, Supervising US Attorney Kevin O'Regan, Dr. Thomas Rocco, Dr. Thomas Graboys, US attorneys Bill Welch and Ariane Vuono, along with many more, were honored by the VA with the *Eagle Award* in June 2001 for their efforts in bringing Gilbert to justice.

SA Plante, Detective Murphy, Ariane Vuono and Bill Welch later received the *Director's Award,* for their "outstanding contributions in law enforcement," from the Attorney General's Office in Washington, DC.

Judge Michael Ponsor ended up fining Gilbert $1.5 million, noting that she would also have to "reimburse her victims' survivors for funeral expenses."

Based on her pay scale at the Carswell, Texas, penitentiary where she is incarcerated, working an eight-hour day, five days a week, it will take Gilbert more than thirty-five hundred years to pay off her fine.

Several civil suits were ultimately filed by victims' families against the Leeds VAMC. In June 2002, however, Judge Ponsor allowed a government motion to dismiss the suits filed by the families of Stanley Jagodowski, Ed Skwira, Angelo Vella, along with the families of Carl Rauch and Ralph McEwen, two veterans who were not named in the indictments against Gilbert but had also died—like many, many more—while under her care.

The civil suits, Ponsor ruled, were filed after the statute of limitations had run out. The families argued that they didn't know there had been malpractice because Gilbert's crimes weren't made public for some time after the deaths.

"By 1996," Ponsor wrote, "each plaintiff knew—at least—that an investigation into the unusually high number of deaths from cardiac arrests at the VAMC was under way." The families were devastated by this.

But Kenny Cutting's wife, Nancy Cutting, filed a lawsuit *within* the time frame of the statute, Ponsor ruled.

Her case continues.

The United States is home to more than twenty-five million veterans of military service, about three million of whom are treated every year for various reasons at some twelve hundred government medical facilities nationwide. All fifty states have veteran patient care centers of some sort.

With an average of twenty-five million outpatient visits and one million inpatient discharges yearly, the Department of Veterans Affairs, Veterans Health Administration, is the largest healthcare system in the world. With a budget of $20 billion, and a staff of more than one hundred and eighty thousand— sixty thousand of which are nurses—it prides itself on the quality of the people it employs.

Practice, Quality of Care and *Performance* stand at the top of the VHA's mission statement.

To some, however, these words mean nothing. Many times, when there is a problem nurse, for example, the VA does little to discipline him or her and, like the Catholic Church, simply relocates the problem person.

"[The VA] has a way of never getting rid of anybody," one nurse who has worked for the VA for more than twenty years and chooses to remain anonymous for obvious reasons says. "If you're a bad nurse, the worse I've ever seen them do to anybody is move them to another ward."

About six months after I began researching this book, I called the VAMC in Leeds and asked the Public Relations Director if I could come up to the hospital for a tour. Ward C had been dismantled by then, but I wanted to get a feel for the place, its sounds and smells, the color of the paint on the walls, the ebb and flow of the hospital, and the people who work there.

I wanted to walk the same halls as Kristen Gilbert.

"I'm writing a book about the Gilbert murders," I said. "A tour of the facility would help color the background of my book."

After a brief silence, "Absolutely not!" she shouted.

She was, obviously, appalled that I had the nerve even to ask.

"Well, I would just want to look around to get a feel for the place, ma'am. I mean, a majority of the book takes place inside your facility."

"You are not welcome here. We would *never,*" she said, raising her voice again, "allow someone to come up here for that reason. It is against policy."

I could hear her huffing and puffing. *How dare you!*

A week or so later, I had coffee with a local reporter who had covered the Gilbert story.

"I understand you spoke to [the Public Relations Director]," he said as we sat down.

Stymied, I looked at him. *How the hell did you know?*

I didn't say anything at first, though. Then, after collecting my thoughts, "Yes," I said, "and boy, was she pissed."

"I saw her yesterday," he said, leaning back in his chair, smiling, gloating. "She said that if *I* were to write the Gilbert book she would have no trouble allowing me full access to the hospital."

He took a bite of his bagel, eyeing at me the entire time.

"Do you think that I didn't go up there already and poke around before calling her?" I asked.

"What?"

"I've been up there two times," I said. "Inside the hospital, looking around, asking questions, taking notes . . ."

"How did you get in?"

"I walked."

As the weeks went by and I began to make my way through town, visiting all of the locations involved in this story, beginning the process of interviewing people, I learned quickly that the VAMC in Leeds would rather wish away the fact that Kristen Gilbert went on a murderous rampage under its nose for—as some have suggested—seven years, rather than confront it.

"Push it all underneath a very large rug," one nurse told me. Ever since coming forward with their allegations, the three nurses responsible for initiating the investigation into the deaths at the Leeds VAMC—Renee Walsh, Kathy Rix and John Wall—have been treated as if they have broken some sort of sacred vow.

Wall, Walsh and Rix did something many of their coworkers, for years, had the opportunity to do, but, for whatever reason, chose not to. Their photographs should be on the walls in the entrances of all the VA medical centers throughout the country, visible as soon as you walk in. A caption above each photo should praise their integrity, their courage, their honesty. These people are *heroes*.

Throughout Renee Walsh's VA career, she has received several monetary awards for, she told a reporter one day, "just doing her job." One time, she received a $250 award for attending a meeting to help a ward merger; a second time, she was awarded $500 for working with two younger nurses, helping them deal with hospice patients who were dying.

Yet though Walsh stuck her neck and career on the line and turned in Gilbert, to this day, neither she—nor Kathy Rix nor John Wall—has received anything from the Leeds VAMC other than animosity and silence.

It's not about the money, Walsh told that same reporter. It's about being recognized for coming forward and "doing the right thing."

Three nurses turn in a coworker and save more lives in one day than anyone at the VAMC will save in their entire careers, and the Leeds VAMC acts as if it never happened, shunning Rix and Walsh every chance it can. (John Wall no longer works for the VA.)

According to documents I obtained later, in late 2001, the National Forensic Nursing Conference, held yearly in Colorado, sent an e-mail notice to all of the VA medical centers across the country with instructions to notify the nursing staffs in all its facilities that the annual conference was coming up. Renee Walsh and Kathy Rix, along with former nursing manager Melodie Turner, had received similar messages about similar conferences and VA-related matters routinely throughout the years.

The 2001 NFN conference, however, was quite a bit different

from years past: The entire conference was dedicated to discussing Kristen Gilbert and, in general, serial killers in hospitals.

Yet neither Melodie Turner, Renee Walsh nor Kathy Rix received the e-mail announcement. It was as if the Leeds VAMC didn't want them to attend—and, more sinisterly, didn't even want them to know about it.

But it didn't end there.

The Leeds VAMC not only failed to tell Rix, Walsh or Turner about the conference, but it paid for and sent William Boutelle, Chief of Staff, and David Levin, chief of Quality Management. In fact, the two men were keynote speakers.

Kathy Rix and Renee Walsh were directly responsible for the apprehension, and partly responsible for the conviction, of Kristen Gilbert, thus initiating the subject matter of the conference in the first place. If *anyone* from the Leeds VAMC should have been speaking at that conference, one would think it would have been Rix, Walsh, or both.

It must be noted that US Attorney Ariane Vuono, who, in my opinion, was often treated poorly by the local press—many times being pushed to the side in post-trial stories, leaving the reader to believe that Bill Welch tried the case by himself—played as big a role in Gilbert's conviction as any other member of the government's team.

In addition, Gilbert's former attorney, David Hoose, in a post-trial newspaper story, likened US attorney Bill Welch to a "Nazi." Hoose was upset because Welch pursued the death penalty in the Gilbert case so vigorously, and made it sound as though he had a personal vendetta against Gilbert. I spent some time with Mr. Welch, studied his entire career, reviewed hundreds of pages of documents he prepared for the Gilbert trial, and spoke to many people who know him. I can say that Bill Welch is one of the most considerate, well-spoken, truth-seeking, and justice-driven lawyers I have ever met. David Hoose could not have been more unprofessional and ridiculous with his comments.

* * *

Nearly everyone I spoke to while writing this book asked me the same question: *Why did she do it?*

There is no definitive answer to that question. There's plenty of speculation. Rumor. Gossip. Theories. But it is all *spin.* My answer, after spending years studying the minds of the criminally insane and more than a year and half researching Kristen Gilbert's entire life, is still the same as it was from day one: Adults don't one day wake up and decide to become serial killers; they are wired at some point—usually during childhood—so that they might later cultivate a malevolence and perpetrate crimes based on what they have been taught. Only Kristen Gilbert knows when, where and by whom that evil seed was planted. She is the only person on this earth who can honestly say if there even was a reason behind her brutality—and to this day, Gilbert continues to deny having anything to do with the VAMC murders for which she was convicted.

—M. William Phelps
October 21, 2002

Acknowledgments

Working on a book like this, one meets a variety of people from all walks of life. Although a few of my encounters were hostile, the majority of the people I met were kind, and helpful in a number of ways.

There is, naturally, a long list of people for whom thanking would be impossible, along with many more who assisted me in a variety of ways but choose to remain anonymous. I want to say that I was overwhelmed by the respect, consideration and sincerity many of you demonstrated. Thank you.

I am indebted greatly to, specifically, four people. I cannot name you, but you certainly know who you are. Over a period of weeks and months, we spoke for hours about the VAMC, nursing, law, medical issues and, of course, Kristen Gilbert. Please know that you have my deepest appreciation and gratitude. The time you gave me, the honesty and insight you brought to this book, along with your ability not to be influenced by what others thought of your coming forward to talk, made all the difference. I could not have written this book without you.

In no specific order, I would like to take this opportunity to thank some of those who helped with the book, along with some who did not:

To William Acosta, a true hero in world that is seemingly overflowing with them today: I salute you, sir. Every American owes you part of their freedom. You have put away more trash than any lawman I have ever met, known or read about. You got me started in the business of writing books—and I can *never* thank you enough for that.

David Perkins (a lifelong friend and brother), Susan Lessard, Trina Taylor, Peter Sauer, Laura Sauer, Victoria Getis, from the University of Massachusetts (for helping me locate Lizzie Borden's complete family history), and all those at the Forbes Library (in Northampton) who were helpful, kind and patient as I sat for hours doing research.

Springfield Federal Court Clerk John Stuckenbruck; a very special thanks to Court Reporter Alice Moran; guards at the Springfield Federal Building: Mike and Mike, Bob and Bob, Brendon, John, Jim, and Al; the US Marshal's Office, and all those in the US Attorney's Office who showed me hospitality.

Special Agent Steve Plante (you are a cut above the rest, sir, and a credit to your profession); Massachusetts State Police Detective Kevin Murphy (the world could use a few more cops with the passion and determination you have for solving crimes); Dr. Michael Baden; US attorneys Bill Welch and Ariane Vuono; a very special thanks to Legal Secretary Lorraine Simpson (for locating and photocopying the endless array of documents associated with this case); retired Illinois Highway State Patrol Lieutenant Garry Rice, a man whose knowledge of the criminal mind is, without question, useful to me in more ways than I can say; and the jurors who helped me understand how emotionally taxing sitting on a jury can be.

J.G. (the music); R.K. (the song); A.R. and N.D.W. (the books); my students throughout the years; Josephine and Louis Castellassi; JulieAnn Charest, my editor at *New England Entertainment Digest;* Danny Lemay, my first editor (for not laughing years ago at those terribly written early stories); *Boston Globe* reporter Thomas Farragher (for heading me in the right direction early on).

Of course, my loving mother, Florence Borelli, and her husband, Thomas Borelli, my brothers: Thomas Phelps, Frank Phelps and Mark Phelps; my nephews Mark Jr. and Tyler Phelps; Allison Atwood (for, years ago, listening); my father, Frank Phelps, and his wife, Mary. Frank Mauri and John Brand from Dynamic Technologies, LLC (for resuscitating my computer's hard-drive on several occasions); Ruth, Tom, Laura, and Alexandra Stalgehtis; Martha Brazauskas; Gunther "John Kava" Brazaukas; former Kensington Publishing Corp. senior editor Karen Haas (for pulling this story out of the pile and bringing it to life); Norris Hawkins; Jim Barakos and "the boys" (Bob Hruskocy and Bob Kayan) at Adcom Express in Hartford, Connecticut.

Gregg Olsen and Harvey Rachlin, who believed in me when they didn't even know me.

Editor-in-chief at Kensington, Michaela Hamilton, and senior editor Johnny Crime for their sage advice, understanding, and tender care with my words. I am blessed to be able to work with such wonderfully talented and dedicated people. I have the utmost respect for you both.

A special thanks to Dr. Richard Orris, who helped me understand some of the more complex medical issues involved in the book; and Dr. Sam Vaknin (for his endless well of information about those who suffer from Narcissistic Personality Disorder).

My literary agent, Jim Cypher, from *The Cypher Agency* (for sticking behind me all those years, teaching me how to write, and working all those extra hours). I am lucky to have met such a great man who has not only become my good friend, but an agent I thought never existed.

If there is anyone I've overlooked, I apologize; it wasn't intentional.

Lastly, my wife, Regina, and my children, April, Jordon and Mathew (for never questioning my dreams and goals, for allowing me the time to investigate and write, for not putting any limitations on me, and for accepting the fact that it takes a lot of time away from us to do what I do). With every ounce of my soul, I love you.

HORRIFYING TRUE CRIME
FROM PINNACLE BOOKS

SERIAL KILLER ON WARD C

In Northampton, Massachusetts, at the Veterans Affairs Medical Center, Kristen Gilbert was known as a hardworking, dedicated nurse—so why were her patients dying? So many emergencies and sudden deaths occurred while Kristen made her rounds on Ward C that her colleagues jokingly called her the "Angel of Death." Yet most people didn't suspect the horrifying truth behind the nickname: that Gilbert's polished facade concealed a scheming, manipulative liar and homicidal, narcissistic sociopath.

LETHAL CURE

From August 1995 through February 1996, Gilbert dealt out wholesale death. Her victims were helpless patients who trusted her as a caregiver, only to learn too late that she was a killer, her weapon a drug capable of causing fatal heart attacks. But she got away with murder until three of her fellow nurses could no longer ignore the proliferation of deadly "coincidences" on Gilbert's watch. Investigators believe Kristen Gilbert may have been responsible for as many as 40 deaths. As the law closed in, she struck back, faking suicide attempts, harassing witnesses, stalking her ex-boyfriend and terrorizing the hospital with bomb threats. In March 2001, after being found guilty of four counts of murder and two counts of attempted murder, Angel of Death Kristen Gilbert was sentenced to life imprisonment.

SIXTEEN PAGES OF SHOCKING PHOTOS